D0850475

German Lieder
In the Nineteenth Century

German Lieder
In the Nineteenth Century

Edited by Rufus Hallmark

QUEENS COLLEGE, CITY UNIVERSITY OF NEW YORK

SCHIRMER BOOKS
An Imprint of Simon & Schuster Macmillan
NEW YORK

Prentice Hall International
LONDON   MEXICO CITY   NEW DELHI   SINGAPORE   SYDNEY   TORONTO

Schirmer Books
An Imprint of Simon & Schuster Macmillan
1633 Broadway
New York, NY 10019

Library of Congress Catalog Card Number: 95–31767

PRINTED IN THE UNITED STATES OF AMERICA

printing number
1   2   3   4   5   6   7   8   9   10

LIBRARY OF CONGRESS CATALOGING-IN-PUBLICATION DATA

German Lieder in the 19th century / edited by Rufus Hallmark.
        p.   cm.—(Studies in musical genres and repertories)
    Includes bibliographical references and index.
    ISBN 0–02–870845–8 (hardcover : alk. paper)
    1. Songs, German—19th century—History and criticism.   2. Music
and literature.   I. Hallmark, Rufus E., 1943–   II. Series.
ML2829.4.G47   1996
782.42′0943′09034—dc20   95–31767
                                                      CIP

This paper meets the requirements of ANSI/NISO Z39.48-1992 (Permanence of Paper).

This book is dedicated to the memory of
Christopher Lewis (1947–1992)

Contents

Preface

Du, Lied aus voller Menschenbrust,
Wärst du nicht, ach, was füllte noch
In arger Zeit ein Herz mit Lust?

—Frage, *Justinius Kerner*

Thou, song from the fullness of the human breast,
If thou didst not exist, ah, then what
In grave times would fill a heart with joy?

Not too long ago, when I mentioned to a colleague that I was editing a book on the German lied, he remarked, "Isn't that awfully precious?" Many regard the lied as a genre that is both dated and overrefined. Here is a large body of music, touted in music history texts and specialized studies (vested interests, one might argue), but otherwise neglected. Young singers would generally prefer to move up to opera; song is the spinach they have to eat as growing children (though few of them will make it to the opera stage). Most young pianists care little for the vocal repertory, in which they feel relegated to mere accompaniment. This particular body of song is, moreover, in German, one of the least obliging European languages to sing, much less to learn. Singers begin with the pure vowels and easy consonants of Italian, and they are familiar with that language from the melodious operas of Mozart, Verdi, and Puccini—not to mention the Italianate pronunciation of church Latin. German—with its comparatively harsher and more difficult sounds, a vocabulary with many fewer cognates, and a forbidding grammar—isn't nearly as inviting. (Observers note that the German-speaking émigré generation of the first half of the twentieth century, which constituted—it is argued—the major devotees of the lied, is dying off and not being replaced.)

Then there are the sentiments of the poems these lieder have as their texts. What does a postmodern youth in the age of environmental plunder know of the beauty and allure of nature? When light pollution in large, sprawling urban areas is so severe that one cannot see the stars, who knows the real darkness and mystery of night? Who can hear of Romantic love sickness without feeling one is eavesdropping on incurable neurotics? Can the world of today be congenial to such sentiments as a yearning for the infinite, a belief in a higher, other reality, even hope itself? Even more basically, who reads poetry anymore, in any language—much less memorizes, recites, enjoys, and treasures it?

Furthermore, the musical scene today is not the same as that of the nineteenth century, which, as Carl Dahlhaus has observed (Dahlhaus 1989, 5), provided a very different context for lieder. Although the age's instrumental music and opera are emphasized in performance and teaching today, nontheatrical vocal and choral music was dominant at the time. The nineteenth-century public were readers, quite conversant with poetry, and associated literature with music more freely than today's. Vocal music was performed by the lay public; song was a staple in domestic music-making, and amateurs filled the ranks of ubiquitous community choral groups. So, all told, perhaps the German lied *is* a bit precious for today's world (especially the non-German-speaking one).

I seem to be arguing for the irrelevance of the book that lies before you. Yet nothing could be further from the truth. As a singer as well as a scholar, I am a fervent proponent of the lied, as are many musicians and musical scholars. Why? To put it plainly, in the repertory of the nineteenth-century German lied one finds a wealth of musical beauty. Here we have musical expressiveness in crystallized form, the operation of musical elements—melody, harmony, rhythm, vocal and piano timbre—in a condensed time frame. By "operation," I mean not only the describable, chartable course of technical musical events (though these events and their analysis constitute an important and satisfying part of the musician's study), but also the emotional concomitants of the lied, an affective content that scholars are growing less reluctant to talk about. Nearly every major (and minor) composer wrote songs, and for many their songs are among their best efforts. For some, such as Schubert and Mahler, the lied was a central genre, without which our perception of these composers would be disfigured. For others, such as Hensel, Franz, and Wolf, the lied was their almost exclusive arena of activity, without which they would practically disappear from our hearing. For still others, such as Schumann and Brahms, song was one part of a balanced, multifaceted compositional activity, yet one without which the physiognomy of nineteenth-century music would not be the same. In short, only at the peril of gross musical ignorance does one neglect this repertory.

It is not the purely musical elements alone, but their combination with the verbal text and the interaction with the singer that set the art song apart and imbue it with some of its most special and attractive qualities. Although chamber music has the intimacy of a song recital and opera the beauty of the human voice, in neither is there the unique bond of eye contact between musician and audience. Singers and instrumentalists alike acknowledge this crucial distinction. (The young singer finds this one of the hardest things to become accustomed to.) A good song recitalist becomes the persona in the poem-song and engages each member of the audience in the shared lyrical experience of poet and composer (see Chapter 10 below and Cone 1974, 57–80 and 115–135). To use a hackneyed but apt expression, the singer bares her or his soul and draws the sympathetic beholder-listener into an aesthetic, psychological, and emotional experience evoked by the words and mediated by the music. For some, the words get in the way of the music. But for others, this apparent drawback is the very thing that keeps the lied potent. The lied invites us, as in no other common modern situation (beyond school and college classrooms), to read poetry. It enlivens thoughts and feelings, delineated by the text, that we thought were no longer part of our sensibilities. The music insinuates them, and we discover that this medium defines and releases feelings that are not so outdated or superseded as we had thought. (Consider: Did we once believe that Technicolor, wide screens, flawless special effects, and sexual explicitness had rendered the movies of the 1930s and '40s second rate, outmoded, and irrelevant?) We need not depend for our enjoyment on a museum recreation of what lieder meant when they were new; with intelligence and imagination we can find those possible readings that still speak to us today.

Through lieder, many musicians have their only significant contact with German literature (other than a novel or two in translation)—the native literature of many of the most important and beloved composers in the Western European canon. This is the body of philosophy, prose fiction, drama, and poetry that (together with its English counterparts) gave voice to the cultural consciousness named Romanticism. Though no one challenges the existence of Romanticism in late eighteenth-century and early nineteenth-century Europe, it admits no easy definition dependent on a simple set of traits. An understanding of this phenomenon is best formed inductively, through the slow accretion of impressions. There could be no better place to start than with the poetry and music of the German lied. Here one encounters Goethe and Schiller, the collectors and imitators of German folk poetry, and other poets of the first Romantic generation; then their successors—the spiritual symbolist Eichendorff, the balladist Uhland, and the hard-surfaced and curiously modern Heine, to name but a few. These figures, though active and frequently set to music well before midcentury, persist into the songs of Brahms, Wolf, Strauss, and Mahler. Many who are considered lesser figures by literary historians and critics were nevertheless prized and set to music—for example, the poet Friedrich Rückert, who was favored especially by Schumann and Mahler.

And the pianist? Far from serving as a mere accompanist, the pianist who delves into lieder will soon discover what balanced partners voice and instrument are, and how crucial to the total effect of the song the piano writing is and how gratifying it is to play. By the same token, the singer must not think her- or himself the sole focus of the audience's attention, but must learn the mutual attentiveness and pleasure of chamber music-making.

* * * * *

The nineteenth-century German lied is often said to have been "born" on 14 October 1814, when Franz Schubert composed "Gretchen am Spinnrade." The quantity and quality of Schubert's songs were important, even crucial, determinants in music history, so much so that it is not farfetched to suppose that without his example many of the composers in this book might have ignored this genre altogether or devoted much less creative effort to it. But there are other factors to keep in mind: (1) the predecessors of the eighteenth century: the two "Berlin schools" (the second one including the prolific lied composers Johann Friedrich Reichardt and Carl Friedrich Zelter), as well as the songs of Gluck, Haydn, and Mozart; (2) Schubert's predecessors and contemporaries in the early nineteenth century, such as Beethoven and the Viennese balladist Johann Rudolf Zumsteeg; and (3) the tradition of domestic music-making, the growing popularity of the piano, and the market for accessible keyboard music and keyboard-accompanied song.

Although these factors are not treated in this book,[1] a fourth, crucial factor—the lyric impulse of late eighteenth- and early nineteenth-century poetry—is discussed in the opening essay, by Harry Seelig. Seelig essentially argues for the seminal role of Goethe in launching the new, unbuttoned lyricism in German poetry. In the subsequent chapters on individual composers, the authors treat the six time-honored masters—Schubert, Schumann, Brahms, Wolf, Mahler, and Strauss. These chapters are not superficial surveys but fresh, well-investigated, thoughtful essays that discuss a limited number of songs in detail. The authors have been encouraged to give attention to less well-known repertory and to produce original, provocative, and specific (but not overly technical) discussions that draw the reader into the heart of each composer's style.

Susan Youens begins by tempering the pervasive notion of Schubert's originality with a discussion of his indebtedness to other composers; she then surveys his choices of poets and musical styles in preparation for a meaningful look at selected songs from different periods. In my chapter on Schumann, I argue that he (more than Schubert) offered heavily interpretive readings of the poetry he set to music. Though I deal with the fruits of the 1840 "song year," I also devote much attention to the later songs and try to shake them free of the ignorance and prejudice that shroud so much of Schumann's late music. Virginia Hancock, writing about Brahms, also offers a corrective essay that treats his folk-tune and folk-lyric settings on an equal footing with his *Kunstlieder*. Lawrence Kramer looks at the lieder of Hugo Wolf in the broader cultural context of the Vienna of his day, which included the practice of "mental science"; he sees Wolf as involved in nineteenth-century discourse on psychology and sexology and, at the same time, in his own, personal rite of passage. In her chapter on Richard Strauss, Barbara Petersen discusses the great range of poetry and musical aesthetics found in his eight remarkable decades of lied composition. To provide a proper context for his penetrating essay on Mahler's songs, Christopher Lewis does nothing less than present a fundamental reconsideration of the notion of Romanticism, on the basis of which he then draws new inferences about the messages in Mahler's songs. Jürgen Thym's longer chapter is devoted to a representative selection of other composers who are little discussed and seldom performed in English-speaking countries. His discussions of Carl Loewe, Robert Franz, Fanny Mendelssohn Hensel, Franz Liszt, and Peter Cornelius impart the distinctive character of each of these composers, whetting readers' curiosity to hear and learn more about their songs and those of other, comparable lied proponents.

Although I considered organizing this book systematically by genre and form, as in a recent German book on the lied (Dürr 1984), I decided to proceed by composer. But John Daverio's chapter on the song cycle raises conceptual and historical issues, both literary and musical, that merit extended treatment. Finally, Robert Spillman's chapter on performance deals with the practical issue of communicating in what, for most users of this book, is a foreign language; he puts matters related to this problem ahead of questions of musical technique and style. Students will find this chapter tantamount to a series of master classes, and more experienced hands will find themselves nodding in agreement with his helpful ideas.

In late summer 1992, not long after he had submitted his chapter on Mahler, Christopher Lewis was killed in an automobile accident. In accordance with the wishes of the other contributors, this book is dedicated to his memory.

Rufus Hallmark

Notes

1. For a discussion of the piano, see *Nineteenth-Century Piano Music,* ed. R. Larry Todd (New York, 1990), especially Leon Plantinga's essay "The Piano and the Nineteenth Century," 1–15.

Bibliography

(NOTE: The following works are recommended for further reading about the German lied and the art song in general.)

Brody, Elaine, and Robert Fowkes. *The German Lied and Its Poetry.* New York, 1971.
Cone, Edward. *The Composer's Voice.* Berkeley, 1974.

Dahlhaus, Carl. *Nineteenth-Century Music.* Trans. J. Bradford Robinson. Berkeley, 1989.

Dürr, Walther. *Das deutsche Sololied im 19. Jahrhundert.* Wilhelmshaven, 1984.

Fischer-Dieskau, Dietrich. *The Fischer-Dieskau book of Lieder: The texts of over 750 songs in German.* London, 1976.

Gorrell, Lorraine. *The Nineteenth-Century German Lied.* Portland, 1993.

Ivey, Donald. *Song: Anatomy, Imagery, and Styles.* New York, 1970.

Kramer, Lawrence. *Music and Poetry: The Nineteenth Century and After.* Berkeley, 1984.

Landau, Anneliese. *The Lied. The unfolding of its style.* Washington, DC, 1980.

Miller, Philip, ed. and trans. *The Ring of Words: An Anthology of Song Texts.* New York, 1966.

Moser, Hans Joachim. *Das deutsche Lied seit Mozart.* Tutzing, 1968.

———. *The German Solo Song and the Ballad.* New York, 1958.

Prawer, Siegbert S., ed. *The Penguin Book of Lieder.* Baltimore, 1964.

Radcliffe, Philip. "Germany and Austria." In *A History of Song,* ed. Denis Stevens, 228–64. London, 1960. Rev. ed. New York, 1970.

Smeed, J. W. *German Song and its Poetry 1740–1900.* London, 1987.

Stein, Jack. *Poem and Music in the German Lied from Gluck to Hugo Wolf.* Cambridge, MA, 1971.

Whitton, Kenneth S. *Lieder: An Introduction to German Song.* London, 1984.

Winn, James. *Unsuspected Eloquence: A History of the Relations between Poetry and Music.* New Haven, 1981.

Wiora, Walter. *Das deutsche Lied: Zur Geschichte und Ästhetik einer musikalischen Gattung.* Wolfenbüttel and Zurich, 1971.

Acknowledgments

I wish to thank R. Larry Todd, the general editor of this series, for inviting me to produce this book and for his periodic gentle urgings and helpful suggestions. The book owes much to the confidence, patience, and prodding of Schirmer Books editor in chief Maribeth Anderson Payne and to her successor, Richard Carlin. In addition, I most gratefully acknowledge the cooperation of all my fellow contributors, who were able with equanimity and generosity to bear up through the vicissitudes of the production of a book with ten authors, one of whom was also the sometimes foot-dragging editor.

Contributors

JOHN DAVERIO, Associate Professor of Music at Boston University, is the author of *Nineteenth-Century Music and the German Romantic Ideology* and of a forthcoming book on Robert Schumann's life and works. He has written articles on a variety of nineteenth-century topics and is preparing the entry on Schumann for the next edition of *The New Grove Dictionary of Music and Musicians.*

RUFUS HALLMARK, Professor of Music at Queens College, City University of New York, is the author of *The Genesis of Schumann's Dichterliebe* and of a forthcoming book on Schumann's song cycle *Frauenliebe und-leben.* He has also written articles on the songs of Schumann and Schubert, and will edit a volume of songs for the new complete edition of Schumann's works.

VIRGINIA HANCOCK, Associate Professor of Music at Reed College, is the author of *Brahm's Choral Compositions and His Library of Early Music* and of numerous articles on Brahms in scholarly journals and collections of essays.

LAWRENCE KRAMER, Associate Professor of English and Comparative Literature at Fordham University, is the Author of *Music and Poetry: The Nineteenth Century and After, Music as Cultural Practice in the Nineteenth Century,* and, most recently, *Classical Music and Post-Modern Knowledge.* He is working on a book about Schubert's songs. He serves as coeditor of the journal *19th-Century Music.*

CHRISTOPHER LEWIS was an Assistant Professor of Music at the University of Alberta, Edmonton. In addition to his book *Tonal Coherence in Mahler's Ninth Symphony,* Lewis wrote several articles on Mahler, Schoenberg, and late nineteenth- and early twentieth-century tonality, including a study of the compositional chronology of the *Kindertotenlieder.* His article "The Mind's Chronology: Narrative Times and Tonal Disruption in Post-Romantic Music" is forthcoming.

BARBARA A. PETERSEN, Assistant Vice-President for Concert Music Administration at Broadcast Music, Incorporated, wrote *Ton und Wort: The*

Lieder of Richard Strauss. She is the author of articles for both *The New Grove Dictionary of American Music* and *The New Grove Dictionary of Opera.*

HARRY SEELIG, Associate Professor of German Languages and Literatures at the University of Massachusetts, Amherst, is the author of a number of musicoliterary studies, including articles on the character of Suleika in Schubert's songs, Hugo Wolf's settings of Goethe's *Divan* lyrics, nineteenth-century settings of Goethe's "Wanderers Nachtlieder," and a comparative reconsideration of Mahler's Symphony No. 8 and Strauss's *Die Frau ohne Schatten.*

ROBERT SPILLMAN, Professor on the faculty of the College of Music at the University of Colorado, Boulder, is the author of *The Art of Accompanying: Master Lessons from the Repertoire.* More recently he coauthored *Poetry into Song* with Deborah Stein.

JÜRGEN THYM, Professor and Chair of Musicology at the Eastman School of Music, wrote an extended study of Schumann's Eichendorff settings and edited *100 Years of Eichendorff,* an anthology of nineteenth-century songs on his poetry. He has also co-authored articles (with Ann Clark Fehn) on lied settings of sonnets and of Persian *ghasels.* He is the editor of volumes in the collected works of Arnold Schoenberg and co-translator of several treatises of music theory, including Kirnberger and Schenker.

SUSAN YOUENS, Associate Professor of Music at the University of Notre Dame, is the author of *Retracing a Winter's Journey: Schubert's Winterreise, Schubert: Die schöne Müllerin,* and *Hugo Wolf: The Vocal Music.* Her new book is *Schubert and His Poets.*

German Lieder
In the Nineteenth Century

CHAPTER ONE

The Literary Context: Goethe as Source and Catalyst

Harry Seelig

Because the nineteenth-century German lied and German Romantic poetry are both so inextricably associated with music—the lieder most obviously, the poems less explicitly—this introduction will trace their origins in the late eighteenth- and early nineteenth-century literary-musical culture that gave rise to each genre. The very term *lied* clearly indicates a symbiosis of literature and music. In addition to designating a fully independent literary text in and of itself, as well as the art songs that are the subject of this book, it has often been used in the titles of large-scale works in poetry (e.g., Schiller's *Das Lied von der Glocke*) and in music (e.g., Mahler's *Das Lied von der Erde*) that have very little to do with the miniature forms we are primarily concerned with here. Yet the basic and still current understanding of *lied* is that of an autonomous poem either intended to be sung or suitable in its form and content for singing (Garland 1976, 535).

Folk Song Origins

For all its subtlety and complexity, the German lied has its origin in the simple German folk song. German lieder generally consist of two or more stanzas of identical form, each containing either four lines of alternating rhymes or rhymes at the ends of the second and fourth lines only. This pattern also defines the basic four-line stanza of the *Volkslied* or folk song, which—with its abab or abcd rhyme scheme—is arguably the most important source of the nineteenth-century art song. The German term

Volkslied was coined by the philologist, theologian, and translator-poet Johann Gottfried Herder (1744–1803) after reading the spurious popular poetry of "Ossian" as well as the authentic examples in Bishop Thomas Percy's *Reliques of Ancient English Poetry* of 1765. Herder thereupon avidly collected folk songs and in 1778–79 published two volumes thereof. Somewhat later, Romantic theorists such as Friedrich Schlegel and the brothers Grimm took these verses to be a kind of spontaneous expression of the collective *Volksseele* or soul of the folk; this rather mystical term received further conceptualization in their theories on *Natur- und Kunstpoesie,* or nature and art poetry (Garland 1976, 900).

The search for the poetic roots of the German people reached its apex in the work of Clemens Brentano and Achim von Arnim, who collected and published the many folk songs and quasi-folk songs of *Des Knaben Wunderhorn* (1806–8). Goethe—reflecting the nascent nationalism of central European literary Romanticism—felt that this excellent source of lieder had a place in every German home. His praise is understandable, given his experience over thirty years earlier as a student in Strasbourg collecting folk songs in the Alsatian countryside, under the tutelage of his mentor Herder. It was the infectious poetic spirit of Herder—who had meanwhile published a second edition of his seminal *Volkslieder,* now known as *Stimmen der Völker in Liedern* (1807)—and the earlier folk-song versions of "Heidenblümlein" that had inspired Goethe to write one of his best-known early poems, "Heidenröslein." The folk-song-like simplicity and freshness of Goethe's "Sah ein Knab ein Röslein stehn" was so invigorating that Herder had enthusiastically quoted from it in his Ossian-essay of 1773, which introduced the word *Volkslied* and, also, led to the false assumption that "Heidenröslein" was a true folk song. Both real folk song and its imitations, then, ushered in an entirely new lyric style.

Although lieder had been written by German poets during the centuries preceding Herder, it is a peculiarity of the art song's heritage that its presumably primordial forerunner, believed to be a spontaneous expression of the *Volksseele,* arose as a concept only with the Romantic theories of the early nineteenth century. Just as the Romantic lied finds its theoretical origin in the retroactive speculative constructs of Romantic theoreticians, Romantic poetry derives its fundamental impetus from the vast and varied poetic achievement of Johann Wolfgang von Goethe, whose musically inspired lyricism served as the wellspring of German Romantic poetry even while it stood in opposition to some of the Romanticists' lyric intentions.

Goethe's Contribution

Although German literary classicism is all but synonymous with Goethe's vast oeuvre from as early as 1786 onward, and coexists with German Romanticism through the first three decades of the nineteenth century, the word "romantic" was first used only in 1798 by Friedrich Schlegel. In influential public pronouncements, he formulated the quintessentially romantic concept of "progressive *Universalpoesie*" to express the almost infinite scope of German Romanticism's aesthetic aspirations. By "progressive" and "universal" Schlegel meant not only that the basic epic, lyric, and dramatic genres of the literary enterprise should be imaginatively combined and juxtaposed, but also that this endeavor should involve interdisciplinary elements from the other arts, particularly music: "It embraces everything that is poetic, from the most comprehensive system of art . . . to the sigh or kiss which the poetic child expresses in artless song."[1] He singled out Goethe's novel *Wilhelm Meisters Lehrjahre* (*Wilhelm Meister's Apprenticeship*), the first edition of which was published with musical settings of the interpolated lyric passages "sung" by Mignon and the Harper, as one of the seminal events and accomplishments of the (Romantic) age.[2]

"Nur nicht lesen! immer singen!" (Don't ever read it! always sing it!) With these urgent and sonorous words (from his twelve-line poem "An Lina"), Goethe addresses the central cultural-aesthetic issue of the entire art-song century. Although this seventh line has attracted the most attention from critics, it is the last quatrain that actually explains why Goethe feels that lieder should be sung and not merely read:

> Ach, wie traurig sieht in Lettern,　　　Ah, how sad the lied looks to
> Schwarz auf weiß, das Lied mich an,　me, in letters black on white,
> Das aus deinem Mund vergöttern,　　which your voice can sing divinely
> Das ein Herz zerreißen kann!　　　　as it breaks a loving heart!
> 　　　　(Staiger 1949, 93)

And the actual musical performance *qua* lied transcends the mere physical proximity of the lovers, which was primary when she originally played *and sang* his songs to him at the piano (as the first quatrain describes it).

A similarly proto-romantic articulation of this fundamental conception can be found in Herder's writings (Martini 1957, 214): "Melodie ist die Seele des Liedes . . . Lied muß gehört, nicht gesehen werden" (Melody is the soul of song . . . song must be heard, not seen). Goethe's clarion call always to sing his otherwise "incomplete" lieder expresses *in nuce* the aspirations of poets as well as composers throughout the nineteenth century.[3] Goethe's lyric insistence, "immer singen!"—taken together with Schlegel's "artless song" and programmatically "progressive" view of the Mignon and Harper settings by Reichardt (see Schwab 1965, 31)—emphatically anticipates the importance of musical settings of poetry in the late eighteenth and nineteenth centuries.

Musical settings of many kinds of poetry had been a vital part of aristocratic and bourgeois social activity since the optimistic and confident Enlightenment spirit of the mid-eighteenth century had taken hold in the three hundred–odd domains that made up the German territories of central Europe. A five-volume novel published in 1770–73, in which songs are sung—usually at the piano—some fifty times illustrates this literary-musical activity and justifies the conclusion that the accompanied song was the most important aesthetic feature of everyday bourgeois life (Albertsen 1977, 175; cf. Smeed 1987, xii). Numerous theoreticians have sought to explain the interrelatedness of poetry and musical settings throughout this period (and up to the present day).[4] Moreover, the social-aesthetic dichotomy between *Volkslied* and *Kunstlied* (art song), as well as the more modern theoretical distinction between "musical" and (more or less) nonmusical poetry, further complicates an already problematic situation. The latter distinction engages primarily those theoreticians who feel that only less "musical" poems allow enough aesthetic "space" for the lied composer to add something musical and meaningful to the text, achieving a true literary-musical synthesis.

Rationalism and Romanticism

Such antinomies are fundamental to the speculative theorizing of German Romanticism itself. Yet the philosophic basis for Romantic aesthetics is best understood as an inevitable development of the preceding era, the Age of Enlightenment. Seventeenth- and eighteenth-century pan-European rationalism is the logical antecedent of European Romanticism generally, and has provided more than enough "reason" for the aesthetic speculation in abstract and metaphorical terms that has been thriving ever since. From this perspective, it is appropriate that throughout his long life Goethe worked to improve and renew in a rational way the more ordinary literary genres of his day; these efforts proved of great consequence for the development of the lied. He was joined regularly by members of Weimar society, meeting weekly to read and sing poetry; as Max Friedländer (v.31, vii) has attested, some of Goethe's amateur associates in Weimar were more prolific composers of lieder than many professional musicians of the time.

In seeking to ennoble ordinary verse through skillful parodies of existing songs, Goethe inspired and participated in a form of dilettantism that is hard to comprehend today. In Weimar, well before 1800, the poetic lied was thoroughly grounded in the regular practice of group singing, which, in turn, inspired numerous parodies: "Selecting simple and well-known melodies, the poets supplied texts that could be sung at sight to popular tunes" (Sternfeld 1979, 13). "Goethe . . . wrote parodies by creating new text to older tunes and rhythms, without any implication of irony" (Sternfeld 1979, 8) using an age-old technique to generate poetry of first-rate quality. Given this robust activity, it is no wonder that many of Goethe's poems were first published alongside their musical settings (Albertsen 1977, 177). Thus twenty of Goethe's early poems were published in musical settings in the *Leipziger Liederbuch* of 1769.

The ubiquitous folk song "Da droben auf jenem Berge" illustrates the interdependence of literary and musical traditions; Sternfeld (1979, 12) explains, "poems wandered as freely as melodies and by 1802 both the model and Goethe's parody were being widely circulated." Sternfeld documents the popularity and parodistic potential of "Da droben auf jenem Berge" by juxtaposing the first stanzas, respectively, of the folk song itself, Goethe's original parody as well as a second version, and three even more varied parodies by Heine, Uhland, and Brentano.[5] Brentano's version "seems to derive more directly from the folk song" (Sternfeld 1979, 12) even as its first line alters the traditional "droben auf dem Berge" image to the more distinctively Romantic "im Abendglanze," underscoring the vast possibilities inherent in the folk-song tradition. (It was Clemens Brentano, of course, who together with Achim von Arnim collected and published the many folk songs and quasi-folk songs of the consistently popular compendium *Des Knaben Wunderhorn* of 1806–08.)

When Goethe arrived in Strasbourg in 1770, he met Herder, who had rapturously welcomed Johann Georg Hamann's postulation of the primacy of poetry in human language through mystical epigrams like "Die Poesie ist die Muttersprache des menschlichen Geschlechts" ('Poetry is the mother tongue of the human race,' Rose 1960, 159). These attitudes provided the perfect antidote for Goethe's literary experience in Leipzig, where his youthful linguistic exuberance had been criticized by the controlled and mannered rhetoric of conservative figures like Johann Christoph Gottsched and Christian Fürchtegott Gellert, who reigned supreme in matters poetical as well as moral. Herder had heeded Hamann's call to unleash the sensuality of language through the originality of linguistic genius (*Sprachgenie*), and encouraged Goethe to trust his heart and imagination rather than the arbitrary rules and regulations of the Leipzig academic establishment (Blackall 1959, 481).

The crucial difference between Goethe's innovative lyric power and the older mode of poetry (as exemplified in the works of Friedrich Gottlob Klopstock, whose ecstatically poetic religious epic in classical hexameters had catapulted him to fame as the mid-eighteenth-century literary genius par excellence) may be seen in the juxtaposition of two lines from Klopstock's "Die frühen Gräber" of 1764:

> O wie war glücklich ich, als ich noch mit euch
> Sahe sich röten den Tag, schimmern die Nacht.

> O how happy was I when still in your company
> I saw the day's red dawn, the shimmering night.

with the opening quatrain of Goethe's "Maifest" of 1771:

Wie herrlich leuchtet	How gloriously Nature
Mir die Natur!	glows for me!
Wie glänzt die Sonne!	How the sun sparkles!
Wie lacht die Flur!	How the fields laugh!

In Klopstock's poem there is antithesis, but in Goethe's there is reciprocity. Throughout "May Celebration," subjective and objective terms interpenetrate, at times to the point of indistinguishability:

O Erd', o Sonne,	Oh earth, oh sun,
O Glück, o Lust,	Oh bliss, oh pleasure,
O Lieb', o Liebe	Oh love, dear love

"The unprecedented fluency of this rhyming litany seems at a single stroke to render obsolete the gawky sentiment of the previous quarter of a century. It is no wonder that the received chronology of modern German literature dates its beginning from 1770" (Boyle 1991, 157–58).

One of the supreme examples of Goethe's new-found trust in the sensuality of poetic language is Gretchen's lament (at her spinning wheel) for the absent Faust: "Meine Ruh ist hin, / Mein *Herz* ist schwer" (emphasis added). Not only is this ten-stanza sequence of short (mostly iambic dimeter) lines a brilliant example of Goethe's ability to distill "one of the most poignant scenes in all dramatic literature" (Stein 1971, 71) into purest lyricism, but its ingenious structure, as reflected by Schubert's inspired setting, makes it the first and foremost example of what the German lied was to become.

Goethe and Schubert

Many commentators have considered 19 October 1814, the day Schubert actually composed "Gretchen am Spinnrade," the birthday of German art song, but few have seen that the stanza-by-stanza development of Goethe's poem actually dictates—in the perfection of aesthetic symbiosis—a musical form that mediates between strophic and through-composed structure. Just as Schubert's startling composition (at age seventeen) breaks new ground in "musicopoetics" (Scher 1992, 328–37), so did Goethe's seemingly straightforward lyric stanzas probe new depths in human emotion rendered as poetry. The crucial refrain-that-is-not-a-refrain, the stanza that begins the whole, is central to the thrust of the poem.

Meine Ruh ist hin,	My peace is gone,
Mein Herz ist schwer,	My heart is sore,
Ich finde sie nimmer	Never will I find it,
Und nimmermehr.	Nevermore.

It recurs twice at strategic points within the poem but not at the end, as a true refrain would, and obviously inspired both the melody and the onomatopoeic accompaniment, which reflects the spinning-wheel imagery in its relentless sixteenth-note motion. But the text itself, couched in quatrains of increasing intensity and expanding reference—moving from

Gretchen's person and psychic condition to Faust's physical attributes, as she idealizes them, and finally to an emotional agitation of grief that "has become indistinguishable from sexual desire" (Kramer 1984, 152)—calls for varied musical treatment as it builds from an anguished but moderated outcry (the very first instance of the "refrain") to "a violent and open expression of sexual fantasy" (Kramer 1984, 153) in the climactic final quatrain:

Und küssen ihn,	And kiss him
So wie ich wollt,	As my heart would choose,
An seinen Küssen	In his kisses
Vergehen sollt!	To swoon, to die away![6]

The composer ultimately returns to the first two lines of the refrain—"Meine Ruh ist hin, / Mein Herz ist schwer"—as a musically apt denouement, but which nevertheless vitiates the "stunning effect" (Stein 1971, 72) of the poem's deliberately abrupt ending. Goethe achieves this stunning effect, as Jack Stein observes, by ending both poem and scene (in the *Faust* drama) at the moment of highest intensity, on the words "An seinen Küssen vergehen sollt": "The theater audience is left limp with empathy as the curtain closes. But the song is so much more aggressive in impact that the effect of breaking it off at this climax would be brutal. Hence, the necessary tapering off" (Stein 1971, 72).

Schubert's ending can be seen as a combination of *both* possibilities: (1) the "breaking off" has been transferred to the final statement of the refrain, which is then truncated after the "reason" for Gretchen's anguish—in the text—is revealed to be her heavy heart; (2) the "tapering off" results from the reiteration of the very first statement of the song's basic melodic-harmonic substance. Inasmuch as this denouement does *not* contain any trace of the innovative merger of strophic variation and through-composition developed elsewhere in the composer's profoundly progressive setting, the music parallels Goethe's dramatic literary "truncation" in its own terms.

In the earliest form of Goethe's play (the *Urfaust*), the poem's strategic enjambment combines "Und halten ihn" and "Und küssen ihn" into *one* eight-line stanza, which gains even more energy and urgency from the brutally honest words "Schoß" and "Gott!" (womb and God), in place of "Busen" (bosom):

Mein Schoß, Gott! drängt	My womb, God! drives
Sich nach ihm hin.	Me toward him so,
Ach dürft ich fassen	Oh could I clasp
Und halten ihn	And hold him close
Und küssen ihn,	And kiss him
So wie ich wollt,	As my heart would choose,
An seinen Küssen	In his kisses
Vergehen sollt!	To swoon, to die away!

The enjambment itself is brilliantly reflected in Schubert's musical extension, strengthening both enjambed stanzas. Furthermore, the music embodies the spirit of Goethe's earlier, more explicit outburst ("Mein Schoß, Gott!") in an extended ascending melodic sequence that, in its relation to the whole setting, makes this song innovative and archetypal at the same time.

The pivotal position of "Meine Ruh ist hin" in the development of the German lied is thus a function of its unique form—its strategically recurring "refrain"—as well as its ever-intensifying content, which might have been set in the traditional strophic manner by a less comprehending and less sympathetic composer. Goethe's revolutionary sense of dramatic development within the confines of lyric poetry facilitated the advent of through-composed art songs. In reacting musically to Goethe's developmental (dramatic) lyricism, Schubert rendered strictly strophic settings as something less than representative of the German *Kunstlied* at its best. The paradigmatic Romantic lied can be characterized as a modified strophic setting in which a given poem's individual stanzas are autonomous literary-musical entities as well as interrelated units seamlessly integrated into the overall development of the word-tone synthesis.

Goethe's role in fostering this innovation can be seen by comparing Schubert's settings of "Meine Ruh ist hin" (D. 118) and "Als ich sie erröten sah" (When I saw her blush, D. 153), the "light and slight little" song (Capell 1957, 89) that Dietrich Fischer-Dieskau has deemed a "more subjective" Schubertian counterpart to "Gretchen am Spinnrade" (Fischer-Dieskau 1972, 72). Bernhard Ambros Ehrlich's five quatrains of trochaic tetrameter represent a perspective opposite that of "Gretchen": a masculine outpouring of rhapsodical praise, generated by desire for the feminine beloved:

All' mein Wirken, all' mein Leben All my effort, all my life
Strebt nach dir, Verehrte hin! Strives toward you, revered one!
Alle meine Sinne weben All my senses conjure up
Mir dein Bild, o Zauberin! [I] Your image, oh enchantress!

Wenn mit wonnetrunk'nen Blicken When with rapture-laden glances
Ach! und unaussprechlich schön, Oh, how unspeakably beautiful!
Meine Augen voll Entzücken My ecstasy-intoxicated eyes
Purpurn dich erröten seh'n. [V] Behold your crimson blush.

The contrast between Ehrlich's cascade of metaphoric adulation—the muses, a lyre's harmony, the soul's storm, and Aurora's sunset are summoned to descriptive service in stanzas 2–4—and the avoidance of obvious poetic embellishment in "Gretchen" (except in the description of the "magic stream" of Faust's forceful words: "seiner Rede / Zauberfluss") could not be greater. But Schubert chose to give Ehrlich's flowery verses a through-composed setting, revealing the influence a poem can have on a setting. Fischer-Dieskau points to some similarities in the rhythm, melodic shape, and sixteenth-note accompaniment figuration of both, but the effect of "Als ich sie erröten sah" is disappointing: not only are the accompaniment figures empty arpeggios throughout, but the smattering of melodic interest attending the first strophe degenerates thereafter into desultory arpeggiated meanderings as well, particularly in the fourth and fifth stanzas.

These two settings demonstrate that a modified strophic form, however varied and unorthodox, is the more appropriate form for musical settings of lyric poetry, which, after all, usually exists in strophes of one form or another. Yet Romantic lieder are apt to be formally anything other than the simple strophic settings of their eighteenth-century predecessors. Three factors help explain this change. The first, as "Gretchen am Spinnrade" indicates so poignantly, is Goethe's timeless "structural" lyricism itself. The second is the emerging awareness of an individual self, which evolves into the self-consciousness of distinctly Romantic poetry, if the insights of poet *and* literary critic W. H. Auden can be taken at face value.[7] Equally important is a third element in Romantic poetry: reverence for nature. This deeply felt worship of nature, articulated with specific reference to German Romanticism by Madame de Staël in 1810, stresses that—in direct contrast to the classical literary representation of man as determined by external societal forces—Romantic literature sees man's actions and behavior as primarily governed by inner energies and emotions. Although mindful that the Romantic personality tends toward unbridled emotionalism, and that its enthusiasm for the moon, the forest, and solitude runs the risk of mindless faddishness, Staël considers the unusual wealth of feeling coming to the fore in Romanticism as a particular strength of the Germans in poetic, religious, and even moral terms (Peter 1985, 102–3).

These characteristics infuse the specifically Romantic poems chosen by most lied composers, but they are especially prominent in Goethe's lyrics. "Nur wer die Sehnsucht kennt," one of the four Mignon songs from *Wilhelm Meister*, embodies in astonishingly concentrated lyrical form the proto-Romantic emotional fervor and self-awareness:

Nur wer die Sehnsucht kennt,	Only one who knows longing
Weiß, was ich leide!	knows what I suffer!
Allein und abgetrennt	Alone and cut off
Von aller Freude,	from all joy,
Seh ich ans Firmament	I gaze at the firmament
Nach jener Seite.	in that direction.
Ach! der mich liebt und kennt,	Ah, he who loves and knows me
Ist in der Weite.	is far away.
Es schwindelt mir, es brennt	My head reels,
Mein Eingeweide.	my body blazes.[8]
Nur wer die Sehnsucht kennt,	Only one who knows longing
Weiß, was ich leide!	knows what I suffer!

Although Goethe concentrates all of Mignon's passion into only one strophe, the symmetry occasioned by the repetition of rhymes and lines—verses 1–2 and 11–12 are identical—has led most composers to employ strophically varied forms that reflect this ABA structure in their settings. The extreme prosodic economy of employing but two alternating rhymes throughout twelve dactylic trochaic lines is rare enough, but there is also the repeated expression of extreme yearning, in which longing and aloneness have become so poignantly merged that the cause of the anguished suffering—the distant lover—is all but forgotten by the reader. This radical compactness of lyric texture may have influenced Schubert to expand and enrich his early strophic settings so ingeniously.

Another single strophe of utter succinctness, "Über allen Gipfeln ist Ruh," exemplifies two Romantic themes—man's reverence for nature and his self-consciousness—with simplicity, brevity, and profundity, making it "probably the most praised poem in the German language" (Plantinga 1984, 121). Its integration of form and content is so complete and infinitely nuanced as to offer an inexhaustible subject for aesthetic and cultural analysis:

Über allen Gipfeln	Over all summits
Ist Ruh,	Is peace,
In allen Wipfeln	In all treetops
Spürest du	You feel
Kaum einen Hauch;	Hardly a breath;
Die Vögelein schweigen im Walde.	The birds in the woods are hushed.
Warte nur, balde	Just wait, soon
Ruhest du auch.	You too shall rest.

"There is in it not a simile, not a metaphor, not a symbol" (Wilkinson 1962, 21). Yet a profounder poetic paradox is unimaginable: nature and man have here been totally fused and fatefully juxtaposed. Only man can be conscious of how and why: the "Hauch" of breeze and breath is both figurative and literal, since the air of man's breath is dependent on the oxygen of nature's breeze; even the birds are unnaturally mute in the face of this inscrutable existential dichotomy. The topic is timeless even as the persona measures time.

Goethe's title "Ein Gleiches" makes reference to the earlier "Wanderers Nachtlied" of 1776: "Der du von dem Himmel bist," which Schubert set in July 1815 (D. 224). "Über allen Gipfeln ist Ruh" was written in 1780 and set by Schubert before May 1824 (D. 768); its title is therefore best rendered as "Another Wanderer's Night Song." This explicit reference to the night song genre is crucial to a full understanding of the poem, since the pervasive stillness invoked and evoked in it is normally experienced in the evening twilight, in celebration of which countless *Abendlieder* (evening songs) have been written. The theme of night is particularly prevalent in Romantic poetry. *Hymen an die Nacht* (Hymns to the Night), by Novalis

(Friedrich von Hardenberg), the most lyrical and influential of the early Romanticists, undoubtedly inspired countless *Nachtlieder* of later poets and composers; "Nacht," "Nacht liegt auf den fremden Wegen," "Nacht und Träume," "Nachtgesang," "Nachts," "Nachtwandler," and "Nachtzauber" are only some of the titles in Fischer-Dieskau's compilation.

The impact of Goethe's unadorned poem on all subsequent lyric style and lied composition is impossible to exaggerate. Its radically concentrated, nonmetaphorical character or "objective" lyric style seems even leaner when juxtaposed with the first eight lines of a sonnet written in Britain at about the same time and about the same theme by William Wordsworth:

> It is a beauteous evening, calm and free,
> The holy time is quiet as a Nun
> Breathless with adoration; the broad sun
> Is sinking down in its tranquility;
> The gentleness of heaven broods o'er the Sea:
> Listen! the mighty Being is awake,
> And doth with his eternal motion make
> A sound like thunder—everlastingly.

Not only is the poetic language of British Romanticism richer in similes, metaphors, personifications, and symbols than its German counterpart, but the subtle elegance of its diction has little of the direct access to the emotions and *Volksseele* (folk soul) that were the concern of Herder and Goethe in the 1770s and 1780s, and which became the goal of the German Romanticists after the turn of the century. It was the directly affecting, concisely "objective" lyric evocation of evening on Goethe's part that prodded Schubert to a superlative 14-measure setting, in which the all but imperceptible movement from inorganic through organic and animate nature to mankind itself is given the musical "objective correlative" that constitutes another highpoint in the history of the Romantic lied.[9]

The consistently stressed final syllable of each line of Wordsworth's sonnet points to another salient aspect of German Romantic poetry: the propensity for unstressed syllables (whether rhymed or unrhymed) at the ends of lines. The first four lines of Goethe's "Nachtlied" demonstrate the regular alternation of unstressed and stressed rhyme words in final position:

> Über allen *Gip*feln   (unstressed)
> Ist *Ruh,*   (stressed)
> In allen *Wip*feln   (unstressed)
> Spürest *du*   (stressed)

In German prosodic terminology, the term *klingend* (resonating) describes the unstressed verse ending, while *stumm* (mute) designates the stressed alternative. The more frequent occurrence of unstressed rhyme words in

German—as compared to English—is caused by such multisyllabic forms as infinitives (uniformly ending in *-en*), strong participles (e.g., gesproch*en,* sprech*end*), and the plural conjugations of verbs, not to mention all the nominal, pronominal, and adjectival declensions that the three genders and four cases of a highly inflected language require. This structural difference between German and English, which does not offer its poets a superabundance of unstressed final syllables, can explain at least partially why German lyric poetry strikes many ears as particularly "musical."[10]

Romantic Poetry and Romantic Lieder

Ultimately most noteworthy and defining for the poetic structures underlying the nineteenth-century or Romantic German lied is the proportion of line and stanza types in the poetry that was set, as represented in Fischer-Dieskau's *Texte deutscher Lieder* (1968). About half of the 750 song texts consist of quatrains with three or four stresses per line, the form most readers associate with the Romantic poetry of, say, Eichendorff or Heine. There is, then, a substantial number of folk-like, romantic verses in the lied texts set to music. But the other half of the texts demonstrate that composers did not hesitate to set quite diverse poetic forms to music as well. In fact, the variety of forms (and themes) once again points to the multifaceted oeuvre of Goethe as the obvious source of this diverse lyric outpouring.

A history of the German lied might be written on the basis of Goethe's poems alone, so influential on composers and so diverse in content, style, and form were they (Abert 1922, 107; Forbes 1972, 59). No other poet induced Beethoven to attempt four and Schubert seven settings of the same poem, "Nur wer die Sehnsucht kennt." Nor could another poet prompt three composers like Schubert, Schumann, and Wolf to try their hands on the Mignon and Harper poems, or for that matter, even two of them— Schubert and Wolf—to tackle the large-scale, unrhymed, lyrically philosophical "hymns" *Ganymed, Prometheus,* and *Grenzen der Menschheit.*

A good example of the difficulty Goethe's classical lyrics posed for the development of Romantic poetry is Brentano's "Der Spinnerin Nachtlied," which could be seen as a combination of elements from Goethe's "Gretchen am Spinnrade" and "Wanderers Nachtlied":

Es sang vor langen Jahren	Many years ago there surely
Wohl auch die Nachtigall,	Sang the nightingale,
Das war wohl süßer Schall,	That was a lovely sweet sound,
Da wir zusammen waren.	Because we were together.
Ich sing' und kann nicht weinen,	I sing and cannot weep,
Und spinne so allein . . .	And do my spinning so alone . . .

Der Mond scheint klar und rein,	The moon shines clear and pure,
Ich sing' und möchte weinen.	I sing and would like to weep.

In six quatrains Brentano's lovelorn maiden projects the new Romantic sensibility and self-consciousness in a nostalgic and rhapsodic style suggesting strophic setting. Yet its meandering repetitions of the same prosodic sounds—vowels, semivowels, diphthongs, and alliterative words—seem to beg for more than strophic musical treatment.

Such a series of trimeter quatrains is found in many Romantic poems—preeminently by Eichendorff—including those of Schumman's *Liederkreis* Op. 39, to take a familiar example. The poem "Mondnacht" contains three iambic trimeter quatrains; in fact, of the twelve poems in the entire cycle, three are in two quatrains, five are in three, and four are in four. But the meandering and repetitious quality of the Brentano poem is foreign to the structured development favored by Eichendorff:

Es war, als hätt' der Himmel	It was as though the sky
Die Erde still geküßt,	Had softly kissed the earth,
Daß sie im Blütenschimmer	So that in gleaming blossoms
Von ihm nun träumen müßt.	She'd now dream (only)[11] of him.

Die Luft ging durch die Felder,	The breeze ran through the fields,
Die Ähren wogten sacht,	The ears of grain swayed gently,
Es rauschten leis die Wälder,	The woods did rustle faintly,
So sternklar war die Nacht.	The night was so starry and clear.

Und meine Seele spannte	And then my soul spread out
Weit ihre Flügel aus,	Its wings so wide and far,
Flog durch die stillen Lande,	Flew over the quiet landscapes
Als flöge sie nach Haus.	As if it were flying home.

The explicit movement within and between the individual stanzas here is a crucial difference between Eichendorff and other Romantic poets generally.[12] Although "Mondnacht" manifests all the figurative devices—metaphors, personification, onomatopoeia, and "as if" subjunctives—commonly associated with the atmospheric nature imagery of Romantic poetry, it also reveals a carefully crafted structure very much like that of Goethe's "Über allen Gipfeln," where there is an "order of the inner process of nature as known by the mind, an organic order of the evolutionary progression in nature, from the inanimate to the animate, from the mineral, through the vegetable, to the animal kingdom, from the hill-tops, to the tree-tops, to the birds, and so inevitably to man" (Wilkinson 1962, 317). But here the structure is Romantically transmuted from the external order of nature to the internal but equally natural realm of the psyche: in Eichendorff's vision, the persona imagines a "marriage"[13] between heaven and earth in the nighttime sky—sealed by a metaphorical kiss and sanctioned by a continuing dream—that not only causes the grainfields and forests to sway and rustle empathetically in a breeze but also enables his soul to spread its wings and take flight through the nocturnal countryside, as if "flying home"—the utopian goal of virtually all German Romantic poetry.

This combination of poetic order and psychic drama inspired the imaginative musical forms, somewhere between strophic and through-composed, through which Schumann projected the poet's evocatively structured landscapes. The music *feels* as strophic as the poem in fact is, but it *sounds* as rhapsodic as the spatially conceived poetic imagery *seems*. Even when the poem and the setting are both clearly strophic, as in the first song of *Dichterliebe*—where the poem consists of two brief quatrains and the music has "an improvisational quality suggested by the free-flowing accompaniment figures of the piano" (Brody and Fowkes 1971, 119)—the overall effect can be anything but conventionally strophic. It is the prosodic structure of the poem, however, as much as anything else, that portrays the yearning for release that is the overwhelming burden of the verses:

Im wunderschönen Monat Mai,	In the wondrous month of May,
Als alle Knospen sprangen,	When buds were bursting open,
Da ist in meinem Herzen	Then it was that my heart
Die Liebe aufgegangen.	Filled with love.
Im wunderschönen Monat Mai,	In the wondrous month of May,
Als alle Vögel sangen,	When all the birds were singing,
Da hab' ich ihr gestanden	Then it was I confessed to her
Mein Sehnen und Verlangen.	My longing and desire.

The poem's lyric structure goes further toward actual release than does Schumann's setting, which delays the musical release—that is, the dominant-tonic resolution—until the third measure of the next song, "Aus meinen Tränen sprießen" (From my tears burst). The latter contains no fewer than six dominant-tonic cadences, lavishly compensating for the un-resolved harmonic "tension" of the first song. Even if the poetic "bursting forth" of "Im wunderschönen Monat Mai" does not find overt musical real-ization until Schumann's second song, in which fully blossoming flowers literally "burst forth" from the persona's tears, Heine's quatrains provide the structural integrity and varied rhythmic movement that inspired Schu-mann to compose such an evocatively "delaying" musical texture.

Heine's mostly sentimental, often ironic, and occasionally sarcastic poetry contributed markedly to the development of the Romantic lied. A typically German way of dealing with the adversities of life in post-1815 Eu-rope was "sentimental lament," which is—according to Meno Spann (1966)—the prevailing quality in the love poems of Heine's *Book of Songs* that makes them "unbearable to read" in our time. These poems nonethe-less produced exquisite lieder in the settings of Schubert, Schumann, Brahms, and other composers. "What inspired the composers was the per-fect structure, and often elegant antithesis of these ballad-like lyrics, in which unfortunately all of nature with her weeping little flowers and golden little stars and pale roses and saddened larks sympathizes with the unhappy love of the poet whose heart bleeds or breaks whenever rhyme, meter, or climactic effect require it" (Spann 1966, quoted in Komar 1971, 113). A particularly good instance of the perfect poetic structure that Heine could achieve is this jewel-like merging of alliteration and ono-matopoeia:

Leise zieht durch mein Gemüt	Gently through my soul
Liebliches Geläute.	Sweet bells are pealing.
Klinge, kleines Frühlingslied,	Sound, tiny song of spring,
Kling hinaus ins Weite.	Sound out far and wide.
Kling hinaus, bis an das Haus,	Sound out as far as the house
Wo die Blumen sprießen.	Where the flowers are blooming.
Wenn du eine Rose schaust,	And, should you see a rose,
Sag, ich laß' sie grüßen.	Convey from me a greeting.

The first two lines, "with their gorgeous liquid alliteration, are a good example of what an inspired opening will do to make a poem famous forever; apart from Goethe and Eichendorff, hardly any poet was as skilled in extracting such sounds from the German language. But the whole poem continues to be superb. Although it contains not a single pure rhyme, the lattice of near-rhymes and near-assonances gives it a genuine musicality" (Sammons 1969, 182–83). This "genuine musicality," paradoxically, may help explain why there is only one setting (Mendelssohn's Op. 19a, No. 5, "Gruss") of "Leise zieht durch mein Gemüt" listed by Fischer-Dieskau (1972): the metaphorical musicality of poetry may preclude or leave no space for actual music.

Romanticism's Aftermath

Heine's younger contemporary Eduard Mörike (1804–75), though humorous and witty, did not share the older poet's vitriolic tendencies, but embodied instead the "holdes Bescheiden" (graceful resignation) that epitomizes the *Biedermeier* period: a German version of the Realism that reigned in the aftermath of the Vienna Congress of 1815. Germanists are prone to call this general literary movement *Poetic* Realism, which suggests why the lyrical style of a poet like Mörike might not immediately attract the musical interest of cosmopolitan composers like Schumann and Brahms, though both did set several of Mörike's poems.[14] It remained for Hugo Wolf (1860–1903) to discover the modernity and musical utility of Mörike's poetry in general, over a decade after the poet's death.

Two poems, both set by Wolf, express graphically the introspective conservatism and subtle sensitivity of Mörike's paradigmatic nineteenth-century worldview that looks both backward and forward:

Herr! schicke was du willt,	Lord! Send what Thou wilt,
Ein Liebes oder Leides;	Delight or pain;
Ich bin vergnügt, daß beides	I am content that both
Aus deinen Händen quillt.	Flow from Thy hands.
Wollest mit Freuden	May it be Thy will neither with joys
Und wollest mit Leiden	Nor with sorrows
Mich nicht überschütten!	To overwhelm me!
Doch in der Mitten	For midway between
Liegt holdes Bescheiden.	Lies gracious moderation.

Mörike's "Verborgenheit" anticipates the infinitely nuanced psychic ambivalences of a later Freudian and fin-de-siècle age:

Laß, o Welt, o laß mich sein!	Leave, O world, oh, leave me be!
Locket nicht mit Liebesgaben,	Tempt me not with gifts of love,
Laßt dies Herz alleine haben	Leave this heart to have alone
Seine Wonne, seine Pein!	Its bliss, its agony!
Was ich traure, weiß ich nicht,	Why I grieve, I do not know,
Es ist unbekanntes Wehe;	My grief is unknown grief,
Immerdar durch Tränen sehe	All the time I see through tears
Ich der Sonne liebes Licht.	The sun's delightful light.
Oft bin ich mir kaum bewußt,	Often, hardly aware am I,
Und die helle Freude zücket	As pure joy flashes through
Durch die Schwere, so mich drücket	The oppressing heaviness
Wonniglich in meiner Brust.	—Flashes blissful in my heart.
Laß, o Welt, o laß mich sein! . . .	Leave, O world, oh, leave me be! . . .

The ambivalence and importance of "Verborgenheit" for its time—1832, the year of Goethe's death[15]—can be seen in the difficulty of translating its title: the translation by Bird and Stokes (1977) as "Obscurity" insufficiently renders the pleasurable withdrawal from society practiced by mid-nineteenth-century poets in the wake of Goethe's very public aesthetic triumphs. Although many successors no doubt felt intimidated by the legacy of Goethe's lyric achievement, Mörike reacted with a degree of poetic introspection that represents a major step on the road toward late nineteenth- and early twentieth-century symbolist poetry. "His subtle interweaving of thought, mood, emotion, impression, and suggestion; the enchanting mellifluousness of his words, phrases, and rhythms, are unrivaled in any lyric poetry that had gone before" (Stein 1971, 155). Mörike's plea for undisturbed *Verborgenheit* perceptively foresees the subconscious realm of the Freudian age—"Oft bin ich mir kaum bewußt" (often I am hardly aware, line 9)—even as it registers the "unbekanntes Weh" (unknown grief) that this seductive probing of the extremes of the human psyche will entail (line 6).[16]

Another example of Mörike's pre-Impressionist sensitivity is the following two-line excerpt from "Im Frühling" ("In Spring")—

Es dringt der Sonne goldner Kuß	The sun kisses its gold
Mir tief bis ins Geblüt hinein;	Deep into my veins;

—the imagery of which goes further even than Goethe's evocative metaphors, but the theme of which—a lover lying on a hilltop in springtime ("Hier lieg ich auf dem Frühlingshügel," line 1), borne on the wing of a cloud—is unthinkable without the equally cloud-borne spring paean "Ganymed" (Ganymede) that Goethe had written some fifty-four years earlier. Yet Goethe's influence did not guarantee public success by any means. The significance of Hugo Wolf's fifty-three settings, in 1888, for the general popularity *and* critical acceptance of Mörike's poetry some five or more decades after its original publication, is legendary.[17] But although Mörike's fame is indelibly connected with Hugo Wolf, his poetry has not found as many different composers as, say, Friedrich Rückert (1788–1866), whose poetry has been set as often as Heine's and Eichendorff's, though not nearly as often and as consistently as Goethe's (Fricke 1990, 18).[18] Harald Fricke candidly admits that the lyric quality of Rückert's poetry is not as high as that of Goethe, Eichendorff, and Heine: he shrewdly analyzes their lyric structure and finds that—although their diction is typically non-"musical"—they are rich in "varied repetition" (*variierte Wiederholung*) and relatively sparse in themes or subjects. Although Rückert's poems do not stray far from the usual Romantic topics of love, suffering, distress, nature, season, and pious devotion, the use of these themes is carefully limited; no more than "two-and-a-half" such subjects are presented in a given poem.[19]

In addition to the lyrical poem, another poetic genre, the ballad, has been an important source of art song settings. Because this genre can be characterized as a combination of epic, dramatic, and lyric elements, its appeal to composers who want to tell a story as dramatically as possible, even while they evoke a pervasive mood, is obvious. The most celebrated composer of ballads, Carl Loewe (1796–1869), provided many settings of Goethe's ballads, as well as a brilliant alternative to Schubert's famous "Erlkönig." But he is generally given greatest credit for his evocative rendition of the horrific "Edward," a grisly dialogue between a young man and his mother, translated from a Scottish source by Goethe's mentor Herder.[20]

Almost all the poets so far considered wrote ballads as a matter of course, so that Heine's "Die beiden Grenadiere" (The Two Grenadiers) of 1819–20, set by Schumann in a dramatic through-composed version, is not unusual. However, both Heine's Bonapartism (Sammons 1969, 4–5) and Schumann's climactic quotation of the "Marseillaise"—in 1840—represent a response to the era's invidious censorship that emboldened creativity even as it sought to restrict its existence. The Swabian poet Johann Ludwig Uhland (1787–1862), whose "Frühlingsglaube" is the only work of the poet that Schubert set, served the development of the Romantic lied in at least two respects: his folk song-like poems have often been taken to be authentic *Volkslieder*—Uhland's scholarly updating of earlier folk song collections in his *Alte hoch- und niederdeutsche Volkslieder* of 1844–45 no doubt enhanced their apparent genuineness[21]—and his masterly ballads inspired Schumann and Liszt to rhapsodic musical emulations.

Some of the same poems by Goethe and Heine prompted both Liszt and Schumann to compose lieder that are staples of today's art song canon. Another poet who inspired Schumann and Liszt is Nikolaus Lenau (1802–50), an Austrian of German, Hungarian, and Slavic descent, whose poems met with enthusiastic reception in 1832 and thereafter no doubt because "they echoed the *Weltschmerz* of the times" (Brody and Fowkes 1971, 218).[22] Georg Friedrich Daumer (1800–75), on the other hand, reflected another passion of the times: Orientalism. He translated the Persian poet Hafiz (1300–88) and wrote pseudo-Oriental poetry; Brahms set nineteen Daumer poems, including lyric versions of Hafiz's originals. The repetitions of the word *wonnevoll* (blissful) in "Wie bist du meine Königin," Op. 32, No. 9 reflect the Persian *ghazel,* which, in its German realizations, is perhaps the most "unusual and highly patterned structure" (Fehn and Thym 1889, 33) that Romantic lied composers chose to set. Whereas the sonnet's length and meter are strictly limited to fourteen pentameter lines, the *ghazel* can vary in length from four to perhaps fifteen couplets; its meter is freely chosen by the given poet. Only the rhyme is constant, but it binds each *ghazel* absolutely by virtue of its twofold appearance in the first couplet, whereafter it recurs at the end of every subsequent couplet. Friedrich Schlegel was the first German poet to use the *ghazel* in 1803, but it was Joseph Hammer-Purgstall's 1812 translation of the fourteenth-century poet Hafiz, master poet of the *ghazel,* that inspired Goethe's *West-östlicher Divan* of 1819 and established the literary fashion of German Orientalism that enthralled Rückert and Platen in the 1820s, as well as Daumer, Geibel, and Keller (1819–90).

Daumer's Orientalism was by no means the first instance in which more or less exotic (or foreign) prosodic forms were prized in German poetry and art song. Already during the later eighteenth century, odes and sonnets found favor as well. The strict Classical meter of Hölty's ode "Die Mainacht" is reflected in the carefully declaimed melody and richly chromatic harmony of Brahm's Op. 43, No. 2, which conforms to the prosodic strictures of the asclepiadean ode even as it expresses late Romantic musical sensibility. The sonnet, a highly shaped poetic form "not obviously and immediately compatible with the musical idiom of the nineteenth-century lied" (Fehn and Thym 1986, 1), was prized at the end of the eighteenth century by A. W. Schlegel, whose translations of Petrarch were widely read, encouraging Goethe, Platen, Eichendorff, Rückert, Uhland, Heine, Mörike, and Rilke to try their hands at it. Schubert set eight sonnets to music, including three by Petrarch in Schlegel's translation; Pfitzner set

Petrarch's ninety-second sonnet in Förster's translation, and there are two each by Bürger and Eichendorff. Mendelssohn, Wolf, and Strauss set only one sonnet each, Brahms two. (Liszt's three sonnet-settings are not in German translation, but in Petrarch's original Italian.)

As these translations of Petrarch suggest, foreign poems (in well-crafted German equivalents) provided sources for many later Romantic poets and composers. Schubert, Schumann, and Brahms all set translated poems ranging from Anonymous to Burns, Byron, Moore, Pope, Scott, Shakespeare, and the Bible. Schumann used the translations of a Frenchman of noble descent, Adelbert von Chamisso (1781–1838), who fled the Revolution and spent the rest of his life in Prussia. Chamisso left France at age 9 for Berlin, where—among many other literary pursuits—he translated the poems of Hans Christian Andersen and Pierre Béranger into German; these, together with his cycle *Frauenliebe und -leben* (Woman's Love and Life), account for sixteen of Schumann's settings. But it was the translations of Emanuel Geibel (1815–84) and Paul Heyse (1830–1914) that—in addition to numerous Schumann settings—provided the poetic raw material for the ninety settings that make up Hugo Wolf's major cycles of 1891 and 1895: the Spanish and Italian Songbooks. Although translated texts constitute "at least half of Wolf's lieder," as contrasted with 5 percent for Brahms, they account for a modest but significant share of the poems set by Richard Strauss (Petersen 1980, 36).

Naturalism and Dénouement

Even more interesting in literary terms, however, is Strauss's encounter (in the mid-1890s) with the poets—and the poetry—of Naturalism. These socially engaged contemporary poets—particularly Richard Dehmel (1863–1920), John Henry Mackay (1864–1933), and Detlev von Liliencron (1884–1909)—were then considered quite "modern" and even "revolutionary." In 1898–99 Strauss set three of Dehmel's new "social lyrics" (Petersen 1980, 170), "Der Arbeitsmann" (Op. 39, No. 3), "Befreit" (Op. 39, No. 4), and "Am Ufer" (Op. 41, No. 3). The grimly realistic (i.e., "naturalistic") protest of the vainly laboring father, who is nonetheless mindful of nature's bounty and his family's rightful place therein, gains a Nibelungen-like aura of joyless futility in Strauss's darkly Wagnerian setting of "Der Arbeitsmann" (The Laborer):

Wir haben ein Bett, wir haben ein Kind, Mein Weib!	We have a bed, we have a child, My wife!
Wir haben auch Arbeit, und gar zu zweit,	We also have work, and work for two,
Und haben die Sonne und Regen und Wind,	And have the sun and rain and wind,
Und uns fehlt nur eine Kleinigkeit,	And just one bit we lack

| Um so frei zu sein, wie die Vögel sind: | To be as free as are the birds, |
| Nur Zeit. | Just time. |

The second stanza—omitted here—describes a Sunday stroll through nature's fields of grain, where the family's clothing is as fine as that of the birds. The third equates human needs with an impending storm and culminates in the oxymoron that expresses hope and hopelessness simultaneously—human deprivation as a "brief" eternity:

Nur Zeit! wir wittern Gewitterwind,	Just time! We sense windy storms ahead,
Wir Volk.	We People.
Nur eine kleine Ewigkeit;	Just one brief eternity;
Uns fehlt ja nichts, mein Weib, mein Kind,	Naught do we lack, my wife, my child,
Als all das, was durch uns gedeiht,	Save all that flourishes through us,
Um so kühn zu sein, wie die Vögel sind:	To be as bold as are the birds:
Nur Zeit.	Just time.

The extreme economy of rhyming words is a structural feature that makes the unrhymed, single occurrence of *Volk* (people) an emphatic call for social justice in the intimate context of the (nuclear) family. Strauss brightens the gloomy F-minor texture with a major harmony when wife, child, and sun are mentioned, but in the crescendo-enhanced F-sharp-minor context of the anticipated storm, the F-major fortissimo harmony supporting *Volk* underscores the political message as well.

In the poem "Befreit" (Freed), Dehmel displays the psychological ambivalence and ecstatic rhetoric typical of Nietzsche's influence on the poets and composers of this age: although Dehmel said that the three quatrains describe a man speaking to his dying wife, the threefold refrain "O Glück!" (Oh happiness) suggests that the "liberation" involved is the "ultimate devotion which has 'freed' the loving pair from suffering to a point which not death itself can threaten" (Del Mar 1972, 316). An even more Nietzschean utterance of Dehmel's in 1896, "Am Ufer" (On the Shore), evokes a twilight-nighttime hallucination far removed from Goethe's serene nocturnal vision of 1780:

Die Welt verstummt, dein Blut erklingt;	The world grows mute, your blood resounds;
In seinen hellen Abgrund sinkt	Into its bright abyss sinks
Der ferne Tag,	The distant day,
Er schaudert nicht; die Glut umschlingt	It shudders not; the glow engulfs
Das höchste Land, im Meere ringt	The highest land, in the sea wrestles
Die ferne Nacht,	The distant night,
Sie zaudert nicht; der Flut entspringt	It lingers not; out of the tide

Ein Sternchen, deine Seele trinkt	A small star springs, your soul drinks
Das ewige Licht.	The eternal light.

Psychic eons seem to have passed between the late-eighteenth-century simplicity and harmony of Goethe's "Warte nur, balde / Ruhest du auch" (Just wait, soon / you too shall rest) and the anthropomorphic aestheticism of Dehmel's fin-de-siècle conception of the bond between mankind and nature that can be expressed only metaphorically and synesthetically as "deine Seele trinkt / das ewige Licht" ("your soul drinks / the eternal light").

This "shoreline" vision, so fatefully poised on the threshold of the twentieth century, received another setting in 1908, by Anton Webern, that heralds the atonal musical idiom that the younger Strauss's post-Wagnerian chromaticism sought but did not attain (Velten 1986, 464–67). Even more prophetic is a very different "shoreline" vision by an all but ignored earlier German poet who precariously bridges German Classicism and Romanticism: Friedrich Hölderlin (1770–1843). At some time between 1799 and 1803, the tormented Hölderlin wrote a short poem whose imagistic concentration and radically disjunctive view of life, whose intoxicated Romantic lushness and despairing, existential hopelessness, have rarely been equaled, even by deliberate modernists (Hamburger 1970, 268):

Mit gelben Birnen hänget	With yellow pears the land,
Und voll mit wilden Rosen	And full of wild roses,
Das Land in den See,	Hangs down into the lake,
Ihr holden Schwäne,	You lovely swans,
Und trunken von Küssen	And drunk with kisses
Tunkt ihr das Haupt	You dip your heads
Ins heilignüchterne Wasser.	Into the hallowed, the sober, water.
Weh mir, wo nehm' ich, wenn	But oh, where shall I find,
Es Winter ist, die Blumen, und wo	When winter comes, the flowers, and where
Den Sonnenschein	The sunshine
Und Schatten der Erde?	And shade of the earth?
Die Mauern stehn	The walls loom
Sprachlos und kalt, im Winde	Speechless and cold, in the wind
Klirren die Fahnen.	Weathercocks clatter.

Except for the adjective *heilignüchtern* (holy-sober), "Hälfte des Lebens" (The Middle of Life) is written in the language of common speech. But as Hamburger points out (1970, 269), "it creates new rhythms—as the expression of a mood so new as to be terrifying." This dynamic syntax, which became typical of the early twentieth-century Expressionists, literally speaks for itself without any poetic or emotional embellishment. Yet the vast difference between Hölderlin's drastic conjunction of two diametrically opposed seven-line stanzas and Goethe's single eight-line strophe "Über allen Gipfeln" is a measure of the capacity of German poetry to express the vicissitudes of human experience during the extended period when the major Romantic lieder were composed. In his schizoid but lyrically conjoined utterances, Hölderlin pits man's classically discerned oneness with a harmoniously perceived and aesthetically experienced nature (in stanza 1) against a Kafkaesque twentieth-century anxiety (in stanza 2) that calls into question the very existence of such relationships. By contrast, Goethe's late-eighteenth-century confidence in the secure place of man in the natural scheme of things seems a long lost utopian dream.

Given the century that passed before Hölderlin's schizophrenically prophetic poetic insights could be discovered, it is understandable that it took another half-century for them to be set (in 1958) to congenial music by the English composer Benjamin Britten (1913–76).[23] The ingenious use of carefully controlled intervalic movement of the melody and arpeggiated ostinato harmonies to express two contrasting strophes—in radically differentiated ways for summer and winter—makes Britten's setting a paragon of musico-poetic congruence, as well as an apotheosis of Schubert's through-composed lied ideal. Just as the quintessential (musical) Romantic lied is all but unthinkable without the folk song tradition of preceding centuries, it is inconceivable that the many-faceted nineteenth-century lied would not continue to influence receptive composers in the decades thereafter.

APPENDIX: Lyric Poets and Lied Composers

An Explanatory Note on Anthologies

To help establish the literary background against which the individual poems chosen by lied composers can be better understood, Tables 1.1 and 1.2 enumerate respectively the "canonic" lyric poets in German literary history between 1750 and 1920, irrespective of musical settings, and the specifically lied-associated poets listed by Dietrich Fischer-Dieskau (1968). The seventy lied poets in Table 1.2 must be seen together with thirty-four of the literary poets in Table 1.1; Fischer-Dieskau's compendium thus contains a total of 104 lied poets. Yet thirty-four primarily literary poets have produced more than half of the 750 lied texts Fischer-Dieskau considers to be viable art song settings in our time.

Most standard literary anthologies—which cover the entire range of German poetry from the Middle Ages to the mid-twentieth century—average about 350 poems and approximately fifty poets for the period under discussion.[24] But Conrady (1991) greatly increases coverage of the period in question with 567 poems by eighty-four poets. Seminal examples of the nineteenth-century lied repertoire are included, among them three poems

TABLE 1.1.
Major German Lyric Poets 1750–1900[25]

Poet	*Setting*
1. Christian Fürchtegott GELLERT (1715–1769)	[6]
2. Friedrich Gottlieb KLOPSTOCK (1724–1803)	[3]
3. Christian Friedrich Schubart (1739–1791)	[1]
4. Matthias CLAUDIUS (1740–1815)	[3]
5. Gottfried August Bürger (1747–1794)	[2]
6. Ludwig Christoph Heinrich HÖLTY (1748–1776)	[5]
7. Johann Wolfgang von GOETHE (1749–1832)	[67]
8. Friedrich von SCHILLER (1759–1805)	[14]
9. Friedrich HÖLDERLIN (1770–1843)	[5]
10. Novalis (Friedrich von Hardenberg, 1772–1801)	[—]
11. Friedrich Schlegel (1772–1829)	[1]
12. Ludwig TIECK (1773–1853)	[15]
13. Clemens BRENTANO (1778–1842)	[3]
14. Justinus KERNER (1786–1862)	[12]
15. Ludwig UHLAND (1787–1862)	[4]
16. Joseph von EICHENDORFF (1788–1857)	[35]
17. Friedrich RÜCKERT (1788–1866)	[22]
18. August von PLATEN (1796–1835)	[6]
19. Annette von Droste-Hülshoff (1797–1848)	[1]
20. Heinrich HEINE (1797–1856)	[62]
21. Nikolaus LENAU (1802–1850)	[6]
22. Eduard MÖRIKE (1804–1875)	[39]
23. Ferdinand FREILIGRATH (1810–1876)	[3]
24. Friedrich HEBBEL (1813–1863)	[3]
25. Theodor STORM (1817–1888)	[3]
26. Theodor Fontane (1819–1898)	[2]
27. Klaus GROTH (1819–1899)	[7]
28. Gottfried KELLER (1819–1890)	[4]
29. Conrad Ferdinand MEYER (1825–1898)	[8]
30. Detlev von LILIENCRON (1844–1909)	[5]
31. Friedrich Nietzsche (1844–1900)	[—]
32. Richard DEHMEL (1863–1920)	[4]
33. Arno Holz (1868–1933)	[—]
34. Stefan GEORGE (1868–1933)	[15]
35. Christian MORGENSTERN (1871–1914)	[3]
36. Hugo von Hofmannsthal (1874–1929)	[—]
37. Rainer Maria RILKE (1875–1926)	[16]
38. Hermann HESSE (1877–1962)	[4]

NB: The bracketed numbers in right column indicate the number of musical settings included in the *Fischer-Dieskau Book of Lieder* (Bird and Stokes 1977). This includes musical settings of poems by all of the poets above except Novalis (10), Nietzsche (31), Holz (33), and Hofmannsthal (36). CAPITALIZED names indicate that three or more poems have been set.

TABLE 1.2.
Additional Lied Poets[26]

1	Hermann Allmers	(1821–1902)	36	Julius Mosen	(1803–1867)
2	Hans C. Andersen	(1805–1875)	37	Wilhelm Müller	(1794–1827)
3	Achim von Arnim	(1781–1831)	38	Chr. A. Overbeck	(1755–1821)
4	Otto J. Bierbaum	(1865–1910)	39	Alexander Pope	[tr. Herder]
5	G. G. N. Lord Byron	(1788–1824)	40	Joh. L. Pyrker	(1772–1847)
6	A. von Chamisso	(1781–1838)	41	Oskar v. Redwitz	(1823–1891)
7	Karl Candidus	(1817–1872)	42	Fdr. Reil [Schubert: D. 889, 917]	
8	Peter Cornelius	(1824–1874)	43	Robert Reinick	(1805–1852)
9	Felix Dahn	(1834–1912)	44	C. L. Reissig [Beethoven: Op. 75]	
10	Georg F. Daumer	(1800–1875)	45	Ludwig Rellstab	(1799–1860)
11	Emanuel Geibel	(1815–1884)	46	JG. v. Salis-Seewis	(1762–1834)
12	Hermann v. Gilm	(1812–1864)	47	Adolf F. v. Schack	(1815–1894)
13	Heinrich Hart	(1855–1906)	48	J. V. v. Scheffel	(1826–1886)
14	Karl Henckell	(1864–1929)	49	M. v. Schenkendorf	(1783–1817)
15	Joh. G. Herder	(1744–1803)	50	Johannes Schlaf	(1862–1941)
16	Paul von Heyse	(1830–1914)	51	F. X. v. Schlechta	(1796–1875)
17	H. v. Fallersleben	(1798–1874)	52	Hans Schmidt	(1854–1923)
18	Joh. Geo. Jacobi	(1740–1814)	53	G. P. Schmidt v. Lübeck	(1766–1849)
19	Aloys Jeitteles	(1794–1858)	54	Franz Schober	(1796–1882)
20	August Kopisch	(1799–1853)	55	Aloys Schreiber	(1763–1841)
21	Franz Kugler	(1808–1858)	56	Ernst Schulze	(1789–1817)
22	Emil Kuh	(1828–1876)	57	Felix Schumann	(1854–1879)
23	Carl G. Lappe	(1773–1843)	58	Sir Walter Scott	(1771–1832)
24	Christian L'Egru	[Schumann]	59	Joh. Gab. Seidl	(1804–1874)
25	K. G. R. v. Leitner	(1800–1890)	60	Shakespeare	(1564–1616)
26	K. v. Lemcke (b. 1831)	[Brahms]	61	Karl Simrock	(1802–1876)
27	G. Ephr. Lessing	(1729–1781)	62	Josef v. Spaun	(1788–1865)
28	Hermann v. Lingg	(1820–1905)	63	F. L. zu Stolberg	(1750–1819)
29	John H. Mackay	(1864–1933)	64	J. Stoll [Beethoven; Schubert]	
30	Gustav Mahler	(1860–1911)	65	Chr. Aug. Tiedge	(1752–1841)
31	Frdr. Matthison	(1761–1831)	66	Joh. Nepomuk Vogl	(1802–1866)
32	Joh. Mayrhofer	(1787–1836)	67	Chr. Felix Weiße	(1726–1804)
33	Michelangelo	(1475–1564)	68	Josef Wenzig [Brahms: Opp. 48, 43]	
34	Alfred Mombert	(1872–1942)	69	M. Wesendonck	(1828–1902)
35	Thomas Moore	(1779–1852)	70	M. von Willemer	(1784–1860)

NB: Where no dates of birth and/or death are available, the composer or translator associated with a given poet is cited in brackets.

from Chamisso's *Frauenliebe und -leben*, a half-dozen Eichendorff poems (set by Schumann and Wolf), two of Rückert's *Kindertotenlieder*, and two Wilhelm Müller excerpts from *Die schöne Müllerin* as well as three from *Die Winterreise*. A singularly influential anthology—*The Oxford Book of German Verse*—reveals the change in literary and musical taste over the course of the twentieth century: its earlier version of 1915, edited by H. G. Fiedler to draw deliberately on the lied for its contents, contained many musical references in its endnotes as well as an extensive index of lied composers, all of which—because of "the commanding position enjoyed by German composers at the beginning of the present century"—proved to be an "invaluable aid" in Fiedler's successful effort to popularize German poetry for primarily English readers. Yet, in E. L. Stahl's third edition of 1967 the links between German music and poetry "are no longer considered to be of primary importance, . . . nor is music held to be the ideal condition to which poetry invariably aspires" (p. vi). These two editions demonstrate both the close bond between the lied and the lyric poem at the turn of the century and its gradual but inevitable dissolution since then.

Notes

1. "Die romantische Poesie ist eine progressive Universalpoesie. . . . Sie umfaßt alles, was nur poetisch ist, vom größten wieder mehrere Systeme in sich enthaltenden Systeme der Kunst bis zu dem Seufzer, dem Kuß, den das dichtende Kind aushaucht in kunstlosen Gesang." "Athenäums-Fragment" no. 116 (Schlegel 1964, 38–39; trans. from Eichner 1970, 57).
2. "Athenäums-Fragment" no. 216: "Die Französische Revolution, Fichtes Wissenschaftslehre und *Goethes Meister* (emphasis added) sind die größten Tendenzen des Zeitalters" (Schlegel 1964, 48).
3. Goethe's letter to Zelter of 21 December 1809 states that "das Lied durch jede Composition erst vollständig werden soll" (Geiger 1902, 260).
4. See, e.g., Barricelli (1988), Brown (1948), Cone (1957), Kramer (1984), Mosley (1990), and Scher (1990).
5. Goethe's and Heine's parodies retain the original first line (but little else!); Uhland deviates to "Da droben auf dem Hügel," and Brentano ventures farthest afield with "Es stehet im Abendglanze."
6. Translation from Kramer (1984, 152). Kramer's perceptive "deconstruction" of both text and music richly documents the "undeniable effectiveness" of Schubert's radical emulation and transformation of Goethe's progressive "sexual fantasy" (Kramer 1984, 155).
7. According to Auden (1950, xii–xiv) mankind redefined itself toward the end of the eighteenth century so that, by the beginning of the nineteenth, man is clearly self-conscious and—like God, but unlike the rest of nature—can say "I" as he senses his ego to be sovereign over against self, which is part of nature. In this self (apart), man can see or imagine possibilities (other than they actually are); he can even foresee his own death. If self-awareness and the power to conceive of possibility are defining elements in man, Auden concludes, then the hero whom the poet must celebrate is himself, for the only consciousness accessible to him is his own.
8. Literally, "my intestines are burning" (as in the biblical expression "her bowels yearned"), as Brody and Fowkes (1971, 44) helpfully elucidate. They also point out that the seemingly impure rhymes "leide" and "Freude" (lines 2 and 4) would pass muster in Goethe's Frankfurt dialect.
9. T. S. Eliot's felicitous phrase (from *The Sacred Wood*) for the metaphorical

equivalent of particular lyric correspondences has been borrowed by many interdisciplinary scholars for designating musico-poetic congruencies. Prawer (1952, 18) cites this "extreme dictum" in its original context.

10. To cite an extreme example: in Ludwig Rellstab's poem "In der Ferne" (Far from Home), the sixth poem of Schubert's *Schwanengesang,* the heavy use of present participles is poetically unthinkable in English:

> Wehe, den Fliehenden,
> Welt hinaus ziehenden!—
> Fremde durchmessenden,
> Heimat vergessenden,
> Mutterhaus hassenden,
> Freunde verlassenden
> Folget kein Segen, ach!
> Auf ihren Wegen nach!

Schubert was able to make a musical virtue of this by setting the participles to a consistent rhythm of dotted quarter, eighth, and quarter in alternate measures throughout the entire composition.

An example of how the abundance of suffixes can seemingly overwhelm meaning is Mayrhofer's amphibrachic tour de force "Beim Winde":

> Es träumen die Wolken, die Sterne, der Mond,
> Die Bäume, die Vögel, die Blumen, der Strom,
> Sie wiegen und schmiegen sich tiefer zurück,
> Zur ruhigen Stätte, zum tauigen Bette,
> zum heimlichen Glück.

Schubert responded with an inspired setting that assimilates the prosodic-semantic substance of "Beim Winde" even as it transcends the poem's linguistic limitations.

11. Eichendorff's poem has "nun" (now); Schumann's text wrongly reads "nur" (only), which Sams (1969, 98) renders as "must dream of him *alone*" and considers to be either a "mistranscription" or a "revealing error, as in other songs."

12. Seidlin (1978) analyzes in convincing detail the "architectonically" three-dimensional or spatial quality of the typical Eichendorffian landscape; "Mondnacht" is clearly a case in point.

13. According to Sams (1969, 7) a very persuasive case can be made—by way of Schumann's system of musical ciphers—for a musical marriage (*Ehe*) between heaven and earth in notational symbolism of (German) E–H–E (H = B♮; cf. Sams 1969, 98) in the initial measures of the bass line supporting these words in the text.

14. The juxtaposition of "cosmopolitan" and "provincial" could hardly be more apt: the urban and urbane north-German Heine spent the last twenty-five years of his life in exile in Paris, whereas the rural south-German Mörike inhabited rustic villages around Stuttgart throughout his life. Schumann set "Die Soldatenbraut (Op. 64, No. 1), "Das verlassene Mägdlein" (Op. 64, No. 2), and "Er ist's" (op. 79, No. 24); Brahms set two longer Mörike poems, "An eine Äolsharfe" (Op. 19, No. 5) and "Agnes" (Op. 59, No. 5), as well as five humorous quatrains of supposed sisterly harmony: the duet "Die Schwestern" (Op. 61, No. 1).

15. Although "Verborgenheit" was first published in 1838, it was not widely known until Wolf's composition some fifty years later.

16. What Mörike's poetry portends for literary developments of the late nineteenth and early twentieth centuries may be analogous to what Wolf's musical settings signify for the art-song aesthetics of the following century. In a perceptive review of Hans-Herwig Geyer's investigation into Hugo Wolf's Mörike settings (1991), Amanda Glauert (1993) persuasively amplifies on Geyer's passing suggestions.

17. But as Sams (1961, 60–61) points out, it took eight years for Hugo Wolf to "prepare" himself for the sudden burst of creativity that resulted in the fifty-three *Mörikelieder*. This was so, Sams claims, because "Mörike's lyrics demanded (and indeed helped to create) a new tonal language for their satisfactory translation into musical terms. . . . Mörike's poetry had by then [1888] been in print for well over half a century; composers from the pioneering Schumann and Robert Franz onwards, including Brahms, had already set [some of] it to music. By the time that Wolf first read Mörike, in the 1870s, the words of 'Das verlassene Mägdlein' had appeared in some fifty published settings, and those of 'Agnes' in more than eighty."

18. Fricke (1990, 18) adds that in spite of Goethe's overall superiority in numbers of lied settings for each poem, only about twenty-five Goethe poems are successful "hits" as art songs, and Rückert can claim almost that many.

19. Fricke (1990, 20) uses this fraction to indicate that two motives or themes are generally developed individually, then joined in a concluding synthesis, so that the limits of the lied as miniature will not be breached.

20. Both Plantinga (1984, 256–57) and Brody and Fowkes (1971, 183–92) see in Loewe's op. 1 treatment of Herder's problematic translation crucial historical significance.

21. It remained for twentieth-century scholarship to debunk the romantic folk-soul theories and to demonstrate that instead of an anonymous oral-aural folk tradition mysteriously producing uniquely polished lyric utterances, necessarily unknown individuals—often members of the intelligentsia—actually created every so-called folk song, which was often an "abgesunkenes Kunstlied, jedenfalls nie vom Volke selbst gedichtet" (von Wilpert 1961, 679) or "a debased art song, in any case never written by the people collectively." Sternfeld's parody-concept cited earlier is a salient part of this scholarly endeavor (Sternfeld 1979, 8).

22. *Weltschmerz* (sadness over the woes of the world) refers to the sentimental pessimism that flourished in the repressive political climate before and after Goethe's death. Lenau's despair over bourgeois civilization and admiration for the allegedly wild and lonely lives of gypsies found poignant expression in Liszt's setting of Lenau's seven-stanza ballad "Die drei Zigeuner" (Brody-Fowkes 1971, 219–22). Schumann set six Lenau poems in his Op. 90.

23. Britten's arguably non-German compositional idiom can be seen as the viable "alienating" catalyst that makes Hölderlin's almost Kafkaesque vision aesthetically acceptable and even (moderately) popular. By contrast, Harald Genzmer's setting of "Hälfte des Lebens" (in Genzmer 1967, 54–56) demonstrates a less immediately accessible twentieth-century German compositional style similar to that of Hermann Reutter or even Boris Blacher.

24. For example, Echtermeyer and von Wiese (1966), the staple of schools and universities both in Germany and abroad, contains in the section entitled "Auf-

klärung, Empfindsamkeit und Sturm und Drang" 18 *Volkslieder,* 3 *Volksballaden,* and 48 other poems by fifteen poets; in "Höhepunkte Klassischer Lyrik" a total of 99 poems are the work of only four poets—54 by Goethe, 25 by Schiller, 19 by Hölderlin, and 1 by Heinrich von Kleist; among the "Romantiker" one finds 84 poems by fourteen poets; and in "Von der Romantik zum Realismus" fifty poets supply 127 poems. The more scholarly multivolume literature series *Klassische Deutsche Dichtung* divides "Balladen" and "Lyrik" into separate volumes, the first of which includes 171 ballads by forty-four balladeer-authors, and the second includes 297 lyric poems by some fifty-five poets. Reclam UB's 1984 edition of *Deutsche Gedichte* presents 290 poems by 105 poets within the approximate parameters of the lied repertory; a companion (Reclam UB) volume—*Gedichte der Romantik*—presents an up-to-date (1984) compilation of some three hundred exclusively German Romantic poems by thirty-one Romantic poets, only twelve of whom are included in Fischer-Dieskau (1968).

25. As compiled by Fritz Schlawe, *Neudeutsche Metrik* (Stuttgart, 1972), 97–103.

26. From Bird and Stokes (1977). Underlining indicates that in Fischer-Dieskau's view two or more poems by the respective poet have inspired important or successful settings.

Bibliography

Abert, Hermann. *Goethe und die Musik.* Stuttgart, 1922.

Albertsen, Leif Ludwig. "Goethes Lieder und andere Lieder." In *Deutsche Literatur zur Zeit der Klassik,* ed. Karl O. Conrady, 172–87. Stuttgart, 1977.

Auden, W. H., ed. "Introduction." In *Romantic Poets,* xii-xxv. New York, 1950.

Barricelli, Jean-Pierre. *Melopoiesis: Approaches to the Study of Literature and Music.* New York, 1988.

Becker, Peter. "'Nicht nur lesen! Immer singen! Und ein jedes Blatt ist dein!': Versuch über ein liederliches Goethewort." *Musik und Bildung* 18 (1986): 224–26.

Bird, George, and Richard Stokes. *The Fischer-Dieskau Book of Lieder.* New York, 1977.

Blackall, Eric A. *The Emergence of German as a Literary Language 1700–1775.* London, 1959.

Boyle, Nicholas. *The Poetry of Desire (1749–1790).* Vol. 1 of *Goethe: The Poet and the Age.* Oxford, 1991.

Britten, Benjamin. *Sechs Hölderlin-Fragmente,* Op. 61. London, 1962.

Brody, Elaine, and Robert A. Fowkes. *The German Lied and Its Poetry.* New York, 1971.

Brown, Calvin S. *Music and Literature.* Athens, GA, 1948. Reprint. Hanover, NH, 1987.

Bruford, W. H. *Germany in the Eighteenth Century: The Social Background of the Literary Revival.* London, 1971.

Capell, Richard. *Schubert's Songs.* London, 1957.

Cone, Edward T. "Words into Music: the Composer's Approach to the Text." In *Sound and Poetry: English Institute Essays,* ed. Northrop Frye, 3–15. New York, 1957. Reprint, in Edward T. Cone, *Music: A View from Delft,* 115–23. Chicago, 1989.

Conrady, Karl Otto. *Das große deutsche Gedichtbuch.* München, 1991.

Dahlhaus, Carl. *Nineteenth-Century Music.* Trans. Bradford Robinson. Berkeley, 1989.

Del Mar, Norman. *Richard Strauss: A Critical Commentary of His Life and Works.* Vol. 3. London, 1972.

Draper, Hal. *The Complete Poems of Heinrich Heine.* Boston, 1982.

Echtermeyer, Theodor. *Deutsche Gedichte.* Rev. Benno von Wiese. Düsseldorf, 1966.

Eichner, Hans. *Friedrich Schlegel.* New York, 1970.

Fehn, Ann C., and Jürgen Thym. "Sonnet Structure and the German Lied." Presentation at the 1986 conference of the German Studies Association, Albuquerque, 27 September 1986.

————. "Repetition as Structure in the German *Lied:* The Ghazal." *Comparative Literature* 41 (Winter 1989): 33–52.

Fischer-Dieskau, Dietrich. *Texte deutscher Lieder: Ein Handbuch.* Munich, 1968.

————. *Auf den Spuren der Schubert-Lieder.* Wiesbaden, 1972.

Forbes, Elliot. "*Nur wer die Sehnsucht kennt:* An Example of a Goethe Lyric Set to Music." In *Words and Music: The Scholar's View,* ed. Lawrence Berman, 59–82. Cambridge, MA, 1972.

Fricke, Harald. "Rückert und das Kunstlied." *Rückert-Studien* 5 (1990): 14–37.

Friedländer, Max, ed. *Gedichte von Goethe in Compositionen seiner Zeitgenossen.* Vols. 11 and 31 of *Schriften der Goethe-Gesellschaft.* Weimar, 1896 and 1916. Reprint as *Gedichte von Goethe in Kompositionen,* Hildesheim, 1975.

Garland, Henry and Mary. *The Oxford Companion to German Literature.* Oxford, 1976.

Geiger, Ludwig, ed. *Briefwechsel zwischen Goethe und Zelter in den Jahren 1799 bis 1832.* Leipzig, 1902. Vol. 1 of 3.

Genzmer, Harald. "Hälfte des Lebens." In *Lieder und Gesänge in Dichtungen von Friedrich Hölderlin.* Vol. 5: *Schriften der Hölderlin-Gesellschaft.* Tübingen, 1967.

Geyer, Hans-Herwig. *Hugo Wolfs Mörike-Vertonungen: Mannigfaltigung in lyrischer Konzentration.* Kassel, 1991.

Glauert, Amanda. Review of Hans-Herwig Geyer, *Hugo Wolfs Mörike-Vertonungen: Mannigfaltigung in lyrischer Konzentration. Notes* 48 (1993): 1451–52.

Hamburger, Michael. *Contraries: Studies in German Literature.* New York, 1970.

Knaus, Herwig. "Im Reich der Nacht: Wort und Ton im bürgerlichen romantischen Lied um 1870." *Musikerziehung* 42 (October 1988): 19–26.

Kramer, Lawrence. *Music and Poetry: The Nineteenth Century and After.* Berkeley, 1984.

Martini, Fritz. *Deutsche Literaturgeschichte von den Anfängen bis zur Gegenwart.* Stuttgart, 1957.

Moser, Hans Joachim. *Das deutsche Lied seit Mozart.* Tutzing, 1968.

Mosley, David L. *Gesture, Sign and Song: An Interdisciplinary Approach to Schumann's Liederkreis Opus 39.* New York, 1990.

Ossenkop, David. *Hugo Wolf: A Guide to Research.* New York, 1988.

Peter, Klaus. "Der spekulative Anspruch: Die deutsche Romantik im Unterschied zur französischen und englischen." *Jahrbuch des Freien Deutschen Hochstifts* (1985): 101–50.

Petersen, Barbara A. *Ton und Wort: The Lieder of Richard Strauss.* Ann Arbor, 1980.

Plantinga, Leon. *Romantic Music.* New York, 1984.

Prawer, S. S. *German Lyric Poetry.* London, 1952.

Rose, Ernst. *A History of German Literature.* New York, 1960.

Sammons, Jeffrey L. *Heinrich Heine, The Elusive Poet.* New Haven, 1969.

Sams, Eric. *The Songs of Hugo Wolf.* London, 1961.

————. *The Songs of Robert Schumann.* London, 1969.

Scher, Steven P. *Literatur und Musik: Ein Handbuch zur Theorie und Praxis eines komparatistischen Grenzgebietes.* Berlin, 1984.

———. "The German Lied: A Genre and Its European Reception." In *European Romanticism: Literary Cross-Currents, Modes, and Models,* ed. Gerhart Hoffmeister, 127–41. Detroit, 1990.

———. "Musicopoetics or Melomania: Is There a Theory behind Music in German Literature?" In *Music and German Literature,* ed. James M. McGlathery, 328–27. Columbia, SC, 1992.

Schlegel, Friedrich. *Kritische Schriften.* Munich, 1964.

Schuh, Willi. *Goethe-Vertonungen: Ein Verzeichnis.* Zürich: Artemis, 1952.

Schumann, Robert, *Dichterliebe,* ed. Arthur Komar. *Norton Critical Score.* New York, 1971.

Schwab, Heinrich W. *Sangbarkeit, Popularität und Kunstlied: Studien zu Lied und Liedästhetik der mittleren Goethezeit 1770–1814.* Regensburg, 1965.

Seaton, Douglass. *The Art Song: A Research and Information Guide.* New York, 1987.

Seidlin, Oskar. *Versuche über Eichendorff.* Göttingen, 1978.

Smeed, J. W. *German Song and Its Poetry 1740–1900.* London, 1987.

Spann, Meno. *Heine.* New York, 1966.

Stahl, E. L. *The Oxford Book of German Verse.* Oxford, 1967.

Staiger, Emil. *J. W. Goethe: Gedichte.* Vol. 1. Zürich, 1949.

Stein, Jack M. *Poem and Music in the German Lied from Gluck to Hugo Wolf.* Cambridge, MA, 1971.

Sternfeld, Frederick W. *Goethe and Music.* New York, 1979.

Stoljar, Margaret Mahony. *Poetry and Song in Late Eighteenth-Century Germany: A Study in the Musical Sturm und Drang.* London, 1985.

Velten, Klaus. "Doppelinterpretation: Richard Dehmels Gedicht 'Am Ufer' in Vertonungen von Richard Strauss und Anton Webern." *Musik und Bildung* 18 (1986): 464–67.

Whitton, Kenneth. "The *Lied.*" In *Dietrich Fischer-Dieskau: Mastersinger,* 179–255. London, 1981.

———. *Lieder: An Introduction to German Song.* London, 1984.

Wilkinson, Elizabeth M. "Goethe's Poetry." In *Goethe: Poet and Thinker,* 20–34. London, 1962.

von Wilpert, Gero. *Sachwörterbuch der Literatur.* Stuttgart, 1961.

CHAPTER TWO

Franz Schubert: The Prince of Song

Susan Youens

The word *lied* immediately calls Schubert's name to mind, prior to Beethoven, Schumann, or anyone else. This is not because of chronological pride of place—there were numerous lied-composing predecessors and contemporaries—or the staggering size of Schubert's oeuvre—Johann Friedrich Reichardt, for one, produced an even more elephantine body of songs—but because of the quality of the music and Schubert's transformation of received genres. In his brief creative career, Schubert endowed both the lied and the song cycle with a profundity and a musical complexity they had lacked until he began "indefatigably" to compose songs.[1] Later composers would look to Schubert as their Ur-ancestor, the "Shakespeare of song." Although, as both older and new research demonstrate (Friedländer 1902, Alberti-Radonowicz 1923, and West 1989), Schubert did not spring fully formed from Jove's head, he overshadowed all others in his passion for poetry and the brilliance with which he transmuted it into music. The sum total of his harmonic originality, his mastery of melodic beauty (or his willingness to abdicate this in the service of musico-poetic revelation), and the depth to which he delved beneath the surface of his chosen verses constitute nothing less than a new aesthetic of the lied (see Capell 1973, Georgiades 1967, L. Kramer 1986, and Reed 1985).

Schubert's wish to modernize the lied implies a certain indebtedness to prior composers, and indeed many relationships link Schubert's songs with those of his predecessors and contemporaries. For example, at the start of his setting of Goethe's "Der Fischer" (The Fisherman), the Viennese composer Anton Eberl (1765–1807) separates almost every syllable of text by rests. Did Schubert know this song and use this particular device when he set Franz Xaver von Schlechta's "Widerschein" (Reflection, D. 949) in 1819 or 1820? The parallels between the two poems are obvious: in Goethe's poem, a fisherman is lured into the ocean by a siren-like mermaid; in Schlechta's brief poem, a fisherman waits for his beloved on a bridge and stares into the brook. She is hiding in the bushes, and her image is reflected back at him, almost enticing him into the waters. Schlechta both encapsulates Goethe's famous poem within smaller boundaries and rescues his own poetic persona from a watery death, thus revising Goethe. Schubert, like Eberl, breaks his melodic line—its arpeggiated contour already a mimicry of Eberl's—into syllables separated by rests: a musical metaphor for suspense and anxious waiting (Ex. 2.1).

In the giant ballads of Johann Rudolf Zumsteeg (1760–1802), the young Schubert found a model of tonal audacity and virtuoso writing for the piano (Maier 1971). When, in the middle of August Bürger's "Lenore" of 1797, the grief-stricken protagonist tells her mother that life without her beloved Wilhelm is hell and then prays for death, Zumsteeg dramatically breaks off the unharmonized C-minor pronouncement about hell and sets the succeeding prayer "Lisch aus, mein Licht, und ewig aus!" (Go out, my light, and forever) in D♭ major. Schubert might have noted for future reference the semitonal jolt upwards. The progressive tonality in these ballads and their episodic form, the sections of alternating recitative, Gluckian arioso, and operatic blood and thunder, were, for Schubert, an invitation to experiment. Whatever Zumsteeg did, Schubert would outdo (Deutsch 1958, 26–27).* And could Schubert have remembered Reichardt's setting of Goethe's "Erlkönig" when he came to compose Matthias Claudius's "Der Tod und das Mädchen" (Death and the Maiden, D. 531) in February 1817? In this declamatory piece (*Deklamationsstück*), Death sings his mingled enticements and threats as pianissimo recitation—whispers within the boy's fevered mind—mostly on the repeated pitch D, accompanied by block chords that shadow the rhythmic patterns of the vocal part. The elf-king's words are thus stripped of all human lyricism, rendered eerily solemn. In Schubert's song, Death is a raptor of the young and a seducer, if a more comforting one than the apparition in Reichardt's "Erlkönig," and sings in similar chantlike tones. Christoph Wolff has proposed Gluck's *Alceste* and the cemetery scene of Mozart's *Don Giovanni* as influences on "Der Tod und das Mädchen," and the pendant setting of Joseph von Spaun's "Der Jüngling und der Tod" (The Youth and Death, D. 545), both from March 1817 (Wolff 1982); perhaps Reichardt's composition provided in addition a model from the realm of lieder (Ex. 2.2).

Schubert was clearly predisposed to ballad and lied composition from the start. Several of his earliest extant manuscript fragments, probably from

---

*For a discussion of Zumsteeg's and Schubert's related settings of Schiller's "Die Erwartung" (D. 159), see Fehn 1983, 229–44.

EXAMPLE 2.1a. Anton Eberl, "Der Fischer"

Romanze

1. Das
2. Sie
3. Labt
4. Das

Was	-	ser	rauscht',	das Was	-

Was - ser rauscht', das Was - ser schwoll, ein
sang zu ihm, sie sprach zu ihm: "Was
sich die lie - be Son - ne nicht, der
Was - ser rauscht', das Was - ser schwoll, netzt'

cresc.

Fi - scher saß da - ran, sah __
lockst du mei - ne __ Brut mit __
Mond sich nicht im __ Meer? Kehrt __
ihm den nack - ten __ Faß, sein __

EXAMPLE 2.1b. Schubert, "Widerschein" (D. 949)

Langsam, zögernd

EXAMPLE 2.2. J. F. Reichardt, "Erlkönig"

1810, are songs,[2] and it was in this medium that he first won public recognition with his Op. 1, his setting of Goethe's "Erlkönig," D. 328, in March 1821.[3] Although he did not consider himself solely a song composer,[4] he did compose more than six hundred songs in his short life, a feat unmatched by any other lied composer. The songs encompass his entire career: "Der Hirt auf dem Felsen," D. 965, and "Die Taubenpost," D. 965a, of October 1828 were among his last completed compositions, and there are few periods of his life from which song composition is entirely absent. It was his project to elevate song to the rank of a major genre, and he did so with respect to every known category of song: folklike strophic song, extended through-composed songs (*Gesänge*), ballads, and the song cycle.

Because Schubert was so prolific, only the merest fraction of his oeuvre can be discussed here. To avoid list-making and meaningless generalizations, I discuss the principal characteristics of Schubert's songs; the poetry; his revisions and multiple settings; and individual songs from several periods. Though the periods are drawn somewhat arbitrarily for the sake of convenience, the examples nevertheless reflect important divisions of Schubert's songwriting life: the miraculous song year of 1815; the years 1817–21; the special year of brilliance 1822; and the period between the two cycles (*Die schöne Müllerin* D. 795 and *Winterreise* D. 911). Although much is omitted, I compensate by directing attention to worthy if less well-known songs and to Schubert's protean word-tone relationships, in which so much of the pleasure and the power of Schubert's songs reside.

Traits of Schubertian Song

One aspect of Schubert's project to modernize the lied was to remove it in part from the realm of amateur performers. Although Schubert could and did compose simple strophic lieder *im Volkston* (in folk song style) and composed almost one hundred such songs between 1814 and mid-1816, (on this facility see Allen 1989, Frisch 1986, Mainka 1957, and Schnapper 1937), many of his songs far exceed the average technical demands of his day, except in ballad composition; even in balladry, he outdid his peers. As a Leipzig critic wrote, the piano part "is very rarely mere accompaniment" in Schubert's lieder (Deutsch 1946, 718), and the accompaniments he devised for such powerful songs as Goethe's "An Schwager Kronos" (To Coachman Chronos, D. 369) and Johann Mayrhofer's "Auflösung" (Dissolution, D. 807) were not for the inept. Even the "easier accompaniment" (*leichterer Begleitung*) he provided for "Erlkönig" in its third version is surpassingly difficult. Nor did he spare the singer. He liked uncomfortably high tessituras, a predilection that occasionally impelled requests for transposition from his publishers: the setting of Johann Mayrhofer's "Die Sternennächte" (The Starry Nights), D. 670 of 1819, was published as Op. 165, No. 2, transposed down to B♭ major from its original key of D♭ major, in which the vocal line is indeed poised high above the earth.[5]

Another frequent Schubertian trait is onomatopeia, or descriptive music. Although word-painting has occasionally drawn fire from opponents of programmatic elements in music, Schubert's onomatopeia is never an end unto itself. Each instance is explicable both in purely musical terms and as a depiction of external phenomena cited by the poet, or of emotional states. For example, the sixteenth-note breeze that rises from the bass in the piano introduction to Marianne von Willemer's "Suleika I," D. 720, heralding Suleika's initial questions "What does this motion signify? Does the East Wind bring me glad tidings?" includes the dominant-seventh chord of C major, unexplained until later in the song when, to the same harmony, she bids the airy messenger depart (Ex. 2.3). The bell tolling midnight in Schubert's setting of Johann Mayrhofer's "Gondelfahrer" (The Gondolier, D. 808, mm. 24–29), is both the consequence of the harmonic progression in the piano introduction (♭VI–I) and a characteristic patch of word-painting (Ex. 2.4). Similarly, the grace-note figures

EXAMPLE 2.3. "Suleika I" (D. 720)

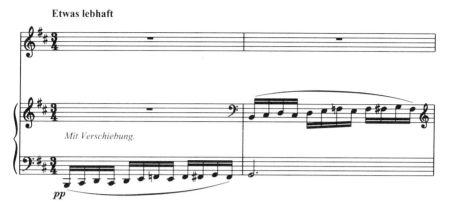

EXAMPLE 2.4. "Gondelfahrer" (D. 808)

in the piano introduction and postlude of the setting of Friedrich von Schlegel's "Der Schmetterling" (The Butterfly, D. 633) simultaneously establish the F-major tonality and depict the butterfly's darting up and down. The perfect fourths and fifths also foreshadow the bagpipe-like country dance strains of the song proper: "Why should I not dance?," the butterfly asks, to rustic figuration.[6] In an especially witty instance of poetic depiction, the pianist in Goethe's "Der Sänger," D. 149, "sings" a miniature Mozartian piano sonata while the minstrel of the song's title comments on the listeners' astonishment in the vocal line. Schubert's contemporaries recognized that his word-painting was more meaningful than most: a critic in 1828 praised him for going beyond the mere imitation of sounds to make the listener aware of "higher things in these impressions" (Deutsch 1977, 759).

As a student in the Royal Seminary, Schubert had been enamored of Gluck's operas, and he not only made many attempts to garner fame as an opera composer but incorporated operatic elements into many of his songs. He even experimented in August 1815 with the fusion of small strophic song with operatic style: his setting of Gabriele von Baumberg's "Der Morgenkuss," D. 264, is a mere nine measures in length but otherwise resembles an aria in style. His reverence for Mozart's operas is evident when he cites the duet "Könnte jeder brave Mann" from *Die Zauberflöte* at the beginning of his setting of Goethe's "Heidenröslein" (Wild Rose, D. 257), one of several Mozartian reminiscences (Sams 1978). More commonly, Schubert interjects recitative into song, as in his third setting of Friedrich von Matthisson's "Der Geistertanz" (The Ghost's Dance, D. 116) of October 1814; at m. 13, Schubert breaks off the $\frac{6}{8}$ dance strains (the faintly Baroque dotted rhythms remind us that these are specters from the past) to ask "Why do the dogs whimper beside their sleeping masters?" in dramatic recitative style. Perhaps the most famous example of recitative in lied was also composed that same month: the end of "Erlkönig," when the horror of the song's denouement is heightened by the sole recitative phrase. There are even songs almost entirely in recitative, such as Schubert's two settings of Friedrich Klopstock's "Die Sommernacht" (The Summer Night, D. 289). Of the piece's fewer than 30 measures, only 6 are purely songlike; Schubert thus toys with the very definition of *lied*.

Although Schubert's musical language throughout his life was founded on Classical form and function, he was also recognized in his own day as one of the most original, even visionary, of new composers in his tonal language. The dialectic between the two tendencies is perhaps the fundamental hallmark of his songs. Contemporary critics often referred, disapprovingly, to Schubert's radical harmonic language, his "disordered and purposeless musical modulation and side-tracking" or the "unwarrantably strong inclination to modulate again and again, with neither rest nor respite, which is a veritable disease of our time and threatens to grow into a modulation-mania" (Deutsch 1946, 166, 355). Others were more positively impressed. In a review of a performance by the great soprano Anna Milder of Schubert's songs in June 1825, the critic of the *Berlinische Zeitung* calls Schubert "a thoughtful song composer, fond of modulation" (Deutsch 1946, 421). He was indeed fond of radical harmonic gestures of many kinds. Sudden semitone shifts both upward and downward, such as one finds in "Auf dem Fluße" (On the Riverbank) in *Winterreise,* would not become commonplace until the last quarter of the century, and Schubert's use of progressive tonality (ending in a different key from the beginning) also belongs to the later era of Liszt and Wagner. The episodic construction of ballads often led to conclusion in a key other than the opening tonality, but such practice in a lied, for example, Goethe's "Ganymed," D. 544, of 1817, was rare; the ascent to a different tonal plane serves here as a metaphor for the youth's apotheosis. Schubert's setting of Mayrhofer's gloomy, powerful "Auf der Donau" (On the Danube, D. 553) of 1817 begins in E♭ major, ends in F♯ minor, and articulates C♭ major in the middle, going against convention and transforming the listener's tonal expectations for three-part song form (Denny 1989). The more irate reviewers could perhaps be forgiven their bewilderment or anger when confronted with such harmonically original songs as "Freiwilliges Versinken" (Voluntary Oblivion, D. 700) of 1817 (?), "Du liebst mich nicht" (You do not love me, D. 756) of 1822, and "Daß sie hier gewesen" (That she has been here, D. 775) (Muxfeldt 1991, 55–70).

Another signature element of Schubert's harmonic language is his fondness for mediant relationships, especially common-tone modulations. In lieder, sudden tonal shifts are often emblematic of removal from one sphere to another, whether from night to day, from waking consciousness to dreams, or from present experience to memory. One example occurs in his setting of the twelfth stanza of Friedrich Schiller's ode "Die Götter Griechenlands" (The Gods of Greece, D. 677) of November 1819, expressing the essence of longing for the "grandeur that was Greece;" Schubert, a schoolmaster's son, was drawn to mythological themes for many of his lieder. From the pantheon of gods and goddesses in this poem, Schubert selected a single stanza in which the poetic speaker laments for a lost springtime world of fable; Schiller's preoccupation with the transience of beauty and the evanescent nature of life are all the more intense for the lack of context. The song is framed on either side by the yearning question "Schöne Welt, wo bist du?" (Fair world, where are you?) in A minor, followed by the plea "Return again" in the parallel major. When the speaker realizes in m. 15 that only in song does the "magic land" live on, F♯ is tonicized as the tonal emblem of the enchanted realm—so near and yet so far in tonal terms. In another example, B major at the beginning and end of Matthäus von Collin's "Nacht und Träume" (Night and Dreams, D. 827) of 1822 (?), one of Schubert's most beautiful songs, is the tonality of dusk and dawn, or of night's arrival and departure at the beginning and end of the poem, whereas the G-major chords of mm. 15–19 are emblematic of full immersion in "holy Night" (*heil'ge Nacht*) (Ex. 2.5).

EXAMPLE 2.5. "Nacht und Träume" (D. 827)

In "Die Götter Griechenlands" one also finds the use of contrasting parallel major and minor keys (Kindermann 1986), one of Schubert's favorite devices. In the songs, the minor mode often symbolizes tragedy, whereas the major represents bygone happiness, the antithesis of dark and light keys that share the same tonic underscoring their kinship. One example from Schubert's last years is all the more moving for the restraint with which the contrast is used. In "Das Lied im Grünen" (Song of the Greenwood, D. 917) of 1827, to a text by Friedrich Reil (1773–1843), the one touch of the parallel minor occurs at the words "Grünt einst uns das Leben nicht fürder" (When, one day, life no longer blossoms for us, mm. 141–44)—not the first but the second time those words are sung, as if further reflection had brought out their inherent darkness (Ex. 2.6). The minor mode is coupled with rhythmic augmentation in the left-hand part, in contrast to the walking bass that prevails elsewhere in the song; the invocation of old age and approaching death is sufficient to slow the previous motion. Reil's poem is a meditation on memories of a bygone youth spent reading "Horace and Plato, then Wieland and Kant" in the countryside, memories to sweeten old age (one notes with amusement the proper progression of the Latin and Greek classics first, followed by German literature and philosophy). Taking his cue from Reil, Schubert refuses to allow more than one telling hint of the darkness of inevitable death, returning seamlessly to A major and the earlier quarter-note motion in the bass. The pastoral achieves its fullest meaning in the underlying awareness of darkness, and the A major at the end shines all the brighter for the one touch of minor.

Of Schubert's melodies, his friend Leopold von Sonnleithner said that their beauty was "an independent, purely musical one . . . even though it follows these [the words] closely in every respect and always interprets the poet's feeling profoundly" (Deutsch 1958, 337–38). Friedrich Schlegel's words in the little-known masterpiece "Der Fluß" (The River, D. 693) about "pure song" (*rein Gesang*)—flowing, curling, transforming, holding the listener enraptured—impelled from Schubert a particularly beautiful example of "pure song" (Ex. 2.7); music itself is the subject in this lied. But Schubert was willing to abnegate conventional melodic beauty in the service of harsher poetic expression, as in his setting of August Graf von Platen-Hallermünde's "Du liebst mich nicht" (You do not love me, D. 756), in which the poetic persona writhes in Wagnerian chromatic anguish and repeats "You do not love me" to a cadential figure (Agawu 1989). The unbearable fact of ending is thus driven home in self-flagellating fashion. If Hector Berlioz's comment that he valued Schubert's music because it "contains nothing of what certain people call melody" is somewhat perverse, there is also an element of truth in it.

Other typical traits include Schubert's fondness for the German and Neapolitan sixth-chords,[7] his characteristically rich pianistic textures, his frequent use of a single unifying figuration in the piano throughout a

EXAMPLE 2.6. "Das Lied im Grünen" (D. 917)

EXAMPLE 2.7. "Der Fluß" (D. 693)

song, and his practice of stating the principal musical material in the piano introduction. The most important hallmark of all, however, is the close poetico-musical correlation. Where Schubert is at his best, both the larger architecture and the smaller details closely reflect his interpretation of the poet's verse. When he sounds nothing but the tonic D-minor chord for the first six measures of Goethe's "Gretchen am Spinnrade" (Gretchen at the Spinning Wheel, D. 118), followed by the chord of the flatted seventh degree (C major), a diminished-seventh harmony dissonant with the continued pedal on C, and a return to D minor, he conveys the violent atmosphere in which this poisoned love will play out its course. Also characteristic is the mingling of descriptive and psychological word-painting: the spinning-wheel figuration in the right hand "spins" restlessly about the third of the tonic chord, not its root, in a manner suggestive of an idée fixe as well as of the circular motion of the wheel.

In another example, Franz Xaver von Schlechta's "Totengräber-Weise" (Gravedigger's Air, D. 869) of 1826, Schubert creates great tension between the chorale model whose conventions he adopts—rhythmic squareness, rigidly symmetrical phrase structure, largely syllabic text setting, block-chordal texture for the piano—and a radical tonal design. The gravedigger who sings this song reassures those he buries that death is not final: even as the body becomes the prey of worms and turns to dust, the sentient heart lives on until resurrection. In Schubert's symbolism, Death in F♯ minor shares the same tonic, the same structural pitches, with the assurance of resurrection in F♯ major—they are opposite sides of the same coin—yet there is no resting place on either one. Even the ending sounds unstable, susceptible to still more change after the final bar, because the tonal shifts that prevail throughout the song continue in the postlude.[8] Schubert creates a new variant of an antique structural premise: the rigidity of the design and the pervasive chromaticism are symbolic of death's all-inclusiveness and mystery. If Schubert does not touch upon all chords and keys, there are more than enough harmonic shifts to make the tonal symbolism apparent (Ex. 2.8). Furthermore, he goes between different registral levels—high, middle, and low—throughout the song, which thus traverses the planes of the grave, the middle earth of the living, and paradise. Every detail mirrors Schlechta's insistence that death is not cessation of life but continued motion and metamorphosis en route to heaven. The song is a demonstration of the essential Schubertian art of lieder: myriad compositional decisions closely reflect the poetic text, but in the language of music.

Schubert and Poetry

Although critics in the 1820s and 1830s praised Schubert's choice of poetry, twentieth-century scholars have found cause for complaint. There is no denying that some of the unidentified poems, such as "Wiegenlied"

EXAMPLE 2.8. "Totengräber-Weise" (D. 869)

Ziemlich langsam

Nicht so dü-ster und so bleich, Schlä-fer in _ der_ Tru-

he, woh-nest nun im stil-len Reich gott-ge - weih-ter Ru - he!

(Cradle Song, D. 498), or the poetry by amateur versifiers in Schubert's circle are negligible. Schubert could and did fashion beautiful songs from mediocre poems whose images appealed to him; his setting of Friedrich Leopold Graf zu Stolberg-Stolberg's "Auf dem Wasser zu singen" (To Be Sung on the Water, D. 774) is one example. However, Eduard Bauernfeld (1802–90), a writer and member of the Schubert circle, thought highly of Schubert's literary sensibilities: "In literature, too, he was anything but unversed," he wrote, concluding that "a man who so understands the poets is himself a poet" (Deutsch 1958, 230). Another of Schubert's friends, Anselm Hüttenbrenner (1794–1868), recalls the composer's saying that, with a good poem, "one immediately gets a good idea; melodies pour in so that it is a real joy. With a bad poem one can't make any headway; one torments oneself over it and nothing comes of it but boring rubbish" (Deutsch 1958, 182–83). Schubert set fifty-nine poems by Goethe and thirty-two by Schiller, many in multiple versions. While he may not have been the first to discover how apt Wilhelm Müller's (1794–1827) poems were for music, he did so soon after their publication and with immortal results. But if Schubert was voracious in his appetite for poetry, and attentive to poetic nuance, he was not averse to editing the poems he set in order to render them more "composable."[9] One of the most drastic examples shows Schubert omitting over half of Mayrhofer's "Erlafsee" (Lake Erlaf) for his 1817 setting, D. 586, fundamentally altering the poem. Schubert omits everything enigmatic in Mayrhofer's poem (such as a "Feenbild" who weeps and a river that will finally submerge a sawmill—Nature victorious over industrial encroachments), leaving only the lyrical description of the lake at sunset and the half-melancholy, half-peaceful effect of its beauty on the poetic persona.[10]

Schubert's songs span the literary gamut from eighteenth-century *Sturm und Drang* and Anacreontic and pre-Romantic verse, to Romanticism and those poets such as Wilhelm Müller and Heinrich Heine who went beyond their Romantic forebears. He began by inheriting the poets of Mozart's generation. Gabriele von Baumberg (1766–1839), known as the "Sappho of Vienna," wrote the text of Mozart's lied "Als Luise die Briefe ihres unvertrauten Liebhabers verbrannt" (As Luise Burned the Letters of her Unfaithful Lover, K. 520) and inspired five completed songs and one fragment from Schubert. Gotthard Ludwig Kosegarten (1758–1818), a mentor and friend to the artists Philipp Otto Runge and Caspar David Friedrich, was a favorite with Austrian and German song composers, and Schubert joined the procession of Kosegarten composers with twenty strophic songs composed between June and October 1815, plus a single more complex creation in May 1817, "An die untergehende Sonne" (To the Setting Sun, D. 457). The poetry of Friedrich von Matthisson (1761–1831) was similarly popular with song composers in Schubert's day for its sentimentality and elegance, and Schubert's twenty-nine settings of Matthisson, mostly composed in 1814–16, constitute an important stage in his development as a composer. Matthisson's friend the Swiss poet Johann Gaudenz von Salis-Seewis (1762–1834) inspired twelve songs in 1816–17 and a masterpiece, "Der Jüngling an der Quelle" (The Youth by the Stream, D. 300), perhaps composed in 1821 (Youens 1989). In 1813–16, Schubert also set twenty-three songs to poems by Ludwig Hölty (1748–76), a founding member of the proto-Romantic poets called the Göttinger Hainbund; these include "An den Mond: Geuss, lieber Mond" (To the Moon: Pour, dear moon, D. 193), one of Schubert's loveliest early songs. Friedrich Gottlieb Klopstock (1742–1803), who left spellbound an entire generation of writers by making, in Schiller's phrase, "everything lead up to the infinite," was a source for thirteen Schubert songs in 1815–16, including the gem-like "Das Rosenband" (The Rosy Ribbon, D. 280). Matthias Claudius (1740–1815) also inspired thirteen songs, eleven of them composed between November 1816 and February 1817, including three extraordinary songs: "An die Nachtigall" (To the Nightingale, D. 497), "Am Grabe Anselmos" (At Anselmo's Grave, D. 504), and "Der Tod und das Mädchen" (Death and the Maiden, D. 531).

In the realm of ballad composition, the fashion for Ossian settings in Schubert's youth is apparent in his nine Ossian ballads composed between June 1815 and February 1816 (Kinsey 1973). These tales, supposedly written by the blind Gaelic bard Ossian, were actually a notorious literary fraud: James MacPherson (1736–96), a Scotsman obsessed with Scottish nationalism, invented a Gaelic challenger to Homer and insisted on the antique authenticity of the works long after the hue and cry had been raised concerning their contemporary origins. In 1815, Schubert was still attracted to ballad composition and had rediscovered Goethe, whose character Werther is a passionate devotee of Ossian. The popularity of this poetry was still so great in the 1820s that Anton Diabelli began the publication by installments of the Schubert *Nachlass* in July 1830 with the Ossian ballads.

However, Schubert soon outgrew the poetic repertoire of his youth, including poets such as Johann Georg Jacobi (1740–1814), although the cluster of seven Jacobi songs in August and September 1816 includes the justly famous "Litanei auf das Fest aller Seelen" (Litany for the Feast of All Souls, D. 343) and the dramatic scena "Lied des Orpheus (als er in die Hölle ging)" (Song of Orpheus as He Went Into Hades, D. 474; see Wing 1993). Schubert and his friends were particularly devoted to the two giants of the era, Friedrich Schiller (1759–1805) and Johann Wolfgang von Goethe (1749–1832). David Gramit has even speculated that the Dioscurii, or twin stars, in Mayrhofer's "Lied eines Schiffers an die Dioskuren" (Song of a Sailor to the Dioscurii, D. 360), are Goethe and Schiller, to whom the reverent sailor-poet dedicates the rudder by which he steers his course (Gramit 1987, 54–55). Schiller's aesthetic concepts were important to the youthful Schubert's circle of friends, and the first true lied, rather than an extended ballade, that can be securely dated is his setting of Schiller's

"Der Jüngling am Bache" (The Youth at the Brook, D. 30) of September 1812, recast three days later in the minor mode; in 1819, he returned to the same poem and set it twice more. Perhaps because Schiller's poetry at times lacks the kind of sensual imagery, rhythm, or motion that most easily quickened Schubert's musical imagination, the composer set seven of the Schiller poems two and even three times in an attempt to capture the right tone (Johnson 1993b). He did not even complete his first attempt to set "Gruppe aus dem Tartarus" in 1816 (Brown 1954) but returned to the poem a year and a half later, composing perhaps the most magnificent of the Schiller songs.[11] The poem begins "Horch!" (listen), and there are sounds and images aplenty to inspire music: the rivers of Hades forced through hollow rocks; the groans and sighs of the dead souls; and eternity sweeping in circles over their heads. Schubert's Schiller songs span the gamut from mammoth ballads such as "Der Taucher" (The Diver, D. 77), to small, insouciant poems like "An den Frühling" (To Spring, D. 283 and 587), to the astonishing chromatic harmonies of "Der Pilgrim" (The Pilgrim, D. 794); there is no one "Schiller style," any more than there is a single "Goethe style" for such variegated poetic oeuvres.

Goethe was a greater catalyst for stylistic experiment on Schubert's part, despite the conservative Viennese literati's faint mistrust of the great writer. Goethe imposed a unity of dominant concerns on a massive body of work, heterogeneous in style and form; he found a way of experiencing and writing in which the thing experienced is always infused with the emotions of the experiencing subject and is therefore rendered symbolic. It seems to have been the seventeen-year-old Schubert's discovery of poetry in general, and of Goethe in particular, that was the catalyst for the "song year" 1815, which actually began with "Gretchen am Spinnrade" in October 1814. If Schubert's attraction to Goethe dwindled over the years (twenty-eight settings in 1815, one in 1824, four in 1826, and none in the last two years of his life), this poet was nonetheless the inspiration for many of the composer's greatest songs, including "Schäfers Klagelied," D. 121; "Rastlose Liebe," D. 138; "Meeresstille," D. 216; "An den Mond," D. 296; "Wandrers Nachtlied," D. 224 and D. 768; "Auf dem See," D. 543; "Ganymed," D. 544; the "Harfenspieler" songs D. 478, 479, and 480; "Geheimes," D. 719; and "Der Musensohn," D. 764. Unfortunately, Goethe was not impressed. Schubert's friends prepared two manuscript collections of songs in 1816 and sent one of them to the great poet; it was sent back without acknowledgement (Dürr 1978). Nine years later, Schubert tried again, sending the Goethe songs of his Op. 19 ("An Schwager Kronos," "An Mignon," and "Ganymed") to the poet and asking for permission to dedicate the opus to him. Goethe did not reply.

Schubert's friends included both professional and amateur poets whose works he set to music. The most notable of those collaborations was with Johann Baptist Mayrhofer (1787–1836), one of the principal intellectual influences on Schubert in his late teens and early twenties. Of the forty-seven Schubert songs to texts by this pessimistic poet, both neoclassical and proto-Expressionist in his enigmatic, idiosyncratic symbolism, almost all are among the composer's best; "Sehnsucht" (Longing, D. 516), "Fahrt zum Hades" (Journey to Hades, D. 526), "Memnon," D. 541, "Einsamkeit" (Loneliness, D. 620), "Die Sternennächte" (Starry Nights, D. 670), "Der Sieg" (The Victory, D. 805), and "Abendstern" (Evening Star, D. 806), are among the many masterpieces from the Mayrhofer songs. Another writer among Schubert's friends was Johann Gabriel Seidl (1804–75), a more conventional poet than Mayrhofer; although Schubert once returned some poems to Seidl, complaining that there was "nothing of music" in them, he found wonderful music in such poems as "Im Freien" (In the Open, D. 880), "Sehnsucht" (Longing, D. 879), "Der Wanderer an den Mond" (The Wanderer's Address to the Moon, D. 870), and "Am Fenster" (At the Window, D. 878), all composed in March 1826 (Schubert had a propensity all his life to compose songs to one poet at a time). Schubert would return to Seidl in 1828 to compose the *Vier Refrainlieder,* D. 866, and "Die Taubenpost," D. 965a, published as the final song in *Schwanengesang,* D. 957.

Others in the Schubert circle were amateur poets who inspired a number of significant lieder. Franz Seraph Ritter von Bruchmann (1798–1867), the son of a wealthy merchant, wrote the poetry for the beautiful "Am See" (On the Lake, D. 746) and "Schwestergruss" (Sister's Greeting, D. 762); Franz von Schober (1796–1882), a wealthy, somewhat dissolute dilettante, provided the poems for "Am Bach im Frühling" (At the Stream in Springtime, D. 361) and the famous "An die Musik" (To Music, D. 547). The songs to texts by Franz Xaver von Wssehrd Schlechta (1796–1875), a government employee and occasional poet, include the charming "Fischerweise" (Fisherman's Song, D. 881) and "Liebeslauschen" (Serenade, D. 698). In 1822 Schubert attended the literary salons of the writer Caroline Pichler (1769–1843), who wrote "Der Unglückliche" (The Unhappy One, D. 713). At her salon Schubert met the Viennese professor of philosophy, playwright, and literary critic Matthäus von Collin (1779–1824), closely associated with the Viennese Romantics and poet of three of Schubert's best songs: "Der Zwerg" (The Dwarf, D. 771), "Wehmut" (Melancholy, D. 772), and "Nacht und Träume," D. 827, as well as the brilliant aria "Herrn Josef Spaun, Assessor in Linz (Epistel)" (To Joseph von Spaun, Taxman in Linz, D. 749). Spaun, one of Schubert's oldest friends, had left for Linz in 1821 and had not written, so Schubert and his friends reproached him with a delightful spoof in best Rossini style.

In the last years of his life, Schubert discovered still other poets for song composition, including Ernst Schulze (1789–1817), whose *Poetisches Tagebuch* (Verse Diary) was the source for ten songs composed in 1825–26. The unhappy Schulze, obsessed by unrequited love for two sisters, recorded his delusions and sufferings in poems such as the powerful "Über Wildemann" (Overlooking Wildemann, D. 884), premonitory of *Winterreise,* and "An mein Herz" (To my Heart, D. 860). Schubert's mastery of varied strophic design is evident in one of his best-loved songs, also from Schulze's *Poetisches Tagebuch:* "Im Frühling" (In Spring, D. 882), whose melody is reminiscent of the theme-and-variations movement of Schubert's Symphony No. 2 in B♭, D. 125 and of a love-duet from his Singspiel *Die Freunde von Salamanka* D. 326 (Johnson 1993a). The year after the Schulze songs, Schubert rediscovered the poetry of Karl Gottfried von Leitner (1800–1890) through his friends the Pachler family in Graz; he had already set Leitner's "Drang in die Ferne," D. 770, in 1823, and now returned to the Styrian poet to set six more lieder, including the exquisite barcarolle "Des Fischers Liebesglück" (Fisherman's Happiness in Love, D. 933) and "Der Winterabend" (The Winter Evening, D. 938; see Feil 1991 and Seebass 1990), which Graham Johnson rightly characterizes as "one of the great song achievements of Schubert's final year" (Johnson 1992a). The ten songs to texts by Ludwig Rellstab (1799–1860) also belong to the last year: according to both Beethoven's amanuensis Anton Schindler and Rellstab himself, the poems came to Schubert from Beethoven's *Nachlass.* The seven songs published in the compilation *Schwanengesang* D. 957 in 1829 include the powerful "Aufenthalt" (Resting Place) and "In der Ferne" (Far Away)—the latter an anti-litany in which an alienated wanderer pronounces not a blessing but a curse upon himself— as well as one of the most famous of all serenades, "Ständchen" and the last of Schubert's "brook songs" and spring songs: "Liebesbotschaft" (Love's Message) and "Frühlingssehnsucht" (Spring Longing). Of the remaining Rellstab songs, "Auf dem Strom" (On the River, D. 943) for tenor, piano, and horn was possibly composed in Beethoven's memory and first performed on 26 March 1828, on the first anniversary of Beethoven's death (Hallmark 1982; Solomon 1979; Dürr 1979).

The autograph manuscript of Schubert's six songs to poems by Heinrich Heine is dated August 1828, but there is reason to believe that Schubert began their composition earlier, perhaps with the initial intent of forming a cycle (R. Kramer 1985 and 1994). The texts were taken from a sequence of poems entitled *Die Heimkehr* (The Return Home), first published in part 1 of the *Reisebilder* (Travel Scenes) in 1826, then in the *Buch der Lieder* in 1827. In these early poems, Heine used the folksong forms he learned from Wilhelm Müller, the poet of the Schubert song cycles, and employed various Romantic ideas to often anti-Romantic ends. His corrosive irony was new to German lyric poetry, and his vivid imagery appealed to composers throughout the century, with Schubert in the vanguard. Both these songs and *Winterreise*—the two sets are similar in many ways— compel one to wonder what could have followed such radical creations, far in advance of their time, had Schubert lived longer. Among the many powerful passages in these songs, harbingers of Schubert's last year, are the un-harmonized B♭s at the beginning of "Ihr Bild" (Her Picture)—which Reed (1985, 261) characterized as a gesture of "runic precision" and Heinrich Schenker as a tonal analogue for the act of staring (Schenker 1921; Kerman 1962)—as well as the fully accomplished fusion of lied and recitative in the declamatory vocal writing of "Der Doppelgänger" (The Spectral Double) and the mysterious introduction to "Die Stadt" (The Town) whose expressionistically repeated diminished-seventh chord is never resolved.

Schubert Revising Schubert

At least 113 songs exist in more than one version (Holländer 1928 and Flothuis 1982), providing ample evidence of this hardworking composer's critical attitude toward his compositions and his willingness to provide new versions for particular singers. Far from composing like a sleepwalker, as the erroneous myth about Schubert's creative processes would have one believe, he felt compelled to revise his music in myriad ways. These ranged from slight alterations of detail—for example, the only changes Schubert made to the second version of Schiller's "An den Frühling," D. 283, was a transposition from B♭ to A major and a slightly altered ending—to the entirely new setting of a given text. The distinctions between alternative versions are not always clear; for example, the so-called second version of Goethe's "Meeresstille," D. 216, is best characterized as an extensive revision rather than a new, independent composition (Jackson 1991). In contrast, the November 1815 version of the Harper's song "Wer sich der Einsamkeit ergiebt" (Whoever Surrenders Himself to Loneliness), from Goethe's *Wilhelm Meisters Lehrjahre* has only its A-minor tonality in common with the two September 1816 settings of the same text.

One of the most striking examples of Schubert's returning to the same poetry many times is the Mignon song "Nur wer die Sehnsucht kennt" (Only One Who Knows Longing), also from *Wilhelm Meister*. Both the adolescent Mignon and her companion, the elderly Harper—later revealed to be her father as the result of an unknowingly incestuous union with his sister—are haunting creatures who symbolize the power of Romantic poetry to cast a magic veil over a squalid existence. In this enigmatic work, whose echoes of Old Testament language are all the more powerful for its brevity, Goethe depicts isolation and suffering so intense that it throws the mind into turmoil. Schubert first set the poem on 18 October 1815 in A♭ major, then wrote a more elaborate version in F major the same day. (Both are numbered D. 310 and are entitled "Sehnsucht," Longing.) The following year, Schubert set the poem two more times, once in D minor under the title "Lied der Mignon" (D. 359)[12] and again in A minor in September 1816 with the title "Sehnsucht" (D. 481). Three years later, he returned to the poem and set it in E major for two tenors and three basses (D. 656), and again in January 1826 (or possibly 1827) as the duet in B minor "Mignon und der Harfner," (D. 877/1). (In the novel, Goethe describes Wilhelm's overhearing the pair singing this poem as a duet, in a strange language that Wilhelm could only imperfectly transcribe.) Schubert was evidently reluctant to compose the duet and did so at the request of the publisher, but it is nevertheless a masterpiece. At the same time, he also composed his last solo version of the song, the "Lied der Mignon" D. 877/4.

The second setting of a text is sometimes a virtual repudiation of the first, as is the case with the two settings of Theodor Körner's "Sängers Morgenlied" (Minstrel's Aubade, D. 163 and 165) of 27 February and 1 March 1815 (Johnson 1989). The first version is a buoyant greeting to the sun in G major, with energetic melismas propelling the vocal phrases forward at strategic points. Schubert took his point of departure from the first stanza, in which the poetic persona ecstatically greets the sun, whose light is "breaking victoriously through the night." But the word "Ach" (Ah) at the beginning of stanza 2 is the signal for a change of tone and greater gravity. Schubert ignored the "Sehnsucht" (yearning) awakened by the arrival of day in the second verse and set the subsequent ponderings on the soul's striving to the merry strains of the first verse, words and music now being at odds with one another. Perhaps disturbed by the discrepancy, Schubert returned to Körner's poem two days later in order to compose a setting in which the musical atmosphere derives from the second stanza, not the first, and therefore reflects the greater part of the poem. This second version, marked *Langsam* and in a far more reverential mood, is a foreshadowing of mm. 16–21 of "Morgengruß" (Morning Greeting) from *Die schöne Müllerin* (D. 795) of 1823, at the words "So muß ich wieder gehen" (So I must go away). The latter's morning mise-en-scène and mood of yearning might have suggested the harmonic, motivic, figurational, and rhythmic resemblances to the song composed eight years earlier.

Schubert occasionally used music composed earlier to one poem as the basis for a setting of another poem by a different poet. In October 1815, Schubert composed three little-known but beautiful songs to poems by Josef Ludwig Stoll (1778–1815) a physician's son and journalist who had died the previous January: "Lambertine," D. 301; "Labetrank der Liebe" (Love's Reviving Potion, D. 302), whose distant echoes of Zerlina's "Vedrai carino" seem appropriate; and "An die Geliebte" (To the Beloved, D. 303). This last is tenderly erotic, the lover drinking his beloved's tears in a symbolic evocation of lovemaking (Heine would use the same symbolism to more corrosive effect in "Am Meer," one of six Heine songs set by Schubert). The poem ends with the ecstatic-melancholy recognition that the lover assumes the beloved's sorrows as well as the rapture of love. In

November 1816, Schubert set Matthias Claudius's "An die Nachtigall" (To the Nightingale, D. 497); the resemblances between the two poems are obvious but the gender is reversed, a male persona speaking in Stoll's poem, a female in Claudius's. The point of view is reversed as well, Claudius's poem presenting a charming depiction of female experience, in which the woman takes delight in her return to herself, to a regained individuality, after love-making. Her love for the sleeping man by her side is not questioned—he is Amor or Love itself—but she has her own guardian spirit and her own capacity for delight apart from eroticism. "To the Nightingale" is a plea for Nature's foremost symbol of love to be silent.

Schubert alters the beginning of "An die Geliebte" to respond to the greater psychological depth of "An die Nachtigall." The earlier song lacks a piano introduction, and the right-hand part in mm. 1–8 doubles the vocal melody, its interlocking descending thirds a variant of what would later become Brahms's "Death" motive for the "little death" of love. When Schubert repeats the first four measures of "An die Geliebte" as the piano introduction to "An die Nachtigall," he refines it with more chromatic gestures and extends the phrase to culminate in a cadence on tonic. One imagines the lover drowsily drifting toward sleep throughout the introduction, his eyes finally closing with the arrival at tonic; there is no cadence on the tonic in "An die Geliebte" until the end of the texted strophe. When the texted body of the song begins, the poetic persona tells us that her beloved has gone to sleep. This is to a repetition of the same music, including the descending chromatic figure in mm. 5–6, that gives the introduction a languid erotic aura. In a characteristic detail of interpretive prosody, Schubert varies the melodic line from mm. 5–8 of "An die Geliebte" to emphasize the poetic persona's gratitude to her guardian angel, who has sung the beloved to sleep. This is accomplished through a grace-note anticipation (m. 18) that produces a touch of *Schwung* just right for the sentiment (Ex. 2.9a).

Since in some contemporary associations of music with gender the subdominant was considered feminine and the dominant masculine, the subdominant emphases in "An die Geliebte" may be emblematic of the woman's presence, and mm. 22–29 of "An die Nachtigall" (Ex. 2.9b) acquire an added significance. Harmonically, this passage to the words "Und ich kann fröhlich sein und scherzen. / Kann Jeder Blum' und jedes Blatt's mich freu'n" is a simple IV–V–I progression in which the subdominant that is her emblem is elaborated by its dominant. The jauntiness of the dotted rhythmic patterns, entirely absent from "An die Geliebte," and the quickened prosodic pace will make any listener smile, and the refusal of strong cadential closure is tantamount to a declaration that *she* will not drift off to sleep as he has done. The vocal line stays poised on and around the dominant pitch (D) throughout mm. 24–34, not descending to the tonic pitch until the last syllable—another indication of a poetic persona

EXAMPLE 2.9a. "An die Geliebte" (D. 303)

O, dass ich dir   vom stil - len Au - ge, in sei - nem lie - be -
Wohl hält sie zö - gernd auf __ der Wan - ge und will sich heiss der

vol - len Schein, die Thrä - ne von der Wan - ge sau - ge,
Treu - e weihn; nun ich sie so im Kuss em - pfan - ge,

determined not to succumb to the erotic languor that has carried off her lover.

In the last vocal phrases (mm. 30–37), Schubert borrows the scalewise contrary motion between the outer voices in m. 13 of "An die Geliebte," extending and repeating it in G minor for the exhortation to the nightingale not to sing. At the climactic prolongation of high G, at the word "A[mor]," we hear the flat submediant harmony that traces its lineage back to the chromatic passing tone in the piano introduction and appears nowhere else in the song. The same linear chromatic figure appears in the postlude, where it has the quickened rhythmic pattern of the woman's laughter and jesting of mm. 24ff. Schubert sounds the 2-measure cadential phrase twice, the second time with the upper neighbor ornamenting the dominant, as if attempting to hold on to the upper register, but each time descending to the tonic. She too, despite her best intentions, has drifted off to sleep. Typically, Schubert not only conveys the poetic protagonist's emotions but adds to the poem in ways that are plausible extensions of the text, although not expressly stated.

EXAMPLE 2.9b. "An die Nachtigall" (D. 497)

Schubert and the "Miracle Year" of 1815

1815 was an *annus mirabilis* in which Schubert composed approximately one hundred fifty songs of every kind: ballads such as Theodor Körner's gripping "Amphiaraos," D. 166; small *volkstümlich* songs in strict strophic form, such as Goethe's "Der Rattenfänger," D. 255;[13] the fusion of ballad and lied in "Erlkönig" (more the latter than the former); and much else. The miracles actually began in October 1814, when Schubert set "Gretchen am Spinnrade" (Gretchen at the Spinning Wheel, D. 118; see L. Kramer 1984, 150–56), which was followed quickly by "Nachtgesang" (Night Song, D. 119), "Trost in Tränen" (Consolation in Tears, D. 120), "Schäfers Klagelied" (Shepherd's Lament, D. 121), and "Sehnsucht" (Yearning, D. 123). The flood tide continued throughout the year to come: while the Congress of Vienna was redrawing the map of Europe, Schubert was redefining the lied.

Goethe's "Die Spinnerin" (The Spinner, D. 247) is one of the many strophic lieder in quasi-folk song style from that year. The song is another example of Schubert's affinity with the female poetic persona, here a young weaver who has been seduced and abandoned, facing disgrace alone. Something of her tragic stoicism—"Wie kann es anders sein?" (How can it be otherwise?), she asks—is embodied in the poet's trochaic rhythms and austere image of the broken strands of thread that symbolize both her lost maidenhood and the rent fabric of her life. John Reed calls this song "a triumphant vindication of Goethe's views on the supremacy of the strophic song" (Reed 1985, 194), and, as Graham Johnson points out, the perception that "one of life's sad old stories is happening yet again is built into the very form of the song" (Johnson 1990). The tessitura is very high; although Schubert might have composed this and other high soprano songs for Therese Grob, with whom he was supposedly enamored and who had a high D, it is difficult to think of a young man in love composing Goethe's cautionary fable of seduction for his sweetheart. Musico-poetic explanations for the song's character seem more compelling, including the association of B minor with mournfulness—it would later be the tonality of "Die liebe Farbe" in *Die schöne Müllerin*, similarly a funeral-march lied—and the use of the high tessitura to convey the poetic persona's gender and her essential innocence.

Despite its small size (eleven measures, with no piano introduction), "Die Spinnerin" is an artful construction. The rhythmic pattern in the accompaniment is that of a pavane, reminiscent of the second movement of Beethoven's Seventh Symphony. Above it, Schubert spins a melodic line in sixteenth notes whose threadlike contours are filled with chromatic inflections, echoed in the piano. For all the simplicity of the B-minor and D-major harmonies, the melodic chromaticism seems quietly indicative of the erotic passion that has produced catastrophe (Ex. 2.10). The spinning motion never stops: where the singer has a quarter note at the end of each

EXAMPLE 2.10. "Die Spinnerin" (D. 247)

Als   ich — still   und   ru - hig   spann,   oh - ne - nur   zu —
Lob - te, — was   zu —   lo - ben   war,   soll - te — das   was

sto   -   cken,   trat   ein — schö - ner — jun - ger   Mann   na - he   mir   zum
scha   -   den?   Mein   dem   Flach - se — glei - ches   Haar,   und   den   glei - chen

Ro   -   cken.
Fa   -   den.

two-measure phrase, the piano fills in the beat with more sixteenth-note motion and continues spinning throughout the postlude. The postlude, furthermore, is an extension and elaboration of the descending motion traced in mm. 1–2 and 5–6, from the high B that appears only at that point to the tonic pitch an octave lower. This symbolism of inexorable descent is quietly powerful, especially when reiterated for the extent of seven stanzas.

From 1817 to 1822

This period includes most of the six-year span commonly called the "years of crisis," during which Schubert was struggling to make a name for himself and to become an independent composer (see Aderhold, Dürr 1985, and Litschauer 1985). During this period, Schubert experimented with progressive tonality in lieder, with the mysticism of Novalis (Friedrich von Hardenberg, 1722–1801) and Friedrich von Schlegel (1722–1829), and with further development of the Romantic lied. His taste in poetry changed, and the large number of strict strophic songs from 1815 gave way to a predominance of other forms, although Schubert would never abandon strophic form altogether (*Die schöne Müllerin* has eight such settings—nine if one includes "Tränenregen").

In a review of the Op. 21 songs, a bemused Leipzig critic wrote, "Herr F. S. does not write songs, properly speaking, and has no wish to do so . . . but free vocal pieces, some so free that they might possibly be called caprices or fantasies" (Deutsch 1946, 353). An example of *Gesang* from another collection (Op. 24) is "Gruppe aus dem Tartarus," D. 583, composed in September 1817 to Schiller's 1782 poem about entry into the underworld. The "group" is an amorphous, unknown mass of dead souls, without names or identities. The terrified new arrivals, deprived of all volition, are forced from horror to horror just as the weeping water is forced through hollows in the rocks. Schiller invites the composer to sound muffled figures in the piano before the poetic speaker bids us "Listen!" The poet then creates a series of magnificent images, especially that of Eternity as a giant avian creature sweeping in unending circles above the bowed heads of the new arrivals and breaking Saturn's scythe in two.

For this powerful poem, Schubert uses, at greater length than anywhere else in his songs, the cliché of linear chromaticism associated with horror, yielding a chromatic fog that envelops the tonality and blankets it from eye and ear. Yet the forces that drive the terrified souls to their confrontation with Eternity are nothing if not purposeful, and so too is the musical design. The first segment of the chromatic sequence in mm. 1–20 begins on the unharmonized pitch C, which will blaze forth in full harmonization at m. 64 with the first invocation of the word *Ewigkeit* (eternity). Long before the souls of the dead ask one another anxiously if the end is nigh, phrases have repeatedly been resolved, attenuating the tension of nonresolution to the utmost, after which the musical engines drive forward again. When the voice enters on D in m. 7, anticipating the D-minor point of arrival at the allegro in m. 21 ("Ach! Schmerz verzerret ihr Gesicht"), it echoes the melodic minor sixth defined by the rising chromatic bass lines of mm. 1–3 and 4–6. As the groaning becomes more audible, the unharmonized texture is replaced by dissonant chords (V of A♭ minor) followed by a chromatic rise to the allegro; the length of the dread journey is symbolized by the tonal distance between V of A♭ and D, tonics separated by a tritone.

In the allegro we finally see and hear the pain-distorted throng. The circling motion of Eternity is already foretold in the wheeling configuration of the vocal phrases, and there are now two chromatic voices, producing chromaticism within chromaticism, symbolic of the *Gruppe* on their last journey; the voice-leading produces augmented triads, associated in the expressive world of Schubert lieder with extremities of anguish. The accented dissonance of E♭ against D on the downbeat of m. 32, at the words "Hohl sind ihre Augen," comes from m. 11, "wie durch *hohler Felsen*": Schubert emphasizes the skeletal analogy in the most direct way possible. The choice of F♯ minor as a temporary resting place in mm. 40–47, the key of the *Trauerlauf,* is as far as possible from the ultimate C major of Eternity; the tritone between keys is again a symbol of the dread length of that "sorrowful course." Not until the word *Ewigkeit* is there a true tonal arrival, and the effect is shattering. In a final instance of tonal symbolism, Schubert repeats the culminating lines "Ewigkeit schwingt über ihnen Kreise, / Bricht die Sense des Saturns entzwei" twice (with internal word repetitions as well), the first time on D♭, the second time on C♯ as V^7 of F♯ (Ex. 2.11). Saturn's scythe is twice broken, once on the flat side, once on the sharp side, and the C of eternity triumphs. The postlude is unforgettable: C major is now C minor, and the tension-fraught ascending chromatic motion is now a descent. The final arpeggiated C-minor chord high in the treble, like a last despairing echo from far away, is chilling. Hugo Wolf would perhaps learn from this song and others like it that *allmählich verklingend* (gradually fading away) postludes are musical metaphors for spatial distance.

EXAMPLE 2.11. "Gruppe aus dem Tartarus" (D. 583)

(*continued*)

Another song from these years is an unicum, Schubert's only solo song to a text by the Viennese writer Franz Grillparzer (1791–1872): "Berthas Lied in der Nacht" (Bertha's Song in the Night, D. 653), composed in February 1819. Grillparzer was in contact with the Schubert circle through his kinship with the Sonnleithner family and his relationship with Katharina Fröhlich and her three musical sisters, although there is no record that he ever met the composer; a great admirer of Schubert's music, he would later write the much-debated epitaph on Schubert's grave: "Music has here buried a rich possession but even fairer hopes." He wrote "Berthas Lied" in 1817 for his play *Die Ahnfrau* (The Ancestress) but did not ultimately include it in this fate-tragedy. The poem is a small, lovely thing in which night and sleep are personified, night as a creature with gently moving giant wings that envelop the hills and valleys, sleep as an "adorable child" who whispers to the sleeper. The fourth line of each stanza rhymes with every other last line on the dark, lulling /u/ sound associated in the German language with rest because it is the defining vowel in the word *Ruhe;* each stanza comes to rest on the most restful sound in the language. In the fourth and final stanza, the poetic speaker turns to the reader to ask whether "you" can sense the approach of Sleep; here, the previous internal rhyming couplets are replaced by the yawning /ah/ sounds of "A*h*nest," "N*ah*en," "*A*lles" and the doubled "slumbering" words *Schlummer* and *Schlummre* in succession: a lulling-to-sleep in rhyme and rhythm.

Schubert sets this poem "Sehr langsam" in $\frac{4}{4}$, each beat prolonged not only by the very slow tempo (a rarity in his songs) but by the subdivision of the beat into eighth and sixteenth notes. The 2-measure piano introduction is divided in half, the first measure in a unison texture and the second harmonized, culminating in a half cadence on the dominant of E♭ minor, prolonged by a fermata. The effect of the semitone motion upwards from the unharmonized B♭ at the end of m. 1, heightened by its leading tone, to the C♭ major chord at the beginning of m. 2 (6 as upper neighbor to 5) continues the rising motion, as if night were spreading outwards and upwards, enveloping more of the musical landscape. The unison texture and the ambiguity of the implied harmonies are beautifully expressive of the mystery of nightfall. Schubert repeats the words of stanza 1 in their entirety; in this twofold setting, the metaphor of night enveloping the landscape and the corresponding metamorphosis within the human soul from care and sorrow to peace are represented by the change—not a jarring modulation but gradually, gently effected—from an ambiguously stated E♭ minor, as veiled and mysterious as night itself, to G♭ major by m. 8. One notices in particular the beautiful use of the flatted sixth degree (E♭♭ foreshadowing the alternation between F♯ minor and F♯ major to follow (Ex. 2.12).

Sleep appears as the enharmonic kin to night, in F♯ major, with occasional harmonies borrowed from the parallel minor in a drowsy motion alternating between the two modes. The texture of this long, soft drifting off to sleep is extraordinary, beginning with an ostinato on the dominant pitch C♯ in the outer voices of the piano in syncopated rhythmic patterns throughout mm. 8–15. (Wolf, who loved *perdendosi* effects of all kinds, would adopt

EXAMPLE 2.12. "Berthas Lied der Nacht" (D. 653)

this pattern as a stylistic hallmark.) The left and right hands do not strike their C♯ simultaneously but alternate, so that the air is filled with a soft, incessant murmuring. Neither piano nor voice reaches the tonic F♯ until m. 15, the singer's phrases ending in mm. 9–10, 11–12, and 13–14 on the second scale degree, drowsily just short of arrival at sleep. In essence, Schubert attenuates an ostinato so as to remove almost every trace of tension and render it lulling; only when the poet invokes eyes wakeful from sorrow does Schubert introduce a rising chromaticism in the tenor part (m. 13), immediately soothed and corrected in m. 14 by the descent to the tonic.

Sleep comes gradually, and the first arrival at tonic restfulness in m. 15 is followed by still more variations on the ostinato and the melodies of sleep and night. When the poetic speaker twice asks "Fühlst du sein Nahen? ahnest du Ruh?" (mm. 15–18), the accompaniment sways back and forth between tonic and dominant harmonies—but without tonic closure in the topmost voice and without resting on the tonic chord. The nearness of sleep and rest is thus promised in tonal terms. In the section marked *langsamer werdend* (becoming slower, mm. 19–27), Schubert makes wonderful use of the lowered leading tone in F♯ although the plagal implications never result in resolution, much less modulation, the restfulness is unmistakable. The syncopated patterns cease in m. 25 as sleep finally weaves its spell, but one notices that the fifth sounds as the topmost voice of the final tonic chord in m. 27, a last, faint invocation of sleep as hovering in midair. In this extraordinary example of Schubert's uses of parallel major and minor keys, the darkness of night and sleep and the comfort they provide for grieving humanity are conveyed in the subtle alternation and admixture of the two modes. Mahler must have learned how to capture the essence of a musical drifting off to sleep and death in his "Die zwei blauen Augen" from songs such as this.

Schubert in 1822

In 1822, the last year Schubert was to enjoy in full health, virtually every text he set turned to gold. One of the most magnificent songs of a magnificent year is "Wehmut" (Melancholy, D. 772), a setting of Matthäus von Collin's "Naturgefühl" (Feeling for Nature). The sight of Nature in springtime awakens both joy and sadness, the alliteration of "wohl" and "weh" underscoring their close relationship.[14] The poetic persona reflects that, just as the beauty surrounding him will die and vanish, so too will humanity and all its works. The poem is an artful construction, its slow, solemn rhythm created in part by the strong syllable at the end of each line and the pause that follows before the next line begins. One notes in particular the long pauses after lines 3 and 6: after each of the rhyming iambic tetrameter couplets in lines 1–2 and 4–5, the following line is clipped shorter, emphasizing both the unquiet heart and spring joy. Lines 7–10 are all tetrameters; the stanza "gains weight," increases in intensity, leading to the final austere *memento mori* in line 11, which is again abbreviated, consisting entirely of verbs whose actions signify the end of all action ("entschwindet und vergeht"—vanish and perish).

Schubert's 2-measure piano introduction states the descending bass tetrachord long associated with lamentation in music, its aura of antique solemnity heightened by the slow tactus in equal half notes, the D-minor tonality, and the flattened seventh and sixth degrees (C, B♭) in the bass descent (mm. 1–2). When the descending tetrachord and its attendant harmonies are restated for the singer's first words, Schubert expands the initial compass upwards for the singer; both the breadth of the woods and fields and the all-embracing nature of the persona's meditation on ultimate things are evoked in the contrary motion between the topmost voice and the bass. When the dominant chord sounds, at the end of the tetrachord, the bass remains on the dominant pitch throughout mm. 5–9; the use of the tonic major chord for "wohl" and the minor for "weh" furnish another example of the most common signification that such contrasts bear in Schubert lieder. The ominous foreboding that melancholy will lead to dread knowledge is evoked by the fixation on the dominant, premonitory of the dominant pedal in mm. 16–18, when the intimations of mortality cannot be staved off any longer. But in the initial section, that underlying knowledge is obscured by present awareness of Nature's springtime array, and therefore the dominant pedal points do not resolve to tonic D minor until m. 25 and the return of the A section—the culmination of a musical architecture in which everything leads to the words *verschwindet und vergeht*. In mm. 10–11, resolution is literally arrested and then transformed at the word *Schönheit* (beauty) into one of the most affecting of all Schubert's mediant harmonic relationships, when the leading tone (C♯) of tonic D minor becomes the (momentary) fifth of F♯ major. We hear a resolution to an apparent tonic but it does not, cannot last, for all its cadential assertions of rootedness and fullness, and instead moves on to D major for the evocation of "Frühlingslust" at the end of the A section. The tonal symbolism is deeply moving: Nature's beauty is defined not in a tonality that is sustained and endures but only as a momentary articulation. Indeed, Schubert's "cadence" occurs before the end of the poetic sentence. "Frühlingslust" and its cadence do not last either, and "wohl" becomes "weh" immediately in m. 15, returning to the dominant chord and to suspenseful foreboding for the beginning of the B section. There is no break, no rest, anywhere in the piano accompaniment: the processes that carry us to our final doom are inexorable, and so too are the slowly shifting harmonic progressions in this lied.

In Schubert's brilliant conception, the enumeration of all that must eventually vanish is set to a chromatically varied reversal of the lamentation tetrachord in the bass, returning the poetic persona to the D-minor resolution that was avoided earlier. Just as the cliché of ascending chromaticism carried the damned souls of Schiller's "Gruppe aus dem Tartarus" to their confrontation with Eternity, it carries the poet/singer to his quiet confrontation with the verb *entschwindet*. A measured tremolando evokes both the sounding winds and the poetic persona's muted agitation, the harmonic rhythm becoming gradually more rapid. Every detail is compelling; for example, the solemn quasi-chanting on a single pitch until the word *Schönheit* (beauty, m. 23) impels both a lyrical blossoming of the melodic line and an E-major harmony rather than the E-minor chord of the preceding measure. Humanity lingers and contemplates Nature's love-liness for an extra two measures, before the harmonic rhythm accelerates alarmingly in m. 24. The portentous rhythms in the vocal line of mm. 16–20, in which the accented syllable of every iambic foot is elongated as a dotted quarter note, are broken in the last half of m. 20 at the first mention of humanity. "Und auch der Mensch" (and humanity too), the singer states, the prevailing rhythmic pattern diminished to half its former duration for the anacrusis on the first three words, so that the crucial word *Mensch* on the downbeat can be prolonged even more.

As he would do later at the end of Müller's "Der Wegweiser" (The Signpost) from *Winterreise*, and throughout "Der Doppelgänger," Schubert accompanies the grim revelation at the end with block chords, one per measure, in funereal succession. (The Neapolitan chord near the end of each of these songs is another point of resemblance.) Only the utmost austerity would do for words that Schubert repeats several times, prolonging the poet's curt conclusion throughout fifteen measures and descending not merely through the tetrachord but the entire length of the octave. There is no more "Schönheit" to deflect the mind and ear from the stark pronouncement that "everything must vanish and perish." In the postlude, the supremacy of minor is starkly confirmed, foreshadowing the manner of the Heine songs.

Between Die schöne Müllerin *and* Winterreise

Although the Midas touch of 1822 is not always evident in the songs composed between the two Müller cycles, there are masterpieces aplenty from this period, including his settings of the Orientalist and poet Friedrich Rückert's "Daß sie hier gewesen," D. 775, "Du bist die Ruh'," D. 776, "Lachen und Weinen," D. 777, and "Greisengesang," D. 778, this last perhaps composed in late 1822 and 1823 (the dating is uncertain). Schubert's setting of Karl Lappe's "Im Abendrot," D. 799, is possibly from 1825, as are his settings of Jacob Nicolaus Craigher's "Totengräbers Heimweh" (Gravedigger's Homesickness, D. 842) and the Walter Scott songs. His much-loved setting of Schlechta's "Fischerweise" (Fisherman's Tune, D. 881) dates from 1826, as do the equally well-loved Shakespeare songs "Ständchen" (Serenade, D. 889) and "An Sylvia" (To Sylvia, D. 891).

In 1824, Johann Mayrhofer's collected poems were published by subscription, but Schubert was not among the subscribers, as the two men had parted company by then. Schubert would, however, have known of the volume and was drawn back to his friend's verses for four more settings, including "Auflösung" (Dissolution), one of Schubert's mightiest songs. One of Mayrhofer's recurring themes, his belief that only artistic creativity could provide consolation for the miseries of existence, is expressed, appropriately, in poetry itself. When creative powers well up from within, the poet of "Auflösung," D. 807, wants all else to disappear, even what is most beautiful in Nature. The sun cannot equal the fiery rapture of poetry, and he imperiously bids it begone; even music and the beauty of spring—his foremost consolations at other times—are unwelcome intrusions. At the culmination of this powerful poem, he wishes that the entire world might dissolve and disappear, leaving only the ethereal choirs of poetry. In graphic illustration of the death-ecstasy that he courts with such intensity (Mayrhofer would kill himself in 1836), the poetic form begins to dissolve as well, the line lengths varying from dimeters—such brief, proto-Expressionistic rhythms are characteristic of Mayrhofer—to tetrameters, and swaying unpredictably between trochees and iambs. There is, in particular, a marvelous enjambment in the final two lines of the poem to emphasize the word *nimmer* (never). Poetic devices such as these are lost in music, but Schubert took note of the poet's emphasis and repeats the word to an arpeggiated vocal phrase spanning an octave and a half and culminating in a downbeat emphasis on tonic high G (mm. 43–44).

In "Auflösung" the poet tells music to be silent ("Verstummet, Töne") in order that "himmlisch singen" (heavenly song) might supersede earthly tones; Schubert contravenes that command by translating the heavenly singing into lied. The poet's engulfing rapture becomes incessant vibratory tone, with tremolandos in the bass and arpeggios that swoop and plunge in the right hand, the essential inwardness of the experience preserved in the piano and pianissimo dynamics at beginning and end. It is the furious injunctions to the outside world to "leave me alone," to "go under," that prompt fortissimo and forzando outbursts. Like Mayrhofer, Schubert creates form in the beginning of dissolution: "Auflösung" is a three-part song-form in which the boundaries between sections dissolve, harmonic events near the ends of the A and B sections fuse with the start of each succeeding section, and the final A section is thoroughly varied. The smallest compositional decisions tell of a universe dissolving in a Turneresque rapture, everything in counterposed, dissolving motion, against which the singer hurls one of Schubert's most grandiose vocal lines: the poet/singer is stronger than Nature at this moment (Johnson 1991). Where Mayrhofer bids "Spring beauty" to go away and leave him alone, Schubert seems as if ready to repeat mm. 7–13, but a diminished-seventh chord replaces the B-minor harmony from before and is followed by a massive semitone shift upwards to the Neapolitan A♭ major. The radical harmonic jolt is unprepared; Schubert understood those words as an outburst that should erupt with special violence, even from music already as turbulent as this. Knowing the misanthropic poet personally, he invested the phrase with maximum intensity. It is as if a black hole had opened and swallowed the detested springtime world of G major.

The "gentle powers" that well up from within in the B section do so on the A♭-major harmony to which the poet-composer bade the world go away (mm. 24–32). Something of both the desperation with which the poet clings to the "powers" and the vulnerability of the experience are registered in the fact that Schubert does not truly establish A♭ by any means other than repetition. He even destabilizes it in mm. 31–32 by means of the C-minor chord and its dominant, which resolves deceptively at the end of the phrase—to an A♭-major harmony. At the moment when the poet invokes heavenly song enveloping him, Schubert begins to dissolve the simultaneously fierce but tenuous hold on A♭; the enharmonic transformation of A♭ into C♯ minor and the subsequent unstable B-major chords prompt the furious-ecstatic imperatives to "go under, world."

When G major returns in the final section, the poet-singer repeatedly attempts to vault into the empyrean and remain there, but finds himself unable to do so; the vocal line leaps to high G repeatedly, but always on the weak beat of the measure and always falling back downwards. In mm. 59–60, the singer, in an Olympian gesture, vaults above the limits of the high G to A and a dominant-seventh chord that has not been heard until this climactic point. The passage is powerful, ecstatic, and desperate—and doomed to failure. The G-major harmonies ascend even higher and more distant than before, then die away, and the final low pleas of "Geh unter, Welt" are tinged with minor coloration and engulfed by tremolandos as the "heavenly song" vanishes.

Surveying the Schubert lied corpus, with its fragments and multiple versions, its poets ranging from mid-eighteenth-century worthies to the "moderns" of Schubert's own generation, its forms ranging from miniatures to mini-operas, one is overwhelmed by its variety and quality. To each element retained from the songwriting traditions that preceded him, whether strict strophic forms, through-composed structures, recitative incorporated within lied, or word-painting, Schubert added his original conception. Everything is subjected to alteration by a creative intelligence that reinvented the lied in a poetic light; even where he warps, ignores, contradicts, drowns out, alters, and obscures aspects of his chosen poetry, Schubert is responding to verse in ways and at depths unavailable to his predecessors or contemporaries.

Schubert's lieder left their impression on later composers. His settings of Friedrich Schlegel's "Der Fluß" (The River, D. 693) and Karoline Louise von Klenke's "Heimliches Lieben" (Secret Love, D. 922) are possible precursors of Robert Schumann's manner of bridging vocal phrases by means of a seamless melody combined with broken chords in the piano interludes, as the latter's setting of Goethe's "Liebeslied" (Love Song, Op. 51, No. 5). Johannes Brahms said, "There is no song by Schubert from which one cannot learn something";* it was perhaps from songs like "Totengräbers Heimweh" that Brahms found his "death motif," the series of falling thirds whose culmination is "O Tod, wie bitter bist du" (Oh

---

*Max Kalbeck, *Johannes Brahms*, 4 vols. (Vienna, 1904), vol. 1, 230.

Death, how bitter thou art) from the *Vier ernste Gesänge* (Four Serious Songs, Op. 121). Adolf Friedrich von Schack's lines "Gib dich zur Ruh', bald stirbt sie auch" (Go to your rest; soon [my heart] will die) at the end of "Herbstgefühl" (Autumnal Mood, Op. 48, no. 7) impelled from Brahms a quotation of the ending of "Der Doppelgänger." Hugo Wolf, who once asked in exasperation "Must I keep silent because a great man lived before me and wrote wonderful songs?," would also convert echoes from Schubert's songs into covert recollections within his own works, as when Schubert's "Geheimes," D. 719, is transmuted into Wolf's "Mein Liebster ist so klein" from the *Italienisches Liederbuch*. Despite their different approaches to song composition, each paid homage in his own way to a composer whom the Viennese rightly dubbed the "Prince of Song."

Notes

1. More than one reviewer of Schubert's songs used the expression "indefatiga-ble" (*unermüdlich*). See Deutsch 1977, 474 (Berlin *Allgemeine Musikalische Zeitung*, 21 Dec. 1825) and 607 (Leipzig *Allgemeine Musikalische Zeitung*, 4 April 1827).

2. Two hefty fragments particularly compel attention: D. 1A, 239 measures of an untexted song in C minor, and D. 39, a setting in C major of twenty-nine lines from Gabriele von Baumberg's "Lebenstraum" (Dream of Life). See Hoorickx (1982–84), Brown (1954 and 1961), and Landon (1969).

3. "Erlkönig" was popular with composers; see Düring 1972. Joseph von Spaun's famous account of Schubert rapidly composing this song in one inspired mo-ment (see Deutsch 1958, 131) is contradicted by other accounts. A fair copy of this song with a simplified accompaniment was made for Goethe in 1816; see Dürr (1978, 43–56).

4. Joseph von Spaun wrote in 1858, "There is a prejudice that Schubert was born only to be a song writer" (Deutsch 1958, 140). Biba (1979, 106–13) points out that Schubert's music was second in popularity only to that of Rossini on the programs of the Gesellschaft der Musikfreunde; that Anton Diabelli paid Schu-bert high fees for his songs; that the most famous instrumental and vocal soloists of the day regularly performed Schubert's works; and that the numer-ous manuscript and album copies of his compositions reflect his renown.

5. On other occasions it was likely the accompaniment that prompted a pub-lisher's request for lowered transposition. The first version of his setting of Goethe's "Der Musensohn," D. 764, is in A♭ major. The appoggiatura-laden ac-companiment is more difficult to play in that key than in its final key of G major.

6. Similar bagpipe figures appear in mm. 67–74 of "Eifersucht und Stolz" (from *Die schöne Müllerin*) to different and bitter effect.

7. Zumsteeg's frequent use of German sixth-chords as the pivot for swift tonal changes might be the origin of Schubert's liking for that same harmony.

8. In November 1822, Schubert had composed another song in the rare tonality of F♯ minor-major, to another text in which humanity is promised a beautiful, ecstatic afterlife: his setting of Franz von Bruchmann's "Schwestergruß," D. 762.

For all their differences of form and figuration, both songs are characterized by the unstable swaying back and forth between parallel modes and even by the "tolling bell" evocation on C♯ in the topmost voice at the beginning.

9. One critic reproached Schubert for making a textual change in the setting of Mayrhofer's "Antigone und Oedip," D. 542: "The treatment of a text should show the same respect for a poet's work with which we honour a composer's creation" (Deutsch 1946, 207).

10. Perhaps the composer's knowledge of the poet's personality influenced the striking prosodic gesture at the beginning; taking his cue from Mayrhofer's syntax in line 1 ("Mir ist so wohl, so weh"), he underscores the poet's solipsism by means of the descending leap of a minor sixth on the anacrusis.

11. An early example of Schubert's discomfiture with Schiller's *Denk-Poesie* or "thought poetry" (versified philosophy) can be found in the setting of "Hoffnung" (Hope, D. 251), composed 7 August 1815. The poem is a miniature philosophical meditation to the effect that the world waxes old and then young, whereas humanity is born to strive for betterment. Schubert, a bit comically, strives for profundity by setting the song in the unusual (for the early songs) key of G♭ major; he reset the poem, possibly in 1817, adopting an entirely different approach (D. 637).

12. Schubert would later use the same type of chordal figuration that one finds in mm. 17–24 of the D-minor "Lied der Mignon," at the words "Ach! der mich liebt und kennt ist in der Weite," in mm. 26–36 of "Am Feierabend," from *Die schöne Müllerin,* in which the beloved is psychologically (not physically) distant and the poetic persona is similarly in turmoil at the realization.

13. Schubert deliberately ignored the whiff of sulfur and brimstone in this poem, and it was left to Hugo Wolf at the end of the century to convey its demonic overtones.

14. In his setting of Ernst Schulze's "Der liebliche Stern" (The Lovely Star, D. 861), composed in 1825, Schubert would be similarly inspired by the compound of "wohl" and "weh" in stanza 1 of that poem.

Bibliography

Adelhold, Werner, Walther Dürr, and Walburga Litschauer, eds. *Franz Schubert— Jahre der Krise 1818–1823: Arnold Feil zum 60. Geburtstag am 2. Oktober 1985.* Kassel, 1985.

Agawu, V. Kofi. "Schubert's harmony revisited: the songs 'Du liebst mich nicht' and 'Dass sie hier gewesen.'" *Journal of Musicological Research* 9 (1989): 23–42.

Alberti-Radonowicz, Editha. "Das Wiener Lied von 1789–1815." In *Studien zur Musikwissenschaft: Beihefte der Denkmäler der Tonkunst in Österreich,* 10: 37–78. Vienna, 1923.

Allen, Robert Trawick. "Franz Schubert's Apprenticeship in the Short Song, 1815–1816." Ph.D. dissertation, University of Michigan, 1989.

Berke, Dietrich. "Schuberts Liedentwurf 'Abend' D 645 und dessen textliche Voraussetzungen." In *Schubert-Kongress Wien 1978: Bericht,* ed. Otto Brusatti, 305–20. Graz, 1979.

Biba, Otto. "Schubert's Position in Viennese Musical Life." *19th-Century Music* 3 (1979): 106–13.

Brown, Maurice J. E. "Some unpublished Schubert songs and song fragments." *Music Review* 15 (1954): 39–102.

———. "Schubert: Discoveries of the Last Decade." *Musical Quarterly* 47 (1961): 293–314.

Capell, Richard. *Schubert's Songs.* London, 1928. Reprint. New York, 1977. 2d ed. London, 1957. 3d ed. London, 1973.

Clercq, Robert O. de. "Schuberts *Erlkönig* in einigen bemerkenswerten Ausgaben." *Schubert durch die Brille* 8 (January 1992): 39–44.

Denny, Thomas. "Directional Tonality in Schubert's Lieder." In *Franz Schubert–Der Fortschrittliche? Analysen–Perspektiven–Fakten,* ed. Erich Wolfgang Partsch, 37–54. Tutzing, 1989.

Deutsch, Otto Erich. *Schubert: A Documentary Biography.* Trans. Eric Blom. London, 1946. Reprint. New York, 1977.

———. *Schubert: Memoirs by His Friends.* Trans. Rosamond Ley and John Nowell. London, 1958.

Dittrich, Marie-Agnes. *Harmonik und Sprachvertonung in Schuberts Liedern.* Hamburg, 1991.

Dürhammer, Ilija. "Zu Schuberts Literästhetik." *Schubert durch die Brille* 14 (January 1995): 5–100.

Düring, Werner-Joachim. *Erlkönig-Vertonungen: Eine historische und systematische Untersuchung.* Regensburg, 1972.

Dürr, Walther. "Aus Schuberts erstem Publikationsplan: Zwei Hefte mit Liedern von Goethe." In *Schubert-Studien: Festgabe der Österreichischen Akademie der Wissenschaften zum Schubert-Jahr 1978,* ed. Franz Grasberger and Othmar Wesseley, 43–56. Vienna, 1978.

———. "Wer vermag nach Beethoven noch etwas zu machen?" In *Musik-Konzepte: Sonderband Franz Schubert,* ed. Heinz-Klaus Metzger and Rainer Riehn, 10–15. Munich, 1979.

———. "Schubert's Songs and Their Poetry: Reflections on Poetic Aspects of Song Composition." In *Schubert Studies: Problems of Style and Chronology,* ed. Eva Badura-Skoda and Peter Branscombe, 1–24. Cambridge, 1982.

———. "Entwurf—Ausarbeitung—Revision: Zur Arbeitsweise Schuberts am Beispiel des Liedes 'Der Unglückliche' (D. 713)." *Musikforschung* 44 (1991): 221–36.

———. "Franz Schuberts Wanderjahre: Einführung in das Generalthema." In *Franz Schubert: Jahre der Krise 1818–1823,* ed. Werner Aderhold, Walther Dürr, and Walburga Litschauer, 11–21. Kassel, 1985.

———. "Schuberts Lied 'An den Tod' (D 518)—zensiert?" *Österreichische Musikzeitschrift* 38 (1983): 9–17.

Fehn, Ann Clark, and Rufus Hallmark. "Text and Music in Schubert's Pentameter Lieder: A Consideration of Declamation." In *Studies in the History of Music,* vol. 1: *Music and Language,* ed. Ronald Broude, 204–46. New York, 1983.

Feil, Arnold. "Franz Schubert 'Des Fischers Liebesglück': Considerazioni sull' analisi strutturale e sull' interpretazione." *Richerche musicali* 4 (1980): 71–80.

———. "Zur Genesis der Gattung Lied, wie sie Franz Schubert definiert hat." *Musikoloski Zbornik* 11 (1975): 40–53.

Flothuis, Marius. "Franz Schubert's Compositions to Poems from Goethe's 'Wilhelm Meister's Lehrjahre.'" In *Notes on Notes: Selected Essays by Marius Flothuis,* ed. Sylvia Broere-Moore, 87–138. Amsterdam, 1974.

————. "Schubert Revises Schubert." In *Schubert Studies: Problems of Style and Chronology*, ed. Eva Badura-Skoda and Peter Branscombe, 61–84. Cambridge, 1982.

Friedländer, Max. *Das deutsche Lied im 18. Jahrhundert: Quellen und Studien*. 2 vols. Stuttgart, 1902. Reprint. 3 vols. Hildesheim, 1970.

Frisch, Walter. "Schubert's *Nähe des Geliebten* (D. 162): Transformation of the *Volkston*." In *Schubert: Critical and Analytical Studies*, ed. Walter Frisch, 175–99. Lincoln, 1986.

Georgiades, Thrasybulos. *Schubert: Musik und Lyrik*. Göttingen, 1967.

Gramit, David. "The Intellectual and Aesthetic Tenets of Franz Schubert's Circle." Ph.D. dissertation, Duke University, 1987.

Hallmark, Rufus. "Schubert's 'Auf dem Strom.'" In *Schubert Studies: Problems of Style and Chronology*, ed. Eva Badura-Skoda and Peter Branscombe, 25–46. Cambridge, 1982.

————, and Ann Clark Fehn. "Text Declamation in Schubert's Settings of Pentameter Poetry." *Zeitschrift für Literaturwissenschaft und Linguistik* 9, Heft, 34 *Das Lied* (1979): 11–80.

Holländer, Hans. "Franz Schubert's Repeated Settings of the Same Song-Texts." *Musical Quarterly* 14 (1928): 563–74.

Hoorickx, Reinhard van. "Schubert's Earliest Preserved Song-Fragments." *Revue belge de musicologie* 36–38 (1982–84): 145–61.

Jackson, Timothy. "Schubert's Revisions of 'Der Jüngling und der Tod,' D. 545a–b, and 'Meeresstille,' D. 216a–b." *The Musical Quarterly* 75 (1991): 336–61.

Johnson, Graham. "Schubert and his Friends." Liner note for *The Hyperion Schubert Edition*, vol. 4, Philip Langridge, tenor, Graham Johnson, piano. Hyperion CDJ 33004 (1989). Includes eight of the Körner songs.

————. "Schubert in 1815." Liner note for *The Hyperion Schubert Edition*, vol. 7, Elly Ameling, soprano, Graham Johnson, pianist. Hyperion CDJ 33007 (1990).

————. "Death and the Composer." Liner note for *The Hyperion Schubert Edition*, vol. 11, Brigitte Fassbaender, mezzo-soprano, Graham Johnson, piano. Hyperion CDJ 30011 (1991).

————. "Lieder der Nacht." Liner note for *The Hyperion Schubert Edition*, vol. 15, Margaret Price, soprano, Graham Johnson, piano. Hyperion CDJ 33015 (1992). [Johnson 1992a]

————. "Schubert and the Classics." Liner note for *The Hyperion Schubert Edition*, vol. 14, Thomas Hampson, baritone, Graham Johnson, piano. Hyperion CDJ 33014 (1992). [Johnson 1992b]

————. "Schubert and the Strophic Song." Liner note for *The Hyperion Schubert Edition*, vol. 18, Peter Schreier, tenor, Graham Johnson, pianist. Hyperion CDJ 33018 (1993). [Johnson 1993a]

————. "Songs to Texts by Friedrich von Schiller (1759–1805)." Liner note for *The Hyperion Schubert Edition*, vol. 16, Thomas Allen, baritone, Graham Johnson, piano. Hyperion CDJ 33016 (1993). [Johnson 1993b]

Kerman, Joseph. "A Romantic Detail in Schubert's *Schwanengesang*." *Musical Quarterly* 48 (1962): 36–49.

Kindermann, William. "Schubert's Tragic Perspective." In *Schubert: Critical and Analytical Studies*, ed. Walter Frisch, 65–83. Lincoln, NE, 1986.

Kinsey, Barbara. "Schubert and the Poems of Ossian." *Music Review* 34 (1973): 22–29.

Kramer, Lawrence. *Music and Poetry: The Nineteenth Century and After.* Berkeley, 1984.

———. "The Schubert Lied: Romantic Form and Romantic Consciousness." In *Schubert: Critical and Analytical Studies,* ed. Walter Frisch, 200–36. Lincoln, NE, 1986.

Kramer, Richard. "Schubert's Heine." *19th-Century Music* 8 (Spring 1985): 213–25.

———. "Distant Cycles: Schubert, Goethe and the Entfernte." *Journal of Musicology* 6 (Winter 1988): 3–26.

———. *Distant Cycles: Schubert and the Conceiving of Song.* Chicago, 1994.

Krebs, Harald. "Tonart und Text in Schuberts Liedern mit abweichenden Schlüssen." *Archiv für Musikwissenschaft* 47 (1990): 264–71.

Kreißle von Hellborn, Heinrich. *Franz Schubert.* Vienna, 1865.

Landon, Christa. "Neue Schubert-Funde: Unbekannte Manuskripte im Archiv des Wiener Männergesang-Vereines." *Österreichische Musikzeitschrift* 24 (1969): 229–332. Translated as "New Schubert Finds," *The Music Review* 31 (1970): 215–31.

Litschauer, Walburga, ed. *Neue Dokumente zum Schubert-Kreis: Aus Briefen und Tagebüchern seiner Freunde.* Vienna, 1986.

Maier, Günter. *Die Lieder Johann Rudolf Zumsteegs und ihr Verhältnis zu Schubert.* Göppingen, 1971.

Mainka, J. "Das Liedschaffen Franz Schuberts in den Jahren 1815 und 1816: Schuberts Auseinandersetzung mit der Liedtradition des 18. Jahrhunderts." Ph.D. dissertation, University of Berlin, 1957.

Motte, Diether de la. "Die Aufhebung von Zeit in Schuberts endlosen Liedern." In *Franz Schubert–Der Fortschrittliche? Analysen–Perspektiven–Fakten,* ed. Erich Wolfgang Partsch, 201–12. Tutzing, 1989.

Muxfeldt, Kristina. "Schubert Song Studies." Ph.D. dissertation, State University of New York at Stony Brook, 1991.

Orel, Alfred. "Die Skizze zu Franz Schuberts letztem Lied." *Die Musik* 29 (1937): 765–71.

Partsch, Eric Wolfgang, ed. *Franz Schubert—Der Fortschrittliche? Analysen–Perspektiven–Fakten.* Tutzing, 1989.

Porhansl, Lucia. "Schuberts Textvorlagen nach Ignaz Franz Castelli." *Schubert durch die Brille* 14 (January 1995): 101–4.

Reed, John. *The Schubert Song Companion.* Manchester, 1985.

Sams, Eric. "Notes on a Magic Flute: The Origins of the Schubertian Lied." *Musical Times* 119 (1978): 947–48.

Schachter, Carl. "Motive and Text in Four Schubert Songs." In *Aspects of Schenkerian Theory,* ed. David Beach, 61–76. New Haven, 1983.

Scheibler, Ludwig. "Franz Schuberts einstimmige Leider, Gesänge und Balladen mit Texten von Schiller." *Die Rheinlande* (April–September 1905): 131–36, 163–69, 231–39, 270–74, 311–15, 353–56.

Schenker, Heinrich. "Franz Schubert: Gretchen am Spinnrade." *Der Tonwille* 6 (1923): 3–8.

Schnapper, Edith. *Die Gesänge des jungen Schuberts vor dem Durchbruch des romantischen Liedprinzipes.* Bern, 1937.

Schwarmath-Tarjan, Ermute. *Musikalischer Bau und Sprachvertonung in Schuberts Liedern.* Tutzing, 1969.

Seebass, Tilman. "Classical and Romantic Principles in Schubert's Lieder: *Auf dem See* and *Des Fischers Liebesglück*." In *Studies in Musical Sources and Style: Essays in Honor of Jan LaRue,* ed. Eugene K. Wolf and Edward H. Roesner, 481–504. Madison, WI, 1990.

Solomon, Maynard. "Schubert and Beethoven." *19th-Century Music* 3 (1979): 114–25.

Spies, Günther. "Studien zum Liede Franz Schuberts: Vorgeschichte, Eigenart und Bedeutung der Strophenvarierung." Ph.D. dissertation, University of Tübingen, 1962.

Steglich, Rudolf. "Das romantische Wanderlied und Franz Schubert." In *Musa-Mens-Musici: Im Gedenken an Walther Vetter,* ed. Institut für Musikwissenschaft der Humboldt-Universität zu Berlin, 267–76. Leipzig, 1969.

Utz, Helga. *Untersuchungen zur Syntax der Lieder Franz Schuberts.* Munich, 1989.

Waidelich, Till Gerrit, ed. *Franz Schubert–Dokumente 1817–1830.* Vol. 1: *Texte.* Tutzing, 1993.

West, Ewan Donald. "Schubert's Lieder in Context: Aspects of Song in Vienna 1778–1828." Ph.D. dissertation, Oxford University, 1989.

Wing, Marjorie. *Schubert's Dramatic Lieder.* Cambridge, 1993.

Wolff, Christoph. "Schubert's 'Der Tod und das Mädchen': Analytical and Explanatory Notes on the Song D 531 and the Quartet D 810." In *Schubert Studies: Problems of Style and Chronology,* ed. Eva Badura-Skoda and Peter Branscombe, 143–72. Cambridge, 1982.

Youens, Susan, "Memory, Identity, and The Uses of the Past: Schubert and Luciano Berio's Recital I (for Cathy)." In *Franz Schubert—Der Fortschrittliche? Analysen–Perspektiven–Fakten.* Tutzing, 1989.

———. *Schubert's Poets and the Making of Lieder.* Cambridge, 1996.

Zeman, Herbert. "Franz Schuberts Teilhabe an der österreichischen literarischen Kultur seiner Zeit." In *Schubert-Kongreß Wien 1978: Bericht,* ed. Otto Brusatti, 283–304. Graz, 1979.

CHAPTER THREE

Robert Schumann: The Poet Sings

Rufus Hallmark

Robert Schumann (1810–56) was probably the most literary and well-read composer of the late eighteenth and early nineteenth centuries. His father was a book dealer in Zwickau, and books were always a part of his life. At fifteen he founded a literary club, as he would one day found a musical journal; at its meetings he and his friends read plays, novels, and poetry aloud to one another. Though a life-long devotee of novelist Jean Paul Richter, his taste was catholic, and throughout his life his diaries disclose almost constant reading on a grand scale. By the time he was twenty, he wrote, "The most significant writers of just about every country were familiar to me" (Eismann 1956, 1:17). For a while the young Schumann even expected he would become a writer. Given this strong literary bent and the musical creativity that subsequently blossomed, it would seem he was destined to combine the two in song.

Early Career and the *Liederjahr*

In his late teens (1827–28), Schumann attended and participated in evening musicales in the home of a local doctor and wrote about a dozen songs for his wife.[1] These compositions show Schumann's early interest in the Swabian poet Justinius Kerner (five settings), to whose work he would return a decade later, but otherwise they bear little resemblance to the later songs. His setting of Kerner's "An Anna" (*Werke*, XIV/1: 34), for example, shows Schumann perfectly capable of joining a text comfortably to an attractive melody, but not yet adept at creating an appropriate mood. The verses are addressed by a soldier dying on the battlefield, to his beloved, yet Schumann wrote it as a polonaise in a major key. The dance rhythm and mood would be well suited years later to the flirtatiousness of Geibel's "Der Hidalgo" (Op. 30, No. 3) or "Botschaft" (Op. 74, No. 8), where similar rhythmic gestures evoke a bolero, but here these effects sound flippant.[2] Schumann does match the music to the words line by line, providing diminished-seventh chords, for example, for the words "carried pale from the battlefield." This rather madrigalesque response, however, is deficient from the perspective of Schumann's later ideal of capturing the mood (*Stimmung*) of a poem as a whole. Brunswick composer Gottlob Wiedebein counseled him to strive for "poetic truth" and to "harmonize all parts together" (Eismann 1:40). Schumann recast the piece some years later as the second movement ("Aria") of his Piano Sonata in F♯ Minor Op. 11. Another Kerner song, "Im Herbste" (*Werke* XIV/1: 36), comes closer to Schumann's later style. Its subdued, *innig* (intimate and sincere) melody and harmony project the poem's sensual and ardent mood rather than its individual images (Ex. 3.1). This song, too, was later incorporated into a piano work, the slow movement of the Piano Sonata in G Minor Op. 22.

EXAMPLE 3.1. "Im Herbste," mm. 1–5

After these youthful efforts, Schumann devoted the first decade of his mature composing career to music for the piano, much of it with literary or extra-musical associations. Allusions, titles, words, even letters assisted the composer with his aesthetic program. *Papillons* is directly related to Jean Paul's novel *Die Flegeljahre; Kreisleriana* refers to Capellmeister Kreisler in E. T. A. Hoffman's novella. *Carnaval* has the masked ball of the pre-lenten Carnival season as its premise, each piece bearing a character's name, and many of the melodies are constructed around permutations of the musical letters common to Schumann's name and the city Asch, where an early sweetheart lived (S [Es], C, H, A = E♭, C, B♮, A). The Variations Op. 1 are based similarly on the pitches in the name *Abegg. Kinderscenen* (Scenes of Childhood), with its famous "Träumerei," contains a piece entitled "Der Dichter spricht"—The Poet Speaks—suggesting that Schumann considered himself a tone poet (*Tondichter*) and that the essence of poetry is the mood or nonverbal message established, whether by linguistic means or, as here, by wordless piano music. Schumann would, however, again appreciate actual poetry as an impetus and opportunity for composition; eventually it would coax the poet to sing.

By his late twenties Schumann was known as the founding editor and frequent contributor to the *Neue Zeitschrift für Musik*—his literary talent harnessed to write musical criticism—and as the composer of piano music too puzzling to please crowds in the concert hall and too thorny for amateurs at home. He felt he was reaching a creative impasse in his piano composition, and he wanted to make a mark in the serious, public genres of symphony and opera. He also was secretly engaged to and determined to marry the esteemed concert pianist Clara Wieck, but her father was throwing up every barrier to their marriage, to the point of making accusations against Schumann's character in court. This personal situation added to the composer's creative dilemma, for one of Herr Wieck's allegations was that Schumann had insufficient income to support his daughter.

During this time, probably in the autumn of 1839, Schumann began to compose songs again, after an eleven-year hiatus. Though no song manuscript of this period is securely dated before January 1840, Schumann, in his letters to Clara, refers to new compositions that do not correspond to any piano music. He describes his composing as being qualitatively different, and in mid-February of the new year he explicitly alludes to lieder. "I've written six notebooks of songs, ballads, and little four-voice pieces." In the course of a little more than one year (late fall 1839 through January 1841), Schumann completed approximately two hundred works for solo voice (or voices). The year 1840 became, in his words, "mein Liederjahr" (see Eismann 1: 147). Schumann felt this body of work to rank among his best achievements, and he published eight sets of songs between the summer of 1840 and the end of 1841 (about a third of the ones he had composed).

In light of the significant turn to song his compositional career was about to take, it is ironic that in mid-1839 Schumann had asked a younger composer, "Have you perhaps, like me, never considered vocal composition to be a great art form?"[3] Schumann's question, much cited and discussed, may simply indicate a generally low opinion of many of the songs that came his way as a reviewer for the journal, or it may imply dissatisfaction with his own early efforts. It may also reflect the pervasive early Romantic view that instrumental music was superior to texted music.

Even if one disregards this pronouncement, Schumann's "conversion" from solo keyboard music to song seems an abrupt turn. A number of explanations have been put forward (see Feldman, Plantinga 1967, Sams 1965, Walsh 1971, and Turchin 1981). One common suggestion is that the composer broke into song because he was inspired by his anticipated marriage to Clara, but the underlying reasoning is fuzzy on several accounts. Robert and Clara had been in love for years and had even made a secret pledge eventually to be wed, in spite of her father's objections. In the winter of 1839–40, when he began to write songs, their marriage was still far from certain. Furthermore, by no means all the poems Schumann set have to do with happy love, or even with love at all. Finally, and most importantly, Clara had already been a constant source of inspiration; he had composed much piano music with her in mind. His feelings toward her cannot logically be advanced to explain a change in genre, though they unquestionably continued to inspire him in whatever he did.[4] But, although rejecting this explanation as facile and sentimental, one may still view Clara as a catalyst; she had been encouraging Robert to compose songs, for example, and he enjoyed hearing her sing.

Subtle changes in Schumann's piano music have been traced; compositions of the late 1830s, such as *Kreisleriana* (Op. 16) and the *Noveletten* (Op. 21), have more songlike melodies than the earlier, more rhapsodic works. Thus the turn to vocal music can be understood as part of a more gradual stylistic change. Another artistic factor may have been Schumann's interest in and ambition to compose an opera. In 1840 he was beginning to look for a suitable subject and libretto, and he may have thought of composing lieder as a prelude to vocal music for the stage.

To these personal and artistic factors may be added economic ones. In 1838–39 Schumann was deeply concerned that the public, and professional pianists (sometimes even Clara), did not appreciate his piano music, and that he needed to compose something to bring in more income and to satisfy Wieck. If one adds this to his dissatisfaction with his recent piano music, to the success of the songs published as supplements to the *Neue Zeitschrift*, and to the sheer fact that success in song composition had made many a nonperforming composer well known, then the cumulative weight of these factors seems ample grounds for his move, whether or not by conscious decision.

Mendelssohn may also have been an influence. On 30 January 1840 the two composers spent the evening together. The next day, Schumann wrote the earliest unambiguously dated song, "Schlusslied des Narren"—the fool's closing song from Shakespeare's *Twelfth Night,* published years later as Op. 127, No. 5. It has been surmised that Mendelssohn, already a published song composer, encouraged Schumann to try his hand at this genre. If we trust inferences from his letters, Schumann had already started to write songs, but a positive word from such a respected colleague could certainly have given his tentative beginning a fresh impetus.

Poets and Poetry

As Schumann began to write songs, he sampled the work of various poets; in the course of his career he set verse by about sixty writers. In his poetic affinities, Schumann has traditionally been characterized as a Romantic lied composer, but recent scholarship has begun to contest this view and to regard him as an artist poised between Romanticism, which had become a dated literary phenomenon and sensibility by the 1840s, and Biedermeier materialism, realism, and resignation (Dahlhaus 1974, Kross 1981). Though one thinks of his mysterious and mystical settings of poems by Joseph Freiherr von Eichendorff, of the distraught lover of his Heine songs, and of his (obligatory?) treatments of the famous lyrics from Goethe's *Wilhelm Meister,* there are few other poems of German Romanticism among his songs, and Heine's status is debatable. Only three by Schiller, six from the *Wunderhorn* collection of folk poetry, and five by balladist Uhland could be properly added to that category, and these are rather slim works.

At the same time there is his attraction to the poems of Adelbert von Chamisso, Friedrich Rückert, and Robert Reinick, which exemplify German middle-class domestic values, tinged with exhausted Romantic imagery. The personae in these poems do not sing of romantic passion and yearning but find meaning in conjugal love, religion, and national pride. Nature is no longer a set of symbols for spiritual realities, as in the poetry of Eichendorff or the paintings of Caspar David Friedrich, but a mirror of human feelings and an index of beauty.

Chamisso's poetic cycle *Frauenliebe und Leben* embodies the age's stereotyped conception of womanhood as subservient wife and mother (Solie); though Schumann's music brings Chamisso's rather flat character to life, the assumptions behind the texts today seem rather unpalatable. In the Rückert songs Op. 37 (jointly composed by Robert and Clara), the artist, anxious that he will be unable to realize his creative goals, finds compensation in love and companionship (Hallmark 1990). The distraught lover of Heine-Schumann does not commit suicide, like Goethe's Werther or Schubert's young miller, but finds consolation and reconciliation.

Schumann also composed songs to poems by Emmanuel Geibel and Justinius Kerner. The poetry of Geibel, especially his translations of Spanish love songs (which inspired two of Schumann's multivoiced cycles, Opp. 74 and 138), is full of earthy realism—humorous, melancholy, angry, flirtatious. Kerner, whose verse the composer had first set as a seventeen-year-old, bears traces of a romantic outlook, but one that has turned somewhat sentimental and pessimistic. Chamisso, Geibel, Kerner, and Rückert, together with Eichendorff, Goethe, and Heine, are the poets on which Schumann drew most heavily for his Lieder; approximately half of his three hundred songs are on texts by these seven poets. Closely following are Robert Burns, Hoffmann von Fallersleben, Elisabeth Kulmann (a German émigré in Russia), and the Austrian Nicholas Lenau, with eleven songs each. These eleven poets are the source of two-thirds of Schumann's songs. From the remaining fifty poets, Schumann often set fewer than five poems, in many cases a single lyric.

Like literature in general, poetry and song can be divided into three broad categories according to their "voice": lyrical, dramatic, and narrative. In the lyric poem or song, the speaking persona is the lyrical self, a first-person voice expressing itself about or in relation to the love of another, of nature, God, and so forth. Dramatic poems are also called *Rollengedichte* in German; in a dramatic song the singer takes on a role, becomes a character. Narrative songs tell a story, and the singer is the neutral narrator; the commonest sort of narrative poem is the ballad (*Ballade*). To these categories it is necessary to add a fourth: folk poems and songs. Folk song is more a mode than basic literary type and can usually be placed in one of the first two categories—a lyrical utterance (e.g., a spring song) or a character type (e.g., a highland widow, a gypsy maiden)—and, of course, the literary ballad is a folk-derived genre. But folk poetry (and its imitations) usually has a distinctive voice, simpler in diction and tone, less artful, more naive than literary creations in lyrical and dramatic veins. For this reason, and because folk song was brought to the fore in this period, it is a useful category for late eighteenth- and early nineteenth-century poetry and lieder.

About half of Schumann's songs are lyrical: for example, the Heine love songs of Opp. 24 and 48; most of the Eichendorff songs, Op. 39; the Kerner, Reinick, and Rückert songs, Opp. 35–37; most of the songs published as *Lieder und Gesänge* (Opp. 27, 51, 77, and 96); the Neun and Lenau songs, Opp. 89 and 90; and the Rückert *Minnelieder*, Op. 101). The remainder are distributed in roughly equal numbers in the other categories. The dramatic songs include *Frauenliebe* Op. 42; the various *Wanderlieder;* the Geibel pseudo-medieval songs, Op. 30; "Der Soldat" and "Der Spielmann," Op. 40, Nos. 3 and 4; "Die Soldatenbraut" and "Das verlassne Mägdelein," Op. 64, Nos. 1 and 2; the *Husarenlieder*, Op. 117; and the Maria Stuart songs, Op. 135. Among the narrative songs are the ballads: the Chamisso and Béranger songs of Op. 31—including "Die Löwenbraut" and "Die Kartenlegerin"—the *Romanzen und Balladen* (Opp. 45, 49, and 53), including "Die beiden Grenadiere" of Heine and "Frühlingsfahrt" of Eichendorff; Heine's "Belsatzar," Op. 57, Goethe's "Die wandelnde Glocke," Op. 79, No. 17, and Schiller's "Der Handschuh," Op. 87; the non-balladesque stories "Die Lotosblume," Op. 25, No. 7, "Zigeunerleben," Op. 29, No. 3, "Im Walde," Op. 39, No. 11, most of the Hans Christian Andersen songs, Op. 40, Nos. 1 and 2, and "Ein Jüngling liebt ein Mädchen," Op. 48, No. 11 and "Die Meerfee," Op. 125, No. 1. The folk and folk-like songs include the various Burns solo songs of *Myrthen,* Op. 25; the duets of Op. 34; "Verratene Liebe," Op. 40, No. 5—a Greek folksong translated by Chamisso; the real folk poems from *Des Knaben Wunderhorn* and the imitations in the *Jugendliederalbum,* Op. 79; and the Spanish folk songs in Geibel's translations in Opp. 74 and 138.

These categories are not firm, and many poems cross from one into another. One could, for example, construe the Burns serenades—set down as dialogues—as dramatic songs; one could consider some non-balladesque narrative poems to be essentially lyrical, with an implicit "I" as an observing persona. But the four-part classification generally holds.

This classification is useful for several reasons. First, it is an enlightening alternative to the use of poets' names as a way of evaluating Schumann's literary interests as a song composer. The exercise provokes certain perceptions, such as the realization that *Dichterliebe* and *Frauenliebe und Leben,* although cycles for a male and female singer, respectively, are not necessarily counterparts, for the former can be thought of as lyrical poetry, the latter as dramatic. One can perform or hear the Heine songs as direct lyrical utterances of the singer, the Chamisso songs as role-playing. Second, it calls attention to the number of non-lyrical songs. Schumann is thought of first and foremost as a lyrical lied composer, and more than half his songs fall into this category; but his interest and creativity in the other categories—particularly the dramatic and narrative songs—is greater than is generally recognized. Third, this apportionment makes clear a significant difference between Schumann and some of the other major lied composers. He drew much more heavily on folk poetry than had Schubert; his interest in the folk "voice" was different from that of his younger protégé Brahms, who drew not only on the texts but on the traditional tunes of folk songs as well. But Schumann did not draw heavily on the most famous folk poetry collection of the century, *Des Knaben Wunderhorn,* from which Mahler and others took many texts.

The Character of Schumann's Songs

In the course of February and March 1840, Schumann set around forty poems by (in alphabetical order) Burns and Byron (both in German translation), Chamisso, Goethe, Heine, Thomas Moore (also in translation), Rückert, Shakespeare, and others. Although his anticipated marriage to Clara may not have prompted his outburst into song itself, it did motivate Schumann in March to gather twenty-six of these songs into a musical bouquet for his bride. He entitled the collection *Myrthen* (myrtles, traditional German bridal flowers), and arranged for an especially decorative title page, the dedication "Seiner geliebten Braut" (to his beloved bride), and publication on their wedding day (September 12).

Though *Myrthen* seems more a special collection than a cycle,[5] many of the other songs Schumann composed in 1840–41 do belong to cycles. Indeed, the composition of groups of songs to poems by a single poet, with a narrative line or a common theme and arranged in related keys, is Schumann's characteristic manner with songs, just as his habit with piano music had been to combine many short pieces into coherent cycles, each with a general title. In this one perceives a continuity that bridges the shift to the composition of lieder. Schumann would often plunge into a frenzy of composition for a few days, and in this way he produced no fewer than seven cycles (a total of seventy-nine songs) in eleven months (February 1840–January 1841; see Table 3.1).

Other published collections of songs from 1840 are also arguably united in varying ways and degrees by poet, theme, genre, and key, even if they are not explicit cycles. Both Op. 30 and Op. 31 are portrait galleries on poems of Emanuel Geibel and Chamisso, respectively. The Op. 40 songs are translations by Chamisso, four of poems by Hans Christian Andersen and one adapted from a Greek folksong; each of these five songs is in only one of two closely related keys (G Major and D minor). The songs of Opp. 45, 49, and 53 are all narratives, as their titles indicate (*Romanzen und Balladen*, sets I, II, and III). There are also detectable poetic and tonal connections between the songs of the two collections of *Lieder und Gesänge*, Opp. 27 and 51. The three part-songs for solo voices, Op. 29, should also be mentioned here. Settings of poems by Emanuel Geibel, they are arranged in a graduated sequence: duet, trio, and quartet.

As Table 3.1 demonstrates, Schumann's opus numbers, which correspond to date of publication, obscure the chronology of his song composition. Though he composed nearly two hundred songs for solo voice(s) in the one year, he did not publish all immediately. The reason was likely both artistic and economic; he withheld songs, both anticipating the need for emendation and probably seeking to spread out his earnings. The old idea of Schumann as a composer swept away with inspirational frenzy, scrawling finished masterpieces at a fevered pace, in in need of refinement. To be sure, Schumann was capable of rapid work. His manuscripts, however, reveal that deliberate and painstaking revision followed the initial notation of a song. From his sketches of the vocal melody, through the full drafts, in which he added the piano part, to the fair copies prepared for the publishers, Schumann emended at every stage, altering and refining details of melody, rhythm, and harmony, changing meters, even omitting whole sections. This thoroughgoing self-criticism extended to entire cycles, both before publication—trimming the twenty Heine songs to the

Table 3.1.
Song Cycles, 1840–41

mid-Feb.	Heine, *Liederdreis*[1]	Op. 24, pub. 1840
early May	Eichendorff, *Liederkreis*[2]	Op. 39, pub. 1842
		(rev. ed. 1850)
mid-May	Heine, *Zwanzig Lieder*[3]	Op. 48 *Dichterliebe*
		pub. 1844
mid-July	Chamisso, *Frauenliebe und Leben*[4]	Op. 42, pub. 1843
July–Aug.	Reinick, *Sechs Gedichte*[5]	Op. 36, pub. 1841
Nov.–Dec.	Kerner, *Zwölf Gedichte*[6]	Op. 35, pub. 1841
January 1841	Rückert, *Zwölf Gedichte*[7]	Op. 37, pub. 1841

1. An integral poetic cycle of Heine's creation, entitled simply *Lieder* and included in the *Buch der Lieder*. On Op. 24, see Höckner.

2. The poems were selected from Eichendorff's novellas *Aus dem Leben eines Taugenichts* and *Ahnung und Gegenwart;* their sequence was reordered. Clara and Robert may have selected the poems together, for they are recorded in the couple's text notebook in Clara's hand. The first edition of the cycle opened with "Der frohe Wandersmann" (D major) and did not contain "In der Fremde" (F♯ minor); the latter was substituted for the former in the second, revised edition of the cycle, and the discarded song was republished as Op. 77, No. 1. See Knaus 1974 and Finson 1994.

3. Schumann set twenty poems from the "Lyrisches Intermezzo" of the *Buch der Lieder* and drafted a title page to that effect. Later he removed four songs and published the remaining sixteen with the familiar programmatic title. The four omitted songs were eventually published as Op. 127, Nos. 2–3 and Op. 142, Nos. 2 and 4. See Komar 1971 and Hallmark 1977 and 1979.

4. Based on the integral cycle of poems by Chamisso. Schumann omitted the ninth poem. See Hallmark (forthcoming) and Solie.

5. Selected from the poet's *Aus dem Liederbuch eines Malers* (From the Songbook of a Painter).

6. Two other 1840 Kerner songs—"Sängers Trost" and "Trost im Gesang"—share themes with the songs of Op. 35 and may have been part of this compositional activity. These were published later as Op. 127, No. 1 and Op. 142, No. 1, respectively, along with other songs, including the Heine songs that were removed from *Dichterliebe*. On Op. 35, see Turchin 1987.

7. Robert composed nine songs in January and Clara, at his request, composed four more, in June. Like most of Schumann's Rückert texts, these are all from the poet's large collection *Liebesfrühling* (Love's Springtime). With one of Clara's songs dropped, the songs were published as Robert and Clara's single joint opus. See Hallmark 1990.

sixteen in *Dichterliebe*—and after, as with the second edition, in 1850, of the *Liederkreis* Op. 39, with the first song replaced, as well as other changes. (See Hallmark 1977, 1979, and 1984, and Hirschberg). Similarly, it appears that Schumann was deliberate about publication, not wanting to "flood the market" and thus bringing out the products of this "Liederjahr" over a period of seven years.

The *Myrthen* collection illustrates many stylistic features of Schumann's songs. Goethe's "Freisinn" (No. 2) is a prototype of Schumann's

Wanderlieder, a major-key marching song propelled by dotted rhythms on weak beats (see Ex. 3.10a below).[6] The song is in ABA form, as are about a quarter of the *Myrthen* songs (Nos. 1, 2, 5, 11, 19, 21, and 25). In "Freisinn" (as in Nos. 1 and 5), the form results from the composer's reprise of the poem's opening strophe (or lines), a not unusual textual gambit for Schumann, for which he is often criticized. In many of Schumann's ternary forms (though not "Freisinn"), the initial section (usually the poem's first stanza) closes on a chord other than the tonic. This makes the form more dynamic; the open-ended first part "leans" more toward a continuation, and the middle section, usually in another key, increases this expectation. The musical reprise is then necessary to close the tonal motion of both preceding parts, and the resultant song is tauter than a simple ternary form in which the initial A section cadences in the tonic. Five of the seven ternary songs in *Myrthen* use this more dynamic tonal construction (Nos. 5, 11, 19, 21, and 25).[7]

"Mein Herz ist schwer" (No. 15) from Byron's *Hebrew Melodies,* is a request by a morose King Saul for the solace of David's harp playing. It exhibits the brand of contrapuntal piano writing that Schumann employed as well in a number of expressive songs,[8] especially in postludes;[9] the diminished-fourth figure in the vocal melody is also characteristic.[10] This song also illustrates Schumann's occasional employment of a declamatory vocal style. In the opening quatrain (mm. 7–16), the phrase structure corresponds to the cesura and enjambment rather than to the lines of the poetry, repeated pitches are used in the manner of recitative, and some words receive marked pitch and agogic accents. These features stand in stark contrast to the song-like setting of the next four lines (mm. 21–36), where the arpeggiations suggest that the harp has begun to play (Ex. 3.2, "Aus den Hebraischen Gesänge," Op. 25/15: see opposite).

Only five of the *Myrthen* songs are stropic (Nos. 14, 17, 18, 20, and 22); two others are modified strophic songs (Nos. 6 and 13). This reflects the much lower proportion of strophic settings among Schumann's songs as compared, for example, with Schubert's. For poems having four or more stanzas, Schumann often employed rondolike structures; in *Myrthen* there are five such songs (see Table 3.2). Schumann used this recursive rather than merely repetitive form with great flexibility, producing unity within

TABLE 3.2.
Rondolike Forms in *Myrthen,* Op. 25

3	Der Nussbaum	AAABA'CD
8	Talisman	ABACA
9	Lied der Suleika	ABABA
15	Aus den hebräischen Gesänge	aABaCB'a (a = piano)
16	Rätsel	ABABA'

(a) mm. 1–3

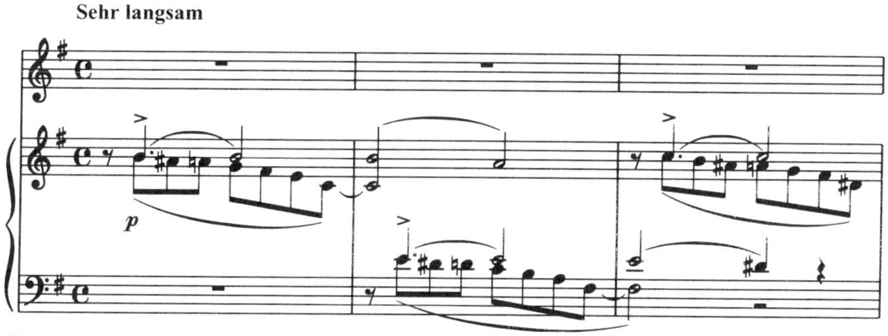

Sehr langsam
p

(b) mm. 7–12

7
p
ritard.
sf
Mein Herz ist schwer! Auf! von der
ritard.
f
sf
Wand die Lau - te, nur sie al - lein mag ich noch hö - ren,
sf

(c) mm. 21–28

21
p
Kann noch mein Herz ein Hof - fen näh - ren,
es zau - bern die - se Tö - ne her,

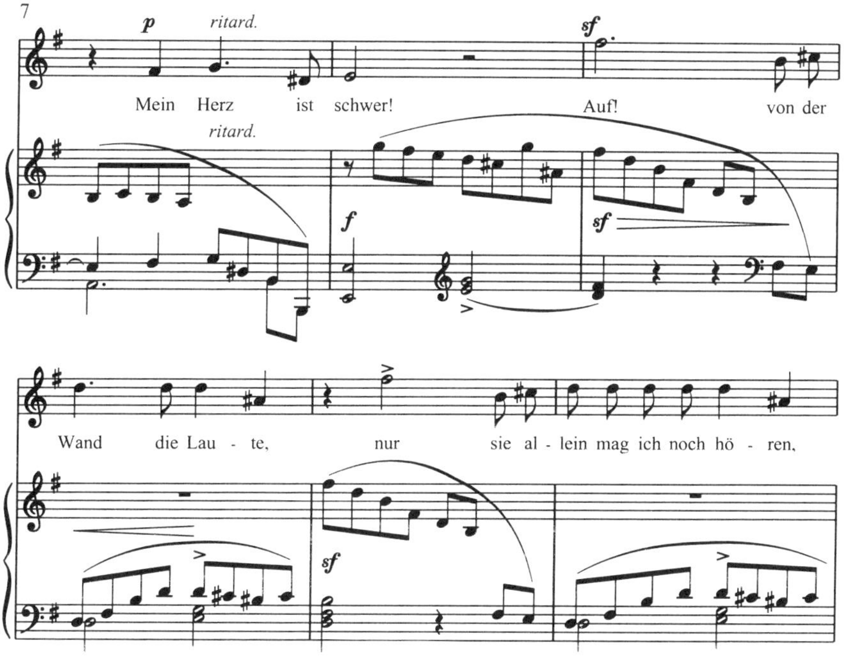

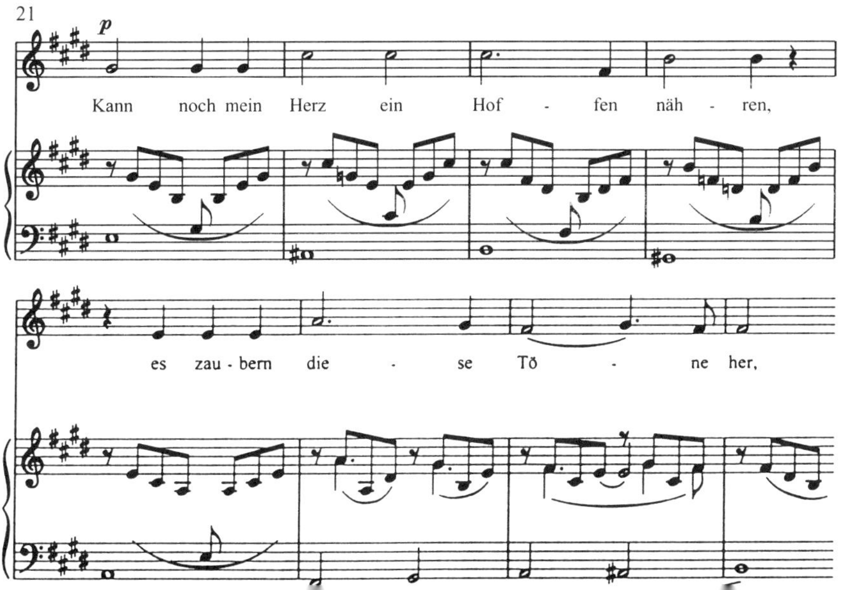

variety in myriad incarnations.[11] Some might designate these simply as through-composed settings, but the recurrence of whole stanzas of music in the tonic seems to conflict with the connotations of the latter term. The idea of rondo or rondolike procedure provides a more concrete formal category in which to place many Schumann settings of longer poems. The dominance of many types of nonstrophic but recursive forms reflects Schumann's grasp of a poem as a whole rather than as a succession of similar parts and his interpretation of the mood of the poem rather than his setting of its external form (cf. Busse 47). Alongside his rich piano accompaniments, this formal complexity reveals Schumann's almost complete rejection of the eighteenth-century lied ideal, though many contemporary composers and critics still held to it.

Schumann was critical of composers who relied too much on pervasive accompaniment figurations. In a song review in the *Neue Zeitschrift* in 1839, he wrote: "With Franz Schubert the retention of a single figure throughout the whole song appeared as something new; young composers should be warned against letting this become a mannerism" (Schumann 1914 1: 432). Yet his songs show that he knew the practice could be winning when used sparingly and with originality. As important as the figuration itself is the inventiveness with which the composer varies it and provides contrast. The justly famous accompaniment to "Widmung" (Op. 25, No. 1) manages not to cloy because the composer stops doubling the rhythmically compelling arpeggiations after three measures and moves them to an inner voice. In "Der Nussbaum" (No. 3) the ascending sixteenth-note arpeggios flow uninterruptedly (as in Mendelssohn's "Auf Flügeln des Gesanges"), but Schumann (unlike Mendelssohn) added a contrasting arch of piano melody that recurs every few measures, sometimes in unison with the voice, and that is developed in the middle of the song.

Twice in the *Myrthen* songs (Nos. 11 and 25), Schumann pervasively used a common accompaniment rhythm (♩ ♫♫ ♩ ♫♫) but in both cases the potential triviality of the figuration is a ground on which arresting features are etched. In "Mutter, Mutter!" (No. 11), the bass line makes a long stepwise descent, initially of thirteen notes (mm. 7–14), then through two octaves (mm. 31–38). In "Ich sende einen Gruss" (No. 25) a right-hand upper-neighbor figure (c–d♭–c) punctuates the vocal phrases, and, seven measures before the end, a line unexpectedly emerges in the piano's uppermost register, first leaping up by a minor seventh and then descending by step to the tonic.

Three songs from *Myrthen*—"Widmung" (No. 1, middle section), "Die Lotosblume" (No. 7), and "Du bist wie eine Blume" (No. 24)—share a distinctive Schumann piano figuration: repeated chords in a moderate or slow tempo, often—as here—in the right hand over more slowly moving notes in the left.[12] The effect is intensified when both hands play the repeated chords, as in portions of these songs and of "Lied der Suleika" (No. 9). In part through the piano writing, these songs present a prototypical Schumann mood of sincerity, warmth, and tenderness. But the prominence of the piano in Schumann's songs has to do with more than just arresting figuration, harmony, and illustration. It has always been recognized that Schumann was a piano composer turned to songwriting. A review of his songs in the *Allgemeine Muiskalische Zeitung,* for example, noted that "Schumann's songs are . . . a continuation of his character pieces for piano, . . . the rich treatment of the piano is retained and often forms in the accompaniment the most important side of these songs. That the author was originally a piano composer is everywhere noticeable" (Eismann 1956, 1: 127).

If with Schubert the piano became equal to the voice, if still separate, with Schumann the voice and piano have become more integrated. The piano now sings as well, in alternation or in combination with the voice. In "Freisinn" (No. 2), the piano anticipates phrases of the vocal melody. In "Der Nussbaum" (No. 3), the high-register piano motive, which is introduced at the outset, is used to complete vocal phrases and to provide transitions between others. It infiltrates the vocal line, undergoes transposition and chromatic modification, and finally serves as the cadencing motive of the concluding stanzas. The voice follows the piano in imitation in "Hauptmann's Weib" (No. 19), and a few measures later the piano bass has a distinct countermelody.

In more than half the songs in *Myrthen,* the piano has a significant postlude, that is, one that does more than simply reiterate the music of the vocal cadence. Such codalike episodes manifest melodic, harmonic, rhythmic, and contrapuntal interest of their own. Many seem to discharge the energy that remains after the singing stops. This pent-up energy may be rhythmic (Nos. 1 and 6; the propulsion must be spent), melodic (Nos. 9, 10, 12, and 19; the vocal endings alone are inconclusive), formal (Nos. 15, 18, and 20; matching prelude and postlude create a frame), and tonal (No. 9; the texted portion ends in a different key). Sometimes the piano seems to add its own afterstatement even when the song is satisfyingly complete at the vocal cadence (Nos. 11, 24). The last two songs (Nos. 25, 26) are the exceptions that prove the rule, for they end with what is essentially a restatement of the cadential vocal phrase. But not even the postlude of the penultimate song sounds repetitious, for it replays the piano's countermelody to the closing vocal phrase as a solo an octave lower.

Interpretations

"Du bist wie eine Blume" (*Myrthen,* Op. 25, No. 24) has a Heine poem as its text. The import of the short, outwardly simple pair of quatrains can easily be misperceived as superficial sentimentality: "You are so sweet and pretty that you bring tears to my eyes: I pray God that you will not change!" But when one considers the poet, the context of his sophisticated *Buch der Lieder,* and the elements of the verse that seem to mock and undercut their sentimentality, one senses that the text cannot be read so simply. Nor does

Schumann do so, though his reading may not accord with what one perceives to be the poet's intent. Heine appears to be thumbing his nose with the hackneyed simile ("Thou'rt like a flow'r") and with the three plain, monosyllabic adjectives. Nevertheless, for "Wehmut" (sadness) to follow these two lines—as if by cause and effect—is unexpected. When Heine utters his prayer and repeats the same three adjectives, a ploy either threadbare or parodistic, it is hard not to read this poem as ironic and sarcastic (especially beside the many less ambiguously ironic poems in this collection).

This is a characteristic Schumann song in many ways. At first glance one might say that the two stanzas of the poem are set strophically, with some modifications: in stanza 2, Schumann subtly alters and revoices the chords, raises them to a higher register, and adds pedal. But in truth the song is not strophic; rather it is a 16-measure period (with introduction and coda); the first stanza (mm. 2–9) ends with a cadence on the dominant (mm. 8–9), and the ending of the second stanza (mm. 10–17) is adjusted to bring about a full close. This is a typical Schumann gambit for a two-strophe poem.[13] Other Schumann staples in this song include the occasional insertion of triplets (mm. 2, 10) for reasons of text setting or rhythmic expressiveness;[14] the turn figure (mm. 3, 11);[15] and the cadential gesture—sol-ti-do—in the voice (mm. 16–17).[16] The song also alters the original poetic text, a frequent occurrence in Schumann's lieder (Hallmark 1987). In his manuscripts and in the first edition, the adjectives in the second line read "So schön, so rein und hold," canceling the rhyme with line 4 ("hinein"; see Ex. 3.3). Whereas many of Schumann's text changes seem to have been consciously planned, this one, like a few others, appears to be a slip of the pen; Heine's word order and rhyme should be restored (as it was in the Peters edition).

Schumann's approach to the half cadence (mm. 7–8) does more than create a stopping point at the end of stanza 1. The melodic tritone (e♭–a) and the harmonic progression—augmented-sixth chord, with the syncopated C♭ in the bass, to V_4^6, a chromatic alteration that is a bit heavy-handed for the purely cadential function—registers the incongruency of feeling "Wehmut" when beholding the young woman. The musical emphases in the second stanza (recitative and chromaticism, mm. 14–16) and the briefly agonizing tone of the postlude also seem to strain against what is otherwise a straightforward setting.

Both Heine and Schumann, in different ways, intend something other than what is immediately apparent in this poem. The poet, one imagines, means that the woman addressed merits no better than his quite conventional description and that this condition is the source of his melancholy. When he imagines a prayer, it is not for her to blossom and mature from the stereotyped creature he sees, but, spitefully, to remain the same! The composer, one conjectures, accepts the opening pronouncement as sincere (note the expressive leap of a seventh at "so schön"), and experiences with

EXAMPLE 3.3. "Du bist wie eine Blume," mm. 1–10

Du bist _____ wie ei - ne Blu - me, so

schön, so rein, ____ und hold; ich schau' dich an und

Weh - muth schleicht mir in's Herz hin - ein.

profound melancholy the inevitability of decay (mm. 7–8). Even as he prays that she might remain young, fair, and pure, he knows the futility of such a wish (mm. 14–16 and postlude). The piano is the agent of this unsettling commentary. Here, as in his great and most famous cycle (*Dichterliebe*), Schumann seeks to reveal the love and pain he sensed in the poet's heart rather than the bitter sarcasm that had formed to cover his hurt. This is a radical misrepresentation of Heine, but not a sentimental trivialization. (For other readings of the song, see Sams 1969, 74, and Brauner 1981, 270.)

By contrast, one seldom feels that Schubert was willfully at odds with a poetic text he set; this may be one of the most significant differences between these two great lied composers. Schubert, it is generally held, chose texts to which he felt sympathetic. Schumann could select a poem that was not a perfect match for his sensibility and proceed to impose his interpretation upon it, whether by subverting its meaning, exaggerating it, or adding a new element. Thus, by reinterpreting a poem musically, Schumann himself became the poet singing his (appropriated) poem.

Schumann's setting of Kerner's "Stille Thränen" (Silent Tears, Op. 35, No. 10) is more nearly in accord with its poet, at least at first. This is surely one of Schumann's most beautiful songs, and also one of the most demanding vocally. Clearly for the tenor voice (the piano stays largely in the tenor range), it has a high tessitura and sustained high Gs, As, and one B♭. Its chromatic passing tones and appoggiaturas add expressive intensity to the melodic line. The piano part is lush, containing repeated chords in the right hand in a slow $\frac{6}{4}$ meter (*sehr langsam*) over pedalled bass notes, often doubled on octave lower (the left hand descends to CC), and an expressive interlude and postlude (Ex. 3.4).

Kerner's three quatrains draw a simile between nocturnal rain and tears, both of which go unnoticed by sleepers who awake to behold only clear sky and clear eyes. Schumann's music illustrates the incongruity between appearance and reality through its own incongruities of musical grammar. First, as the voice passes from g through g♯ to b (as the harmony moves from c major to A minor), the bass remains on C and moves through B down to A only two measures afterward (a motion to which the song draws more attention later). Second, where one might expect a progression from A minor (vi) through D (ii) to a half cadence on G (V) at the midpoint of the stanza (a harmonization that would fit the melody), the music proceeds through a dominant minor triad to a cadence on a C-major chord with minor seventh, V^7 of F (IV). Third, the outer voices move in parallel fifths to this cadence (mm. 8–9), although they are ameliorated by that unexpected B♭ that is held through. The second half of the stanza begins in F with a transposition up a fourth of the first phrase (mm. 11–13 = mm. 3–5), followed by a cadence back to the tonic, C. In this phrase the bass again moves tardily, here from F to D in mm. 12–15. Whereas the vocal melody tells one story to the audience, the piano stands behind, shaking its head and suggesting another.

EXAMPLE 3.4. "Stille Tranen," mm. 1–10

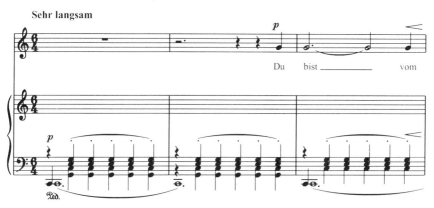

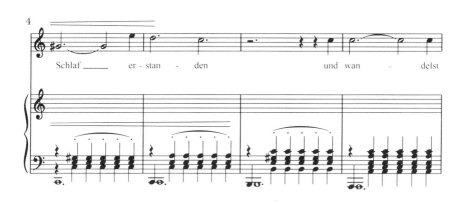

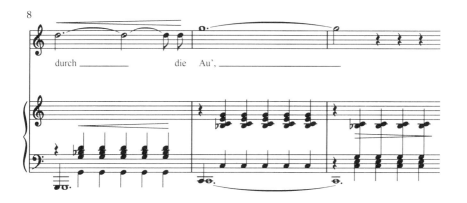

The next stanza, a middle section with contrasting music, moves to A♭, and then to C♭. (Moves to keys related by thirds are typical of Schumann.) This leads through a Neapolitan progression to B♭ as dominant seventh of E♭ major, and we then hear the third stanza set to a reprise of the opening period in this new key. Here the climactic vocal phrase, "In stillen Nächten weinet / Oft mancher aus den Schmerz" (Often in silent nights many a person weeps out his sorrow), peaks on the high B♭ at the word "Schmerz"— the highest note in all of Schumann's songs. The next phrase, instead of proceeding to a close in E♭ approaches a cadence in C minor (through iv⁶ and ii⁶₅) but unexpectedly lands on I⁶₄ in C major—this to the words "Und morgens dann ihr meinet / Stets fröhlich sei sein Herz" (and then, come morning, you think his heart is always happy). Again a musical incongruity underlines the distinction between truth and appearance.

No sooner has the voice cadenced (m. 49) than the piano is off again, now playing the music of stanza 1 in the original C major (and in the tenor register) but without the voice. The tardy bass motion from C to AA is highlighted with a trill. The voice enters at the midpoint of the musical phrase, repeating the closing lines of the poem. Under this line the bass does move down (F–E–D, mm. 57–59) and becomes part of a more natural progression, this time leading convincingly toward the C-major cadence. But again the reality of the music undercuts what seems about to happen, bringing us up short with an unusual deceptive cadence. Prompted by this inconclusiveness, the piano plays a postlude whose complexity belies the simplicity of the voice's melodic cadence. There is no authentic cadence after the one in m. 49; the cadence at m. 63 is deceptive, and the postlude carries us around the circle of fifths (D–G–C–F), ending with a weak plagal cadence in C. There is no clear cessation of the sorrow wept over in the night (of course the fact that this song occurs in a cycle partially accounts for its inconclusiveness).

Although Schumann's music does not go against the grain of Kerner's poem as it does with some Heine lyrics, it goes *beyond* the poem in the depth of its expressivity. Though the sorrowful weeper in Kerner's poem is referred to in the third person, one might infer that the generalized "mancher" (someone) is only a disguise for the speaker. But in Schumann's song, the identification of the singer with the melancholy figure is explicit, as the passion is so great and so personally expressed. The momentous quality of Schumann's music gives a different import to the poem. Whereas Kerner's emphasis is on the irony in the beholder's ignorance of "someone's" grief, Schumann seems to say that the "someone," who is the speaker himself, is concealing his sorrow behind a front of heroic stoicism.

Night is a Romantic theme prominent in Schumann's music, and nowhere is it more magnificently and variously treated than in the Eichendorff *Liederkreis* Op. 39. Unanimity between text and music is probably strongest in Schumann's treatment of this poet (see Thym 1974 and 1980), the prime example being the justifiably beloved and much discussed "Mondnacht" (Op. 39, No. 5; cf. Brinkmann 1990, Sams 1969). In their haunting subject matter, nature imagery, and evocative mood, Eichendorff's poetry, Schumann's songs, and the paintings of Caspar David Friedrich form a constellation of remarkably similar artists in their respective media; Friedrich's *Man and Woman Beholding the Moon* is an apt companion piece for the Eichendorff-Schumann "Mondnacht."

"Zwielicht" (Twilight), the tenth song of the Eichendorff *Liederkreis,* portrays the mysterious, sinister aspect of approaching night. (Cf. Friedrich's *The Great Copse* and *The Evening.*) The poem's first stanza attributes terrifying qualities to dusk, breezes, and clouds, and asks what this dreadful feeling betokens. The second stanza warns against letting a favorite deer graze alone in the forest, where there are hunters. The third stanza counsels against trusting a friend at this hour. The last stanza most gravely warns that many are lost in the night. There is, then, a progression from a vague feeling of uneasiness to explicit fear of loss or death. Dusk imparts a premonition of evil. The hunters are a real danger, but they can be avoided. Human deceitfulness is less easily detectable; hunters blow their horns and we hear their voices, but our supposed friends can dissimulate. Finally we come face to face with the supernatural forces of night; all one can do is to be alert and cheerful, but nevertheless "Manches geht in Nacht verloren" (much vanishes at night).

Schumann's song begins with a single strand of chromatic melody and develops into a two- and three-part contrapuntal texture. Tonally ambiguous for five measures (the 2-measure cell could continue repeating itself sequentially), the piano prelude starts toward a cadence in E minor in m. 6, but even then an F♮ (flat supertonic) threatens the certainty of the close. As the first stanza begins, the piano plays the prelude again, this time with a distinct bass line, but after two notes this breaks off and henceforth appears only sporadically. The voice follows the piano's top line heterophonically. The last line of the quatrain is delivered as recitative, and a distinct half cadence emerges (bass notes C–BB; see Ex. 3.5).

The second stanza is much the same, although the bass notes persist into the stanza a little longer. In the third stanza an active, rising bass line and an excited, higher-climbing vocal line give clearer directedness to the harmony but lead to a momentary stopping point that is—deceitfully—not in E minor but in C♯ minor. In the last stanza the ambiguous polyphonic lines give way to explicit, repeated chords over a distinct continuous bass line in half notes with octave doublings. The gradual crystallization of the harmony stanza by stanza is a musical analog of the progression of thought in Eichendorff's poem. Schumann, moreover, learned from Schubert's "Erlkönig" the chilling effectiveness of ending such a song with a plain recitation of the last line (cf., too, the ending of "Belsatzar," Op. 57). Schumann thus sings this poem very much as one imagines Eichendorff would speak it; Schumann's interpretation neither contradicts nor exceeds the poet. (Much the same could be said of Schumann's settings of his favorite poet, Rückert.)

EXAMPLE 3.5. "Zwielicht," Op. 39/10, mm. 1–15

Of Schumann's narrative and dramatic songs from 1840—besides the well-known "Die beiden Grenadiere" (Heine, Op. 49, No. 1)—the Hans Christian Andersen poems (in Chamisso's translations) should be mentioned. The middle three pieces—"Muttertraum," "Der Soldat," and "Der Spielmann"—are especially poignant, for which the outer two— "Märzveilchen" and "Verratene Liebe"—form light-hearted frame. The first two stanzas of "Muttertraum" tell of a mother holding her baby boy; forgetting life's grief and hardship, she is filled with hope for his future. In the third stanza, a raven with its young predicts a grim future for the boy: "Your angel will be ours; the robber will be our meal." In the piano prelude the right hand traces a chromatic line in sixteenths, the bass entering a measure later in syncopated quarters. As the voice enters, the piano figuration continues, the D-minor key seems odd and sinister for the scene of maternal love. The key turns to F major for the second stanza (hopefulness). The prelude is heard again, pianissimo, and the third stanza begins like the first, but when the raven speaks the piano changes to repeated sixteenth-note chords over quarters; the last line is sung quietly on a reiterated low A. A varied statement of the prelude concludes the bleak song (Ex. 3.6).

The overall means and effect of "Muttertraum" are strongly reminiscent of "Zwielicht." The resemblance provides an opportunity to consider briefly Eric Sams's theory about motives in Schumann's songs (Sams 1969, 11–26 and passim). There are many melodic contours and figures, piano rhythms and textures, and the like, that permeate Schumann's songs (cf. the enumeration of common material in the discussion of "Du bist wie eine Blume" above). Sams identifies many recurring motives but perhaps goes too far in insisting that each figure has a crystallized symbolic meaning, or that each instance of the same figure in different songs means the same (or a similar) thing. Furthermore, he occasionally describes an element inaccurately. In short, although Sams is provocative and helpful, his book should be read with caution.

For example, noting the similarity between the openings of "Muttertraum," "Zwielicht," and "Aus den hebräischen Gesänge" ("Mein Herz ist schwer," Op. 25, No. 15), Sams defines his Motif 33 rhythmically as a string of even notes beginning off the beat, after a rest, and tonally as E minor (Sams 1969, 18). Two of these songs fit this description—"Mein Herz ist schwer" and "Zwielicht"—but they resemble each other less than "Zwielicht" and "Muttertraum" do, even though the latter begins on the beat and is in a different key (D minor). In these two songs, the minor-mode melody regularly falls and rises, mostly in thirds; another voice enters in a staggered rhythm; and the key center is blurred by chromaticism and sequence. In "Mein Herz ist schwer" the lines all descend, mostly by step and half step; there is no staggered counterpoint; and despite the chromaticism, the E-minor tonality is never in doubt because the lines and implied harmonies all hover around the dominant.[17]

EXAMPLE 3.6. "Muttertraum," Op. 40/2, mm. 1–8

Sams also claims that "Muttertraum" shares a "rocking figure" (at the word "Wiege," cradle, mm. 9ff.) with "Hochländisches Wiegenlied" (Op. 25, No. 14), "Schöne Wiege meiner Lieder" (Op. 24, No. 5), and "Lust der Sturmmacht" (Op. 35, No. 1). He defines this motive (Motif 35A) as "prolonged bass notes . . . together with a rocking movement in both hands" (Sams 1969, 18). I can perceive no similarity between the opening of "Highland Lullaby" and the passage in "Muttertraum," nor do I find that either fits the description of Motif 35A. Op. 24, No. 5 and Op. 35, No. 1, on the other hand, correspond loosely to Sams's motive: both have sustained tonic pedals, and the left thumb and right hand alternate notes of the superimposed chords. In only one of the songs (Op. 24, No. 5) does the text refer to a cradle, and Sams offers no explanation for the use of this motive in the other (Op. 35, No. 1). Furthermore, in neither song does the piano part particularly resemble rocking; the tempos are simply too fast (*bewegt* in Op. 25, No. 4, *kräftig, leidenschaftlich* in Op. 35, No. 1).

Songs for Multiple Solo Voices

A substantial but largely ignored body of Schumann songs is for two or more solo voices with piano.[18] Some of these songs were published separately as duets and trios (Op. 29, 34, 43, 78, 103, and 114), but many are parts of cycles (Opp. 37, 74, 101, and 138) or of the *Liederalbum für die Jugend* (Op. 79). Though one tends to think of the later multivoice cycles ("für ein und mehrere Singstimmen") in this regard—the *Spanisches Liederspiel* Op. 74, the *Minnespiel* Op. 101, and the *Spanische Liebeslieder* Op. 138—Schumann's interest in multivoice songs began in 1840.

These songs deserve to be better known and more frequently performed because of their sheer beauty; Schumann lavished far more musical imagination than his contemporaries on such compositions, and they should be considered part of his lied production proper.[19] Many duets of the time are relatively simple strophic parlor songs with two treble voices singing in rhythmic unison—often in parallel thirds and sixths—over unremarkable accompaniment. Among Schumann's some nineteen duets, about half would fit this description except that their melodic charm and harmonic-contrapuntal ingenuity surpass the merely pretty, and their pianism exceeds the conventionally accompanimental. The rest of the duets exhibit more interesting musical form and richer polyphonic texture.

Schumann had great fun with poems that are dialogues or that implicitly suggest two characters, such as the soprano-tenor duets of Op. 34. "Liebesgarten" (Reinick, Op. 34, No. 1) is in the first person plural: "wir zwei, mein Lieb und ich" (we two, my love and I). The two voices begin each stanza together in parallel melodic lines but then have solo phrases and independent counterpoint. "Liebhabers Ständchen" and "Unterm Fenster" (Op. 34, Nos. 2 and 3), both translations of Robert Burns poems, are serenade dialogues between an impetuous youth (tenor) beseeching admission and a maiden (soprano) refusing it. During much of "Liebhabers Ständchen" the two voices sing their respective text portions simultaneously, creating complicated rhythmic counterpoint; this, together with the minor key and fast tempo, match the turbulence of the winter storm from which the boy seeks a haven. In "Unterm Fenster" the question-and-answer dialogue proceeds in a rollicking $\frac{6}{8}$ meter, with melodic phrases that alternate between the soprano and tenor; at the conclusion the voices overlap, and the duet is concluded by a piano postlude.

In "Familien-Gemälde" (Family Portrait, A. Grün, Op. 34, No. 4) a young couple—hence the duet—contemplate their future as they gaze at the maiden's grandparents. Though Schumann's melody seems a bit too sweet, converting the poem's sentimentality to notes, the song is notable for its dueting technique and the piano postlude. The tenor sings the first stanza alone; when the second voice, the soprano, enters at the second stanza, it sings the original tune, the tenor providing a countermelody. This technique later served Schumann in "In der Nacht," Op. 74, No. 4 and "Ich bin dein Baum," Op. 101, No. 3 (see below). The song also exhibits one of Schumann's longest postludes. After several stanzas, the singers end on a dominant-seventh chord, and the piano concludes the song by playing the opening stanza alone, varied and developed. This wordless, leisurely close suggests the contemplation by each couple of their past and future, respectively. (The procedure and effect are similar to the famous reprise in *Frauenliebe und leben* of the first song as postlude to the last, and to the postlude in "Mein Wagen rollet langsam," Op. 142, No. 4, one of the four songs from the 1840 *Twenty Lieder* of Heine omitted when the songs were published as *Dichterliebe*.)

The *Drei Gedichte von Emanuel Geibel* Op. 29, for two, three, and four voices must be mentioned among the multivoice songs of 1840. "Ländliches Lied," No. 1, treats the theme of romancing youth, here in a descriptive poem about springtime, when couples go dancing in the village. The piano plays a spirited duple-meter dance, and the two treble voices chase each other in close imitation, as two dancers might mimick each other's steps. The strophic form is rounded off by a coda in which the young lovers praise Maytime. The second song, entitled simply "Lied," is a small masterpiece. Geibel's poem describes through suggestive images the sadness of a person whose beloved is far away: the garden flowers have wilted (stanza 1), the hearth fire has gone out (stanza 2), the world is decayed, the heart dead (stanza 3). Schumann's song, cast in Bar or AAB form, portrays the mood in a dolorous tempo and minor key and in languorous counterpoint full of dissonant suspensions and overlapping phrases. Though scored with three undesignated treble clefs, this song is beautifully effective with one male and two female voices; this is the natural solution if one assumes that a conventional quartet is on hand to perform the last song (Ex. 3.7).

EXAMPLE 3.7. "Lied," Op. 29/2, mm. 1–11

"Zigennerleben" (Gypsy Life), No. 3, the only quartet Schumann composed in 1840, quickly dispels the enervated mood of the second song with its vivacious nature. The piece opens with a pounding dance rhythm (stanzas 1–2); this music returns at the end (stanza 7), making a large ternary form. The middle section (stanzas 3–5) describes the gypsies' activities around their evening campfire—cooking, eating, drinking, storytelling, singing, dancing, and finally sleeping. Schumann distinguishes each activity with differing melodies, keys, tempos, accompaniments, and textures, even featuring a series of one-line solos and duets.

Late Songs

After the burst of song composition in 1840–41, Schumann composed almost no lieder until 1847. Many find Schumann's later songs—like his later music in general—wanting, in comparison with his earlier compositions. But it is harsh to fault Schumann because his style evolved or because the late songs are not carbon copies of the early ones. One should perhaps speak of his late lied *styles*. Moreover, he was drawn to new and different poets in his later years. Of his previously favored poets, only Goethe and Rückert continued to interest him significantly, and the number of settings by Geibel increased. In the later years there are practically no songs on poems by Heine, Eichendorff, Kerner, Chamisso, or Burns. The only new poets on whom Schumann drew for more than five poems were the popular Hoffmann von Fallersleben (Op. 79, selections), the Austrian Nicholas Lenau (Opp. 90, 117), and Elisabeth Kulmann (Opp. 104, 114). Otherwise Schumann sampled Mörike, Uhland, Platen, and a number of other, relatively undistinguished, poets.

There were strong new currents in lied aesthetics at midcentury, and Schumann was demonstrably affected by them. Among these, according to Ulrich Mahlert's brilliant study, was an interest in more realistic and dramatic declamation of text. Mahlert (1983) quotes at length from lied criticism from the years around 1848, showing, on the one hand, that there were conservative viewpoints that still preferred the strophic song with melodious vocal lines shaped into regular phrases and, on the other, that progressive opinion preferred songs with more dramatic, theatrical, even operatic settings of poetic texts and musical forms that followed the sense rather than the structure. Schumann's songs had always admitted irregular, dramatic declamation and malleable forms, but Mahlert argues that these are more pronounced in later songs, and he cites examples from the *Spanisches Liederspiel* (Op. 74) and the *Wilhelm Meister* songs (Op. 98a).

The opening of "Melancholie" (Op. 74, No. 6, marked *Mit Affekt)* unfolds less as a melody than as a series of exclamations, in metrically displaced and strongly accented notes, culminating with a melisma, more operatic than lied-like (Ex. 3.8). These qualities, compounded with the ir-

EXAMPLE 3.8. "Melancholie," Op. 74/6, mm. 1–11

regular phrase structure (2 + 6) and the suspensions in the piano bass, impart a supercharged, dramatic character to the song. Later, mid-phrase leaps of ninths and tenths intensify the mood still more. Though he uses motivic repetition, Schumann does not base whole phrases on repeated rhythms or melodic repetition and sequence, abandoning another recognizable feature of conventional lieder. Even the reprise at the end, so often literal in Schumann's songs, is completely overhauled.

The late lyric songs, in particular, are usually found wanting, whereas the dramatic songs, such as "Melancholie"—the songs in which the singer assumes a role—are less criticized for failing to live up to earlier standards. The two Mörike settings in Op. 64, each presenting a different young female persona, are good examples in a very different vain. "The Soldier's Girl" ("Die Soldatenbraut") brags about her uniformed boyfriend: "For the King he would shed his blood, but for me he'd do just as well"—a remark shaded with a possible double-entendre.[20] She pines for his discharge from military service and for their wedding. Schumann gives the song a jaunty march, which alludes to the soldierly boyfriend and gives his sweetheart a plucky personality at the same time. In the middle section the girl gets a bit starry-eyed, thinking of marriage; the music is slower and the vocal melody loses the dotted rhythms of the march (they remain in the piano's tenor). Drum rolls bring us to the reprise of the first stanza. Although one cannot prove that Schumann was thinking of the ribald reading suggested above, his music gives the words the right harmonic and rhythmic accents and offers listeners five opportunities to make the inference—at the ends of the first and last stanzas and again (to different music) in the postlude (Ex. 3.9).

"Das verlassne Magdelein" (Op. 64, No. 2; also set by Wolf) is a very different maid who has been forsaken by a faithless boy. In the first stanza she matter-of-factly tells of rising early at the cock's crow to light the hearthfire; in the first couplet of the second stanza she remarks on the beauty of the flames but stares into them sorrowfully in the second couplet; in the third stanza it suddenly comes to her that she dreamed of the "treuloser Knabe" all night, and now (fourth stanza) she weeps as day breaks, and wishes it were over. Schumann has matched the bleak mood of the poem with austere music—three-part harmony, a minor key, and relentless repetition of motives: the descending and rising phrases of the tune and the continuously sinking bass line. The song construes the sixteen lines of the four quatrains as 6 + 6 + 4: mm. 1–12 (lines 1–6) are transposed up a fourth in mm. 13–26 (lines 7–12), with an altered ending, and mm. 27–35 (lines 13–16) are a varied reprise of mm. 1–9. The partition of stanza 2 conflicts with the poem's form but agrees with its sense. The music gradually becomes more oppressive: Schumann eventually expands from three- to four-part harmony (m. 23 to the end), and each return of the opening music is intensified with greater dissonance (mm. 12–13 and mm. 26–27).

EXAMPLE 3.9. "Die Soldatenbraut," Op. 64/1, mm. 6–11

Mahlert (1983) notes Schumann's tendency in some late songs to greater openness. Although many 1840 lyric songs reflect the subjective world of the Romantic artist in their sentiments and technique, in his later songs Schumann—and here again Mahlert finds him in harmony with mid-century progressive aesthetics—often uses an intentional simplicity and straightforward manner to make his songs accessible. In this connection, Mahlert discusses selections from the *Liederalbum für die Jugend* (Op. 79), a major lied project for Schumann in the late 1840s. These songs for children, composed and assembled in 1848–49, account for over a quarter of the late songs. His notebooks suggest that he composed or sketched more songs for this project than he ultimately used in the publication; some manuscripts of rejected lieder exist.[21] Schumann was committed to the creation of good pedagogical material, as he had already demonstrated with the piano *Album für die Jugend* Op. 68. The *Liederalbum* is a collection of twenty-eight solo songs and duets, largely folk and folklike texts from *Des Knaben Wunderhorn* (three) and by Hoffmann von Fallersleben (ten), Goethe (two), and Geibel (two), together with single poems in the same vein by Andersen, Hebbel, Mörike, Rückert, Schiller, and others.

The musical settings, nearly all strophic, are graduated in difficulty for both voice and piano, ranging from the utterly simple 8-measure "Der Abendstern" (No. 1) to the sophisticated "Kennst du das Land" (Mignon's Lied, No. 28, also published in the *Lieder und Gesänge aus Wilhelm Meister*, Op. 98a; see Finson 1990).

The Op. 79 songs, however, like the pedagogical music of other great composers, are not without interest for mature performers. Many of these songs possess great beauty and charm. Despite a certain cultivated naiveté, nearly every song contains artfully nuanced elements that make for satisfying performance. "Marienwürmchen" (No. 13), for example, has a pleasingly irregular phrase structure (6 mm. + 3 + 6 + 2) created by word repetition, relatively long notes, and rests, and by a short piano codetta. Its charm also comes from the mock-tragic chords in the piano during the vocal rests in mid-stanza and the rapid patter of the closing lines. The spirit of the Op. 79 *Jugendlieder* dwells also in late songs like the *Mädchenlieder* Op. 103, the *Fünf heitere Gesänge* Op. 125, and even to a certain extent in the *Sieben Lieder* by Elisabeth Kulmann, Op. 104, where Schumann sought a childlike voice for these premonitions of an early death (Kulmann died at seventeen). Such simplicity, frequently cited as a waning of creative power, was more likely a conscious artistic choice. One may question Schumann's judgment, but one should not fault him for failing to accomplish what he did not set out to do, or upbraid him for artistic growth and change.

Some accounts of Schumann's late songs exaggerate their differences from his earlier vocal compositions. Certain works definitely approach the 1840 manner. "Die Hütte" (Gustav Pfarrius) of 1851 (Op. 119, No. 1 in G major, Ex. 3.10b) could be mistaken for an early *Wanderlied* in the style of "Freisinn" (Op. 25, No. 2, E♭ major, Ex. 3.10a). Both songs have the typical chordal accompaniment in dotted rhythms, regular phrase structure, and simple harmonic ductus. Both are also of the same formal type, returning to the opening music after some contrast ("Freisinn" is in ternary form; "Die Hutte," having more stanzas, is a rondo.) In another vein, "Ihre Stimme" of 1850 (Op. 96, No. 3, A♭ major) uncannily recalls "Lied der Suleika" (Op. 25, No. 9, A major) in its melody and arpeggiated accompaniment (Ex. 10.11). Though the chromaticism of the later song is arguably bolder, both have the same character and comparable formal procedures.

Such similarities raise the question of whether correspondences in the poetry elicited the musical resemblances. If so, was Schumann writing the same songs to different words? Though Goethe's "Freisinn" is a true wanderer's song, the Pfarrius is about living contentedly in a cabin in the woods. Common to both, however, are the sentiments of independence, solitude, and communion with nature that underlie most *Wanderlieder*. So Schumann drew on well-established genre characteristics to bring out what for him were the implications of the Pfarrius poem, coincidentally making palpable an affinity with earlier songs. Goethe's Suleika lyric and Platen's

EXAMPLE 3.10.

(a) "Freisinn," Op. 25/2, mm. 1–4

(b) "Die Hutte," Op. 119/1, mm. 1–4

"Ihre Stimme" both portray communication between lovers, indeed the power of the absent lover's voice (in the Goethe, the lover's poetic voice in his songs; in the Platen, the recollection of the actual sound). How the music of these songs is related to the meaning of the poems is less easily explicable, there being no external genre characteristics to point out, though the rhythmic irregularity of the text setting in both cases individualizes and personalizes the lyricism. Again, however, is Schumann just recycling slightly varied music in the service of related ideas?

Two things distinguish "Ihre Stimme" from the Suleika song. Melodically and harmonically, the junctures of its phrases are concealed, and thus a more nearly continuous musical flow is created. Whereas the first stanza of the Goethe setting divides neatly in the middle, with a cadence on the diatonic ii chord (B minor, echoed in the piano, m. 4), the Platen setting at this point moves through an augmented-sixth chord to an altered major II (B♭ major, m. 4). This, coupled with the syncopated vocal line, prevents any sense of rest here. After this is yet another unexpected move: instead of functioning as a V of V (E♭), the B♭ chord progresses to G

EXAMPLE 3.11.

(a) "Lied der Suleika," Op. 25/9, mm. 1–8

(*continued*)

(b) "Ihre Stimme," Op. 96/3, mm. 1–8

major (altered vii). Only then, at the end of the stanza, does Schumann allow a conventional half cadence to V, and even this is undercut by the deceptive move up c in the bass (m. 8). The sense of an almost unsegmented musical flow continues in the new music of the middle stanzas; thoughts of the distant lover possess the lyric protagonist and will not let go.[22]

A second distinction concerns thematic construction. The piano's bass c (m. 8) begins a restatement of the initial motive of the vocal melody, a recurring, fragmentary musical idea that functions like a leitmotif, here emblematic of the beloved's voice. Its ghost is then heard in the upper register of the piano, at the words "Doch drängt auch nur von ferne dein Ton zu mir sich her" (Yet if the sound of your voice reaches me even from afar; m. 17). The motive occurs twice more in the last stanza (which is set to a varied musical reprise of the opening section) and, finally, varied and augmented in the short postlude (mm. 24, 31, 36–38).[23]

Many of the later songs have an economy of emotion that distinguishes them from their older cousins. This may be what Fischer-Dieskau and others identify as a greater objectivity in Schumann's later works. This understated quality can be heard in the songs of Op. 107 (1850). The poems are by lesser poets, with the exception of "Der Gärtner" by Mörike, but they are not without appeal. Most of the poems are tinged with sadness, but Schumann does not give melancholy free rein (which he does, say, in "Hör' ich das Liedchen klingen" or "Ich hab' im Traum geweinet" from *Dichterliebe*). Sams takes this for a failure of nerve (Sams 1969, 259–62, 268–9) when just the opposite may be true: all of Schumann's traditional skill is at work, but in a new vein.

Opus 107 begins with "Herzelied" (Titus Ullrich), portraying the torment of a "miserable dreamer" on the brink, but stopping short, of suicide. Its delicate tissue of dissonant counterpoint and appoggiaturas, the vocal melody continued by the piano between text phrases, the voice's inconclusive ending resolved by the piano, the two stanzas cast as a period—all recall a quintessential 1840 composition, "Im wunderschönen Monat Mai" (Op. 48, No. 1). The second song, "Die Fensterscheibe" (also by Ullrich) has the everyday circumstantial quality of a Mörike poem, and Schumann's music is proto-Wolfian in its economy and austerity. A young woman washing her windows is so startled when "he" passes by that she breaks a pane; she reflects that though the noise drew his attention, he never noticed that he had broken her heart. Schumann tailors his B-minor music to this modest affect: a short introduction with mild dissonance; speechlike melody within a small compass; vocal silence, chromatic harmony, and major tonic that set up and underscore the telling line "Da gebt er stolz vorbei!" (mm. 9–11). The last stanza—the one drawing the analogy between windowpane and heart—does not overdramatize the maiden's sadness or mope in an extended postlude.

"Der Gärtner" (No. 3) has a naive quality attributable to the exuberant and obvious portrayal of the horse's prancing and the plain harmony coupled with chordal texture. By placing it among other songs that are explicitly about loneliness, Schumann invites us to consider that the gardener's delight in the princess's beauty may mask his sense of isolation from people of her social class. In "Die Spinnerin" (No. 4), Goethe's Gretchen has been transposed from her solitary chore to cottage industry, her passionate grief transmuted to a young girl's dejection over not having a sweetheart; the pathetic heroine of *Faust* has been objectified to a lower middle-class everywoman.

After continued study, these songs, by different poets and about different protagonists, cohere more and more. One perceives that Schumann has fashioned a song group about different kinds of loneliness—suicidal depression, rejection in love, social isolation, and friendlessness. One might even argue that the protagonists also have in common a lower social class with which a post-1848 Schumann hereby expresses sympathy: a *Putzfrau* or cleaning maid, a gardener, a cottage-industry weaver, a farm boy (as evidenced by the folk imagery and diction and strophic variation of this poem). Thus the "objectivity" of these songs is due partly to the fact that they are not the confessions of a single, subjective lyrical self—the poet—but the thoughts and feelings of several different people. Rather than the plight of the isolated or alienated Romantic artist, these songs portray the general human condition. By linking these poems together, the poet in Schumann sings a social message that is not inherent in any of the poems taken alone. In common with Schumann's earlier songs, however, these end with implied consolation. In the last song—"Abendlied," with a starlit night and the spiritual (*Engel Füsse?*) embodied in the piano triplets—Schumann leaves us with his closing thought: "Cast off, my heart, what ails you and what frightens you!"

Schumann's nascent interest in the multivoice song cycle in 1841 (expressed in his and Clara's cycle for soprano and tenor from Rückert's *Liebesfrühling* Op. 37) grew stronger in the late 1840s and prompted the two cycles on Geibel's translations of Spanish poetry, Opp. 74 and 138, and the *Minnelieder* Op. 101, again on poetry of Rückert. These cycles contain a number of fine solo songs, such as the passionate "Melancholie" (discussed above) and the ebullient "Der Kontrabandist" (both from Op. 74); the pair of tenor solos "O wie lieblich ist das Mädchen" and "Weh, wie zornig ist das Mädchen" from Op. 138, which continue the character of the *Jugendlieder*; and "Mein schöner Stern" (Op. 101, No. 4), with its lush seventh- and ninth-chords in circle-of-fifths motion (for a moment one thinks of Fauré). But the most beautiful pieces in these cycles are the duets, which expand the technique and expressiveness of Schumann's earlier achievements in the genre.

The opening song of the *Spanisches Liederspiel* Op. 74 is a vivacious soprano-alto duet ("Von dem Rosenbusch, O Mutter"). Though the voices always sing together rhythmically, the propelling triplets and luscious melodic intervals and harmonies make the music irresistible. The real pièce de résistance, however, is "In der Nacht" for soprano and tenor (later set by Hugo Wolf as a solo). The poem's persona is wakeful with care while others sleep, and his/her thoughts turn always to the absent beloved. The poem is a solo lyric, but by setting it as a duet Schumann makes it the simultaneous expression by the two separated lovers of their yearning for each other. The mood is set by the slow 7-measure piano prelude, which exhibits a neo-Bachian motivic melody in G minor, after which the soprano sings the six-line poem alone in an expansive setting (mm. 8–50!). One is unaware that the piece is a duet until the tenor enters dramatically at the height of the soprano's cadential phrase (see Ex. 3.12). As the tenor sings the original melody, the soprano repeats the verse, her new notes forming a disjunct, expressive counterpoint to the tenor line (e.g., note the intertwining *nur nicht dus*, mm. 57–60).

A similar procedure is used in "Ich bin dein Baum, O Gärtner," Op. 101, No. 3. Rückert's poem portrays a male-female relationship in an almost Biblical metaphor of tree and gardener (reminiscent of the *Song of Solomon*), and the two-stanza dialogue—one stanza spoken by each—suggests a musical setting for two voices. Schumann gives the soprano (tree) a melody that remains pretty much the same, but after one stanza the tenor (gardener) joins in, singing a different countermelody to each repetition of the soprano's song.

There is no denying that Schumann's catholic taste and emotional disposition occasionally led him to set flimsy, sentimental, even bathetic poetry. When his music merely matches rather than surpasses such verse, the result may be a disappointment.[24] Even so, it is hard not to appreciate Schumann's noble attempt. In "Resignation" by Julius Buddeus, Op. 83, No. 1, the first stanza professes ardent love as evidenced by numerous physical manifestations, but the second stanza deflatingly reveals that "You will never embrace me." Though his love is hopeless, the persona is consoled by the expectation of reunion in the hereafter (Ex. 3.13). The bathos is not helped by the fact that the circumstances and the feelings of the addressee are not clarified; it is ambiguous whether she simply does not love him or is prevented from doing so.

Schumann alternates a very declamatory and quasi-recitative style (for the exclamations and rhetorical questions) with a more lyrical vocal line and flowing accompaniment (for the despondent statements and responses). The melody and harmony are full of chromatic passing tones and appoggiaturas, which flavor the song but never seriously obscure the keys (D♭ major and the parallel enharmonic minor, C♯). A four-note rising chromatic line (often in dotted rhythm in the tenor register) is a perceptible motive throughout the song (mm. 1, 4, 14, 16, 25, 31–32, 42–44), reflected in the vocal line (mm. 3, 8, 10, 18–19, 20–21) and imitated diatonically in the bass (mm. 19–20, 21–22) and in inversion (mm. 8, 10, 35, 37). One comes away with admiration and affection for the song, a desire to hear it performed really well, and wishing that its text had been worthy of the loving musical interpretation that Schumann gave it.

EXAMPLE 3.12. "In der Nacht," Op. 74/4, mm. 42–52

EXAMPLE 3.13. "Resignation," Op. 83/1

(a) mm. 1–6

(*continued*)

(b) mm. 18–21

Notes

1. These early songs do not appear in the practical editions (such as Peters). Three were edited by Brahms and published in 1893 as a supplement to the complete edition of Schumann's works (*Werke*, XIV/1: 34–37). Six more were edited by Karl Geiringer (*Robert Schumann: Sechs frühe Lieder*, Vienna; 1933), and one was published as a supplement to *Neue Zeitschrift für Musik* 100 (1933), Notenbeilage 1. Another was edited by the present author (Hallmark 1984, 101–2). One remains unpublished and one is lost.

2. Another early song, "Lied für ***" (Hallmark 1984, 101–2), composed to Schumann's own poem for a girlfriend, is also a polonaise. Both poem and music gush with teenage infatuation but little real substance. These pieces are probably related to an early set of eight polonaises for piano, some of which were used by the composer in *Papillons* Op. 2.

3. ". . . sind Sie vielleicht wie ich, der ich Gesangskomposition . . . nie für eine

grosse Kunst gehalten?" *Robert Schumanns Briefe: Neue Folge,* ed. Gustav Jansen (Leipzig 1886), 143.

4. Of course one can read personal significance into the songs. Indeed, whatever Schumann was composing was probably bound up with his personal feelings, in many cases about Clara. For example, in his manuscript of "Ich sende einen Gruss" (Op. 25, No. 25), beside the setting of the lines "Aus Schmerzensstürmen, die mein Herz durchtosen, / Send' ich den Hauch, dich unsanft rühr' er nicht!" (out of storms of pain, which rage through my heart, I send a breath; may it not touch you untenderly), Schumann wrote in the margin: "In Erwartung Claras" (in expectation of Clara). The fact that Schumann makes a point of a connection to Clara in a few specific cases confirms the interpretation that *in general* she was not the instigating cause.

5. *Myrthen* arguably has a coherent succession of keys but none of the other unifying characteristics of song cycles, such as a single poet, shared poetic theme or mood, narrative linkage, or prominent shared motives. Schumann's title, however, may allude to other collections. Schumann drew five of the poems from Friedrich Rückert's large compendium of love poems *Liebesfrühling,* which is subdivided into "Sträuße" (bouquets). Bridal myrtles were traditionally woven into a garland or *Kranz,* and *Liederkranz* was a common designation for song collections. In the final song, titled by Schumann "Zum Schluss" (in conclusion), Rückert's poem reads "Hier . . . hab' ich dir den unvollkomm'nen Kranz geflochten, Schwester, Braut!" (Here . . . have I woven an imperfect garland for you, sister, bride). For further discussion of cycles, see chap. 9.

6. Cf. "Wanderlied" (Op. 35, No. 3), "Frühlingsfahrt" (Op. 45, No. 2), "Der frohe Wandersmann" (Op. 77, No. 1; originally the opening song of the Eichendorff *Liederkreis* in its first edition), "Ins Freie" (Op. 89, No. 5), "Die Hütte" (Op. 119, No. 1). The march topos also figures in the ballad "Die beiden Grenadiere" (Op. 49, No. 1), but without the leavening of the regular dotted rhythms. "Mein altes Ross" (Op. 127, No. 4) is a rare minor-key version. See Turchin 1987 on *Wanderlieder* cycles, including Schumann's Op. 35.

7. Compare "Intermezzo," "Die Stille," "Wehmut," and "Frühlingsnacht" in the Eichendorff *Liederkreis* (Op. 39, Nos. 2, 4, and 9). The cadence at the end of the A section may also be to a key other than the dominant, as in "Dein Angesicht" (Op. 127, No. 2).

8. Cf. "Auf einer Burg" and "Zwielicht" (Op. 39, Nos. 7 and 10), "Im Rhein, im heiligen Strome" (Op. 48, No. 6), "Stirb, Lieb' und Freud'" (Op. 35, No. 2), and "Muttertraum" (Op. 40, No. 2).

9. E.g., "Intermezzo" (Op. 39, No. 2), "Er, der herrlichste von allen" (Op. 42, No. 2), "Und wüssten's die Blumen," "Hör' ich das Liedchen klingen" (Op. 48, Nos. 8 and 10), "Frühlingsfahrt" (Op. 45, No. 2), and "Tragödie" (Op. 64, No. 3).

10. Cf. "Mutter, Mutter" ("Lied der Braut I," Op. 25, No. 11, mm. 8 and 32), "Ich sende einen Gruss" (Op. 25, no. 25, m. 15), "Süsser Freund" (Op. 42, No. 6).

11. As in "Schöne Wiege meiner Leiden" (Op. 24, No. 5): AABA'CDA'; "Familiengemälde" (Op. 34, No. 4): AA'BA''CDA'''; "Wanderlied" (Op. 35, No. 3): AAABCA; "An den Sonnenschein" (Op. 36, No. 4): ABA'CA; "Er, der herrlichste von allen" (Op. 42, No. 2): AABA'CC'A; "Du Ring an meinem Ringer" (Op. 42, No. 4): ABACA; "Helft mir, ihr Schwestern" (Op. 42, No. 5): ABACA; "Frühlingsfahrt" (Op. 45, No. 2): AAA'BBA''; "Die beide Grenadiere" (Op. 49, No. 1): ABA'CA''B'DEF, where E and F quote the "Marseillaise."

12. Cf. *Dichterliebe,* Op. 48 (Nos. 5 and 7), *Frauenliebe und -leben,* Op. 42 (passages in Nos. 2, 4, 5, and 6), "Sonntags am Rhein" (Op. 36, No. 1), "Stille Thränen" (Op. 35, No. 10), and "Mein schöner Stern" (Op. 101, No. 4).

13. The two stanzas of "Ich will meine Seele tauchen" (Op. 48, No. 5) are set in the same way. The half-cadence ending may be used in longer poems, too, as in the three stanzas of "Schöne Fremde" (Op. 39, No. 6), "Mondnacht" (Op. 39, No. 5), and "Ich hab' im Traum geweinet" (Op. 48, No. 13); and on an expanded, but still analogous scale, for the four stanzas (grouped in pairs) of "Waldesgespräch" and "In der Fremde" (Op. 39, Nos. 3 and 8). On a still larger scale, compare "Warte, warte, wilder Schiffmann" (Op. 24, No. 6); the through-composed music for the first three stanzas ends on the dominant (m. 54), after which the last two stanzas are set to the same music as the first three (the piano playing the first eleven measures alone), with a tonal adjustment at the end. The process is not unrelated to Schumann's way with ternary forms; see above.

14. Compare Op. 25, No. 11. See also Op. 24, Nos. 3, 4; Op. 39, No. 3; Op. 42, No. 6, and Op. 48, No. 5.

15. Compare other uses of the turn in *Myrthen,* Nos. 1, 9, 11, 21, 24, and 25. See also Op. 39, Nos. 2, 3; Op. 42, Nos. 2, 5; and Op. 48, No. 5.

16. The same figure occurs in *Myrthen,* Nos. 8, 11, 12 (piano), 24, and 25, and also, for example, in Op. 37, No. 6 and Op. 127, No. 2. A similar stock melodic cadence is la-sol-do, as in Op. 25, Nos. 1, 18 (piano); Op. 39, No. 12; Op. 42, No. 7; Op. 48, No. 3; and Op. 79, No. 16.

17. Perhaps as significant as the "twilit melancholy" (Sams 1969, 18) resemblance between "Zwielicht" and "Muttertraum" is the motivic connection between them and their major-key counterpart "Mondnacht," also beginning with a descending melody in skips, with another voice syncopated against it. This E major/E minor juxtaposition of similar motivic material in the same cycle, contrasting two different poems about night, seems a more important textual and musical parallel than the other cited instances.

18. A number of the male-female duets are recorded by Jan DeGaetani and Leslie Guinn, with Gilbert Kalish, piano (Nonesuch H-71364, 1979).

19. Eric Sams's work-list in the New Grove Dictionary (1980, 16, 857–64) includes all the songs for solo voice—one or more—as it should. It is unfortunate that the prominent discussion of the songs in Sams 1969 omits the multivoice songs, especially when they are parts of integral cycles; even more lamentable is the dispersal of such cycles in practical editions. In Walker 1972 discussion of vocal duets, trios and quartets is included illogically in Louis Halsey's essay on choral music!

20. Even if it is unlikely that the maiden might be suggesting the flowing out of another body fluid, and if the expression *Blut lassen* means "to die," the line might still evoke dying as the age-old metaphor for orgasm. Another possible reading is that the maiden fears her soldier might throw his life away in the mistaken belief that his death is an act of courage for country and sweetheart, whereas in reality (stanza 2) his life is cheap; she longs for his release from military service to save him from his own bravado. Schumann's jaunty music arguably does not support this interpretation.

21. E.g., "Der weisse Hirsch," "Das Schwert" (Uhland), and "Die Ammenuhr" (*Des Knaben Wunderhorn*) are unfinished songs probably intended for the *Jugendliederalbum;* a completion of "Das Schwert" has been published (Hallmark 1984).

22. Similar melodic-harmonic fluidity and a tendency away from distinct phrase endings characterize "Liebeslied," Op. 51, No. 5; "Die Blume der Ergebung," Op. 83, No. 2; "Die Tochter Jephthas" and "An den Mond," Op. 95, Nos. 1, 2; and "Liebster, deine Worte stehlen," Op. 101, No. 2.

23. Similar prominent melodic motives in voice and piano occur in "Liebeslied," Op. 51, No. 5, "Gesungen!," Op. 96, No. 4, and "Mein schöner Stern," Op. 101, No. 4.

24. Schumann's taste lapsed occasionally in 1840, too. Consider "Nur ein lächenlnder Blick" by Zimmermann and "Der Nussbaum" by Mosen. In the latter, Schumann's musical conception surpassed the poet's meager offering; the former song, however, reminds us that Schumann could be quite ordinary.

Notes on Editions of Music and Texts

The nineteenth-century complete edition is the most reliable source for Schumann's songs: *Robert Schumann Werke*, ed. Clara Schumann, Johannes Brahms, and others, series X, XI, XIII (vols. 1–4), and XIV (supplement). (Leipzig, 1882–93. This edition was reissued by Gregg Reprints, and portions have appeared in the Lea Pocket and Kalmus Study Scores series. A new critical edition of the complete works is in progress (*Robert Schumann: Sämtliche Werke*, Mainz).

The old three-volume practical or performance edition of the solo songs by Max Friedländer is still issued by Peters. (The International edition is essentially the same.) Peters has begun to issue what are basically reprints of its earlier editions of individual cycles, with the addition of excellent critical notes by Joachim Köhler.

A publisher's practice that interferes with our understanding of Schumann's songs is the gathering of the most famous groups and cycles (Opp. 25, 39, 42, 48) intact in the first volume of practical editions, but breaking up other groups in order to add to the first volume a selection of favorite, individual songs. Thus, for example, the Peters edition includes the final, ninth song of the Op. 24 Heine *Liederkreis* in volume 1, but puts the first eight songs in volume 2. Just as confusing is the breaking up of cycles made up of songs for one to four voices (e.g., Opp. 37, 74, 101, 138) which get divided up systematically into solo, duet, trio and quartet anthologies!

There is no edition from the original literary sources of the poems Schumann set, but such a valuable reference is projected as a volume in the new Schumann edition. Most books and anthologies that print texts for Schumann's songs furnish the version of the text that appears in the published song (e.g., the appendix of the German edition of Fischer-Dieskau's book listed below) rather than the poetic text as it appeared in the literary source. Though Eric Sams did not print the original poems in his book, careful consultation of his annotations enables one to reconstruct the original poem in most cases; Thilo Reinhard similarly notes discrepancies between Schumann's song texts and the poets' originals. Individual scholarly studies of songs are usually careful to compare the original poem to Schumann's emended text.

Bibliography

NOTE: The standard English book-length surveys of the songs are those by Desmond, Fischer-Dieskau, Sams (1969), and Walsh.

Agawu, V. Kofi. "Structural 'Highpoints' in Schumann's *Dichterliebe.*" *Music Analysis* 3 (1984): 159–80.

[Anonymous]. "Robert Schumanns Gesangkomposition." *Allgemeine Musikalische Zeitung* 44 (1842): 30–33, 58–65.

Brauner, Charles S. "Irony in the Heine *Lieder* of Schubert and Schumann." *Musical Quarterly* 67 (1981): 261–81.

Brinkmann, Reinhold. "Lied als individuelle Struktur: Ausgewählte Kommentare zu Schumanns 'Zwielicht.'" In Analysen Beiträge zu einer Problemgeschichte des Komponieren. Festschrift Hans Heinz Eggebrecht zum 65 Geburtstag, ed. Werner Breig, Reinhold Brinkmann, & Elmar Budde, 257–75. Stuttgart 1984.

Burkhart, Charles. "Departures from the Norm in Two Songs from Schumann's *Liederkreis.*" In *Schenker Studies*, ed. Hedi Siegel, 146–64. Cambridge, 1990.

Busse, Eckart, *Die Eichendorff-Rezeption im Kunstlied,* Würzburg, 1975.

Cone, Edward T. "Words into Music: The Composer's Approach to the Text." In *Sound and Poetry*, ed. Northrup Frye, 3–15. New York, 1956.

Cooper, Martin. "The Songs." In *Schumann: A Symposium,* ed. Gerald Abraham, 98–137. Oxford, 1952.

Dahlhaus, Carl. "Romantic and Biedermeier." *Archiv für Musikwissenschaft* 31 (1974): 22–41.

Desmond, Astra. *Schumann's Songs.* London, 1972.

Eismann, Georg. *Robert Schumann: Ein Quellenwerk über sein Leben und Schaffen.* 2 vols. Leipzig, 1956.

Feldman, Fritz. "Zur Frage des 'Liederjahres' bei Robert Schumann." *Archiv für Musikwissenschaft* 9 (1952): 246–69.

Finson, Jon. "Schumann's Mature Style and the 'Album of Songs for the Young.'" *Journal of Musicology* 8 (1990): 227–50.

———. "The Intentional Tourist: Romantic Irony in the Eichendorff *Liederkreis* of Robert Schumann," in *Schumann and his World,* ed. R. Larry Todd, 156–70. Princeton, 1994.

Fischer-Dieskau, Dietrich. *Robert Schumann: Words and Music: The Vocal Works.* Trans. Reinhard Pauly. Portland, OR, 1988. Originally published as *Robert Schumann: Wort und Musik: Das Vokalwerk.* Stuttgart, 1981.

Hallmark, Rufus. "The Sketches for *Dichterliebe.*" *19th-Century Music* 1 (1977): 110–36.

———. *The Genesis of Schumann's Dichterliebe: A Source Study.* Ann Arbor, MI, 1979.

———. "Die handschriftlichen Quellen der Lieder Robert Schumanns." in *Robert Schumann: Ein romantisches Erbe in neuer Forschung,* ed. Robert-Schumann-Gesellschaft, 99–117. Düsseldorf, 1984.

———. "Schumann's Behandlung seiner Liedtexte: Vorläufiger Bericht zu einer neuen Ausgabe und zu einer Neubewertung von Schumanns Lieder." In *Schumanns Werke—Text und Interpretation: 16 Studien,* ed. the Robert-Schumann-Gesellschaft, 29–42. Düsseldorf, 1987.

———. "The Rückert Lieder of Robert and Clara Schumann." *19th-Century Music* 14 (1990): 3–30.

————. "Schumann and Rückert." In *Schumann in Düsseldorf: Werke—Texte—Interpretation,* ed. Bernhard R. Appel, 91–118. Mainz, 1993.

————. *Schumann's Frauenliebe und Leben: Context, Composition and Interpretation.* Oxford, forthcoming.

Hindenlang, Karen. "Eichendorff's *Auf einer Burg* and Schumann's *Liederkreis,* Op. 39." *Journal of Musicology* 8 (1990): 569–87.

Hirschberg, Leopold. "Merkwürdiges aus einem Schumann-Erstdruck." *Die Musik* 21 (1929): 731–36.

Höckner, Berthold. "Spricht der Dichter oder der Tondichter? Die multiple Persona and Robert Schumanns *Liederkreis* Op. 24." In *Schumann und seine Dichter,* ed. Matthias Wendt, 18–32. Mainz, 1993.

Knaus, Herwig. *Musiksprache und Werkstruktur in Robert Schumanns Liederkreis.* Schriften zur Musik, 27. Munich, 1974.

Komar, Arthur. *Schumann: Dichterliebe.* New York, 1971.

Kross, Siegfried. "Robert Schumann im Spannungsfeld von Romantik und Biedermeier." *Bonner Geschichtsblätter* 33 (1981): 89–109.

Mahlert, Ulrich. *Fortschritt und Kunstlied: Späte Lieder Robert Schumanns im Licht der liedästhetischen diskussion ab 1848.* Munich, 1983.

McCreless, Patrick. "Song Order in the Song Cycle: Schumann's *Liederkreis,* Op. 39." *Music Analysis* 5 (1986): 5–28.

Moore, Gerald. *Poet's Love: The Songs and Cycles of Schumann.* New York, 1981.

Mosley, David L. *Gesture, Sign, and Song: An Interdisciplinary Approach to Schumann's Liederkreis Opus 39.* New York, 1990.

Neumeyer, David. "Organic Structure and the Song Cycle: Another Look at Schumann's *Dichterliebe." Music Theory Spectrum* 4 (1982): 92–105.

Ostwald, Peter. *Schumann: The Inner Voices of a Musical Genius.* Boston, 1985.

Plantinga, Leon. *Schumann as Critic.* New Haven, 1967.

————. *Romantic Music.* New York, 1984.

Reinhard, Thilo. *The Singer's Schumann.* New York, 1989.

Sams, Eric. "Schumann's Year of Song." *Musical Times* 106 (1965): 105–7.

————. *The Songs of Robert Schumann.* London, 1969. 3d edition. Bloomington, IN, 1993.

————. "The Songs." In *Robert Schumann: The Man and His Music,* ed. Alan Walker, 120–61. London, 1972.

Schumann, Robert. *Gesammelte Schriften über Musik und Musiker.* 5th ed. Ed. Martin Kreisig. 2 vols. Leipzig, 1914.

Solie, Ruth. "Whose Life? The Gendered Self in Schumann's *Frauenliebe* Songs." In *Music and Text: Critical Inquiries,* ed. Steven Scher, 219–40. Cambridge, 1992.

Thym, Jürgen. "The Solo Song Settings of Eichendorff's Poetry by Schumann and Wolf. Ph.d. dissertation. Case Western Reserve University, 1974.

————. "Text-Music Relationships in Schumann's 'Frühlingsnacht.'" *Theory and Practice* 5 (1980): 7–25.

Turchin, Barbara. "Schumann's Conversion to Vocal Music: A Reconsideration." *Musical Quarterly* 67 (1981): 392–404.

————. "Robert Schumann's Song Cycles: The Cycle within the Song." *19th-Century Music* 8 (1985): 231–44.

————. "The Nineteenth-Century *Wanderlieder* Cycle." *Journal of Musicology* 5 (1987): 498–525.

Walker, Alan, ed., *Robert Schumann: The Man and His Music.* London, 1972.

Walsh, Stephen. *The Lieder of Schumann.* New York, 1971.

CHAPTER FOUR

Johannes Brahms: Volkslied/Kunstlied

Virginia Hancock

Johannes Brahms (1833–97) composed lieder all his life. Among the portfolio of pieces that impressed Robert and Clara Schumann when he arrived on their doorstep in September 1853 were a number of songs. In 1896, at a gathering of friends after Clara's funeral, Brahms played through his latest compositions, the *Vier ernste Gesänge* Op. 121.[1] In all, the works he published for solo voice (or voices) and piano number 196 solo songs, twenty duets, sixty quartets, and fifty-seven arrangements of German folksongs (WoO 31, 33).[2] Posthumous publications include twenty-eight additional folk song arrangements (WoO 32) and a few additional art songs, including the five Ophelia songs (WoO 22).

Brahms's practice was to accumulate songs over a period of time, then to publish a group or several groups at once, sometimes reaching back to pieces composed many years earlier. Although it is clear from the correspondence with his publishers that the order of songs within opus numbers, which he assembled like "bouquets," was important to him, in only a few instances is there evidence of advance planning.[3] Moreover, it is generally difficult to identify individuals or occasions that inspired Brahms to song composition. There are a few occasional songs, like those written to celebrate the births of children to Bertha Faber ("Wiegenlied," Op. 49, No. 4) and Amalie Joachim (Op. 91, No. 2). The poem "Komm bald" was a birthday gift to Brahms that he immediately provided with a setting (Op. 97, No. 5) for the celebrated contralto Hermine Spies. Two poems by Felix Schumann (Op. 63, Nos. 5, 6) were set as a gift for the eighteen-year-old poet and his mother, and a number of songs from the late 1850s were written for Agathe von Siebold, an amateur soprano with whom Brahms was briefly in love. His friends sometimes discerned other personal connections that the reticent Brahms would not willingly have admitted: for example, in 1867 the depressed tone of a pair of new songs (Op. 48, No. 7 and Op. 49, No. 5), composed when Brahms was feeling his rootlessness especially keenly, so alarmed Clara Schumann that she strongly advised him to get married (13 November 1867).[4] But mostly his inspiration seems to have come from the poems themselves.

Brahms was an omnivorous reader, and poetry—especially modern poetry—was a special enthusiasm.[5] Initially he read a poem as an uncritical aficionado, trying to adopt the poet's point of view (Jacobsen 1975, 76–77). Once a poem had attracted his attention as a candidate for musical setting—had "forced itself" on him, as he wrote to Mathilde Wesendonck (Jacobsen 1975, 56)—he evaluated it more critically, considering, among other factors, whether it was already perfect in itself and thus provided no latitude for a composer.[6] Indeed, after his early years, Brahms seems to have avoided setting works by "great" poets (as well as poems set by other major composers); rather, he made a distinction between what "might be called 'poetic music' (self-sufficient poetry) [and] 'musical poetry' (poetry that invites musical elaboration)" (Braus 1988, 128).

This point of view helps to account for the fact that Brahms set many poems considered inferior by literary authorities. Although he selected texts by Tieck, Heine, Eichendorff, Hölty, Goethe, Platen, Mörike, Brentano, and Storm, critics have inclined toward Jack Stein's judgment that "well over half of his songs use mediocre-to-bad poems" (Stein 1971, 131). Among the poets who incur such criticism are several whose texts Brahms set repeatedly: Carl Candidus (6), Klaus Groth (11), Friedrich Halm (6), Karl Lemcke (7), and, above all, Georg Friedrich Daumer (1800–1875), a prolific author and translator whose poems Brahms used for nineteen of his solo songs and for the *Liebeslieder-Walzer,* as well as all but the last (by Goethe) of the *Neue Liebeslieder-Walzer.*[7] The eroticism of some of the Daumer texts occasionally offended Brahms's friends, and the quality of his verse has been assailed by numerous critics, but despite its weaknesses, this poetry evoked some of Brahms's most compelling songs. As Malcolm MacDonald (1990, 351) observes, the listener cannot but be "impressed by his ability to identify with the emotional truth behind often undistinguished poems and place them in a setting that imparts the memorable resonance lacking in the words themselves."

Brahms has been accused of lack of respect for his poetic texts, especially with regard to declamation and the repetition of words, phrases, and lines, and is often cited—usually in contradistinction to Hugo Wolf—as a composer who let the music outweigh the text. There are undoubtedly instances where Brahms was carried away by his own enthusiasm, several in the *Magelone-Lieder* Op. 33, where already ungainly songs are taken to extremes by textual repetition. But in many songs, repetition of the final line of a stanza or poem, often at a slower declamation rate (Platt 1992, chap. 2), helps to provide a satisfactory conclusion, and individual words are often repeated for emphasis.

From the time of his earliest published songs, Brahms was aware of the criticism of his declamation. Thus it seems clear that "faulty" declamation in his lieder is the result of conscious decisions. Certainly he studied the poems; according to his only composition student, Gustav Jenner, "he demanded first of a composer that he know his text thoroughly," recommending recitation of the text and analysis of form and meter, with special attention to the location of pauses (Jenner 1990, 35). In many cases, Brahms's critics have failed to recognize a rhythmic element long acknowledged in his instrumental music: his frequent disregard of bar lines. Apparent misaccentuations disappear when temporary, unnotated changes of meter, shifts of bar line, and hemiola are taken into account. In some instances, one must concede that Brahms chose to ride roughshod over the text for musical reasons. He clearly felt that it was possible to carry fidelity too far, and in one of his few recorded remarks about Wolf, he told Heuberger (1971, 41), "Well, if one isn't worried about the music, the declamation of a poem is very easy."

According to his own statements, once Brahms had decided to attempt a musical setting, he committed the poem to memory, spoke it aloud repeatedly, analyzed its meter, structure, and meaning, and waited for a kernel of melodic inspiration. After allowing the idea to germinate, he committed the song to paper, developing the complete vocal melody together with a contrapuntally convincing bass line. He continued with the remainder of the piano part and concluded with a ruthless revision of the whole (Henschel 1907, 22–23, 39; Jenner 1905, 35, 40–41; see also Finscher 1983b, 33, and Bozarth 1978 and 1983b for the most detailed work on Brahms's compositional process).

Brahms's original melodic ideas were often derived from or closely related to the German folk music that was his lifelong passion. He knew that many of his favorite tunes were not genuine folk music but eighteenth- and nineteenth-century "improvements" or downright inventions; but their style was, as he told Clara Schumann, his "ideal" (27 January 1860). A great number of his melodies are constructed on incomplete arpeggiations of triads and seventh-chords—*jodlerhaft* melodies like that of "Minnelied," Op. 71, No. 5 (Mahlert 1992, 89; Musgrave 1980 shows that Brahms's supposed motto F–A–F, often cited as a source of such melodies, was a figment of Max Kalbeck's imagination). The soaring melodies beloved of singers are mostly of this type, often with wide leaps that usually ascend but may also descend, especially at cadences. A melody of narrow compass often reflects an anxious or melancholy text. Further echoes of folk music include patches of modal coloring, hemiola, and occasional use of irregular meters. Text illustration also influences the construction and course of melodies, from obvious madrigalisms like ascent and descent to affective chromaticism or appoggiaturas.

Much has been made of the fact that in evaluating the songs of others Brahms first looked at the melody and bass (Henschel 1907, 44; Jenner 1905, 40), but it is also clear that he gave careful thought to his accompaniments. Many are illustrative of the text, using the common currency of the lied—rushing waters, blowing winds, rustling leaves, singing birds, serenading guitars, and so forth. Other types of "musical images," as Eric Sams calls them, can represent an almost unconscious response to the text, as in the case of "the idea of vision or dream expressed in slow upward arpeggios in the left hand, like a vague notion drifting up from sleep towards the borderlands of consciousness" (Sams 1972, 9). An accompanimental figure can continue throughout a song or change in response to the text or for musical reasons.

Changing an accompaniment pattern is one way Brahms articulated form in his songs. According to Jenner (1905, 30–31), he felt that a composer who failed to follow the form of the poem demonstrated "a lack of artistic understanding or insufficient penetration of the text." Although he claimed to prefer strophic form, recommending the study of Schubert's songs as a basis for deciding when to write a strophic setting, relatively few of Brahms's art songs are in simple strophic form. But in nearly every case where there is a division in the text, it is somehow clearly reflected in the musical setting; textual demarcations are obscured only for good reasons.

Rudolf Gerber, whose article (1932) remains the most useful short discussion of form in Brahms's songs, describes the ways in which Brahms set strophic poems. Simple strophic settings occur when the poem has few stanzas and little or no progression of ideas. The remaining songs are classified as open or closed forms. Open form—strophic variation—can range in degree from slight modification in the last stanza to a radically progressive series of variations. Sometimes the common element undergoing variation is not readily audible, although Brahms said, "If I want to retain the same idea, then it should be clearly recognized in each transformation, augmentation, inversion" (Frisch 1984, 31–32). In closed or rounded form—ternary or rondolike songs—motivic relationships between the outer sections and the central part or parts range from obvious to imperceptible. Only a few songs—principally some of the *Magelone-Lieder*—are unequivocally *durchkomponiert.* Gerber observes that if there is any hint of formal return in the poem, Brahms's setting is invariably closed and his desire for musical closure occasionally overrides the sense of an "open" poem. The ternary form in which "the core idea of the first strophe is subtly varied to create a contrasted but related second strophe or central group, prior to the varied reprise of the first," is "perhaps Brahms's most characteristic contribution to the German tradition" (Musgrave 1985, 44).

This discussion treats selected songs in four groups, emphasizing lesser-known songs that deserve wider exposure, particularly those with texts by minor poets. Nearly half of Brahms's songs reflect his preoccupa-

TABLE 4.1.
Folklike and Hybrid Songs, Listed by Opus Number

Folklike Songs (Group II)	*Hybrid Songs (Group III)*
op. 7/4, 5	op. 3/1, 4
op. 14/1, 2, 5, 6, 7	op. 7/1, 2, 3
op. 43/3, 4	op. 14/3
op. 47/3	op. 19/2, 3, 4
op. 48/2	op. 48/1, 3, 4
op. 49/4	op. 49/1
op. 59/5	op. 69/1, 5, 7, 9
op. 69/2, 3, 4	op. 84/1, 2, 3, 4
op. 84/5	op. 85/3, 4
op. 97/4, 6	op. 95/1, 4, 5, 6
op. 105/3	op. 97/3
	op. 107/3, 5

tion with folk music; because the folk-related songs are often neglected, they receive here more attention than they are typically accorded. Group I comprises his settings (approximately eighty) of traditional texts with their preexistent tunes, whereas Group II contains settings of folk texts for which Brahms composed his own melodies in imitation of folk tunes (twenty). Group III is made up of songs with folk or folklike texts set in a manner more characteristic of art songs while retaining *volkstümlich* qualities (thirty). (A list of the songs included in Groups II and III is found in Table 4.1.) The remainder, lyric songs or *Kunstlieder*, a little more than half the total (148), make up Group IV (see Table 4.2).

Folk Songs

Brahms's lifelong favorite source, Kretzschmer and Zuccalmaglio's *Deutsche Volkslieder mit ihren Original-Weisen* (1838, 1840), provided the texts and tunes for the fourteen *Volkskinderlieder* dedicated to the Schumann children (WoO 31, 1858) and the twenty-eight settings in a manuscript sent to Clara in June 1858 (WoO 32, published 1926). He published no more solo arrangements for thirty-five years, although he maintained an enthusiastic interest in folk song, collecting and studying numerous additional sources and providing arrangements for the choral ensembles he conducted.[8] But scholarly attacks on the Kretzschmer-Zuccalmaglio collection finally became more than he could bear, and he came to the defense of his old favorites, revising some of his earlier settings and adding new

TABLE 4.2.
Lyric Songs Listed by Opus Number
(with references to published analyses)

Key to references:

a. Beller-McKenna (1994)	k. Jacobsen (1975)
b. Bozarth (1978)	l. Jost (1992b)
c. Bozarth (1983b)	m. Mahlert (1992)
d. Bozarth (1983a)	n. Pisk (1976)
e. Braus (1988)	o. Platt (1992)
f. Draheim (1992)	p. Sams (1972)
g. Finscher (1990)	q. Schmidt (1984)
h. Frisch (1984)	r. Sick (1992)
i. Horne (1992)	s. Stein (1971)
j. Goldberg (1992)	

Op.	*No.*
3	2, $3^{e,1}$ 5^{gko}, 6^{eg}
6	1^{j}, 2^{g}, 3, 4^{g}, 5, 6^{e}
7	6^{l}
WoO 21^{k}	
14	4
19	1^{m}, 5^{kos}
32	1^{eis}, 2, 3, 4os, 5^{e}, 6^{o}, 7, $8^{e,2}$ 9
33^{3}	1, 2, 3^{k}, 4, 5, 6, 7, 8, 9^{kos}, 10, 11, 12, 13, 14, 15
43	1os, 2^{hkmpqs}
46	1^{h}, 2, 3^{ehm}, 4^{km}
47	1, 2, 4, 5^{k}
48	5^{k}, 7^{di}
49	2^{m}, 3, 5^{d}
57^{b}	1, 2, 3, 4, 5, 6, 7, 8
58^{b}	1, 2, 3, 4, 5^{l}, 6, 7^{c}, 8^{d}
59	1^{s}, 2, 3^{o}, 4^{o}, 6, 7, 8
WoO 23	
63	1, 2, 3, 4, 5, 6, 7, 8, 9
69	6^{eo}, 8^{ks}
70	1, 2, 3, 4
71	1^{j}, 2, 3, 4^{o}, 5^{km}
72	1, 2, 3, 4, 5^{s}
85	1^{ej}, 2^{ej}, 5, 6^{o}
86	1^{ks}, 2, 3, 4^{i}, 5, 6
91	1, 2
94	1^{o}, 2^{e}, 3, 4^{f}, 5^{o}

(continued)

95	2, 3, 7
96	1[jns], 2, 3[jo], 4[jk]
97	1, 2[o], 5
105	1, 2[ino], 4[e,4] 5
106	1, 2, 3, 4, 5
107	1, 2, 4
121[a]	1, 2, 3[h], 4

---

1. An earlier version of this article appeared as "Brahms's *Liebe und Frühling II*, Op. 3, No. 3: A New Path to the Artwork of the Future?" in *19th-Century Music* 10 (1988): 135–56.
2. Braus (1992) presents a revised version of the same analysis.
3. See references in chap. 9 of this volume.
4. Also published as "Poetic-Musical Rhetoric in Brahms's *Auf dem Kirchhofe*, Op. 105, No. 4" in *Theory and Practice* 13 (1988): 15–30. Schenker's analysis of op. 105/4 appears in the same issue.

ones. In June 1894 he published the forty-nine *Deutsche Volkslieder* (WoO 33), of which forty-two are for solo voice and piano.

Two songs from this collection exemplify the range of style in Brahms's folk-song settings. The simple accompaniment of "Da unten im Tale" (No. 6, earlier set in a cappella versions for women's and mixed choirs), with its interpolated off-beat pitches and steady eighth-note pulse, essentially follows the vocal line. Although the postlude that ends each stanza seems a natural continuation, it is in fact taken from another, original setting of the same text, "Trennung," Op. 97, No. 6 (1886); the beginning of its melody, a three-note descent, provides the seed for the interlude the two settings share. (Brahms's other settings of folk texts with original and traditional tunes are "Vor dem Fenster" [Op. 14, No. 1; WoO 33, No. 35], "Gang zur Liebsten" [Op. 14, No. 6; WoO 33, No. 38], "Spannung" [Op. 84, No. 5; WoO 33, No. 4], and "Dort in den Weiden" [Op. 97, No. 4; WoO 33, No. 31].)

"Gunhilde" (No. 7), a tale of the flight, degradation, contrition, and redemption of a young nun, receives a much more elaborate setting. The folk melody begins in G major and ends in E minor. Four versions of the accompaniment are heard. The first, in stanzas 1–3, is taken largely from an earlier setting. The pace of the piano quickens for stanzas 4–6, which otherwise maintain the diatonic harmonies and plagal cadence of the first three stanzas. Following an interlude marked by imitation by inversion, the setting of stanzas 7–9 turns, surprisingly, to chromaticism and a concluding authentic cadence. The last stanza recalls the slower pace of the beginning but with less reliance on G major, and the disappearance of the angel that has substituted for the nun during her absence occurs in a choralelike phrase in block chords over a dominant pedal, with a final plagal cadence in E minor.

Brahms's settings of folk texts to his own folklike melodies (Group II) display a comparable range in style. Although his melodies sound like folk tunes, the songs sometimes diverge from strophic form, as in "Die Trauernde" (Op. 7, No. 5, 1852), a lament in Swabian dialect by a girl who has no lover. The three stanzas are in the form of a *Reprisenbar* (AABa; see Ex. 4.1) in A minor. Each of the first two stanzas is set to a predictable, even monotonous *Stollen*. As the *Abgesang* starts, however, the range shifts upward, beginning on the previous high pitch C and ascending to E, which is harmonized with an unexpected, even shocking, A-major chord. The cross-relation C–C♯ is emphasized when these two measures are repeated, but the outburst is brief and the song ends with a reprise of the end of the *Stollen*, a return to resignation.

EXAMPLE 4.1. Op. 7, No. 5, entire

(continued)

The songs of Op. 14, though not published until 1861, were all composed in 1858, the year of Brahms's most energetic early involvement with folk song. Five are of the *volkstümlich* type, the largest number in any Brahms opus. Another "Trennung" (No. 5) is a lively song in which lovers must separate as dawn breaks. Its opening melodic gesture, an ascending fourth, recurs as a motive throughout the setting. Although stanzas 1–3 and 5 are identical, stanza 4 has a new melody, accompanied in the piano by descending chromatic lines as the text describes separation—"as hard as death"—and a few measures in the submediant major. This apparently simple song contains several features characteristic of many of Brahms's lieder: variation of the first part to produce a contrasted but related middle section, derivation of an important motive from the beginning of the melody, affective chromaticism, and use of chromatic third-related keys.

Most of the folklike settings among the songs published in 1868 (Opp. 43, 46, 47, 48, and 49) were composed earlier. Only the famous "Wiegenlied" (Op. 49, No. 4) comes from 1868—and Brahms had learned the Viennese waltz song that inspired its accompaniment almost twenty years before. The earliest, Op. 48, No. 2 (1853), "Der Überläufer," is the plaint of a lover jilted by his sweetheart for—whom else?—a hunter. Its strophic setting in the natural minor mode, uncolored even by leading tones, oddly lacks any musical reference to the hunter's horn. Brahms declaimed the text of "Das Lied vom Herrn von Falkenstein" (Op. 43, No. 4) repeatedly and loudly while hiking on the Falkenburg near Detmold in 1857 (Kalbeck 1912–21, I: 313). His setting, with its unpredictable phrase lengths in the seven martial outer stanzas and its unexpectedly lyrical fifth and sixth stanzas, was a favorite of his friends, although the lengthy narrative lacks the same appeal today. The two imitation-Renaissance lieder "Ich schell mein Horn ins Jammerthal" (Op. 43, No. 3) and "Vergangen ist mir Glück und Heil" (Op. 48, No. 6), both arranged from a cappella choral pieces, and the popular "Sonntag" (Op. 47, No. 3) all date from the years of Brahms's activity with the Hamburg Frauenchor.

For the remainder of his career, Brahms continued to produce these folklike songs slowly but regularly, usually one or two at a time every few years. "Agnes" (Op. 59, No. 5), composed in 1873, sets a poem by Mörike on the deserted-maiden theme. The nine lieder of Op. 69, published in 1877, all have texts that are folklike in theme, language, and structure, although the melodies and piano parts present the widest possible variety of treatments. Of the three songs in Group II, the second "Klage" (Op. 69, No. 2), another maiden's lament, shows Brahms in his gypsy mode but hides skillful counterpoint under the exotic surface. "Des liebsten Schwur" (No. 4) is thoroughly Germanic (in spite of its Bohemian text) in the defiant maiden's arpeggiated vocal part, the thumping piano, and the many secondary dominants in the final line. "Abschied" (Op. 69, No. 3), in contrast, is an unassuming but beautiful song on the "ferne Geliebte" theme, distinguished by the economy with which the melodic material is developed from the first four notes of the vocal part.

The last of Brahms's essays in folk style, "Klage" (Op. 105, No. 3), is rarely performed. As in "Gunhilde," the opening melody begins in the major and ends in the relative minor, followed by an interlude that returns to the original key. But when Brahms uses the passage as a postlude, the song unexpectedly ends in the major. This lied, marked "einfach und ausdrucksvoll" by the composer, exemplifies the idealized concept of an artful folk music that led him to his *Deutsche Volkslieder.*

Hybrid Songs

"Liebestreu," the song that Brahms chose to open his first set of lieder (Op. 3), is also the first of the group with texts on standard folk themes, melodies more artificial than folk tunes, and elaborate and varied accompaniments. Despite what Sams (1972, 18) calls "Reinick's sentimental magazine rhymes," it is a splendid song. In other early songs, however, Brahms yielded to the temptation to write overblown settings containing tremendously difficult piano parts and, as Finscher puts it (1983b, 35), "an excess of chromaticism" unmotivated by the text.

Op. 3, No. 4, "Lied," composed in July 1853, is a case in point. The text is an extended metaphor in which innocent creatures are threatened by beasts of prey; in the last stanza we learn that the singer is a girl trying to protect her endangered heart. The three stanzas—connected to one another by a short recurring interlude in unharmonized octaves (Ex. 4.2a)[9]—are set identically until the conclusion of the third, where three interpolated measures provide a grandiose chromatic finale (Ex. 4.2b). The final phrase starts with an ascent by half steps in E♭ major (mm. 27, 43); the interpolation begins with a half-step slide upward and a sequential repeat of the ascent. The dominant-seventh chord on C♭ (lacking its third) that harmonizes the last pitch of the sequence becomes a German augmented sixth resolving to a tonic six-four chord in E♭ major; this moves through the parallel minor (the song's tonic) on its way to the expected

EXAMPLE 4.2. Op. 3, No. 4
(a) mm. 27–31

(*continued*)

EXAMPLE 4.2. (*continued*)
(b) mm. 43–48

dominant seventh. The song ends with a slower version of the conclusions of the previous stanzas—what had been a minor subdominant chord is altered to an augmented fifth—and settles finally on an open fifth. Into these few measures is concentrated a treasury of ideas that Brahms exploited throughout his life of song writing. At this stage, however, he had not yet learned a sense of proportion.

The late 1850s saw the composition not only of Opp. 14 and 19, but of Op. 48, Nos. 1 and 3. The latter were not published until 1868, but a version of Op. 48, No. 1, "Der Gang zum Liebchen," appears in the partbooks of the Frauenchor. In this strophic song, the motus perpetuum of the accompaniment in the second half also serves as a postlude. The abandoned girl of "Liebesklage des Mädchens" (Op. 48, No. 3) sings an odd, indeterminate song that never settles down to a clear key. Although a few of Brahms's great songs are tonally ambiguous, this is not one of them. Two more songs published in 1868 have unknown dates of composition. "Am

Sonntag Morgen" (Op. 49, No. 1) hides sorrow under a cheerful face, concluding with a classic affective Neapolitan-sixth cadence ($\flat$II^6-V^7-i). The same harmony colors the similar and equally attractive "Gold überwiegt die Liebe" (Op. 48, No. 4).

Four of the songs of Opp. 85 and 95 are settings of translations of Eastern European folk texts by Siegfried Kapper. Two of the three translations from the Serbian, "Das Mädchen" (Op. 95, No. 1) and "Mädchenlied" (Op. 85, No. 3), are set in irregular meters; in "Mädchenlied," trochaic tetrameter ("Ach, und du mein kühles Wasser!") is transformed into $\frac{5}{4}$ when the last two syllables of each line are lengthened. At first glance, "Vorschneller Schwur" (Op. 95, No. 5) is an obvious example of varied strophic form: in the first stanza the girl swears off carrying flowers, drinking wine, and kissing boys, all in D minor; in the second she reneges on all three pledges in D major. The relationship of setting to text is more complicated, however. The poem is divided into two sections: the first, six lines long, is the girl's oath (two repetitions are part of the poem), and the second begins with two connecting lines ("Gestern schwor das Mädchen— / heute schon bereut es") and continues with the six lines of her retraction. The musical parallels, then, are between the first section and the last six lines of the second; the setting of the two central lines is almost recitative, based on the ascending third that opens the song, but also accomplishing recitative's traditional narrative and modulating functions. (The same formal technique appears in the very different "O kühler Wald," Op. 72, No. 3, where the first line of the poem's second stanza is isolated and declaimed.) "Ade!" (Op. 85, No. 4, translated from the Bohemian) is an unusually cheerful song of farewell; for much of the song, a duet between the voice and a countermelody is masked by layers of rhythmic activity in the difficult accompaniment.

"Entführung" (Op. 97, No. 3) seems to be a throwback to Brahms's earlier excesses of the ballad type. The galloping-horse accompaniment, with its syncopated bass, is effective, and his friends like the song; Elisabeth von Herzogenberg, for whose opinions he had great respect, thought the words "splendid" and the music "delicious" (Brahms 1909, 230). Several writers have suggested that the image of the hero riding into the night with his lady represents wishful thinking by the composer (Sams 1972, 56; MacDonald 1990, 348); the song's title has been translated as both "abduction" and "elopement," but Frau von Herzogenberg's approval proves the latter correct.

Brahms's last published opus of songs includes two songs with women narrators. The girl of "Mädchenlied" (Op. 107, No. 5) is spinning, but unlike Schubert's Gretchen she has never had a lover. Her melancholy is in sharp contrast to the exuberance of the young bride who sings the leaping melody and fractured rhythms of "Das Mädchen spricht" (Op. 107, No. 3). (Brahms did not assume performances by women; Op. 107, No. 3 was premiered by the tenor Gustav Walter.) The poem is in two stanzas of identical meter, each containing five lines of three feet, with a variable number of syllables per line. The first stanza:

Schwalbe, sag mir an,	Swallow, tell me,
Ists dein alter Mann,	Is it your old husband
Mit dem dus Nest gebaut?	With whom you have built a nest?
Oder hast du jüngst erst	Or have you just recently
Dich ihm vertraut?	Entrusted yourself to him?

The song begins with an introduction that gives no clue to its meter (Ex. 4.3, pp. 133–34); is it triple, as notated, or duple with two fermatas? The voice enters in unambiguous triple meter, but the third line, sung twice and accelerated so that its three accents fit into three adjacent beats, is a hemiola in both voice and piano. The shift to C major on the second beat of m. 11 provides a striking accent, so that the perceived downbeat moves to beat 2, where it is supported by the piano part until m. 15. The repositioned downbeat provides accentuation—previously unclear—for the text "o-der hast du jüngst erst." But the line is then broken with a rest, and the enjambment into the next line is ignored. The two remaining beats of m. 15 lead to two bars in which the piano part contains a harmonic hemiola: the first beat of m. 16 is the diminished-seventh pivot that restores the original tonic, A major, and in that key the chords of mm. 16–17 fall into two-beat groups, $vii^{o4}_{3}/V–V^{6}$, $vii^{o7}/vi–vii^{o7}/V–I^{6}_{4}$. The voice does not have the hemiola pattern, however, and when the last line of text is repeated the piano falls into line, returning briefly to simple triple meter.

Art Songs

Whereas Brahms maintained objectivity in his songs for and about women by conforming to the conventional genres of folk poetry, he expressed more personal feelings in his *Kunstlieder.* These form roughly half of his output of songs, although only about a third are performed frequently. (Table 4.2 includes references to analyses of individual songs.) The songs discussed below have been selected largely because of their relative neglect, although for a few well-known songs earlier analyses are expanded or clarified. Settings of texts by lesser-known poets are emphasized, with special attention given to the Daumer songs.

Brahms is often characterized as a grim composer—preoccupied with thoughts of lost youth, unhappy love, and death. Although many of his greatest songs treat such topics, he occasionally exhibits moods of optimism—even exuberance—in such well-known songs as "Botschaft" (Op. 47, No. 1), "O liebliche Wangen" (Op. 47, No. 4), "Meine Liebe ist grün" (Op. 63, No. 5), and "Ständchen" (Op. 106, No. 1).

The lyric songs include a few settings of folk or folklike texts so elaborate that any sense of the *volkstümlich* is essentially absent. "Von ewiger

EXAMPLE 4.3. Op. 107, No. 3, mm. 1–19

(continued)

EXAMPLE 4.3. (*continued*)

Liebe" (Op. 43, No. 1) and "Verrat" (Op. 105, No. 5) are narratives—the former frequently performed, the latter, a grisly tale of revenge, almost never. Other such elaborate settings are "Sehnsucht" (Op. 49, No. 3), an overwrought setting of a slight poem; "Blinde Kuh" (Op. 58, No. 1), in which a game of blindman's buff becomes a chase between the pianist's two hands; and "Die Spröde" (Op. 58, No. 3), an artful setting of a text "aus dem Calabresischen" by August Kopisch that was revised after the first edition by Paul Heyse (Bozarth 1978, 140–42). The last two songs of this type are on texts by Lemcke: "Salamander" (Op. 107, No. 2) and "Willst du, daß ich geh?" (Op. 71, No. 4), in which the protagonist, ignoring barline meter, disingenuously asks whether he really must go out into the hostile night—depicted by a stormy piano part and numerous cross-rhythms. Elisabeth von Herzogenberg disapproved of this serious approach to the poem, saying that only a setting "in Volkslied style" would have been appropriate (Brahms 1909, 23).

Brahms's first opus consisting entirely of lyric songs is the *Lieder und Gesänge* Op. 32 (1864), on texts by Daumer and the respected August von Platen. This set, a watershed in Brahms's career as a composer of lieder, is described by Kalbeck (1912–21, 2:138) as "a sort of lyric *Novelle*, . . . a highly personal history of the heart." In the powerful first and fourth songs, both expressing alienation and futility—linked by Goldberg (1992, 192) to Platen's homosexuality—the feeling of rootlessness is reflected in passages of uncertain tonality. The other Platen songs, Nos. 3, 5, and 6, respectively unite in text and music emotions of despairing numbness, violent escape from unspecified fetters, and bitter resignation.

Brahms's first setting of a poem by Daumer, "Nicht mehr zu dir zu gehen" (Op. 32, No. 2), represents a remarkable change in style from anything he had composed earlier; Friedlaender (1928, 33) describes Brahms's ternary setting as less a song in the traditional sense than "a declamation hesitating between a recitatif and an aria." Indeed it is effectively *anti*-lyrical: in the first of the three stanzas (Ex. 4.4), the vocal melody sounds almost spoken, the second and fourth lines are interrupted by pauses (the repetition of "denn jede Kraft," which extends the already longer fourth line, is Brahms's), and the vocal part has no discernible meter. The only stable presence is the passacaglialike bass. Next to the ascending scale of mm. 1 and 4 (inverted in the middle section), the most striking motive is the one in the piano associated with the words "beschloß ich"; other three-note figures in the voice are heard as variants of this one. The harmony is as indecisive as the vocal rhythm: V–i cadences are colored by alteration of the dominant (as with the augmented fifth in m. 8) or evaded, and there is only one authentic cadence. Kalbeck's description (1912–21, 2:140) of the trapped, hapless lover—"on each syllable hangs a drop of blood"—seems appropriate.

The ninth and last song, "Wie bist du, meine Königin," renowned as one of Brahms's most beautiful lieder, is almost equally notorious for its

EXAMPLE 4.4. Op. 32, No. 2, mm. 1–10

faulty declamation. Daumer's four stanzas are in iambic tetrameter; every stanza ends with the word *wonnevoll* and has an enjambment between the third and fourth lines. Brahms's modified strophic setting preserves the enjambment, isolates and emphasizes through repetition the final "won-nevoll" of each stanza, and disrupts the meter, placing unaccented sylla-bles on strong beats, although there appears to be no justification for this on grounds of shifting downbeats or ambiguous accentuation. Bell's sug-gestion (1979, 43) that Brahms's idea for the main melody may have come from the first phrase of the last stanza—"Laß mich vergehn in deinem Arm!"—and that he found it too good to relinquish despite its poor fit with the other stanzas, seems plausible. It is supported by the fact that minor changes in the rhythm within strophes, often prompted by chang-ing accentuation, occur only in the second and fourth lines of stanzas and not in the first and third, which are always set to that melody or variants of it.

The third stanza (Ex. 4.5), with its contrasting affect, provides in its brief course a virtuoso display of modulation, exploiting the enharmonic

EXAMPLE 4.5. Op. 32, No. 9, mm. 44–60

(*continued*)

EXAMPLE 4.5. (*continued*)

identity of dominant-seventh and German augmented-sixth chords (see chap. 9 on the use of the "Neapolitan complex" in this passage). The shift from E♭ minor (parallel minor of the tonic) to E major in m. 47 is accomplished by reversing the conventional pattern: the chord on the first beat, V_3^4 in E major, is the German sixth of the previous key. (This reverse German-sixth progression, rarely used by Brahms, is by no means unique; see, for example, Schumann's "Im leuchtenden Sommermorgen.") The change of mode in mm. 49–50 is reinforced by the linkage between the voice's descending half step in m. 49 and the knell-like sixfold echo of the half step in the piano part;[10] the same motive is reflected in the half-step slip from V^7 in E minor to V^7 in E♭ minor between mm. 52 and 53.[11] The return to the tonic minor is interrupted in m. 55 by one of Brahms's favorite devices, a dyad that belongs equally to two keys, here used to move to C♭ major. A seventh is added to the resolution to C♭ in m. 58, and the resulting chord—enharmonically the same as that heard in m. 47—is the

German sixth that, used conventionally this time, returns the song to E♭ major for its final stanza.

Two songs composed in May 1867 on texts by Adolf Friedrich von Schack rank, with *Ein deutsches Requiem,* most of which Brahms had just completed, among his most serious works. "Herbstgefühl" (Op. 48, No. 7), the first of the songs often dubbed "autumnal," was written when he was only thirty-four years old. The tonality is obscure until the end, and although it appears that D major will prevail (foreshadowing later death-as-refuge songs and confirming the message of the *Requiem*), the final phrase is in F♯ minor; Brahms acknowledged its resemblance to Schubert's "Doppelgänger" (Friedlaender 1928, 75). Hugo Wolf might have recognized a premonition of his "Um Mitternacht" in the long prelude to "Abenddämmerung" (Op. 49, No. 5), one of Brahms's most powerful songs of nostalgia, in its low range, rocking piano figuration, and poignant dissonance.

The eight songs of Op. 57 (1869–71) are settings of Daumer texts—Brahms's only opus except the *Magelone-Lieder* devoted to the works of a single poet. The poems as a group express "hot passion and undisguised sensuality" (Friedlaender 1928, 83). Like Op. 32, the set might be read as a cycle, beginning with the breathless urgency of No. 1, "Von wald-bekränzter Höhe," in which love is avowed, followed by several masterful songs expressing doubt and hesitation: "Wenn du nur zuweilen lächelst" (No. 2), "Es träumte mir" (No. 3), and "Ach, wende diesen Blick" (No. 4). The deserted lover of No. 5, "In meiner Nächte Sehnen"—more akin to Schubert's Gretchen than the wistful maidens of Brahms's folklike songs—recalls previous sexual encounters in the ceaseless accompaniment and ascending tessitura. The form is ternary, with two stanzas of the original four combined in the middle section, at the end of which a climax of rhythmic intensity coincides with the recollection of physical climax. In contrast, "Strahlt zuweilen auch ein mildes Licht" (Op. 57, No. 6) is a lovely miniature setting of a single stanza: the glances from the poet's beloved do not, finally, convey the message he desires. The seventh song, "Die Schnur, die Perl an Perle," in which the lover's hope is rekindled, reaches a root-position tonic triad only in its final measure; much of this passionate song is over dominant pedals (often tonic six-four chords) in a variety of keys.

The lover at last reaches fulfillment in "Unbewegte laue Luft" (No. 9), a song on the scale of some of the *Magelone-Lieder* but more successful because of its musical unity. Elisabeth von Herzogenberg told Brahms that she had "broken many lances" (Brahms 1909, 34) in defense of its erotic text (the last two lines: "Komm, o komm, damit wir uns / himmlische Genüge geben!"). The setting, filled with yearning chromaticism, is distinguished by a contrapuntally derived French augmented-sixth chord heard four times in the first four measures (Ex. 4.6a). This chord would normally lead to E♭ major or minor; here, however, it functions as neighbor and sub-stitute dominant to the tonic E major and is instantly recognizable as un-usual—perhaps even unique—in Brahms's style.[12] Memorable on its own, it is underlined whenever the voice is present by the dissonant flat sixth degree of the scale, C♮, sung against the tonic chord (m. 4). The languid beginning is briefly enlivened (although remaining dolce) by the plashing of a fountain in B major. At this point one expects continuation in the dominant or a common-tone shift to a third-related key; unanticipated, however, is a circuitous return to the original tonic (Ex. 4.6b) by way of chords that resemble French sixths (mm. 20–21) and a momentary toni-cization of the Neapolitan key, F major (foreshadowed in the introduc-tion). The diminished seventh of m. 24 leads not to the expected dominant seventh in E major but to its tonic six-four, which disappears as the tempo quickens to *Lebhaft*; the dominant seventh finally arrives in m. 30 and leads to a twofold repetition of the initial melody and harmony. In the quiet but triumphant conclusion (Ex. 4.6c), three more appearances of the aug-mented sixth form part of the prolongation of the final tonic.

Carl Candidus, an often-criticized poet, provided the text for the pow-erful, unhappy "Schwermut" (Op. 58, No. 5) and several other excellent songs (the best known of which is "Alte Liebe," Op. 72, No. 1). The mood and the piano introduction are reminiscent of Schubert's "Rast," while a Wolfian key change on the word *gedenkensatt*—a common-tone shift be-tween third-related minor keys (E♭ minor and B minor)—is unique in Brahms's songs, although such shifts between major keys are a normal part of his style. The song is built on a circle of descending major thirds, E♭ minor to B minor to G minor to E♭ major; in the final key, death is anticipated as a release from suffering. On the other hand, "Auf dem See" (Op. 59, No. 2), on a poem by Carl Simrock, presents a mood of cheerful tranquility, enlivened by hemiolas that ruffle the smooth waters a trifle. This opus demonstrates the range of Brahms's choice of poets for lied texts. Single poems by Goethe, Mörike, Simrock, and Daumer—whose coy "Eine gute, gute Nacht" (Op. 59, No. 6) is set to music that in several re-spects resembles Schumann's "Im wunderschönen Monat Mai"—are joined by four poems by his north-German compatriot Klaus Groth, whose poetry often evoked a nostalgic mood in Brahms. Although "Dein blaues Auge" (Op. 59, No. 8) is more often performed, the paired songs "Regen-lied" and its shorter and better echo "Nachklang," Op. 59, Nos. 3 and 4, are well known because of their reappearance in Brahms's G-Major Violin Sonata Op. 78.

One of Brahms's best Lemcke settings is another nostalgic song, "Im Garten am Seegestade" (Op. 70, No. 1). Here, sounds heard in a seaside garden—trees, waves, and melancholy bird calls— combine to produce music "like a song of lost love and eternal longing." Bird song appears again in the setting of Candidus's "Lerchengesang" (Op. 70, No. 2), whose first line generates the languid mood and rhythm of the vocal part. The

EXAMPLE 4.6.

(a) Op. 57, No. 8, mm. 1–5

(b) Op. 57, No. 8, mm. 20–27

(*continued*)

EXAMPLE 4.6. (*continued*)

(c) Op. 57, No. 8, mm. 63–70

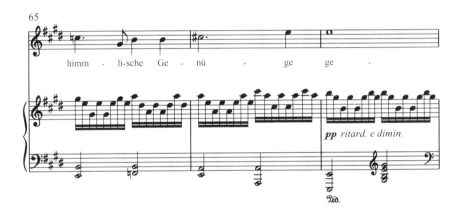

piano begins (Ex. 4.7) over a tonic pedal with a high, descending melody interrupted by rests; each accented treble pitch is an appoggiatura or dissonant passing tone belonging to the previous chord. The voice echoes the descending melody, but its triplets come from the rhythm of the word *ätherische.*

Brahms's only setting of a poem by Theodor Storm is "Über die Heide" (Op. 86, No. 4, 1882), a short, densely constructed song based on a stepwise three-note motive; it is dramatic without overstatement—a far cry from the kind of setting Brahms might have written thirty years earlier. Another song of lost youth is the powerful "Mit vierzig Jahren" (Op. 94, No. 1), composed just before Brahms's fiftieth birthday and one of his few settings of a text by Rückert, in which a man at forty looks back at his youth, then presses toward his final destination—represented, as so often in Brahms, by a turn to the parallel major. In the progressively varied strophic setting, the first two syllables of the first and third lines of each of the three four-line stanzas are set to the falling fifth F♯ to B, harmonized differently each time.[13] The most striking harmonization occurs at the re-

EXAMPLE 4.7. Op. 70, No. 2, mm. 1–12

(*continued*)

EXAMPLE 4.7. (*continued*)

turn to the tonic B minor, at the beginning of the third stanza (Ex. 4.8): a modulation to D minor during the second stanza, confirmed in a passage of unharmonized octaves (mm. 23–25), is reversed when B♭ is enharmonically changed to A♯, the third of the dominant of the original key.

Brahms's last two Daumer settings are "Schön war, das ich dir weihte" (Op. 95, No. 7) and the well-known "Wir wandelten" (Op. 96, No. 2, the only non-Heine text in this opus, which includes "Der Tod, das ist die kühle Nacht," Op. 96, No. 1). The text of the underrated Op. 95, No. 7 is a single six-line stanza in irregular meter, with the last line longer than the others. Gerber (1932, 41) calls the form a *Reprisenbar*: lines 1–2 and lines 3–4 are set to the same music, which is heard again, partially reharmonized, when line 6 is repeated at the end of the song. A sense of urgency and imbalance results from persistent left-hand syncopation, augmented- and diminished-fourth leaps in the vocal line, and musical as well as textual enjambments.

The last songs Brahms published before the gap that preceded the *Vier ernste Gesänge* (he was occupied with the *Deutsche Volkslieder* during some of this time) are the three sets Opp. 105, 106, and 107, which appeared in October 1888. Op. 105, for low voice, includes "Immer leiser

EXAMPLE 4.8. Op. 94, No. 1, mm. 21–29

wird mein Schlummer" (No. 2), one of the most frequently performed of Brahms's songs and the most often analyzed after "Die Mainacht" (Op. 43, No. 2, whose many analyses have been prompted by Brahms's use of its first phrase as the subject of his "seed-corn" analogy). The text, his only setting of a poem by Hermann Lingg, was recommended by Eduard Hanslick (Kalbeck 1912–21, 4: 136); its two stanzas receive what might be described as a transformed strophic setting. The series of second-inversion triads underlying the rapid key changes at the end of each strophe drew the wrath of Elisabeth von Herzogenberg, who complained shortly after the song was composed, "You surely never wrote anything of the kind before? I know of no other passages to equal it for harshness in the whole of your music, and flatter myself you will find some other means of expressing the passionate yearning of the poem at that point" (Brahms 1909, 291). She remained unreconciled when the song was published two years later in 1888 (Brahms 1909, 358), the same year that Brahms told Jenner to "underline every six-four chord and consider carefully whether it is in the right place" (Jenner 1905, 37). In the first stanza (Ex. 4.9a) the bass descends by step, from a root-position E-major chord (relative major of the tonic, C♯ minor) to D (bass of a G-major six-four) and C (F-major six-four); the voice continues the sequence, but the accompaniment interrupts it, moving not to B♭ (V of E♭ major) but to B♮ as bass of an E-minor six-four chord that resolves to a dominant seventh in that key. The end of the second stanza begins in the same way (Ex. 4.9b, p. 148), but this time the six-four chords remain unresolved (compare m. 44 to m. 17); the voice and the bass move upward through a circle of minor thirds (G major, B♭ major), and the climax of the song comes with fulfillment of the sequence: the voice's highest pitch, initially harmonized by an augmented triad (m. 46), now in D♭ major, the parallel major of the original tonic.

Postlude: The *Vier ernste Gesänge* Op. 121

The texts of the *Four Serious Songs* are fruits of Brahms's lifelong study of the Lutheran Bible. He was proud of his accomplishment in setting them, telling Heuberger, "You know, prose is difficult to set to music," and showing him where the musical setting had been particularly difficult, but then going on in a contradictory vein, "Isn't it good to speak and to sing?— really obvious? One could hardly compose more simply!" (Heuberger 1971, 104–5).

At the beginning of the cycle, death appears bleak and terrible, the outcome of a pointless existence. It is depicted musically in the dragging, stepwise melody that opens the first song; similar melodies appear in several of Brahms's choral works (the most frequently cited is the second movement of *Ein deutsches Requiem*) and in "Nicht mehr zu dir zu gehen" (Op. 32, No. 2), a song, also in D minor, about hopeless love (see Ex. 4.4,

EXAMPLE 4.9. Op. 105, No. 2

(a) mm. 14–22

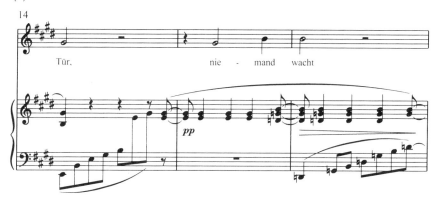

(*continued*)

EXAMPLE 4.9. (*continued*)

(b) mm. 41–47

mm. 1 and 9–10 [bass]). The second song conveys the dreariness of its text through descending arpeggios formed from unharmonized octaves like those heard in "Mit vierzig Jahren" (Op. 94, No. 1).[14] However, in the *Vier ernste Gesänge,* as in Op. 94, No. 1 and a number of other songs (for example, "Schwermut," Op. 58, No. 5 and "Auf dem Kirchhofe," Op. 105, No. 4), death is ultimately a haven for the weary. The third song in the cycle ends in the parallel major of its original minor key, and the message of comfort is confirmed in the triumphant concluding song.

These songs, the last works Brahms published, present a synthesis of ideas that had preoccupied him for decades in lieder and choral music, much as the *Deutsche Volkslieder* sum up his devotion to folk music; they demonstrate his conviction that the principles of life and art are unaltered by time and even by death. As he wrote to Clara Schumann in August 1894 (Schumann and Brahms 1927), pointing out to her that the last of the *Volkslieder* was a setting of a song he had quoted in his Piano Sonata Op. 1, "It ought to represent the snake that bites its own tail, thus saying symbolically: the tale is told, the circle closed."

Notes

1. See McCorkle (1984) for opus numbers, dates and details of composition and publication, poets and text sources, information on manuscripts and editions, and references.
2. Included in this number are the four songs in Op. 84, which can be sung as duets, and the two in Op. 91, for alto, viola, and piano. Of the vocal quartets, all but twelve belong to the sets of *Liebeslieder-* and *Neue Liebeslieder-Walzer* or the *Zigeunerlieder.* Brahms also arranged eight of the *Zigeunerlieder* for solo voice. The last seven songs of WoO 33, not included in the total, are for *Vorsänger* and chorus.
3. Fellinger (1990) summarizes the evidence and discusses the implications of Brahms's collective titles: *Lieder, Gesänge, Romanzen,* and *Gedichte.*
4. The correspondence with Clara Schumann (Schumann and Brahms 1927) is cited by date because the English edition does not include all letters found in the German edition. See Bozarth 1978, 73–78, for an assessment of Brahms's state of mind at this time.
5. Musgrave 1983. The original versions of the texts of all the vocal works of Brahms were collected by Gustav Ophüls at Brahms's suggestion and first published in 1898.
6. In an oft-cited passage from the memoirs of George Henschel (1907, 45), Brahms is quoted as saying that Schubert's Suleika songs are "the only instance where the power and beauty of Goethe's words have been enhanced by the music." Max Kalbeck (1912–21, 3: 87) also quotes Henschel's memoirs; his version of the same passage narrows the reference to the last stanza of the song "Was bedeutet die Bewegung?"
7. Braus (1992, 158) cites information that Daumer did not know Persian and that his Hafis "translations" were based on authentic translations by Platen and Rückert. Whether his other translations come from German sources or are his inventions remains unanswered.
8. The best-known choral setting is "In stiller Nacht," the melody of which has been attributed to Brahms, although in fact he found both text and tune in an unpublished collection by Friedrich Wilhelm Arnold (see McCorkle 1984, 552).
9. Many writers have linked Brahms's use of such octaves, particularly when they outline falling thirds, with the idea of death. This early example supports that "tonal analogue" (Sams's phrase), since on both appearances it immediately follows a description of the probable fate of the innocent. A much better-known song that provides an example is "Feldeinsamkeit" (Op. 86, No. 2).
10. The "linkage technique" defined by Schenker is described by Frisch (1984, 15–16). It may be significant that in stanza 4 the half step sets the word *Tod.*
11. This is an unusual maneuver for Brahms; in most cases his changes of key can be accounted for in functional terms or as common-tone modulations. See also Op. 3, No. 4.
12. Schumann had used the same harmonic figure in the Goethe song "Heiß mich nicht reden" (Op. 98a, No. 5) and the first movement of the Piano Trio Op. 110.
13. Friedlaender (1928, 157) refers to "the six times repeated but always differently harmonized fifth," saying "it is as though Brahms . . . wished to take farewell of

his own youth, expressing his resignation in the notes A–D." He means the pun on "Ade"—but he refers to the transposed version of the song for high voice, in D minor.

14. Daniel Beller-McKenna (1994) argues that the first two songs of Op. 121 represent Brahms's reaction to the pessimistic philosophy of Schopenhauer, that the surprising change in key near the end of the second song, at the point of the text's "darkest utterance," marks "a pivotal moment in the cycle," and that the final two songs show Brahms's ultimate resolution in favor of an earlier Romantic ideal of death.

Bibliography

Atlas, Raphael. "Text and Musical Gesture in Brahms's Vocal Duets and Quartets with Piano." *Journal of Musicology* 10 (1992): 231–60.

Bell, A. Craig. *The Lieder of Brahms.* Darley, Yorkshire, England, 1979.

Beller-McKenna, Daniel. "Johannes Brahms's Later Settings of Biblical Texts, 1877–1896." Ph.D. dissertation, Harvard University, 1994.

Bozarth, George S. "The *Lieder* of Johannes Brahms—1868–1871: Studies in Chronology and Compositional Process." Ph.D. dissertation, Princeton University, 1978.

————. Introduction to *Johannes Brahms: Three Lieder on Poems by Adolf Friedrich von Schack: A Facsimile of the Autograph Manuscripts.* Washington, 1983. [Bozarth 1983a]

————. "Synthesizing Word and Tone: Brahms's Setting of Hebbel's 'Vorüber.'" In Pascall (1983), 77–98. [Bozarth 1983b]

————, ed. *Brahms Studies: Analytical and Historial Perspectives.* Oxford, 1990.

Johannes Brahms: The Herzogenberg Correspondence. Ed. Max Kalbeck. Trans. Hannah Bryant. New York, 1909. Reprint, with introduction by Walter Frisch, New York, 1987.

————. *Sämtliche Werke.* Ed. Eusebius Mandyczewski. Vols. 23–26. Leipzig, [1926]. Reprint. New York, 1979–80.

Braus, Ira, "Textual Rhetoric and Harmonic Anomaly in Selected Lieder of Johannes Brahms." Ph.D. dissertation, Harvard University, 1988.

————. " '*Skeptische Beweglichkeit*': Die Rhetorik von Wort und Ton in *So stehn wir, ich und meine Weide* op. 32/8." In Jost (1992a, 156–72).

Daverio, John. "Brahms's *Magelone Romanzen* and the Romantic Imperative." *Journal of Musicology* 7 (1989): 343–65.

Draheim, Joachim. "Die Welt der Antike in den Liedern von Johannes Brahms." In Jost (1992a, 47–64).

Fellinger, Imogen. "Cyclic Tendencies in Brahms's Song Collections." In Bozarth (1990, 379–88).

Finscher, Ludwig. "Songs for ensembles of solo voices with piano." Liner note for *Johannes Brahms Vokal-Ensembles* 9–10. Ed. Christiane Jacobsen. Trans. Mary Whittall. Polydor International/Deutsche Grammophon. German version reprinted in *Johannes Brahms: Leben und Werk,* 153–54. Wiesbaden, 1983. [Finscher 1983a]

————. "Songs for Solo Voice and Piano." Liner note for *Johannes Brahms: Lieder.* Trans. Mary Whittall. Deutsche Grammophon (2740 279) (1983). German version reprinted in *Johannes Brahms: Leben und Werk,* 139–43. Wiesbaden, 1983. [Finscher 1983b]

———. "Brahms's Early Songs: Poetry Versus Music." In Bozarth (1990, 331–44).

Friedlaender, Max. *Brahms' Lieder: An Introduction to the Songs for One and Two Voices.* Trans. C. Leonard Leese. London, 1928. Reprint. New York, 1976.

Frisch, Walter. *Brahms and the Principle of Developing Variation.* Berkeley, 1984.

Gerber, Rudolf. "Formprobleme im Brahmsschen Lied." *Jahrbuch der Musikbibliothek Peters* 39 (1932): 23–42.

Goldberg, Clemens. "Vergänglichkeit als ästhetische Kategorie und Erlebnis in Liedern von Johannes Brahms." In Jost (1992a, 190–211).

Harrison, Max. *The Lieder of Brahms.* New York, 1972.

Helms, Siegmund. "Die Melodiebildung in den Liedern von Johannes Brahms und ihr Verhältnis zu Volksliedern und volkstümlichen Weisen." Ph. D. dissertation, Freie Universität, Berlin, 1967.

Henschel, George. *Personal Recollections of Johannes Brahms.* Boston, 1907.

Heuberger, Richard. *Erinnerungen an Johannes Brahms: Tagebuchnotizen aus den Jahren 1875 bis 1897.* Ed. Kurt Hofmann. Tutzing, 1971.

Horne, William. "Brahms' Heine-Lieder." In Jost (1992a, 93–115).

Jacobsen, Christiane. *Das Verhältnis von Sprache und Musik im Liedern von Johannes Brahms, dargestellt an Parallelvertonungen.* Hamburg, 1975.

Jenner, Gustav. *Johannes Brahms als Mensch, Lehrer und Künstler.* Marburg, 1905. Portions translated by Susan Gillespie in *Brahms and His World,* ed. Walter Frisch, 185–204. Princeton, 1990.

Jost, Peter, ed. *Brahms als Liedkomponist: Studien zum Verhältnis von Text und Vertonung.* Stuttgart, 1992. [Jost 1992a]

———. "Brahms und das deutsche Lied des 19. Jahrhunderts." In Jost (1992a, 9–37). [Jost 1992b]

Kalbeck, Max. *Johannes Brahms.* 4 vols. Rev. ed. Berlin, 1912–21. Reprint. Tutzing, 1976.

Krones, Hartmut. "Der Einfluß Franz Schuberts auf das Liedschaffen von Johannes Brahms." In *Brahms-Kongress Wien 1983,* ed. Susanne Antonicek and Otto Biba, 309–24. Tutzing, 1988.

MacDonald, Malcolm. *Brahms.* London, 1990.

Mahlert, Ulrich. "Die Hölty-Vertonungen von Brahms im Kontext der jeweiligen Liederhefte." In Jost (1992a, 65–92).

McCorkle, Margit L. *Johannes Brahms: Thematisches-Bibliographisches Werkverzeichnis.* Munich, 1984.

Musgrave, Michael. *"Frei aber Froh:* A Reconsideration." *19th-Century Music* 3 (1979–80): 251–58.

———. "The Cultural World of Brahms." In Pascall (1983, 1–26).

———. *The Music of Brahms.* London, 1985.

Ophüls, Gustav. *Brahms-Texte: Sämtliche von Johannes Brahms vertonten und bearbeiteten Texte.* Berlin, 1898. Reprint, ed. Kristian Wachinger, Ebenhausen bei München, 1983.

Pascall, Robert, ed. *Brahms: Biographical, Documentary, and Analytical Studies.* Cambridge, 1983.

Pisk, Paul. "Dreams of Death and Life: A Study of Two Songs by Johannes Brahms." In *Festival Essays for Pauline Alderman,* ed. Burton L. Karson, 227–34. Provo, UT, 1976.

Platt, Heather. "Text-Music Relationships in Lieder of Johannes Brahms." Ph.D. dissertation, City University of New York, 1992.

Quigley, Thomas. *Johannes Brahms: An Annotated Bibliography of the Literature through 1982.* Metuchen NJ, 1990.

Sams, Eric. *Brahms Songs.* London. 1972.

Schmidt, Christian Martin. "Überlegungen zur Liedanalyse bei Brahms' 'Die Mainacht' Op. 43/2." In *Brahms-Analysen: Referate der Kieler Tagung 1983,* ed. Friedhelm Krummacher and Heinrich W. Schwab, 47–59. Kassel, 1984.

Schumann, Clara, and Johannes Brahms. *Clara Schumann–Johannes Brahms: Briefe aus den Jahren 1853–1896.* Ed. Berthold Litzmann. Leipzig, 1927. Abridged translation by Grace E. Hadow as *The Letters of Clara Schumann and Johannes Brahms, 1853–1896.* New York, 1927. Reprint. New York, 1973.

Schwab, Heinrich W. "Brahms' Kompositionen für zwei Singstimmen mit Pianofortebegleitung." In *Brahms-Analysen: Referate der Kieler Tagung 1983,* ed. Friedhelm Krummacher and Heinrich W. Schwab, 60–80. Kassel, 1984.

Sick, Thomas. "*Unsere Liebe muß ewig bestehn!*" In Jost (1992a, 173–89).

Stark, Lucien. *A Guide to the Solo Songs of Johannes Brahms.* Bloomington, IN, 1995.

Stein, Jack. *Poem and Music in the German Lied from Gluck to Hugo Wolf.* Cambridge, MA, 1971.

CHAPTER FIVE

Crosscurrents in Song: Five Distinctive Voices

Jürgen Thym

The historiography of the German lied has been aptly described (Marx-Weber 1977, 177) as a hike through the high-peak area of a mountain landscape where the trail along the ridge leads from one glorious peak to the next. The present volume is no exception. Its organization confirms the ascent of Schubert, Schumann, Brahms, Wolf, and, to a lesser extent, Mahler and Strauss to the Parnassus of lied composers. To stand on the mountaintops with these canonical figures—whose long reception history sustains critical discourse of considerable sophistication—engenders a feeling of elation and offers breathtaking perspectives on the terrain below. But ravines and trees often obscure this broader view, and the explorer of these nether regions cannot always rely on trails. Much bushwhacking is needed to reach a clearing or an intermediate elevation where orientation is possible.

The forces unleashed by Schubert and others near the beginning of the nineteenth century resulted in a deluge of song publications in the following decades, flooding the market with repertory suited for performance in the homes of the middle class. Many amateur composers entered the field, including some of noble birth, and some gained the sincere respect of their professional colleagues for an inspired moment or two. That so many composers, some with little training, turned out competent songs was the natural result of the song as then conceived. The aesthetic requirements of the genre during the Goethe era—simplicity, singability, popularity (Schwab 1965)—were repeatedly invoked throughout the century as corrective norms whenever centrifugal forces seemed to detract the lied from what was regarded as its proper course (as Brahms was to do in a letter to Clara Schumann of 1860, cited in Wiora 1971, 15). In addition, a preexistent text provided a frame on various structural levels as well as expressive ideas, both general and specific, for song composers, many of whom would have had trouble coping with larger or freer forms of instrumental music. Thus the lied lent itself to mass production.

This discussion cannot do justice to the many noncanonic composers of the lied. But searching for hidden treasures among those musicians can unearth a whole host of little masterpieces, as several anthologies of lieder of lesser-known composers, focused on individual poets (Friedländer 1896–1916, Finck 1903, Moser 1957, Komma 1967, Thym 1983, Smeed 1992, and Green forthcoming) or on music by women (Briscoe 1987), have shown. Songs by composers well known for genres other than the lied can also prove rewarding. Wagner's *Wesendonck-Lieder,* usually relegated to the status of compositional exercises preparing the musical idiom of *Tristan,* and Mendelssohn's setting of the Goethe sonnet "Die Liebende schreibt," perhaps the composer's most adventurous statement among his lieder, stand up well to the settings of the poem by Schubert and Brahms. In Clara Schumann's "Liebst du um Schönheit" (Rückert), the seamless interweaving of voice and piano makes the setting one of the true gems of the lied literature. But few know Zelter's Goethe song "Um Mitternacht," a nostalgic evocation of childhood memories composed within the stylistic confines of the Second Berlin Lieder School, or Meyerbeer's "Sie und ich," which reveals an intimacy and subtlety entirely appropriate to the Rückert text but unexpected from a master of grand opera. And who has heard, or even heard of, Curschmann's or Jensen's "Frülingsnacht" (Eichendorff) or Otto Scherzer's "Ein Stündlein wohl vor Tag" (Mörike). Similarly forgotten are the delightfully witty Heine settings by Vesque von Püttlingen, which prove, if proof were needed, that irony can be rendered in music. The list of forgotten masterworks could easily be extended.

Rather than tramp through low-lying and disorienting terrain, I have chosen to explore some less-elevated peaks: five artists not generally admitted to the canon of lied composers. Their work, often first-rate, offers interesting perspectives that differ from the views gained from the highest mountaintops. The first, Carl Loewe, cultivated more than any other lied composer the art of the narrative ballad. Fanny Hensel, after more than a century of neglect by scholars and performers, seems to emerge as perhaps the most important composer of a Third Berlin Lieder School; she is also representative of other neglected women composers of the nineteenth century, including two other prolific song composers: Louise Reichardt and Josephine Lang. Franz Liszt, thanks in part to his international experience as a keyboard performer, opened the rather insular and provincial genre of the lied to cosmopolitan influences as did no composer before him. Robert Franz pursued a decidedly retrospective trend, yet maintained considerable artistry. Finally, Peter Cornelius, a poet-composer like Wagner, carved out a position of his own as a lied composer during a period of great controversy about the direction of musical composition (much of it around Richard Wagner). In the following portraits I have tried to interweave genre history, cultural and political history and biography with discussions of these composers' individual contributions. This approach permits a view from a path leading to the "high peaks" discussed elsewhere in this book.

The Storyteller: Carl Loewe (1796–1869)

Historians have been consistent in their ambivalence toward the music of Carl Loewe. Already during his life, he was both praised by Vesque von Püttlingen as "the North German Schubert" (Loewe 1870, 357) and marginalized by Robert Schumann as the cultivator of a remote musical island with little wider influence (quoted in Althouse 1971, 1). The comparison with Schubert might be dismissed as a polite toast, like flattery of the visiting artist at a post-recital reception in Vienna in 1844, but, in more than one way, it rings true. The two composers were born just one year apart into abject poverty, and they burst onto the musical scene at almost the same time, each with a remarkably mature setting of Goethe's ballad "Erlkönig" later published as each composer's Op. 1. Both men, too, later acknowledged their indebtedness to the ballads of Zumsteeg in finding their voices. But whereas Schubert grew from there, successfully conquering other vocal and instrumental genres, Loewe—despite respectable attempts at writing operas and oratorios—was never able to shed the label "ballad composer."

Loewe was marginalized in another way: having received a fine musical education in Halle with Daniel Gottlob Türk, author of a notable *Clavierschule*—Reichardt, who spent his declining years nearby, must also be considered a mentor—Loewe accepted in 1820 the position of civic music director in Stettin, the capital of Pomerania near the Baltic Sea, notorious in the nineteenth century as a cultural backwater. Loewe stayed in Stettin for more than forty-five years, teaching music and other subjects at the civic high school on weekdays and providing organ and choral music for the main local church on Sundays. He contributed significantly to improving musical life in that region through concerts and music festivals. (Loewe was instrumental in the revival of the oratorio in the early nineteenth century; see Stanley 1987, 121–49.) But he was several days by coach removed from Germany's major musical centers, such as Dresden and Leipzig, and this distance ultimately had an adverse effect on him. Loewe seems to have been perfectly happy with his life and never seriously considered a change (Loewe 1870, 100); only occasionally did nostalgia for the cultivated ambience of his native Saxony or daydreams of a career different from that of a schoolmaster (Loewe 1870, 187 and 259) enter his letters. At heart he remained a provincial, largely content with his small-town surroundings and domestic existence.

Loewe nevertheless attempted to overcome the limitations imposed by his occupation in Stettin. A highly educated humanist and a gifted conversationalist and raconteur (also evidenced by his autobiography) and blessed with considerable social grace and an amiable character, Loewe early developed a network of friends and acquaintances, mostly musicians and publishers, who supported his endeavors as composer and performer. Especially in the 1830s and 1840s, he left Stettin during summer vacations to conduct his oratorios and, more frequently, to perform his ballads, accompanying himself at the piano, in such cities as Vienna, Mainz, Cologne, Leipzig, Dresden, and Weimar. Loewe had a fine tenor voice and considerable pianistic skills. His one-man shows attracted educated citizens of social prominence (the *Bildungsbürgertum*) as well as members of the aristocracy. Prussia's crown prince, who later became King Friedrich Wilhelm IV, was a Loewe fan; at the end of his career as touring artist, Loewe also sang for Queen Victoria and Prince Albert in London. His recitals bore little resemblance to the concerts of keyboard lions then dazzling mass audiences all over Europe; they were intimate affairs, directed to audiences that numbered between one and two hundred at most (see Althouse 1971, 48). Although most of Loewe's ballad recitals were highly satisfactory for him personally and artistically, they could not provide the public acclaim that usually resulted from the performance of larger works such as symphonies and operas.

Loewe faced the same problems associated with small musical genres as did other lied composers in the first half of the century, including Schubert. The lied, perhaps more than any other musical genre, is representative of the Biedermeier period, an era of complacency, enforced by police state methods, that began with the Vienna Congress of 1815 and ended abruptly in the revolutionary year of 1848. During these years the bourgeois class, after the great expenditure of political and military energy of the Napoleonic wars, turned inward to escape into cultural niches removed from the politics of the time. One such niche was the performance of lieder in the parlors and drawing rooms of the middle and upper classes: Loewe's political vita as well as his art are representative of this broader trend.

While the Napoleonic wars and the uprising of the German people in 1813 released pent-up feelings of nationalism and the desire for democratic political institutions, Loewe remained bound to the status quo. Royal intervention had seen to it that he got a good musical education: Napoleon's brother Jérôme during his brief reign as King of Westphalia had provided a stipend for the talented youngster; at several later junctures, too, Loewe's career was furthered by his connections with royal acquaintances and the aristocracy. Throughout his life he was a monarchist

(Loewe 1870, 98–100), glorifying in many historical ballads the magnanimity of crowned heads of all ages, including the then still-ruling Habsburg and Hohenzollern dynasties (see the works in Loewe 1898–1904, Vols. 4–5). Although he set works by a number of poets associated with the *Junges Deutschland* literary movement, such as Heine, Anastasius Grün (Alexander Graf von Auersberg), and Freiligrath, all of whom opposed the police-state methods of the Metternich era, the poems he selected were usually free of political undertones; the anti-slavery message of Freiligrath's "Mohrenfürst auf der Messe" was sufficiently removed from German political concerns to be appropriated as a human interest story. Although the sounds of folksongs, Prussian marches, chorales, and even plainchant melodies are heard occasionally in Loewe's music, he never—unlike Schumann and Wagner—quoted the "Marseillaise." (After Loewe visited Freiligrath in London in 1847, he characteristically blamed Freiligrath's wife for the exiled poet's radical political views. See Loewe 1870, 430.)

Loewe's total output as a composer of songs and ballads exceeds that of Schubert. Seventeen volumes edited by Max Runze around the turn of the century contain more than 550 compositions, approximately 350 of which are songs; the remaining 200 are based on narrative poetry and thus are ballads of various types. But in length, not to mention significance, the narrative settings outweigh the songs two to one: although about eleven of the seventeen volumes in the *Gesamtausgabe* are ballads, only six contain settings of a lyrical nature. Loewe set a wide variety of poets (see the list in Althouse 1971, 286–90): Goethe, whom Loewe visited in Weimar in 1820, is represented by fifty-one settings, half of them ballads; Rückert by twenty-five; Uhland by eighteen; Chamisso by ten, including the nine songs of the *Frauenliebe* cycle; Heine by nine; and Herder by seven. More surprising are the names represented by only a few settings or missing altogether, such as Wilhelm Müller, Hoffmann von Fallersleben, Eichendorff, and Mörike—poets who figure prominently in song settings in the first half of the century. It seems that narrative poetry was less frequently cultivated by Romantic poets—Uhland being the exception—than by an earlier generation of poets who had received the impulse from Herder's ballad revival around 1770. Perhaps for this reason, Loewe turned to poets of lesser significance, such as Alexis, Freiligrath, Grün, and Vogl; among them were versifiers from his circle of friends in Stettin and other cities, including Giesebrecht—who also provided the librettos for some of Loewe's oratorios—Kugler, and Telschow.

Loewe's Op. 1, which, besides Goethe's "Erlkönig," contains settings of Herder's translation of the Scottish ballad "Edward" and Uhland's "Der Wirtin Töchterlein," is a surprisingly mature work. Without much preparation and experimentation, Loewe reveals himself here as a master of the form, overcoming the limitations of his predecessors in the art of ballad composition: the strophic simplicity of composers associated with Goethe in Weimar (Corona Schröter, Reichardt), on the one hand (see Friedländer 1896), and on the other the richly illustrative through-compositions of Zumsteeg and others, who set lengthy ballads in cantatalike sequences of recitatives and arias, often without a compelling overall structure. (See A. B. Marx's review of Loewe's Op. 1 in Althouse 1971, 150–61.) Loewe charted a middle course between the "Weimar impoverishment and the splurging of storm-and-stress illustrators" (Moser 1958, 537). He always maintained a strophic design or, at least, composed against the background of the stanzaic organization of the poems. But he juxtaposed contrasting materials in voice and piano in accordance with the protagonists or the situations presented in the ballad texts.

Loewe's setting of Herder's "Edward" is a case in point. The seven stanzas of the text, each consisting of eight lines, are grouped four-by-four, in the form of a dialogue between mother and son. They describe two large developmental spans, each concluding with a wild emotional outburst: at the admission of patricide (stanza 3) and at the accusation of maternal coconspiracy in the murder (stanza 7). Whereas the first such span, in E♭ minor, juxtaposes the voices of mother and son with different musical material (most obvious in the contrast between $\frac{6}{8}$ and $\frac{2}{4}$ meters, the second—taking both meter ($\frac{4}{4}$) and key (G minor) from the son's confession in stanza 3—unifies the continuing dialogue through a descending scalar motive. This motive is modified at important structural junctures, appearing in the right hand of the piano for the mother's questions and in the left for the son's responses. Loewe's materials are flexible enough to underscore differences and parallelisms of the text, yet they also account for the emotional intensification that progresses relentlessly from beginning to end: the ballad returns for the concluding climax to E♭ minor, the key that unifies most of the first section. The conciseness of the setting is underscored by the absence of any piano solos; the piano's sole function is to present sharply delineated accompanying materials, in order to portray the dialogue between the two protagonists.

Loewe's "Erlkönig" is similarly conceived from the perspective of dramatizing the different voices of the ballad's protagonists (father, son, and Erlking) and shaping the dialogue into a coherent whole through motives in the piano part, appropriately suggesting storm and galloping horse. (See Dürr 1984, 203–18, and Althouse 1971, 145–73, for comparisons of Loewe's and Schubert's "Erlkönig" settings.) The same can be said about "Herr Oluf" (Op. 2, No. 2) of 1821, a variant of the Erlking story, and of the relatively late "Odins Meeresritt" (Op. 118), composed after Loewe had retired as a concertizing artist. Throughout his life Loewe was drawn to ballad texts that introduced their protagonists through direct speech. Indeed, he flattered Goethe at his visit in Weimar by saying that he considered "Erlkönig" the finest of all German ballads because all persons were introduced in the poem in dramatic form; according to Loewe, Goethe concurred (Loewe 1870, 76–77).

In the years following his success with "Edward" and "Erlkönig,"

Loewe combed the literature for poems on other horrific subject matters, often taken from Nordic legends (*Geisterballaden*). It is here that his compositional output can be most clearly linked with contemporary Romantic trends emphasizing the ghostly and supernatural. Another aspect, perhaps equally Romantic in nature, gained prominence over the years: Loewe's turning to poems commemorating and celebrating historical figures, not only from German history—distant ones, such as the medieval emperors, as well as those closer to his time, like Frederick the Great—but also from other countries. Legends of saints, fairy tales, and fables provided further material for musical settings. Indeed, Loewe was an incredibly prolific storyteller who could turn any subject matter into a pretext for a musical setting; during his recitals, he frequently improvised ballads on texts given to him before the concert by members of the audience.

In general, Loewe's ballads are short, sharply delineated settings lasting no more than five minutes. Occasionally they extend into larger structures, several sections being juxtaposed, in the manner of a cantata, as in "Die Heinzelmännchen," Op. 83; "Die Waffenweihe Kaiser Heinrichs IV," Op. 122; and "Archibald Douglas," Op. 128, one of Loewe's last and finest ballads. "Die Gruft der Liebenden," Op. 21, based on a Visigothic legend, amounts to a veritable operatic scene with a duration of over fifteen minutes. Occasionally Loewe gathered his ballads into cyclic structures supported by the narrative thread of the individual poems as well as by key sequence. "Der letzte Ritter," Op. 124—three vignettes from the life of Emperor Maximilian—as well as the three settings of Freiligrath's "Mohrenfürst" poems, Op. 97, and "Karl V," Op. 99, is such a cycle. Opus 99 consists of settings of four poems by three poets, including Platen, on one of the most fascinating early modern rulers, who abdicated his throne after more than thirty years, concluding his life in a monastery. (Ernst Krenek fashioned an opera from this subject matter in the 1930s.)

Even closer to a true ballad cycle is "Gregor auf dem Stein," Op. 38, based on a legend from the *Gesta romanorum*, faintly resembling the Oedipus myth but Christian in its resolution to forgiveness and redemption. (Thomas Mann was attracted to this subject matter in his novels *Doktor Faustus* and *Der Erwählte*.) The legend was cast into five "acts" by Loewe's friend Franz Kugler as follows: (1) Announcement of the Queen, (2) Victory Celebration and Courtship, (3) Dialogue with Shocking Revelations, (4) Gregory's Penitence and Prayer on the Rock Island, and (5) Gregory's Ascent to the Papal Throne and Final Redemption. Loewe designed a symmetrical structure for the cycle. The dialogue between Gregory and his spouse-mother is assigned the central position; the longest and weightiest of the five vignettes, it progresses in cantatalike sections from a conversation juxtaposing C minor and E♭ major (representing Gregory and the Queen, respectively) to a first condemnation, and proceeds then to the gradual acknowledgment not only that Gregory has married his own mother but that he is the offspring of another incestuous relationship, a revelation that leads to a second (and more intense) condemnation in F minor. This central cantata—a latter-day "Edward," so to speak—is preceded by a ballad, again in dialogue form, celebrating victory, courtship, and marriage, in E♭ major, and followed by Gregory's Prayer on the Rock in B♭ major (perhaps the strongest of the five movements). Both settings are haunted by a descending lower-sixth neighbor-note figure. In the second song, the figure is introduced as an ominous symbol for the imaginary presence of a third person, namely Gregory's father, in the otherwise happy courtship processional; it pervades the fourth song as an equally ominous leitmotif of Gregory's guilt. These three internal songs are framed by two ballads in B♭ major, the first with the festive music of heralds announcing the Queen's decision to seek help in times of turmoil and the last with equally festive music of another kind: Gregory has been elected pope in Rome and, under the sounds of a plainchant hymn, absolves his mother from all wordly sins. The modal turns of the *tonus peregrinus* at the end of the setting give the cycle a somewhat open, other-worldly conclusion in G.

Unlike his ballads, Loewe's lieder have come in for considerable criticism. There can be no doubt that he is often overly sentimental ("Die Uhr") or trivial ("Frauenliebe," after Chamisso) and occasionally mediocre ("Tom der Reimer"). The lieder, however, for the most part were written not for himself, the professional ballad performer, but for friends and acquaintances—in short: the amateur. Measuring Loewe's lieder against those of Schubert may not be appropriate; Loewe composed songs in the tradition of the Berlin Lieder School, favoring strophic design and simple accompaniment.

The best of Loewe's lieder can be found among his Goethe settings. The wide-ranging "Meine Ruh' ist hin" ("Gretchen am Spinnrade") of 1822 for alto voice, a song full of passion and longing, holds up quite well next to Schubert's Op. 2. In "Ganymed" of 1836, enthusiastic melismas express the protagonist's emotional rapture at the prospect of union with the Deity. Some numbers from the Heine *Liederkreis* Op. 9 of 1828—one of the earliest attempts at setting a substantial body of Heine's poetry—deserve attention as settings contemporaneous with Schubert's, predating Schumann's settings of that poet by twelve years. Loewe's "Lotusblume," for example, is a gem and withstands comparison with Schumann's setting (for a different opinion, however, see Althouse 1971, 176). The simplicity and conventionality of the setting of stanzas 1 and 2 contrast nicely with the luxuriant abundance—in terms of both harmony and texture—of the last strophe. Provided with colorful harmonies by the piano, the voice delivers the text in broken fragments ("sie blüht—und glüht—und leuchtet . . . sie duftet—und weinet—und zittert") that find their melodic context in the longing melodic phrases of the instrumentalist's right hand. Heine's peculiar poetic mixture of irony and eroticism has found here an appropriate match.

Making Her Voice Heard:
Fanny Hensel (1805–47)

Fanny Mendelssohn Hensel and her music have been the focus of several publications in recent years (Quin 1981, Sirota 1981, Citron 1983, Weissweiler 1985, and F. Hensel 1987); her biography and the inattention her works received both during her life and after her death make a particularly poignant case study of a composer who has been neglected because of her gender. Early on, Fanny displayed the same musical talent as her brother Felix, and both were privileged to receive the best possible education, including first-rate musical training under Friedrich Zelter and Ludwig Berger. Nonetheless, their father Abraham Mendelssohn made it clear to Fanny that music could be only an ornament of her life, not a profession; he admonished her to prepare herself for the duties of a proper *Hausfrau* (S. Hensel 1882, 1: 82 and 84). Her brother continued the patriarchal family tradition by voicing reservations when she considered going public with some of her works in 1837 and, when she finally had the courage to do so in the last year of her life, by sending his "professional blessing" somewhat reluctantly (S. Hensel 1882, 2: 325–26). He did this even though he valued his sister's talent and not infrequently sought her advice in musical matters. There can be no doubt that the lack of encouragement from her family undermined her confidence; unable to gain experience as a composer outside the domestic sphere to which she was confined, she occasionally even questioned whether she had sufficient talent and perseverance to be a composer (Weissweiler 1985, 149–50 and 202–3).

Yet Hensel found support and role models within her family that modified and, to a certain extent, countered its patriarchal tendencies. Her mother Lea (née Salomon), born into a family of considerable wealth and cultural interests, seems to have taken Fanny's side a number of times, encouraging the musical aspirations of her daughter. Lea's aunt, after whom Fanny was named, married into the Viennese aristocracy and, as Fanny Arnstein, became the leader of one of the most celebrated salons during the Vienna Congress, tremendously influential as a philanthropist and patron of the arts (Quin 1981, 32). Closer to home were women relatives from both parents' sides who either headed salons in Berlin and thus became important figures in the cultural life of their community or thwarted patriarchal expectations by going their own way. One of Abraham's sisters, Dorothea Veit, divorced her husband of a prearranged marriage, turned Catholic, and lived with Friedrich Schlegel. Another, Henriette, remained unmarried and became a school principal in Paris. These women, some of them at the forefront of emancipation, provided alternatives to traditional gender roles and, no doubt, were on Fanny Mendelssohn's mind in her quest for a role of her own.

Fanny Mendelssohn acceded to her father's wishes: in 1829 she married the court painter Wilhelm Hensel, and a year later a son was born (named Sebastian); domestic duties now prevailed over artistic aspirations. Fanny found an outlet for her musical talent in the *Sonntagsmusiken*, Sunday musicales that had taken place on a biweekly basis in the Mendelssohn mansion since the 1820s. Originally, these events functioned mainly as a platform for showing off the musical talents of the Mendelssohn children, especially Fanny and Felix, to an invited group of Berlin notables and prominent guests. But after 1831, when Felix left the Mendelssohn household to assume positions outside of Berlin, the *Neue Sonntagsmusiken* assumed a new character under the leadership of Fanny Hensel. On the one hand, the concerts provided her with a private forum to perform on the piano, to conduct small chamber groups of vocalists and instrumentalists, and even to try out some of her own compositions; on the other hand, the Sunday musicales continued the salon tradition that had blossomed in Berlin around the turn of the century, bringing together aristocrats and members of the bourgeois class, men and women, Christians and Jews, under the auspices of tolerance and magnanimity (Hertz 1988). During the 1830s and 1840s, the Mendelssohn household, under the aegis of Fanny Hensel, became a center of cultural life in Berlin, attracting some of the most outstanding scientists and artists of the day, among them Droysen, Humboldt, Heine, Eichendorff, and Liszt, as guests of the Sunday musicales.

The *Neue Sonntagsmusiken* kept Fanny Hensel artistically alive while confined to the domestic sphere. Only after her father's death in 1835 did she gradually free herself from the restraints imposed on her. She performed in public for a charitable cause, and—despite the raised eyebrows of her brother—published two of her songs in an almanac. Most important for her artistic development, however, was a yearlong trip to Italy undertaken with her family in 1839–40, which brought her into contact with other artists, including Charles Gounod, a *Prix de Rome* recipient that year. (There is some reason to believe that it may have been Fanny Hensel who suggested that Gounod compose his infamous "Ave Maria" to the accompaniment of Bach's C-major prelude from part 1 of *The Well-Tempered Clavier*, see Krautwurst 1973, 659.) The beauty of the Italian landscape, the artistically rich environment of Venice, Florence, and Rome, and the support she received from her husband—Wilhelm Hensel was refreshingly unpatriarchal—and like-minded friends made this year the happiest of her life. She returned to Berlin with new energy and increased confidence,in her abilities as an artist (Weissweiler 1985, 204). After a second journey to Italy in 1845 she began to publish her works. Her newfound assertiveness might have led to a successful professional career in music, but her path was cut short by her death in May 1847 during a rehearsal of her brother's *Walpurgisnacht* for a Sunday musicale.

Lieder, the musical genre of the domestic sphere par excellence, are the most numerous part of Fanny Hensel's oeuvre, many having been composed for the Sunday musicales, with Fanny frequently accompanying her sister Rebecca. In the last year of her life, two collections (Opp. 1 and 7) containing six songs each were published in Berlin; two more (Opp. 9 and 10), with six and five songs, respectively, were issued in Leipzig after her death. Two songs came out in almanacs in the late 1830s, and six (one of them a duet) appeared under Felix's name as part of his Opp. 8 and 9 (see table 1 in Citron 1983, 574). Thus the songs published during her life and shortly after her death amount to barely thirty settings for solo voice and piano. This is, however, only the tip of the iceberg. About 180 songs written between 1822 and 1841 (some in multiple versions) are contained in several manuscript volumes (*Sammelbände*) in the Mendelssohn Archive in Berlin (Elvers 1972, 169–74); an additional hundred or so songs are inaccessible in private collections in Germany (Elvers 1975, 215–20, and Citron 1983, 574). Although it is premature to attempt a comprehensive study of Hensel's songs, enough of her work is available to sketch the outlines of her development. The quantity and quality of her work make her an equal to other song composers just below the level of canonization.

Fanny Hensel shared with her brother a familiarity with and deep appreciation of a wide range of literary trends. Some of the most important poets of the second half of the eighteenth and the first half of the nineteenth century are represented (see Citron 1983, 577, for a table of poets). Goethe tops the list with twenty-five settings, followed by Tieck with fourteen, Eichendorff with thirteen, and Uhland with ten; Klopstock, Voss, and Hölty were chosen nearly as frequently as Lenau, Wilhelm Müller, and Heine. Some of these poets were family friends. Goethe, trusting the judgment of his musical mentor Zelter, was touched by Fanny's settings of his poetry and, after granting her an audience in Weimar in 1822, honored her with a poem. Eichendorff, who from 1832 to 1844 worked in Berlin in the Prussian civil service, was a frequent guest at the Sunday musicales; Fanny set his poems especially in the later years of her life. Her reaction to Heine (who likewise attended the musicales in Berlin) was ambivalent; she detested his egocentric and affected behavior but admired his poetic way with words (S. Hensel 1882, 1: 173); his poetry inspired some of her best songs in the 1830s. Among her settings are some composed on English (Byron and the Heine translations by Mary Alexander), French, and Italian texts (Citron 1983, 579).

Because of her sensitivity to literary matters Fanny Hensel, like Schumann and others, knew that appropriating a poem for a musical setting occasionally made it necessary to change the poetic text. Repetition of the last line(s) of a stanza or even the entire poem (if it is brief) serves to support a sense of closure (see "Schwanenlied," Op. 1, No. 1; "Bitte," Op. 7, No. 5; "Bergeslust," Op. 10, No. 5). Sometimes lines in the center of a stanza are restated to gain verbal material for extended middle sections that balance the framing outer sections ("Vorwurf," Op. 10, No. 2; "Im Herbste," Op. 10, No. 4); sometimes the initial line of the poem is restated as a refrain, to function as a formal divider, supporting a rondolike musical structure ("Dein ist mein Herz," Op. 7, No. 6). Lines are sometimes also transposed ("Morgenständchen," Op. 1, No. 5).

In a few cases Fanny Hensel deliberately censored or altered a poem. Eichendorff's lengthy "Durch Feld und Buchenhallen" loses its first three stanzas in "Bergeslust," Op. 10, No. 5; as a result, this *Wanderlied* turns more quickly from its earthbound imagery toward transcendence and the heavenly home. This changes its form without misinterpreting its message. Heine's wit and irony must have struck a chord in Fanny Hensel, whose letters are full of gently humorous observations, but the morbidity and sardonic quality of some of his verse drew a less sympathetic response. The accusatory tone of Heine's "Warum sind denn die Rosen so blass?" is softened considerably in her setting (Op. 1, No. 3) by the substitution of *verwelkter Blütenduft* (fragrance of wilted blossoms) for *hervor ein Leichenduft* (a corpselike smell arises). And in her setting of "Ach die Augen sind es wieder" (in *Sammelband* MA Ms. 45)—a poem about the loss of interest in a former beloved—the last stanza, describing sexual relations in the absence of emotional closeness, is eliminated. Relatively minor but equally telling is Hensel's subtle alteration in "Verlust" ("Und wüssten's die Blumen"), published as her brother Felix's Op. 9, No. 10: by altering *nur eine kennt meinen Schmerz* (only one knows my pain) to *einer,* she changes the poem's persona from male to female, thereby "signing" her work.

Fanny Mendelssohn began writing songs in the style of the Second Berlin Lieder School as represented by Reichardt and her teacher Zelter. Zelter espoused the lied aesthetic of his great contemporary Goethe, for whom simplicity and singability were the essence of song; anything too elaborate, in voice or piano, would overload a basically simple genre. Zelter's deliberate ignorance of Schubert's works was of no little influence on Goethe and certainly had an impact on his two students Fanny and Felix Mendelssohn. Almost without exception, Fanny's songs composed in the 1820s are simple strophic settings with subordinate piano accompaniment. The posthumous Op. 9 collection on texts by eighteenth-century poets constitutes a representative sample of the song style found in the *Sammelbände* from those years. The vocal parts have a certain predictability, relieved occasionally through unusual melodic twists and exuberant melismas, often at the end of songs. The chordal accompaniment is rendered flexible by various types of arpeggios in the right hand; occasionally the piano accompaniment is handled in imaginative ways: the low register for the accompaniment of Klopstock's "Die frühen Gräber" (Op. 9, No. 4) sets the mood for a meditative poem about early death, and the melodic fragments highlighted by hand-crossing in the piano part of "Die Mainacht" may be thought of as a musical response to the image of silvery moonlight being cast over the landscape. The Op. 9 collection also exhibits a fondness for compound meter that Fanny shares with her brother Felix.

As the impact of Zelter's teaching began to wane, other influences made themselves felt. Probably in the late 1820s, Fanny and Felix Mendelssohn became familiar with Schubert songs (Werner 1963, 74 and 84). The encounter resulted in her beginning to shed the restrictions imposed on lied composition by Goethe and his followers, and after 1840 she must have encountered Schumann's lieder, resulting in more elaborate piano parts. Her Heine lieder of the 1830s and her Eichendorff songs, mostly composed after 1840, indeed show a new synthesis as well as, occasionally, an experimental quality.

Published as Op. 1, No. 1, "Schwanenlied" (ed. Citron in Briscoe 1987), perhaps her best known song, is representative of Hensel's lied style in her last decade. The four quatrains of the Heine poem are set to two musical strophes, each encompassing two stanzas; the harmonic disposition of the strophes underscores the stanzaic organization of the poem as well as smaller subdivisions. The setting of stanzas 1 and 3 is quite traditional, exhibiting a four-plus-four-measure phrase structure marked by half and full cadences on the dominant. The music for stanzas 2 and 4 expands to 15 measures through repetition of lines and melismas in the vocal part. The melismas fall appropriately on the words *treiben [damit ihr Spiel]* (carry on [their games]) and *verklungen* (faded away). Harmonic interest is added in these sections through brief chromatic ascents and descents. The accompanying arpeggios of the piano part gain prominence at the conclusion of each musical strophe. Hensel has nicely captured the subdued melancholy of Heine's poem in an elegant, gently moving setting.

"Nachtwanderer" (Op. 7, No. 1, ed. in Thym 1983) moves further in the direction of structural and textural complexity. Based on an Eichendorff poem of two six-line stanzas (rhyming aabccb), the setting shows the composer's casting aside the formal and textural restraints of the Second Berlin Lieder School. The piano is an equal partner, exploring a wide range of textural possibilities, at times doubling the vocal part in the bass line and in the chordal accompaniment, at times alternating melodic statements with the voice, sometimes even offering true countermelodies. In the setting of the second stanza the piano becomes forthrightly descriptive, illustrating the sounds of the night through extensive tremolos. By contracting the prevailing $\frac{9}{8}$ meter to $\frac{6}{8}$ in this section and presenting rhythmic groupings in both voice and piano that suggest $\frac{3}{4}$ rather than $\frac{6}{8}$, Hensel finds a musical correlate for the image of unreality and confusion evoked by the nocturnal sounds. The song is through-composed, preserving certain elements of the stanzaic organization of the poem without resorting to schematic repetitions. At the beginning of the second strophe, the piano, rather than restating its introduction, appropriates the first vocal phrase, thereby forcing the voice to begin with the second phrase superimposed on the countermelody of the piano. This foreshortening of the first stanza's materials in stanza 2 allows Hensel to introduce earlier than before the tremolo that thus pervades so much of the second stanza.

The remainder of this strophe bears little resemblance to the first, apart from the pattern of sequential phrases in alternation during the tremolo.

These few examples show that Hensel had found her voice by the 1840s. Although her impact on the history of the lied was negligible because of her isolation, many of her songs show that she participated in the development of the genre from self-imposed limitations at the beginning of the century toward more complex structures and greater variety of texture. She participated in this evolution perhaps more wholeheartedly than her brother, for whom the lied remained a sideline throughout his career. If we are to accept the idea of a Third Berlin Lieder School (Rosenwald 1930 and Gudewill 1960)—a group that would include the Zelter students Mendelssohn and Bernhard Klein, as well as Ludwig Berger and Friedrich Curschmann—we must insist that the name of Fanny Hensel be included in it. In many ways, she is the most interesting of its lied composers.

Cosmopolitan Infusions: Franz Liszt (1811–86)

When Liszt settled in Weimar in 1848, after many years as a traveling virtuoso, he not only brought his pianistic legacy into order—by teaching and by publishing definitive versions of his hand- and ear-challenging keyboard works—but also tackled in his symphonic poems one of the great issues of nineteenth-century music: the relation between music and literature. No doubt inspired by the philosophy of Hegel, he considered the latter works, as well as Wagner's music dramas and the dramatic works of Berlioz from which both composers drew sustenance, as evidence supporting a grant evolutionary scheme in which music and literature were viewed as drawing ever closer together, eventually to shed their separate identities and merge in a historically necessary synthesis.

There is no evidence that Liszt saw the lied—despite its intrinsic possibilities for uniting literature and music—as participating in this ambitious enterprise. His Schumann essay (Liszt 1855a), published in installments in the *Neue Zeitschrift für Musik* in 1855, focuses on the composer's music criticism and instrumental works and mentions the songs only in passing. His Franz essay, also published in the *Neue Zeitschrift* that year, discusses Franz's position as a lied composer with great sensitivity, but, in deference to the ailing lied composer, politely expresses the hope that Franz will find an outlet for his genius in some more public musical genres (Liszt 1872, 28–29). Reacting to the mass production of lieder in the second half of the century, Hans von Bülow, a member of Liszt's Weimar school is more forthright, suggesting, in an intentionally provocative review of 1860, that the lied may have passed its peak as a musical genre and that further enrichments might not be possible (cited in Youens 1992, 198).

In view of Liszt's inclination toward larger musical forms in his quest for securing music a place in history and society, it is surprising that the lied figured in his oeuvre at all. In fact, the composition of songs was an important facet of Liszt's creativity, although it has been disregarded by all but a few scholars (Raabe 1931, Montu-Berthon 1981, Dömling 1981, and Riethmüller 1991 are the notable exceptions; see also Saffle 1986, 271–72, for a survey of the most recent literature). It sheds light not only on Liszt's development as a composer—especially the numerous revisions to which he subjected his songs—but also on the history of the lied and its varied reception in the nineteenth century.

Liszt's familiarity with the lied preceded his first song compositions. In 1835 he began transcribing Schubert lieder for piano solo, thereby expanding the repertory of his instrument as well as exposing in the concert hall and to an international public a major musical art form that otherwise would have remained in the domestic sphere, limited, by and large, to German-speaking audiences. By the time he abandoned the career of traveling virtuoso, he had "translated" for piano some of the most important songs, not only those of Schubert—including six songs from *Die schöne Müllerin*, twelve from *Winterreise*, and the entire *Schwanengesang*—but also lieder by Robert and Clara Schumann, Mendelssohn, Franz, and Beethoven (including the cycle *An die ferne Geliebte*). With considerable imagination, he incorporated the vocal part in the pianistic textures, sometimes giving it to an inner voice whose notes are played in alternation by the two thumbs, sometimes having it appear in briefly struck peak tones atop turbulent arpeggios. He often modified the strophic form through illustrative devices depicting aspects of the poetic imagery. In our age, which looks askance at such bald derivativeness, Liszt's transcriptions are regarded with some disdain. But there can be no doubt that Liszt's productive encounter with the lied repertory, which resulted in *Lieder ohne Worte* of a distinctly Lisztian type, not only opened up avenues for his own song compositions but also—by the sheer force of Liszt's authority as a performer—contributed to the reception of German lieder across Europe.

The close connection between piano piece and song appears to be typical of Liszt's oeuvre. During the 1840s he published transcriptions of his own songs under the title *Buch der Lieder für Klavier allein* (alluding to Heine's famous collection of poetry). Some works were published nearly simultaneously in two versions, as piano pieces and as songs: for instance, the *Tre sonetti di Petrarca*. The *Liebesträume* for piano stand in a similarly symbiotic relation with some of Liszt's lieder (including the well-known "Liebestraum" No. 3, based on the rather conventionally sentimental song "O lieb, so lang du lieben kannst" after a poem by Freiligrath). It has been suggested that Liszt may have intended "from the very start such dual artistic manifestation" (Dömling 1981).

Liszt's composition of lieder was not accompanied by as much fanfare as his symphonic poems—Raabe speaks of his "peculiarly silent activity" in this domain (Raabe 1931, 2:129)—but, as Dömling (1981, 2) has pointed out, it was also "a peculiarly persistent activity" to which the composer returned throughout his life, suggesting that Liszt felt compelled by an inner need to express himself also in this genre. Over the course of forty years he composed about eighty songs, nearly half during the 1840s, also the decade of his most intense encounter, in the form of piano transcriptions, with the songs of other lied composers. Another third of his song output originated during the Weimar years, between 1848 and 1861, in addition to the many revisions, second versions, and recompositions of earlier settings. Sixteen songs were written in the last fifteen years of his life. Nearly three quarters of Liszt's songs are on texts in his native German (the language spoken in the early part of the nineteenth century in western Hungary, where Liszt was born), with Heine and Goethe topping the list of poets. Fourteen songs are on French poems (many of them by Victor Hugo), the others being on texts in Italian (4), Hungarian (3), and English (1).

Liszt's cosmopolitan temperament manifests itself not only in his settings of poems in languages other than German, but also in his infusing the lied with elements from styles and genres outside of the lied proper. The operatic bel canto of Bellini and Donizetti makes its appearance not only in the lullaby of "Angiolin dal biondo crin" and the amorous bliss of the "Tre sonetti de Petrarca" but also in the serenade "Kling leise, mein Lied" (Nordmann) and the refrain of Goethe's "Mignons Lied" ("Kennst du das Land"). Liszt captured the graceful and elegant tone of the French *romance* not only in his much-admired Hugo setting "Oh! quand je dors," but also in his love songs on German texts: for instance, "Es muss ein Wunderbares sein" (Redwitz), "Wieder möcht ich dir begegnen" (Cornelius), and the afore-mentioned "O lieb, so lang du lieben kannst." These occasionally exhibit a somewhat formulaic musical language that is not always free of traces of nineteenth-century salon music. Liszt's openness to non-German musical cultures allowed him also to incorporate in his setting of Lenau's "Die drei Zigeuner" (The Three Gypsies) elements of Hungarian dance or *verbunkos* music. Liszt also brings to the lied the rich and colorful pianistic textures of his keyboard music, full of pictorialisms and occasionally even bordering on the impressionistic (as in the Heine setting "Im Rhein, im schönen Strome") or containing gestures that mesmerize and dazzle the audience. In short, he invades the parlors of German *Hausmusik* with the styles and genres of different performance settings: the opera house, the elegant salon, and the concert hall. Liszt's cosmopolitan infusions result in lieder that no longer cultivate inwardness of expression but direct their utterances to the outside. As Riethmüller (1991, 185) points out, the theatrical character of Liszt's songs foreshadows the tone of those composed by Richard Strauss half a century later. It is perhaps because of this quality that a number of Liszt's lieder succeed, and are perhaps more compelling, as orchestral songs: for instance, "Loreley," "Mignons Lied," "Die drei Zigeuner," and "Die Vätergruft" (whose orchestral version was Liszt's last composition).

Liszt favored ballad texts that allowed him to display his considerable talents as a musical dramatist. Two of the three songs from Schiller's *Wilhelm Tell* are ballads, "Der Fischerknabe" and "Der Alpenjäger," the latter being a particularly dramatic specimen. Goethe's "Der König von Thule" and Heine's "Loreley" become elaborate dramatic scenes, stripped of their folksong qualities. Even "Mignons Lied" of longing for a distant land develops in Liszt's hands into an operatic aria, concluding with an extrovert coda in which—because of the need for additional verbal material—textual repetitions merge the addresses of the three stanzas ("Vater," "Beschützer," and "Geliebter"—father, protector, and beloved) in one climactic synthetic statement—an interpretation of the poem as questionable as it is psychologically intriguing.

Not all of Liszt's songs have the extrovert character of dramatic settings. Occasionally in the 1840s he succeeded in setting texts of subdued and inward character (for instance, Heine's "Du bist wie eine Blume"). But the ability to set such poems in sharply delineated structures, without false climaxes and dramatic gestural props, seems to have come to him only during his Weimar years. The return to song composition was prompted by Liszt's preparation for the 1860 edition of his lieder, which led to revisions of many of his earlier settings. A comparison of earlier and later versions of his songs, the later sometimes leading to what must be considered a new composition, is instructive for studying Liszt's growth as a song composer (see Mueller 1988). In nearly all cases, the later versions not only have more focused musical structures but also show subtler text-music relations.

The greater compositional sophistication of the Weimar years may have led to a refinement in his approach to text setting, but biographical circumstances can be invoked as well. As he was approaching the fiftieth year of his life, a number of disappointing experiences soured his existence: the failure of his reform work in Weimar, the death of his son, and seemingly endless problems in overcoming obstacles to his marrying the Princess Wittgenstein. An air of resignation hovers over almost all the songs he set or revised during that time: "Es rauschen die Winde" (Rellstab), an agitated lament over love lost; "Lasst mich ruhen" (Hoffmann), a call for solace in nature and reminiscence; "Wanderers Nachtlied" (Goethe), about life's transitoriness; and "Der du von dem Himmel bist" (Goethe), a deeply moving prayer for spiritual peace. Even his 1847 setting of Herwegh's tragic poem in pentameters about death's inexorability, "Ich möchte hingehn" (which Liszt considered his "youthful testament"), occupied him again around 1860. The allusions in that song to the chromatic idiom of Wagner's *Tristan* (composed 1857–59)—extending even to a brief quotation of the Tristan chord—may be considered a creative anticipation; a similar foreshadowing can be found in "Loreley," one of his earliest songs, also from the 1840s (Riethmüller 1991, 191). But the brief quotation, at least, may well have been, as Fischer-Dieskau has suggested

(Klein 1981, 6), a reverential gesture to Liszt's great friend, added in the process of revising the song. (The deathbound, sensual imagery of *Tristan* is not that far removed from Herwegh's hymnic verses.)

In Liszt's last years the process of concentration and reduction continued, giving his lieder at times an austere, even barren appearance. Etreme brevity, avoidance of textual repetition, unresolved dissonances, unaccompanied recitative, unison passages in the piano accompaniment, and even a certain monotony are characteristic of the songs of his later years. These features can be found as early as in the second setting of Goethe's "Wer nie sein Brot mit Tränen ass" (composed around 1860), but they become more prominent in the very last blossoms of Liszt's lyricism, such as "Einst" and "Gebet" (both on poems by Bodenstedt), as well as his 1880 setting of Saar's wonderfully soothing poem of evening and farewell, "Des Tages laute Stimmen schweigen."

Few of Liszt's lieder use strophic structures; "Wieder möcht ich dir begegnen" comes closest to approximating that form. Some songs establish simple rondo forms ("Angiolin," "Das Veilchen"), but striving for simplicity was not a central concern in Liszt's approach to the lied. On the other hand, he was not insensitive to the stanzaic organization of a poem, which he tried to capture through repetitive strategies of various kinds. Each of the three stanzas of "Mignons Lied," for instance, repeats the same sequence of musical materials, parallelling the ternary division of each poetic strophe: (a) elaborate question ("Kennst du das Land," ". . . Haus," ". . . Berg"); (b) question intensified ("Kennst du es wohl?"); and (c) expression of longing ("Dahin, dahin . . ."). "Es rauschen die Winde" pursues a similar strategy in juxtaposing, at least initially, two contrasting musical sections within each of the first two stanzas of the poem.

Rounding off a song by returning to material or a section presented earlier is one of the stock-in-trade devices of lied composers. Liszt occasionally made use of this gambit. When the text did not suggest a recapitulatory effect, he sometimes just repeated one or more poetic stanzas at the end of a musical setting (without doing violence to the poem), as in the serenade "Kling leise, mein Lied." Often, however, Liszt showed considerable ingenuity in finding the right textual phrase for the musical return. Goethe's "Der du von dem Himmel bist"—basically a double quatrain with alternating rhymes—was set by Liszt around 1860 (there is an inferior earlier version) as an ABA structure. The middle recitative section, setting lines 5 and 6, contrasts with the choralelike outer sections. The B section is lengthened to the proportions of the first section through textual repetition of both lines and by the responses in the left hand of the piano to the question of line 6 ("Was soll all der Schmerz und Lust?"), using the vocal melody to "Der du von dem Himmel bist" from the A section and thereby preparing the return. The recapitulation proper does not occur until the setting of line 7 ("Süsser Friede"), which provides the real answer to the problem pondered by the entire poem. Here the piano plays the succession of chords from the beginning of the song, now in augmentation, thereby sustaining the invocation of peace.

"Loreley" is composed entirely from the perspective of the culmination of the poem, that is, the shipwreck described in the first two lines of the sixth and last stanza. Even in this very dynamic and fluent narrative, Liszt establishes a sense of closure by returning to material from the introduction and to the parlando setting of stanza 1 at the dramatic climax, and by recapitulating the "fairy-tale" music of stanza 2 for the textual repetitions of the last two lines of the poem ("Das hat mit ihrem Singen / die Lorelei getan"). This strategy not only enables the lied to return to its initial texture, reminiscent of recitative and arietta (Riethmüller 1991, 185–92). It also distances the composer from this ballad about the gruesome effects of female attractiveness on innocent males, by means of a tongue-in-cheek gesture and a tone of make-believe.

Despite his tenure in Weimar between 1848 and 1861, Liszt seems to have been unconcerned with the lied aesthetics of Goethe and Schiller, his famous predecessors in that city who had established German literary Classicism more than half a century earlier. Giving the lied the appearance of simplicity through folklike melody, plain diatonic harmony, and frankly strophic organization—in short, by pursuing the ideal of purity of genre—was alien to his artistic disposition. Concerns that were still upheld by such contemporaries as Robert Franz (or even composers of a later generation, such as Brahms) were non-issues for him. As a cosmopolitan and free spirit, Liszt was not bound by the shackles imposed on the genre by the aesthetics of a bygone era. Mixing and multiplying musical genres and styles stimulated his creativity. He was a true non-classicist.

In Search of "Chasteness": Robert Franz (1815–92)

From 1843, when his Op. 1 received a warm welcome from Robert Schumann in the pages of the *Neue Zeitschrift für Musik*, to 1884, when he gave Op. 52, his penultimate work, to the press, Robert Franz published about two hundred eighty songs for voice and piano. Most songs are on texts by Heine (sixty-seven, nearly one fourth of his output) and by his childhood friend Wilhelm Osterwald (about fifty settings); Lenau (eighteen), Burns, in German translation (fifteen), Geibel (thirteen), and Eichendorff (twelve) are also represented. In many ways, Franz is the lied composer par excellence, a specialist who, due to the extraordinary focus—others might say limitations—of his musical talent, wrote almost exclusively songs. Of his fifty-three numbered *opera*, forty-four consist of song collections, nearly all containing six or twelve settings each. The others are choral works, many of them secular and thus closely allied to the lied.

Such concentration on just one genre is rare among the major lied composers. Wolf, whose reputation as a composer is based mainly on his lieder, ventured into opera, symphonic poem, and string quartet. Throughout his brief life, Schubert was well aware that, to be considered an equal of the Viennese Classical masters, he needed to avoid being pigeon-holed as a composer active only in small, intimate genres. Although both these composers succeeded, to differing degrees, in shedding their reputations as mere lyricists, Franz proudly retained his self-imposed limitations. He did not accept the hierarchy of musical genres typical of the nineteenth century, which favored public over private genres; for him the eternal laws of true art could be revealed in the small and intimate, far from the hustle and bustle of the world with its often ephemeral noisy productions (Franz 1895, 40–41). He was firmly convinced that his songs would live.

For a while he appeared to be right. During the last three decades of the nineteenth century, Franz was considered, in much of Germany, the third in an illustrious triumvirate of lied composers, together with Franz Schubert and Robert Schumann, whose song techniques (as well as whose first names!) he seemed to synthesize. Across the Atlantic, a faithful congregation of Franz admirers formed around the Mendelssohn student Otto Dresel, who, after his emigration to the United States in 1848, worked in New York and Boston. The Boston firm of Oliver Ditson published in 1879 a Franz album containing more than one hundred settings, with footnotes pointing out noteworthy features of chosen passages. Some of the finest singers at the end of the century, including Livia Frege, Eugen Gura, Johanna Jachmann (Richard Wagner's niece), Amalie Joachim (Joseph Joachim's spouse), Helene Magnus, and Julius Stockhausen, lent their voices to the performance of Franz's lieder, especially after it became known that deafness—presumed to have been triggered by the whistle of a locomotive—forced the composer to resign from his posts as organist and director of the Singakademie in his native Halle, which he had occupied since the early 1840s. Some of the leading musicians of the time contributed to a fundraising effort on his behalf spearheaded by Arnold Freiherr Senfft von Pilsach, a businessman and singer of considerable renown; they did this as much out of respect and admiration for his work as out of compassion for his unfortunate plight.

It was not easy for Franz to find his niche in the musico-political turbulence of Germany after 1850, which was the result of partisan battles between the *neudeutsche Schule* and the adherents of a more academic musical tradition. By upbringing—he studied with the rigorous Friedrich Schneider in Dessau—and disposition, he tended toward the latter group, that is, toward Mendelssohn, perhaps even more than toward Schumann. In the mid-1840s he made this clear by dedicating several of his works to Leipzig-based composers: his *Schilflieder* (after Lenau), Op. 2, to Schumann, his Opus 3 to Mendelssohn, and his Opus 4 to Niels Gade. But his innate fairness and unwillingness to be appropriated by any group made him a poor partisan in later decades. Besides, Liszt, who had been the dedicatee of Franz's Op. 7 in 1846, developed an admiration for the composer's songs and supported his art through his performances—Liszt arranged several of Franz's lieder as piano solos—and writings. Liszt's article on Franz in the *Neue Zeitschrift für Musik* was later expanded into a little monograph (Liszt 1872); Liszt hailed Franz as a "guiding star of German lyrics" (Franz 1895, 288). Even Richard Wagner, although setting out to take music to completely un-Franzian horizons, acquired a taste for Franz's muse and encouraged the composer to write musico-dramatic works (Franz 1985, 74; further on the Franz-Wagner connection in Franz 1895, 24–25 and 42–44, and in Franz and Senfft 1907, 239). Franz wisely resisted such bear-hugs and—equally wisely—refused to follow Wagner's advice. But he honored the composer of *Lohengrin* with the dedication of his Op. 20, a gesture that in the 1860s must have raised eyebrows in some quarters. Despising the cliquishness of musical life during his time, Franz was unwilling to take sides and trusted that his songs would speak for themselves.

Franz believed, with some justification, that his songs represented a direction in lied composition different from that of Schubert and Schumann. Although he admitted "that without these two I would not have composed my songs the way I did" (Franz 1895, 107), he criticized much in their approach to text setting. In Schubert's songs, he felt, the composer frequently freighted the poem with music inappropriate to the text; in "Trockene Blumen," from *Die schöne Müllerin*, for instance, he considered the jubilant setting in major of the last stanza—a fantasy in which the miller envisions flowers springing from his grave (a response to his beloved's belated recognition of her wrongdoing)—out of step with the basically melancholy mood of the poem (Franz 1895, 129, also 107). This blindness to Schubert's smiling-through-tears effect reveals a certain myopia caused by literal-mindedness on Franz's part. Schumann, he asserted, emphasized the declamatory and details of the poem's imagery at the expense of the whole, and he suggested that a comparison of his and Schumann's Heine songs might demonstrate his more compelling approach to text setting (Franz 1895, 107).

The Heine settings of Schumann and Franz indeed provide instructive examples. Of the sixteen Heine poems from the *Buch der Lieder* that Schumann gathered in his cycle *Dichterliebe*, Franz set ten. Perhaps more revealing than a comparison of the texts that both share is a consideration of those poems not set by Franz, including the multilayered and sharp-edged "Ich grolle nicht" as well as "Das ist ein Flöten und Geigen" and "Ein Jüngling liebt ein Mädchen." These last two poems about love triangles were set by Schumann in the distancing manner of a waltz parody and a narrative operetta song, respectively. Franz shied away from those Heine poems with a decided ironic thrust, preferring texts in which the poet presented his sentiments in a more straightforward manner. Even when Franz did set poems in which Heine used a filter of irony and wit, his settings almost always disregard elements at odds with what he perceived as the basic mood expressed in each poem. Schumann's setting of "Im Rhein, im heiligen Strome," in his opinion, emphasized the "Gothic arches and columns" of the Cologne cathedrale and downplayed the central image of the beloved (Franz 1895, 107). Franz's setting, in contrast, expresses loving devotion, with the concluding punchline, "die gleichen der Leibsten genau," sung almost in a blushing whisper, as if the protagonist is ashamed of comparing the features of the image of the Madonna with those of his beloved (Pfordten 1923, 68). Liszt (1872, 24) speaks in another context of Franz's tendency to "bend back" the punchline in a song (*zurückbiegen der Pointe*). Without denying entirely the legitimacy of Franz's dreamy-eyed reading of the poem, we can rescue Schumann's: although Schumann takes the image of the cathedral perhaps more seriously than he needs to, his one-sided evocation of the archaic, the rigorous, and the monumental through his stark counterpoint puts music in a state of expressive dissonance with the text, highlighting the blasphemous nature and irony of the conclusion of Heine's poem.

Franz's avoidance of extreme poems as well as of adventurous readings jibes with his general approach to song settings. He abhorred self-indulgent and sensual music; "crassly materialistic" is how he frequently characterized the musical approaches of most of his contemporaries, including those of Brahms, Bruch, and Wagner (Franz 1895, 6; Franz and Senfft 1907, 169–70 and 271–72). Tending decidedly toward cultural conservatism, he espoused an art that maintained equilibrium, simplicity, beauty, and—a peculiarly puritanical quality in this context—"chasteness" (Franz and Senfft 1907, 270). He wished his songs not to excite the nerves but to help people find peace and tranquility (Franz 1895, 8). Rare indeed are songs with a passionate outpouring of emotions, such as "Sonnenuntergang," Op. 2, No. 4 (Lenau); "Er ist gekommen," Op. 4, No. 7 (Rückert); "Gewitternacht," Op. 8, No. 6 (Osterwald); and "Im Herbst" ("Die Haide ist braun"), Op. 17, No. 6 (Wolfgang Müller). He did compose a few hits; the exuberance of "Willkommen, mein Wald," Op. 21, No. 1 (Roquette) and "Wenn der Frühling auf die Berge steigt," Op. 42, No. 6 (Mirza-Schaffy) turns these songs into sure applause catchers, appropriately placed at the end of a recital. But the majority of his settings turn their expressive ardor inward. Inspired by the Romantic nature lyrics that he favored, Franz's songs exhibit warm, gently passionate sentiments, often tinged with feelings of nostalgia and melancholy.

The "ascetic" quality (Pfordten 1923, 36) of Franz's muse is evident also in the technical aspects of his songs. The ideal of the purity of the genre, which informed the songs of many composers of the Goethe era, made its impact felt throughout the nineteenth century (Thym 1983, ix–x; Smeed 1992, ix–xii), but in few cases did it take such a peculiarly retrospective bent as with Franz. Franz's guiding principles seem to have been the simplicity and vigor of folk song, especially the old German tunes of the fifteenth and sixteenth centuries—Franz published arrangements of six songs from the Lochamer Liederbuch and the Ott Collection (ed. in Franz 1880; see Pfordten 1923, 95–96)—and the Protestant chorale. During his childhood in Halle he had been exposed to the latter in the embellished versions of the Freylinghausen editions; the modal character of his songs, however, has been exaggerated in the literature about Franz.

The accompaniment in many of his songs reveals the background of four-part chorale settings, sometimes very much at the surface, in order to evoke religious sentiments (as in "Bitte," Op. 9, No. 3 [Lenau] and "Sonntag," Op. 1, No. 7 [Eichendorff]), sometimes dissolved in arpeggios and other forms of diminution, as in "Es klingt in der Luft" and "Wenn drüben die Glocken klingen," Op. 13, Nos. 2 and 5, after Waldau; and "Abends," Op. 11, No. 6, after an anonymous poet (see Franz's list of chorale-inspired settings in Prochazka 1894, 40). Chorale textures give some of Franz's songs a peculiarly archaic quality. Free-voiced accompaniments, idiomatic to keyboard instruments, are not absent from Franz's piano parts, but rigorous principles of four-part voice-leading prevail in his accompaniments. The adherence to four-part voice-leading allowed Franz to transcribe without much ado some of his solo songs for mixed chorus; his last published work is a collection of choral settings based on the Mörike songs, Op. 27.

Franz noted with some pride that his lieder owed much to Handel and Bach, two masters from his native Halle and nearby Leipzig whose music he studied throughout his life (Franz 1895, 14). He published numerous highly controversial editions of their works—lovingly Romanticized arrangements that earned him the wrath of the newly established discipline of musicology as represented by Chrysander, Spitta, and others. Many of Franz's songs are pervaded by Baroque-inspired techniques for developing musical ideas, such as sequence, melodic diminution, and fragmentation. These motivic techniques not only render his piano parts flexible and add to their richness but also integrate both voice and piano in a polyphonic texture, inasmuch as the voice frequently takes part in the motivic interplay; "Wenn drüben die Glocken klingen," Op. 13, No. 5, is a fine example. Some of Franz's songs indeed sound as if Bach is looking over his shoulders, infusing the lied with the principles of the two- and three-part inventions. But pictorial elements, referring to details of the poem's imagery, are rare in textures conceived in this way.

Franz not infrequently criticized his contemporaries for conceiving their vocal parts instrumentally. He attributed the smooth singability of his songs to the influence of the Italian bel canto tradition, which he believed himself to have inherited from Handel—another instance of his backward glance's proving beneficial for the composition of lieder. His vocal parts indeed follow the ideal of singability espoused in the theory and practice of the German lied since the eighteenth century: the tessitura is usually that of a mezzo-soprano, avoiding extremes on either end of the range, and the words are most often set syllabically and without extensive ornamentation. It is no accident that amateurs were active in furthering his fame in the nineteenth century. Franz had no objection to performance of his songs by both female and male singers: "The lied," he stated, "belongs to the field of lyricism, and lyricism is, in its sentiments, without gender" (quoted in Pfordten 1923, 46). But he was opposed to transpositions of his songs; the key and, by implication, the vocal range in which he had conceived the song were integral parts of the mood he tried to convey, and thus of the composition. Only grudgingly did he proofread editions of his songs for low voice, which overly eager publishers put together against his expressed wishes (Franz and Senfft 1907, 198–200 and 236–38).

Consistent with the ideals of singability and simplicity, the forms of Franz's songs lack the complexities of those by many of his contemporaries. Through-composed structures appear mostly in his earliest publications, for instance in the second and fifth of the *Schilflieder* Op. 2, and even then the stanzaic organization of the poetry remains audible. "Vöglein, wohin so schnell," Op. 1, No. 11 (text by Geibel) is almost unique in Franz's output in its rapid juxtaposition of four different sentiments in a relatively short setting. The majority of his settings are strophic, often making minimal adjustments in rhythm, harmony, and melody to later strophes. Even where the music digresses from a previously set mood, the differences are subtle rather than blatant.

Throughout his life, Franz published his songs in groups incorporating poems by various authors. Only eight works gather songs on texts by a single poet: Opp. 2 (the *Schilflieder* of Lenau), 13 (Max Waldau), 25 (Heine), 27 (Mörike), and 33 (Goethe), and Opp. 34, 38, and 39 (all Heine). Opus 23, which Franz dedicated to his wife Marie, can also be considered as of this type, all its poems being based on folksong texts. But cyclic structures similar to those encountered in the works of Schubert, Schumann, and other contemporaries are absent. The five *Schilflieder* Opus 2 perhaps come closest to forming a song cycle. Based on a poetic cycle by Lenau, the settings follow a well-calculated sequence of keys. Franz even changed Lenau's ordering of the poems to produce a dynamic curve of nature sounds reaching, as he put it, from the "softest whispering of a lament to wildest roaring of desperate passion [in song 4] and returning in resignation to its point of departure" (Franz/Senfft 1907, 246–47).

Reluctant Wagnerian: Peter Cornelius (1824–74)

Among the composers of the lied in the second half of the nineteenth century, Cornelius is unique: more than half of his nearly eighty songs are on his own texts. Born into a family of actors, he was steeped from an early age in literary matters, and his dual talent as both poet and composer defined his artistic career. Not only did he write poems that he as well as others (for instance, Liszt) set as songs, but he also wrote the librettos for his operas, an accomplishment that he shares with his contemporary and friend Richard Wagner (and with a composer both he and Wagner admired: Hector Berlioz). The librettos, especially the one for his comic opera *Der Barbier von Bagdad*, have been praised by literary scholars for their poetic and dramatic merits (see Just 1977).

After several years of studying composition and counterpoint in Berlin with Siegfried Dehn, Cornelius left the conservative artistic climate of that city to join Bülow, Draseke, Raff, and others in establishing the artistic community headed by Liszt at Weimar. From 1852 to 1859 he gave freely of his time and energy as a writer and translator in furthering the causes of Liszt, Wagner, and Berlioz and in turn received important impetus from that community for his career as an artist. (Niemöller 1977) In particular, Liszt's generosity of spirit, open-mindedness, and encouragement were a nurturing presence during these formative years. Furthermore, the religious convictions of Liszt and the Princess Sayn-Wittgenstein must have struck a resonant chord in the young composer as well, who throughout his life remained a devout Catholic. In fact, Liszt saw in Cornelius mainly a composer of church music who could further Liszt's goals of reforming the liturgical music of the Catholic church, incorporating contemporary musical styles and Gregorian elements. After Liszt resigned his post in Weimar—ironically, the premiere of Cornelius's comic opera *Der Barbier von Bagdad* in 1858 led to an administrative vendetta that ultimately made Liszt throw in the towel—Wagner became a sometimes overbearing artistic presence in Cornelius's life (Bauer 1977). Cornelius devoted himself to causes Wagnerian, even struggling to improve his pianistic skills in order to work his way through Bülow's piano reduction of *Tristan*, and infecting Brahms with his enthusiasm. In the mid-1860s, after Wagner's fortunes had turned, thanks to King Ludwig II of Bavaria, Cornelius was rewarded, on Wagner's recommendation, with a teaching position at the reorganized Royal Music Academy in Munich.

Cornelius seems to have experienced in overpowering ways what literary critic Harold Bloom calls the "anxiety of influence." Although aware and proud of his great talents, he was frequently tortured by lack of confidence. The Wagnerian connection may well have sapped his time and creative energies in the last decade of his life. But for the most part he seems to have resisted being appropriated by his powerful mentors and friends, even to the extent of insisting on maintaining some distance from them in order to preserve his individuality and creativity. Neither his opera *Barbier* nor his songs are particularly Wagnerian, and his less than flamboyant but always functional pianistic idiom has little in common with Liszt's. Only after 1859 is the gravitational attraction of Wagner measurable in some of his works. The opera *Der Cid* can be considered a descendant of *Lohengrin*, and the unfinished *Gunlöd* approaches the Wagnerian orbit in the mythological aspects of the libretto (Just 1977, Abert 1977). The chromaticism of some of the later songs, most of them unpublished during his lifetime, can, moreover, be attributed to his acquaintance with the harmonic idiom of *Tristan*. Although his artistic profile was more lastingly shaped by his association with Liszt and Wagner than by his contrapuntal studies with Dehn, historians agree that Cornelius was a most reluctant member of the *neudeutsche Schule* (Niemöller 1977, Bauer 1977, and Mahling 1977; also Moser 1958). Earlier training and natural disposition made him avoid the extremes often characteristic of his peers in Weimar; even after intoxicating himself with *Tristan* harmonies in the early 1860s, he charted for himself a path of greater sobriety. At heart he remained a classicist.

The brevity of Cornelius's creative career, which spanned little more than twenty years, and the small number of works he composed may make any attempt at periodization seem forced. Caution is also indicated by the fact that Cornelius revised earlier settings later in life. Nevertheless, as far as his song output is concerned, three stages can be observed, as marked by the years 1852, when he joined Liszt's *école de Weymar*, and 1859, when Wagner became a more prominent force for him. The early songs, including his Op. 1 (which originated in Weimar), appear to be conventional settings, often strophic, of second-rate Romantic poets. The Weimar years show growth and maturity in the settings of *Gedankenlyrik* from his own pen, often of a religious nature, which he grouped into cycles. The years after 1859 in Vienna and Munich are characterized by his embracing, with caution, the harmonic idiom of *Tristan* in his songs and by greater use, again, of poetry other than his own. (The cycle *An Bertha* as well as the revisions of two *Weihnachtslieder* are exceptions to both these trends.)

In his choice of poetry Cornelius differs strikingly from the Mendelssohn-Schumann generation of song composers. The near-absence of nature lyrics (Massenkeil 1977), including Goethe's, is particularly notable. Eichendorff, whose nature lyrics were the inspiration of Schumann and many of his followers, produced no major musical response in Cornelius, although both men met in Berlin during the 1840s. The composer had little use for poems evoking the mysterious and mystifying forces of nature and their impact on the human psyche. (The only Eichendorff setting is the relatively late ballad *Die Räuberbrüder*.) Heine, whose poetry of Romantic and post-Romantic sentimentality and irony was a staple of composers throughout the nineteenth century, is represented by only two settings, one of them a very early song. When Cornelius sets nature lyrics, as in the early songs of 1848 and, to a certain extent, Op. 1 of 1852, it is on texts by Paul Heyse (another acquaintance from his Berlin years) or the composer himself—texts somewhat derivative in their Romanticism, with the obligatory touch of folk-song influence. The settings are conventional if occasionally charming.

The song composer Cornelius was particularly attracted by what we may call *Gedankenlyrik*, his own as well as that of others. He set eighteenth-century poets such as Bürger, Hölty, and Hölderlin (Cornelius's *Sonnenun-*

tergang is one of the earliest settings of this enigmatic poet), as well as nineteenth-century lyricists such as Platen, Droste-Hülshoff, and Hebbel. Although the poems Cornelius set after 1852 are not completely lacking in nature imagery, their tone is primarily meditative and introspective. Rather than fictionalizing and mystifying nature, the poems describe real-life situations; they cast into verses elevated moments of human existence in an equally elevated poetic language—in other words, they are worlds away from the *Wunderhorn*-inspired blossoming of German lyric poetry in the nineteenth century, which resulted in an unprecedented flowering of lied compositions. The poetic forms favored by Cornelius are more intricate and urbane than those used by the average song composer. Pentameters and five-line stanzas are not infrequent, as are complicated verse schemes with asymmetries and irregularities. Nor did Cornelius shy away from the ode (Platen, Hölderlin, Hölty) or sonnets (three by Bürger), a rather recondite form in the repertory of the German Lied. Through his choice of poetry he intentionally sought to open new areas of form and expression for the song.

Cornelius found his voice as a song composer in the fall of 1854 with his *Vater unser* settings, Op. 2 (Hasse 1922–23, 148–64). The nine poems of the cycle are poetic meditations on the various sections of the Lord's Prayer, occasionally interspersed with references to Biblical stories, such as Christ's miracles or that of the prodigal son. Cornelius employs considerable virtuosity in handling various poetic forms and meters; no less intricate is the music. The composer derives the motivic material for each of the settings from plainchant formulas, taken from N. A. Janssen's *Lehrbuch des gregorianischen Kirchengesangs*, a nineteenth-century source for Gregorian melodies (see the facsimile of the first page of the cycle in Hasse 1922–23, 1: 157). These pervade the piano part in various guises; each formula is given a rhythmic shape and then transformed through augmentation and diminution as well as other principles of variation, including frequent canonic voice-leading. Although the Gregorian element is completely absorbed by Cornelius's mid-nineteenth-century musical language, modal turns at various junctures provide an archaic flavor appropriate to the religious subject matter. The musical forms of the nine settings are determined, without exception, by the stanzaic organization of the poetry; poems of three stanzas are usually set as ABA or AAB forms, or in a simple strophic form (No. 9); poems of four stanzas are rendered as ABAB or ABAC. The most daringly through-composed structure is perhaps "Vergib uns unsere Schuld" (No. 6), which is shaped into a coherent musical discourse by the systematic use of thematic transformation. Throughout the cycle, and here in a particularly striking manner, Cornelius reconciles Liszt's device of thematic transformation with the cantus firmus technique of earlier ages, within the context of a song composition.

Quite a number of Cornelius's songs are grouped into larger units. The nine prayer meditations of the *Vater unser* clearly constitute a cycle, not only because of the poetry and its chant-based motivic material, but also because the individual songs are chained to one another in a tonally closed sequence of related keys: E♭–E♭–c–D♭–C–f–F–B♭–E♭. Only the fourth song, "Dein Wille geschehe," stands in a relatively remote (Neapolitan) relation to its neighbors; in contrast to the more pleading character of the other prayers, this song communicates confidence in the righteousness of God's will, an affirmation most clearly expressed through the rhythmic profile of its principal motive).

Trauer und Trost Op. 3 (also composed in 1854) is a cycle progressing in various stages from grief to consolation. It, too, is bound together by a key sequence: e (with a Phrygian flavor) D, e, b, G, and e (again Phrygian). By beginning and ending the group with songs containing strong modal inflections, Cornelius creates a definite frame for his cycle. In the third song, "Ein Ton," the voice hovers throughout on the pitch b. On the surface, this seems a one-sided interpretation of the song's title—the indefinite article is turned into a number—and critics have spoken condescendingly of this type of text-music relationship (see Diez 1968, 10). But the monotony of the voice makes sense here, in view of the stage of the grieving process: by reducing the voice to one pitch, the composer forces the listener—and, by implication, also the singer, as the lyric subject—to listen to the piano part, which presents, as if from outside, a ray of hope. In addition, the harmonies are anything but monotonous, alluding to E-major and G♯-minor tonalities. More importantly, the pitch b is the pivotal tone common to all keys of the cycle; each song begins (and many conclude) with b in the voice, the piano, or both. The "monotonous" quality of the third song—which reverberates in other songs as well, especially in the fourth, in the piano part—thus underscores a particularly poignant structural feature of the cycle (see Dürr 1984, 301–4; the second song, however, is not in F!).

Brautlieder (composed 1856–59) comprises six settings that follow a young bride through various stages of prenuptial and marital bliss, though from a less patriarchal perspective than Shumann's *Frauenliebe.* The *Weihnachtslieder* Op. 8 (composed 1856, revised 1870), six vignettes on the celebration of Christmas, includes the chorale melody "Wie schön leuchtet der Morgenstern," which Cornelius inserted, at Liszt's suggestion, to accompany the three kings on their way to Bethlehem. Each is held together by another sequence of closely related keys, as are the four songs of *An Bertha* Op. 15, which Cornelius composed for his bride on their engagement in 1865. Whether Cornelius planned to make cycles of his settings of Bürger sonnets, or of the Droste and Hebbel poems, all but three of which remained unpublished during his lifetime, must remain an open question, although these settings clearly can be grouped into larger structures. There is also some evidence that Cornelius planned to complement his two cycles of religious *Hausmusik*—the *Vater unser* settings and the *Weih-*

nachtslieder—with song cycles for other Christian holy days, such as Easter, Pentecost, and Ascension (Hasse 1922–23, 1: 179).

"Die Hirten," the second of the *Weihnachtslieder*, is a charming example of Cornelius's lyrical genius, in both its poetry and its music. Although the earlier versions of the song of 1856 (see Hasse 1922–23, 1: 183) were by no means failures, the revised version of 1870 excels because of its greater conciseness, showing the composer's ability to give artifice the appearance of simplicity. The poem outlines the events of Christmas night in four stanzas: the shepherds watching their flock, the angel's announcement of Christ's birth, the singing of the angels, and the shepherds worshiping the child. Musical elements evocative of nature and simple, rustic life—in short, of the pastoral character—abound, including the siciliano-like motion in $\frac{6}{8}$ and $\frac{9}{8}$ meters, the horn-call motive, the juxtaposition of third-related keys in the song's middle section, and a pedal point in the last section. Although through-composed, the song alludes to a strophic musical structure. In the second stanza, both the bass and the vocal line are largely identical with those in the first strophe; by omitting the interjections of the horn-call motive, Cornelius arrives at a contracted setting of the second stanza (7 rather than 12 measures). The fourth stanza has the character of a recapitulation, not only because of its return to D major, but also because of the reappearance of the horn-call motive that had been absent since the end of the first stanza.

Cornelius's skill in interweaving poetic and musical structures is evident also on a local level. Each stanza of the poem consists of four lines, the first three being trimeter lines, the last having only one accent. The sudden fall to the cadence causes a contraction of the temporal rhythm established in the beginning of the stanza. In the settings of all stanzas, Cornelius compensates musically for the shortening of the verses by repeating lines 3 and 4, thereby also dwelling on their end rhymes. The changes of meter characteristic of the setting, as well as the shortened statement of the horn call in m. 8, can be interpreted as musical responses to the asymmetry caused by the irregular fourth line.

How much the encounter with Wagner—their first meeting took place as early as 1853—affected the musical language of Cornelius can be seen in several settings composed after 1859. Biographical circumstances faintly reminiscent of the Wagner-Wesendonck situation found their artistic outlet for Cornelius in, among other works, a sonnet cycle for the singer Rosa von Milde, with each poem reflecting on an operatic role she had sung in Weimar (Cornelius 1905b, 209–22), as well as the composition of three sonnets by Bürger, some in multiple settings. Bürger's poem "Der Entfernten" (To the Distant One), the soliloquy of a lover tormented by his passion for an unreachable partner, may have led the composer to the intoxicating eroticism of harmonic idiom similar to that of Wagner's *Tristan*. The two measures of piano prelude are the song's signature. Harmonically a conventional prolongation of the dominant-seventh, these measures introduce an appoggiatura motive, the dissonant note being resolved both upward and downward, which pervades the entire song; the motive defines the song's harmonic idiom, in which downbeats on various levels are generally dissonant. Despite its roving harmonies, the sonnet and its various sections are clearly articulated through tonal, motivic, and textural means, resulting in one of the finest statements of Cornelius as a lied composer. He anticipates here not only the harmonic idiom of his opera *Der Cid*—forming another parallel to Wagner, who foreshadowed his opera *Tristan* in his Wesendonck-Lieder (Hasse 1922–23, 2: 67–69)— but also the musical language of Hugo Wolf, who a generation later achieved similar text-musical utterances in his Mörike settings.

Simpler in its harmonic means but no less Wolfian is Cornelius's exquisite setting of Hölty's "Auftrag," an ode in the Alcaic meter, composed in 1862 and published as Op. 5, No. 6 in 1865 (facsimile of first page in MGG II 1952, col. 1687, and in Hasse 1922–23, 2: 105). In accordance with the mood of resignation that hovers over the verses ("Ye friends, fasten when I am dead and gone the little harp of mine by the altar here"), Cornelius sets the ode in an almost static harmonic language characterized by pedal points on D, Eb, and A for the three stanzas, with quartal harmonies functioning as structural markers at the beginning and end of the song, as well as between sections. (Schoenberg would use quartal sonorities in a strikingly similar way in his first *Chamber Symphony*.) The voice declaims the poem in recitative superimposed on chords whose harmonic drive seems to be arrested by the pedal points. Only at the end does the piano sing in imitation of the harp, its music reminiscent of both the Valhalla motive from Wagner's *Ring* and the second movement of Schubert's "Unfinished" Symphony.

Bibliography

EDITIONS OF MUSIC

Briscoe, James R., ed. *Historical Anthology of Music by Women*. Bloomington, IN, 1987.

Cornelius, Peter. *Musikalische Werke*. Vol. 1: *Einstimmige Lieder und Gesänge*. Ed. Max Hasse. Leipzig, 1905. [Cornelius 1905a]

———. "Ein Ton." From *Trauer und Trost*. In Finck (1903, 103–5).

———. "Die Hirten." In Moser (1957, 99–101).

———. "Sonnenuntergang." In Komma (1967, 10–12).

Finck, Henry T., ed. *Fifty Mastersongs*. Boston, 1903. Reprinted as *Fifty Art Songs by Nineteenth-Century Masters*. New York, 1975.

Franz, Robert. *Ausgewählte Lieder*. 4 vols. Leipzig, n.d. (probably after 1876).

———. *Album of Songs: Old and New*. Boston, 1880.

———. Six Songs, including "Bitte," "Wonne der Wehmut," and "Es hat die Rose sich beklagt." In Finck (1903, 89–102).

———. "Aus meinen grossen Schmerzen." In Moser (1957, 102).

———. "Abends" and "Am Strom." In Thym (1983, 16–21).

———. "Wonne der Wehmut." In Green (forthcoming).

Friedländer, Max, ed. *Gedichte von Goethe in Compositionen.* 2 vols. Weimar, 1896–1916.

Green, Richard, ed. [*Goethe Songs*]. Madison, WI, forthcoming.

Hensel, Fanny. *Lieder für eine Singstimme mit Begleitung des Pianoforte.* Berlin, 1895. Reprint of the original editions of Opp. 1 (Berlin, 1846) and 7 (Berlin, 1848).

———. Nachtwanderer. In Thym (1983, 13–15).

———. *Schwanenlied.* Ed. Marcia Citron. In Briscoe (1987, 115–18).

———. *Ausgewählte Lieder.* Ed. Aloysia Assenbaum. Düsseldorf, 1991.

Komma, Karl Michael, ed. *Lieder und Gesänge nach Dichtungen von Friedrich Hölderlin.* Tübingen, 1967.

Liszt, Franz. *Thirty Songs.* Ed. Carl Armbruster. Boston, 1911. Reprint. New York, 1975.

———. *Musikalische Werke.* Vol. 7: *Lieder und Gesänge.* Ed. Peter Raabe. 3 vols. Leipzig, ca. 1922.

Loewe, Carl. *Loewe-Album: Ausgewählte Lieder und Balladen.* Ed. L. Benda. 4 vols. Braunschweig, n.d.

———. *Werke: Gesamtausgabe der Balladen, Legenden, Lieder und Gesänge.* Ed. Max Runze. 17 vols. Leipzig, 1898–1904.

———. *Die drei Lieder.* Ed. in Moser (1957, 74–79).

Moser, Hans-Joachim, ed. *Das deutsche Lied und die Ballade.* Cologne, 1957.

Smeed, J. W., ed. *Famous Poets, Neglected Composers.* Madison, WI, 1992.

Thym, Jürgen, ed. *One Hundred Years of Eichendorff Songs.* Madison, WI, 1983.

LITERATURE

Abert, Anna Amalie. "Zu Cornelius's Oper *Gunloed.*" In Federhofer and Oehl (1977, 145–56).

Althouse, Paul L., Jr. "Carl Loewe (1796–1869): His Lieder, Ballads, and Their Performance." Ph.D. dissertation, Yale University, 1971.

Bauer, Hans-Joachim. "Cornelius und Richard Wagner." In Federhofer and Oehl (1977, 93–104).

Citron, Marcia. "The Lieder of Fanny Mendelssohn Hensel." *Musical Quarterly* 64 (1983): 570–94.

———. "Gender, Professionalism, and the Musical Canon." *Journal of Musicology* 8 (1990): 102–17.

Cornelius, Peter. *Literarische Werke.* Ed. A. Stern. 4 vols. Leipzig, 1905. [Cornelius 1905b]

Diez, Werner. *Hans Pfitzners Lieder.* Regensburg, 1968.

Dömling, Wolfgang. "Der unbekannte Liszt: Die Welt seiner Klavierlieder." Liner note for *Franz Liszt: Lieder.* Dietrich Fischer-Dieskau, voice, Daniel Barenboim, piano. Deutsche Grammaphon 2740254 (1981).

———. *Franz Liszt und seine Zeit.* Laaber, 1985.

Dürr, Walther. *Das deutsche Sololied im 19. Jahrhundert.* Wilhelmshaven, 1984.

Elvers, Rudolf. "Verzeichnis der Musik-Autographen von Fanny Hensel in dem Mendelssohn-Archiv zu Berlin." *Mendelssohn-Studien* 1 (1972): 169–74.

———. "Weitere Quellen zu den Werken von Fanny Hensel." *Mendelssohn-Studien* 2 (1975): 215–20.

Engel, Hans. "Cornelius." In *Die Musik in Geschichte und Gegenwart.* Vol. 2, cols. 1683–89. Kassel, 1952.

Federhofer, Hellmut, and Kurt Oehl, eds. *Peter Cornelius als Komponist, Dichter, Kritiker und Essayist.* Regensburg, 1977.

Franz, Robert. *Gespräche aus zehn Jahren.* Ed. Wilhelm Waldmann. Leipzig, 1895.

Franz, Robert, and Arnold Freiherr Senfft von Pilsach. *Ein Briefwechsel 1861–1888.* Ed. Wolfgang Golther. Berlin, 1097.

Gudewill, Kurt. "Lied." In *Die Musik in Geschichte und Gegenwart.* Vol. 8, cols. 745–75. Kassel, 1960.

Hasse, Max. *Der Dichtermusiker Peter Cornelius.* 2 vols. Leipzig, 1922–23. Reprint. Walluf, 1972.

Hensel, Fanny. *The Letters of Fanny Hensel to Felix Mendelssohn.* Ed. Marcia Citron. New York, 1987.

Hensel, Sebastian. *The Mendelssohn Family (1729–1847).* Trans. Carl Klingemann. 2 vols. New York, 1882.

Hertz, Deborah S. *Jewish High Society in Old-Regime Berlin.* New Haven, 1988.

Just, Klaus Günther. "Peter Cornelius als Dichter." In Federhofer and Oehl (1977, 19–30).

Klein, Ursula. "Liszt als Liederkomponist: Gedanken eines Interpreten." Liner note for *Franz Liszt: Lieder.* Dietrich Fischer-Dieskau, voice, Daniel Barenboim, piano. Deutsche Grammophon 2740254 (1981).

Krautwurst, Franz. "Fanny Caecilia Hensel." In *Die Musik in Geschichte und Gegenwart.* Vol. 16, cols. 658–62. Kassel, 1979.

Liszt, Franz. "Robert Schumann." *Neue Zeitschrift für Musik* 42 (1855): 133–37, 145–53, 157–65, 177–82, 189–96, 213–21, and 225–30. Reprinted in *Gesammelte Schriften,* vol. 4, 103–85. Leipzig, 1982. [Liszt 1855a]

―――. "Robert Franz." *Neue Zeitschrift für Musik* 43 (1855): 229–35 and 241–47. [Liszt 1855b]

―――. *Robert Franz.* Expanded version of Liszt 1855b. Leipzig 1872. Reprinted in *Gesammelte Schriften,* vol. 4, 207–44. Leipzig, 1882.

Lowe, Carl. *Carl Loewes Selbstbiographie.* Ed. C. H. Bitter. Berlin, 1870. Reprint. Hildesheim, 1976.

Mahling, Christoph-Hellmut. "'. . . in Dichtung und Komposition auf eigenem Boden gesachsen': Cornelius und sein Verhältnis zur 'Neudeutschen Schule.'" In Federhofer and Oehl (1977, 105–11).

Marx-Weber, Magda. "Cornelius' Kritik des Liedes." In Federhofer and Oehl (1977, 169–78).

Massenkeil, Günther. "Cornelius als Liederkomponist." In Federhofer and Oehl (1977, 159–68).

Montu-Berthon, Suzanne. "Un Liszt méconnu." *La revue musicale* 1 & 2 (1981): 342–46.

Moser, Hans-Joachim. *Musikgeschichte in hundert Lebensbildern.* 2d ed. Stuttgart, 1958.

Mueller, Rena Charnin. "Reevaluating the Liszt Chronology: The Case of *Anfangs wollt ich fast verzagen.*" *19th-Century Music* 12 (1988): 132–47.

Niemöller, Klaus W. "Cornelius und Franz Liszt." In Federhofer and Oehl (1977, 81–92).

Pfordten, Hermann Freiherr von der. *Robert Franz.* Leipzig, 1923.

Prochazka, Rudolf Freiherr. *Robert Franz.* Leipzig, 1894.

Quin, Carol L. "Fanny Mendelssohn Hensel: Her Contributions to Nineteenth-Century Musical Life." Ph.D. dissertation, University of Kentucky, 1981.

Raabe, Peter. *Franz Liszt.* 2 vols. Stuttgart, 1931.

Reithmüller, Albrecht. "Heines *Lorelei* in den Vertonungen von Silcher und Liszt." *Archiv für Musikwissenschaft* 48 (1991): 169–98.

Rosenwald, H. H. *Das deutsche Lied zwischen Schubert und Schumann.* Berlin, 1930.

Saffle, Michael. "Liszt Research Since 1936." *Acta musicologica* 58 (1986): 231–81.

Schwab, Heinrich. *Sangbarkeit, Popularität und Kunstlied: Studien zu Lied und Liedästhetik der mittleren Goethezeit 1770–1814.* Regensburg, 1965.

Searle, Humphrey. *The Music of Franz Liszt.* New York, 1966.

Sirota, Victoria R. "The Life and Works of Fanny Mendelssohn Hensel." D.M.A. dissertation, Boston University, 1981.

Stanley, Glenn. "Bach's *Erbe*: The Chorale in German Oratorio of the Early Nineteenth Century." *19th-Century Music* 11 (1987): 121–49.

Weissweiler, Eva. *Fanny Mendelssohn: Ein Porträt in Briefen.* Frankfurt, 1985.

Werner, Eric. *Mendelssohn.* Trans. Dika Newlin. London, 1963.

Wiora, Walter. *Das deutsche Lied.* Wolfenbüttel, 1971.

Youens, Susan. *Hugo Wolf: The Vocal Music.* Princeton, 1992.

CHAPTER SIX

Hugo Wolf: Subjectivity in the Fin-de-Siècle Lied

Lawrence Kramer

Hugo Wolf occupies an anomalous position in the canon of "classical" music. He is the only standard composer whose reputation rests entirely on his songs, and he enjoys enough critical esteem to suggest that he parallels Chopin as a genre specialist. Unlike Chopin, however, he is not a popular composer; his songs are more often praised than sung. Concomitantly, though his reputation is high, he has attracted only a modicum of critical attention. And though his music is expressively and sometimes structurally elusive, reflecting, moreover, the composer's notorious penchant for complex texts, Wolf's small cadre of critics—its chief English-language members including Ernest Newman, Eric Sams, Mosco Carner, and Frank Walker—has found only one story to tell about him. This is what might be called the Wolf legend: the tale of the moody, sensitive, but esthetically disciplined artist who submerged himself in first-rate literary texts, understood them preternaturally well, and "expressed" them to perfection by repeating their sound and meaning in the form of music.[1]

It would be foolish to deny that the Wolf legend contains a measure of truth. Wolf was more intent on perfect declamation than most lied composers, and he made a point of demanding high-quality poetry. He seemed to assume that an important poem could (or should) have a single definitive setting, and thus avoided setting material for which he felt other composers, especially Schubert and Schumann, had fully accounted. As a recitalist, he liked to point up the interrelationship of music and poetry, prefacing the performance of each of his lieder with a recitation of its text.

In passing from recitation to song, and from a silent background to an accompaniment notable for its individuality and independence from the voice, Wolf would in effect stage the lied as a reproduction of meaning and figuratively re-enact its composition.

Nonetheless, the Wolf legend contains less truth than truism. Its initial weak point is the somewhat heavy-handed narrative structure that posits, in the style of nineteenth-century evolutionism, a teleology in the history of the lied of which Wolf is the fulfillment. (Wolf might have agreed, but that only makes him the first partisan of his own legend.) The central, organizing truism of the Wolf legend, however, is something less obviously questionable. It is the core assumption that the artistic purpose of the lied, peerlessly served by Wolf, is to "express" musically the meaning or affect of a lyric poem. This expressive ideal can supposedly provide a self-sufficient artistic end because the poetry deals in timeless human truths, transcendent of history and society, which the universal language of music can reproduce and enhance. No idea about the lied is more commonplace than this one. In practice, though, its application generates only a limited range of text-music analogies that have little value for satisfying interpretations of either poetry or music, let alone interpretations of their interaction. The idea works better as encomiastic rhetoric than as critical principle. Moreover, the canonical composers of lieder, especially Wolf's primary models Schubert and Schumann, have no qualms about treating their texts quite brutally when the purposes of a song require it. Whenever the song is expressing, it is not something proper to the poem.[2]

But even if the expressive ideal is taken as normative, Wolf's compositional practice does not seem to follow it. Wolf's declamation does transfer the text into the song with minimal verbal breakage. But it does so only to highlight the rhythmic, melodic, and even expressive discontinuities between the voice intoning the text and the enveloping musical texture created by the piano. Wolf does not so much "express" the text as scrutinize it, as explained below. To put it another way, Wolf treats the singing voice as equivalent to the voice of the text and treats it on the model of Wagnerian music-drama. He envelops the voice of the signer with an extratextual music that may incorporate, but always transcends, the point of view embodied in that voice itself.

It is hard to see the motives for this songwriting practice in a self-contained esthetic or an ideal sphere of timeless verities. History and culture need to be consulted. Like the leading poetic genres of the nineteenth century, the dramatic lyric and dramatic monologue, the lied by definition has no voice of its own. Rather than speak for itself, it represents someone else speaking; the lyric or dramatic utterance is always distanced, framed as a speech act.[3] The effect of this distancing, however, depends on its extent, which varies widely. The smooth, sensual lyricism of, say, Tennyson and Schubert tends to reduce the sense of distance and to invite the reader or listener to identify with the speaker. By contrast, the brainy colloquialism of Browning and the sustained discontinuity between voice and piano typical of Wolf tends to enlarge distance and invite reflection on the motives behind the speech act.

Insofar as they embrace an esthetic of distance and reflection, both the lied and its poetic counterparts reproduce a key practice of nineteenth-century clinical psychology, or "mental science" as it was called. For English poetry, at least, as Ekbert Faas (1988) has shown, this "interdisciplinary" link was explicitly recognized by a wide circle of poets and critics. As it would later do for psychoanalysis, literature formed a body of evidence for mental science, the practice of which, it turn, overlapped with literary criticism. Many psychologists, then known as "alienists," published analyses of dramatic poetry in order to illustrate the workings of the disordered mind and to exemplify the laws governing mental life. Poets began to write with this type of reading in mind, which critics, journalists, and alienists gradually supplied, eventually giving rise to the first waves of psychobiography and modern pop psychology.

Shakespeare was by far the favorite object of study, in Germany no less than England, but contemporary authors also made a good showing. The alienist John Charles Bucknill, for example, drawing on the work of his colleague Joseph Guislain, developed a theory of the "psychopathic origin of insanity" and published readings of both Shakespeare and Tennyson to support his findings. Shakespeare's *King Lear* showed how "morbid emotion," and not merely impairment of the intellect, has "an immense influence . . . in the causation of insanity" (Faas 1988, 109); Tennyson's atypically distanced *Maud* showed the complex etiology and symptomatology of madness "in that period when [it] is threatening and imminent, but not actually present" (Faas 1988, 32). Nietzsche, a subtler and less compassionate interpreter than Bucknill, liked to subject important figures from intellectual history to this same mode of literary psychologizing—his favorite targets were Plato, Kant, Goethe, Schopenhauer, Wagner, and himself—and he deploys an allegorical version of it throughout his *Also Sprach Zarathustra*. Wolf, who knew his Nietzsche, could have taken hints from that source, or, for that matter, from the shrewd dramatic lyrics of his favorite poet, Eduard Mörike. But the practice was sufficiently "in the air" to require no specific sources.

Wolf's choice of this "scrutinizing" mode as the basic rhetorical configuration of his songs involves him even further in the discourse of nineteenth-century psychology—and sexology. Even more involving, however, and probably the cultural formation most basic to Wolf's songwriting practice (not the autonomous "esthetic" of the legend), is a rite-of-passage scenario writ large across Wolf's culture, his life, and his work. This is the scenario of a certain coming to manhood: of a youth who leaves home to establish his independent identity, to succeed in a hostile world both vocationally and sexually, to inherit and even to exceed his father's example and authority.

The name of this scenario, as it would be codified in the early twentieth century, is the Oedipus complex. To say this is not to suggest that the secret of Wolf's art lay in neurosis, even though Wolf had neuroses to spare. Nor am I suggesting that Wolf's songs center around what would be his unsurprising fantasies, in childhood and early adolescence, of sexualized attachment to his mother and jealous violence against his father. Although such fantasies are the starting points for the classical Freudian account of the Oedipus complex, they are not the whole story or even its most prominent part. My focus, instead, is on the oedipal narrative as the normative script for the formation of masculine identity in Western culture. In recent years, cultural theorists have emphasized, usually from an oppositional standpoint, the historical importance of this script. Their formulations, however, have shifted the main venue of oedipal relations from individual psychology to the social construction and regulation of subjectivity.[4]

At no time was the oedipal script more important than during the period of bourgeois social and cultural hegemony that peaked around the time of Wolf's maturity in the late nineteenth century. Privileged as a norm, yet under siege from declining birthrates and agitation about gender and class, the middle-class (Western) nuclear family of this period made exceptionally strong demands on its sons (while obsessively walling up its daughters). The task of emerging from the family nucleus as man of means (*ein vermögender Mann*, both sexually and economically potent), around whom another family could be formed, became, with great visibility, the true test of manly character as well as a source of heightened vulnerability to failure or, even worse, to modest success interpreted as failure.

Wolf's songs are probably more caught up in oedipal issues than any comparable body of music in the "classical" canon. In order to make this claim credible, I will first outline the dynamics of oedipal identity formation and sketch their manifestations in Wolf's career and character. A turn to the music will follow: a further account of the rhetorical configuration typical of Wolf's songs, counterpointed against the precedent of Schubert's; a survey of Wolf's innovative songbooks—collections framed as neither anthologies nor cycles, but including features of both—from an oedipal perspective; and, finally, detailed discussion of a quartet of well-known songs each of which is engaged with a cardinal oedipal problem.

The Oedipal Regime

From puberty on, writes Freud (1966, 337),

> the human individual has to devote himself to the great task of detaching himself from his parents, and not until that task can be achieved can he cease to be a child and become a member of the so-

cial community. For the son this task consists of detaching his libidinal wishes from his mother . . . and in reconciling himself with his father if he has remained in opposition to him, or in freeing himself from his pressure if . . . he has become subservient to him. These tasks are set to everyone; and it is remarkable how seldom they are dealt with in an ideal manner.

The wry last sentence is no mere throwaway; its worldliness is a point of theory. The oedipal regime of culture is structured precisely by, and derives its often destructive energies from, a set of demands that are impossible to satisfy fully. In this fairy tale even the lucky third son loses his—head.

The fulcrum of the oedipal structure is the Freudian superego: the masculine image that consolidates the young boy's character and becomes the internal representative of paternal law when the boy accepts the cultural interdiction against his eroticized attachment to the mother (or, more broadly, to being mothered). To say, as Freud sometimes did, that the superego is the vehicle of conscience is to give conscience a bad name. The superego is censorious and oppressive. Its primary means for structuring both the son's identity and the father's power of cultural transmission is a sense of guilt and inadequacy that often crosses into "moral masochism"; the superego, writes Freud (1960, 44), is often "super-moral" and "cruel," so that "even ordinary normal morality has a harshly restraining, cruelly prohibiting quality."

In order to ward off its punitive violence, oedipal sons typically seek to win the superego's love and approval by adopting a passive, compliant attitude toward its cultural representatives—personified or abstract ideals and institutions. This attitude is regarded as feminine, with the radical implication that femininity is primarily constructed not in order to serve the needs of women but to supply the authority administered by the superego with a paradigmatic object. "For Oedipal sons," as I have suggested elsewhere (1991, 353), "the social subject-position inscribed as masculine is countered by a psychic object-position inscribed as feminine." The oedipal son, we might say, represents the normalized version of a favorite nineteenth-century pathological type, the sexual "invert" said to bear a woman's spirit in a man's body. Normal masculinity arises when the woman's spirit cross-dresses as a man's.[5]

Two broad strategies are available to mitigate this contradiction. The oedipal son can be a model of feminine compliance to cultural authority, even if that means enforcing it brutally on both others and himself. Or he can revolt, sometimes by identifying cultural authority with himself, more often by staging his transcendence of the feminine position by staging his dominance over women. If these strategies seem disturbingly sadomasochistic, they ought to. Drawing on the work of Jessica Benjamin (1983), we can connect them with the struggle for a validating recognition that, in Hegel's *Phenomenology of Mind,* is said to plot the primary relationship between Self and Other. The masochistic Self tries (and fails) to deserve recognition by satisfying all of the Other's desires, no matter how cruel. The sadistic Self tries (and fails) to compel recognition by submitting the Other to a domination that stops only a hair short of annihilation. The same oedipal son may play both Selves, but with equal lack of ultimate success. The superego always withholds its final gifts.

The Lucky Third Son

Wolf's relationship with his father, Philipp, was close and intense, fed through intimate correspondence once Wolf had left home. As the correspondence shows, Wolf was preoccupied with convincing Philipp that he, Hugo, was man enough to achieve independence, success, and fame. Burdened by the heritage of two ne'er-do-well brothers, Wolf was determined to prove that he was indeed the lucky third son. His task was the more urgent because of his vocation. Philipp Wolf was a gifted amateur musician and Hugo's first music teacher; he was literally the man to whom Hugo had played second fiddle in the Wolf family orchestra. For Hugo to succeed, his father must be surpassed, a goal that the oedipal regime mandates but that the superego tends to regard as equivalent to parricide.

Philipp Wolf was not easy to please. Wolf would write him with a flourish:

> Courage! Courage! We will present a brow of iron to all affliction. Now, when everything conspires against me . . . now for the first time I am come to consciousness of my strength. . . . I will extinguish my unlucky star and replace it with a star of fortune.

Philipp would reply:

> Oh, the consciousness that I have reared with great sacrifices only good-for-nothing scamps is galling. Even more so is the derision and mockery of the people among whom I have to live . . . You, to be sure, shake yourself free like a wet poodle, but I can't do that. Your education was a Sisyphean labor. Graz, St. Paul, Marburg, the Conservatoire—the stone came always rolling back. . . . It will roll over me, over my useless life.

Given the literariness of the correspondence (quoted from Walker 1952, 125–26) it is tempting to read that poodle as an allusion to Goethe's Mephistopheles—a veiled but stinging insult that neatly leaves Philipp retaining the role of Faust.

Ironically, Philipp Wolf died in 1887, on the eve of his son's real success. It is not clear how either man, had the father lived, would have handled the son's oedipal graduation. Almost six years later Wolf wrote to his sister Kathe, "Ah! why do I go on composing when he can no longer hear?" (Walker 1952, 195). But the full flowering of Wolf's creativity came precisely when his father could no longer hear and seems to have coincided with the end of the mourning period in 1888, when Wolf began composing the fifty settings that would make up his Mörike songbook.

Wolf continued the oedipal dialogue with his father by addressing himself to substitute interlocutors, staging for them his superego-driven habit of vacillating between self-aggrandizement and self-debasement. At work on the Mörike songs, he would issue grandiose proclamations in letters to friends (Walker 1952, 203):

> Today . . . I created my masterpiece [,] "Erstes Liebeslied eines Mädchens" (Eduard Mörike). . . . Compared with this song everything earlier was child's play. The music is of so striking a character, and of such intensity, that it would lacerate the nervous system of a block of marble.

> I retract the opinion that "Erstes Liebeslied eines Mädchens" is my best thing, for what I wrote this morning, "Fussreise" (Eduard Mörike), is a million times better. When you have heard this song you can have only one wish—to die.

When not in the heat of labor "at a thousand horsepower," he could perform a shocking *volte-face* (Sams 1980, 485):

> I really and truly shudder at the thought of my songs. . . . What does it signify but reproach that songs are all I ever write, that I am master of what is only a small-scale genre?

As a young man, Wolf had been advised by Wagner, Brahms, and Liszt to apprentice himself to the larger forms. What could that signify but reproach from the very voice of Father Culture itself? Yet, although Wolf tried his hand at opera (*Der Corregidor,* the unfinished *Manuel Venegas*) and symphonic poem (*Penthesilea*), he never did stop specializing in songs.

Wolf's life in and around Vienna also played itself out according to the oedipal script. He supported his musical career as an admitted vagabond and sponger, losing old patrons because of his abnormal sensitivity to slights and winning new ones by sheer charm and talent. This bohemian way of life can be taken as a wholesale rejection of the respectable, psychosexually muddled middle-class family represented by his father, and to some degree Wolf must have taken it in that sense. A man who manages to have no apartment of his own, while at the height of his powers (between 1887 and 1896), is clearly making a political statement. Yet Wolf's vagabondage also served him as a means of becoming "adopted" by idealized families cut to the same pattern, families in whose homes he formed special alliances with the children. In this way he could return, in fantasy, to the supposedly blissful period of childhood that falls between the infantile and adolescent oedipal crises. This pattern was repeated often, notably in the early years of Wolf's career with the family of Josef Breuer, later Freud's collaborator in the epochal *Studies in Hysteria,* and with the Preyss and Werner families, with whom Wolf spent two idyllic summers in the summer resort town of Mayerling.

Wolf's "adoptions" reached their acme in his relations with the Köchert family: Heinrich, the Viennese court jeweler, his wife, Melanie, and their three children. In this, the most enduring case, Wolf was able to combine his fantasy of childhood bliss with something further. He and Melanie became devoted secret lovers, creating a scene of supreme oedipal triumph. As the figurative son, Wolf won and kept recognition as a man of means from the figurative father, Heinrich, while at the same time attaching himself erotically to the figurative mother, Melanie. It was Melanie, not Wolf, who at considerable personal cost kept this frail bubble from bursting.

On at least one occasion, with the help of his Goethe song "Epiphanias," Wolf stage-managed as "epiphany" of his Oedipal relationship with the Köcherts. Composed in 1888 for Melanie's birthday, the song was first performed in costume by the Köchert children, each one taking a verse, while the composer played the piano behind a screen. Wolf regarded "Epiphanias" as a composition "for the *home*"; "The lady," he said, "must be present" (Walker 1952, 277). The song is a processional for the three Magi, who are humorously introduced as freeloaders. Like children, and like Hugo Wolf, they partake of family intimacies and mysteries, but do not pay for their meals:

> Sie essen gern, sie trinken gern,
> Sie essen, trinken and bezãhlen nicht gern.

> They're glad to eat, they're glad to drink,
> They're not glad to eat, drink, and pay.

The next verse, being mere bantering doggerel, forms the perfect means to give veiled expression to Wolf's position within the family:

> Die heil'gen drei König' sind kommen allhier',
> Es sind ihrer drei und sind nicht ihrer vier;
> Und wenn zu dreien der vierte war,
> So war ein heiliger drei König mehr.

> The holy three kings have all come here,
> There are three of them, there aren't four,
> And if to the three a fourth there were,
> There'd be a holy three king the more [*sic*].

The identity of the absent-present, which is to say the hidden, fourth king, is virtually an open secret. Wolf sang the introductory verses at the birthday pageant and claimed his place among the Magi by echoing, on the piano, his own vocal cadence at "drei Konig mehr." The extra king comes out of hiding, at least musically, when Wolf ends the song with an extended piano postlude for himself. Big postludes in Wolf's songs are usually reserved for tragic or transcendental effects; this one, all genial playfulness, is only an apparent exception. The postlude gently upstages the Köchert children by recapitulating and, with small, sophisticated variations, appropriating virtually all their music. Figuratively, Wolf, too, is a child, a child-king, a member of the procession and, moreover, the privileged member, the lucky son in whom the procession is summed up. Meanwhile, being a man regardless, Wolf as the fourth king is also a substitute for the official "king" of the household, the court-connected Heinrich Köchert. Heinrich is neatly elided from the fantasmatic scene, which allows only for the lady of the house and three kings plus one: Melanie, her children, and Wolf.[6]

"Epiphanias" accomplishes frankly and jovially what Wolf's other nativity songs, including "Auf ein altes Bild" and "Schlafendes Jesuskind" from the Mörike songbook, and "Ach, des Knaben Augen" and "Die ihr schwebet" from the *Spanish Songbook,* do covertly and lyrically. The latter songs also devote themselves to the family romance, in Freud's telling phrase. Combining the imagery of the holy family with what, despite an ostentatiously *religioso* style, is the secularizing expressivity typical of the lied, they fantasmatically center the modern middle-class family on the figure of the child-king.

The Scrutinizing Mode: Confession and Recognition

Wolf's distinctive approach to the rhetorical scheme of the lied, the scrutinizing mode set up by the marked separation of voice and piano, forms a further means of perpetuating the structure of oedipal dialogue. Whereas Schubert and his heirs regard the text as a source of expressive potential and mine it even at the cost of fracturing it or melting it down, Wolf regards the text as a bid for expressive or discursive authority and interrogates it with the least possible damage to the evidence. Using the voice to assert the claims of the text, he employs the piano accompaniment to grant or deny them a validating recognition. In so doing, he builds an oedipal dynamic into the lied as a form independent of the expressive content of particular lieder. He does not, of course, do this equally with (or even within) every song; we are dealing here with dispositions, not ironclad laws. Wolf can write like Schubert or Schumann when the spirit moves him. Sometimes, moved more by the letter than the spirit, he can even write like C. F. Zelter.

Strangely enough, Wolf's scrutinizing mode gives him something in common with Zelter, a commonality that forms the kernel of truth in the Wolf legend's invocation of the expressive ideal. Zelter (together with his colleagues in the Second Berlin School) was trying to invest the lied with the prestige that early Romantic criticism and the example of Goethe had newly granted to lyric poetry. His songwriting practice, accordingly, was an attempt to reproduce in music the explicit expressive intentions of the text, which were presumed to be transparent in themselves. Schubert's practice, so often described as a harmonically and texturally enriched means of doing the same thing, created the modern lied by doing just the opposite. For Schubert, the expressive intentions that count belong to the music, not the poetry. The lied derives its legitimacy as an art form not from the poet's authority but from the composer's interpretive power to appropriate and transform poetry. Schubert's "Gretchen am Spinnrade," by common consent the prototype of the modern lied, can stand as emblematic: a song that not only ends, famously, by repeating a refrain that Goethe pointedly omits, but also drives toward that end by compacting Goethe's stanzas and rewriting his text.[7]

Wolf's practice is grounded in the tortuous path he must take in order to gain Schubert's appropriative power. Like Zelter, though for different reasons, he is bound to the letter of the text. As the discourse of the ego in an oedipal dialogue, of the Self in its desire for recognition, the text must be neither obscured nor changed—to do either would falsify it—but may only be given a voice. The authority of the lied as a whole will depend on the power of the piano to act as a superego: the power, that is, to stand voicelessly over against the textual voice and to authorize or deauthorize its utterance. This process will necessarily be complicated when the voice is female, suggesting not what the normatively masculine ego wants to say but what it wants to hear. The underlying oedipal dynamic, however, remains unchanged.

Whatever the sex of the voice, that dynamic goes forward as the music seeks to discover and project the full truth of the text: not only the truth the text reveals, but also the truth it hides, even from itself. Like the alienist of mental science, like the detached observer who hovers over the dramatic monologue, the scrutinizing subject figured by the piano part of a Wolf song trades in unexpected and often unwelcome insight. This is, I take it, the point of the composer's well-known credo: "For me the sovereign principle in art is rigorous, harsh, and inexorable truth, truth to the point of cruelty" (Sams 1980, 492). The superego in person could hardly have put it better.

As Michel Foucault has argued, this same principle was diffused across nineteenth-century culture through the disciplines of clinical medicine, psychology-psychiatry, criminology-penology, and (especially) sexology. Its diffusion enforced a general epistemic transformation in which the religious institution of confession was recast as secular and scientific and utilized as the foremost engine for the "production of truth." "If one had to confess," Foucault writes (1980, 66–67), this was not merely because the person to whom one confessed had the power to forgive, console, and direct, but because the work of producing the truth had to pass through this relationship if it was to be scientifically validated. The truth . . . was constituted in two stages: present but incomplete, blind in the one who spoke, it could only reach completion in the one who assimilated and recorded it. . . . The one who listened was not simply the forgiving master, the judge who condemned or acquited; he was the master of truth.

Freud's concept of the superego represents this master of truth as a stern father who listens to one's inner thoughts; the piano parts of Wolf's lieder represent what the same master hears when he listens.

Wolf's scrutinizing mode drastically alters both the social and the expressive values traditionally proper to the lied. Socially, the domestic *Liederabend* and the semi-public salon performance emblematized by the Schubertiad give way, at least ideally, to a public concert into which Wolf's songs can condense the illusionary, mythographic theater of Wagner's Bayreuth. Hence the activity of the Vienna Wolf-Verein, which in the eight years of its existence (1897–1905) arranged twenty-six such concerts of Wolf's songs. Expressively, the field of subjectivity once shared by voice and piano is split apart into separate and possibly incommensurate domains.

On this point, it is once again Schubert whose innovations best clarify Wolf's. The piano accompaniment of the pre-Schubertian lied is essentially the stage on which the voice is heard to soliloquize; the music tactfully keeps out of the text's way while evoking its mood. Schubert advances the piano part to a role resembling that of the chorus in classical Greek drama. Engaging the voice in dialogue, the piano serves partly as an onstage personage in its own right, partly as a reflection of the voice's condition, and partly as a personification of the audience's understanding. The voice, however, remains the central figure; it is privileged as the source of melody, which the piano may echo, exchange, counterpoint, anticipate, recollect, double, or forego.

Wolf modernizes the implicit theater of song by depriviledging the voice. Schumann can be said to have paved the way by enlarging and complicating the role of the piano, but Schumann does not, like Wolf, change the very nature of that role. Wolf's changes are conceptual and rhetorical, not stylistic; he can make do equally well with piano parts simple and complex, prominent and discreet. Appropriating the voice's former power over melody, the piano part in Wolf acquires an autonomy that identifies it with, or as, the music of the song. The music of the voice embodies the "music" of the poetry—hence another reason for Wolf's usual practice of neither altering the text nor fragmenting it by expressive repetitions of words or phrases. If the piano part still resembles a Greek chorus, it is one that has been mythologized and dematerialized on a Wagnerian model. It arises, like the music of the invisible orchestra at Bayreuth, as a kind of floating consciousness, a site of subjectivity with which the audience is meant to identify.

Wolf does not produce this effect of ambient subjectivity as Wagner does, by literally severing the music from its material production. His procedure is figurative, even abstract, and can unravel in performances that unilaterally showcase the voice. In general, Wolf projects the impression of an enhanced musical autonomy by casting his songs in a notably unyielding periodic mold. As Mosco Carner has observed (1982, 8), "In the majority of his writings [Wolf] adheres to a rigid 2 plus 2 or 4 plus 4 design, in which he goes at times so far as to add a completely superfluous pause bar at the end of a song. . . . An irregular phraseology is comparatively rare in Wolf." The tight frame is articulated primarily by the piano; its effect is to contain (include and limit) the energies of the voice, even at the risk of being appropriated by them. In this way Wolf capitalizes on the semiotics of nineteenth-century musical life, in which the piano—or, more exactly, the piano of professional public performance—already figures as the symbol and primary vehicle of autonomous musicality.[8] Piano sonority is basic to the success of Wolf's songs, which, unlike Mahler's, have not traveled well in their composer's orchestral arrangements.

Wolf's procedure fosters two types of song that may be either realized in undiluted form or intermingled dialectically. The more frequent type enhances the distance between voice and piano. It casts the voice as the subject of a Foucaultian confession, which the piano exacts and expresses; the piano empowers itself by recognizing the voice only as a medium, not as a knower, of truth. The effect of distance in such corrective songs may include, but is by no means limited to, ironic distance. The four numbers that close the sacred half of the *Spanish Songbook* ("Mühvoll komm ich und beladen," "Ach, wie lang die Seele schlummert," "Herr, was trägt die Boden hier," and "Wunden trägst du, mein Geliebter") are punitive, not to say sadistic, in attitude. The voices speak of sin and repentance; the piano parts envelop them with gratingly dissonant ostinatos repeated mechanically like accusations that can never be fully revoked. "Um Mitternacht," from the Mörike songbook, takes up a transcendentalizing stance. The piano evokes a realm of tranquility and mystery that the voice, musing allegorically on the world of night, believes itself to intuit but actually, with its strongly profiled melody, obscures. "Kennst du das Land," from the Goethe songbook, is analytic, almost psychoanalytic, in approach. Its text is the famous lyric from Goethe's novel *Wilhelm Meister's Apprenticeship* in which the waif Mignon longs eagerly but naively for a storybook Italian paradise. Wolf's piano part is overwhelmingly intense, with an orchestral sweep that the composer twice tried to capture with a real orchestra; it exposes Mignon's lyric as a thin veneer covering wave on wave of repressed sexual desire and the guilty knowledge, repressed alike, that this desire is linked to, contaminated by, incest.

EXAMPLE 6.1. Wolf, "Wer nie sein Brot" (Goethe), mm. 22–26

The rarer (but more popular) type of Wolf lied is concessive. It enacts a process of oedipal capitulation in which the piano, as if involuntarily, yields to the recognition that the voice, this time, rings true. The concessive songs depend on the collapse of the distance that sustains the corrective songs. They are always highly intense, sometimes religio-mystical, sometimes erotic or eroticized. "Ganymed," from the Goethe songbook, offers a striking example in part because it forms an antithesis to "Kennst du das Land." Ganymede, the beautiful boy abducted by Zeus, continually sexualizes his perceptions of the natural world, almost as if to compel the abduction. The piano is gradually drawn to ratify him in this, especially in the last of the song's three sections; here the piano recapitulates its melodic gestures from the first section as a continuous series of tremolos betokening the uncontrollable quaver of desire.[9]

Finally, "Wer nie sein Brot mit Tränen ass," another song from Goethe's *Wilhelm Meister,* impressively exemplifies the mixture of concessive and corrective features. The voice belongs to a wandering harper, Mignon's father, who makes the typically oedipal accusation that those who hold authority over destiny, in this case the pagan gods, take abuse as their end and guilt as their means. The voice seeks to cast this accusation as an ascent from hard-earned judgment to righteous indignation; the piano casts it as "a descent into an all-consuming rage of almost infantile ferocity" (Kramer 1990a, 118). Largely concessive in the first half of the song, the piano in the second half draws slowly but inexorably apart from the voice. The point of crisis comes with the last two lines: "dann überlasst ihr ihn den Pein: / denn alle Schuld rächt sich auf Erden" (then abandon [the wretch] to pain: / for all guilt calls forth its retribution upon the earth). The voice is heard forte, but the piano hammers at it with heavy chords rising from fortissimo in syncopation to triple forte in two-hand rhythmic unison (Ex. 6.1). It is as if the piano, half mesmerized, half horrified, were hearing through the voice's moral integrity to a core of narcissistic fury. The postlude, a study in melodic disintegration that closes in parallel fifths, announces icily that the fury has been futile at best, at worst self-destructive.[10]

One cautionary word. Like all oedipal frameworks, Wolf's cannot always keep femininity from becoming a wild card. Concessive songs for woman's voice do not necessarily signal the triumph of the ego nor corrective ones its defeat.[11]

Oedipal Careers: The Songbooks

It is commonly said, and fairly, that Wolf's songbooks, not the songs they contain, are his primary works, and that their amplitude constitutes a microcosm with which he can imitate, if not emulate, the Wagnerian macrocosm. But if the songbooks are works, that is, real totalities, it is not at all clear what kind of works they are. They have neither narrative nor musical coherence; none would hang together in performance, even if the *longueur* of such a thing were acceptable. Yet they do contain coherent pairs or groups of songs and they constitute perceptible totalities of some kind, however elusive. Perhaps it is indeed best to think of them as microcosms, subject to an indefinite number of fragmentary realizations amid performers and listeners who have (in the ideal world) studied them as wholes.

In sum, the songbooks are works conceptually but not pragmatically. Wolf organizes them, in varying degrees, by the topics of the songs they include, particularly of the songs that begin and end them. The framing songs in each case imply an unarticulated narrative, and, not surprisingly, the narratives can be situated in the wider field of oedipal narrative.

The Mörike songbook, its fifty-three songs composed in 1888, has the loosest and simplest structure but also the luckiest. The opening is epigraphic and allegorical. The first song, "Der Genesene an die Hoffnung," makes an earnest and, at the climax, militant declaration of victory over a nearly mortal illness that the gods would not cure. The piano overrides the voice's humble plea to be enfolded "like a child" in the arms of Hope and claims a mastery that is both personal (marked by the elevated expressive level) and musical (marked by an elevated level of chromaticism). The closing song is the comical "Abschied," in which the voice, for once happily doubled by the piano, claims ownership of the blatantly phallic "World-Nose" on behalf of the poet-composer (Ex. 6.2) and ends by narrating how a well-placed kick on the behind propelled the Nose's self-appointed critic down a flight of stairs. The piano rounds off the narrative with a rollicking waltz tune. Coarse to the core, the self-affirmation of "Abschied" is relaxed and confident, a clear practical advance on the more portentous triumph of "Der Genesene." The narrative implied by these framing texts is thus one of coming to full manhood by passing from symbolic to worldly mastery. The topics of the songs within the frame suggest that this end is reached via an initiatory journey through the realms, roughly speaking, of love, religion, nature, and the supernatural.

The Goethe songbook, a skein of fifty-one songs composed in 1888–89, forms a complement to the Mörike volume; its structure is elaborate but its attitude, in the end, is self-abnegating. Wolf's frame consists of two trilogies of songs. The first of these belongs to Goethe's harper and traces his step-by-step descent into the impotent rage that closes "Wer nie sein Brot mit Tränen ass." The songs form a clear narrative unit and are linked by their dispirited clinging to slow tempos. The second trilogy is a group of large-scale mythological songs, "Prometheus," "Ganymed," and "Grenzen der Menschheit," that reexamine the problem of divine authority that so obsesses the harper. The songs articulate a conspectus of oedipal attitudes. "Prometheus" is a corrective song that, most unusually, stages the failure of the piano to dominate the voice. (Wolf rightly felt that his orchestral arrangement went wrong because it undid that failure.) Prometheus brutally mocks and defies the paternal god, who storms noisily on the keyboard in a series of vain attempts to intimidate his accuser

EXAMPLE 6.2. Wolf, "Der Abschied" (Mörike), mm. 47–52

into silence and obedience. "Ganymed" reverses the situation, erotically yielding to and even seducing the "all-loving Father" in an ambience of diffuse bliss. "Grenzen der Menschheit" closes the volume by sublimating Prometheus's defiance and Ganymede's erotic submission into an attitude of sacred awe. The linear progression of the harper trilogy is thus counteracted and replaced by a dialectical spiral.

The framing trilogies of the Goethe songbook deal exclusively with men. This is indicative of another primary feature of the oedipal paradigm, its identification of human agency with masculinity. Oedipal negotiations always proceed between men; women are either elided altogether or construed as relay stations for masculine desire.[12] ("Ganymed" is an intriguing case; the song is usually performed by tenors, but Wolf thought of it as a *Hosenrolle* for soprano. It is meant to channel the male listener's homosexual desires by heterosexual means.) The Mignon of "Kennst du das Land" is chosen for elision and relay alike. Her hysteria, as registered by the piano, can be interpreted as belonging initially to the pianistic subject himself, who cannot avow it precisely because it is feminine. Mignon's paradisal longings, in turn, understood as feminine in their excess, are sublimated by the chastened, de-eroticized avowal of reconciliation in "Grenzen der Menschheit." The "feminine" masochism of the ego in relation to the superego is thereby normalized and idealized, its passive suffering recast as spiritual illumination.

The middle of the Goethe songbook consists of a rather cerebral miscellany followed by a group of amatory-exotic numbers from the *West-östlicher Divan*. The latter gives a cue to the Spanish and Italian songbooks, which focus primarily on the (mis)fortunes of sexual love. The *Spanish Songbook*, composed in 1889–90 to sixteenth- and seventeenth-century Spanish texts translated by Paul Heyse and Emanuel Geibel, is organized by contradiction. The first part of the volume consists of ten religious poems, four of them tender evocations of the holy family, the rest anguished studies in the consciousness of sin. The sinner's monologues cannot automatically be linked to oedipal modes of guilt and inadequacy latent in the nativity songs, but the overwrought quality of Wolf's settings make such a link credible.

Sacred love is countered by the secular variety in the second part of the volume, the thirty-four songs of which reinscribe the contradiction between religious bliss and torment within the battle of the sexes. Songs for male voices dominate here by about a three-to-one ratio, and their burden is the traditional test of virility: winning a woman's love, satisfying her sexually, insuring her submissiveness and fidelity. The result is a fiasco. Most of the men portrayed are, as Frank Walker notes (1952, 256), "tormented by desire, unhappy and embittered." The women, with less time onstage, have far more vitality. They are frankly indomitable—Wolf uses the Spanish setting to give them an exoticized hot-bloodedness—equally capable of strong passion and strong invective.

The secular part of the *Spanish Songbook* is framed by songs for woman's voice that project an implicit narrative of independent feminine sexuality. In the opening song, "Klinge, klinge, mein Pandero," a woman tries to "drown her sorrows of love in a dance accompanied by the tinkle of a tambourine" (Carner 1982, 45). Though she complains that her heart is not in the dance, the piano's persistent dance rhythms and mimic jingling have the effect of buoying her up, suggesting a latent vitality and resiliency that is sorely lacking in the songbook's men.

The extended and highly concessive closing song, "Geh', Geliebter, geh' jetzt," is an aubade expressing a woman's sexual and emotional happiness. In urging her illicit lover to leave her house to avoid discovery, she envisions a microcosm that joins the morning bustle of a market town with a future ascent through purgatory toward "heaven's glory"—thus joining the two halves of the songbook. The presence of the lover, to whom the woman is genuinely devoted, dwindles before her imaginative energy, which Wolf's piano realizes with what Carner (1982, 48) justly calls "magnificent sweep and grandeur and most intense feeling . . . an illustration of Wolf's autonomous, 'symphonic' writing at its most impressive." In this context, the refrain "Geh', Geliebter, geh' jetzt / Sieh, der Morgen dämmert" (Go, darling, go now, / See, the morning dawns) no longer aims at practical security but rather at the bliss of self-sufficient solitude. The first line of the refrain appears four times in the course of the song, each time to the same music. With each appearance, a measure on a chromatic auxiliary for "Geh', Geliebter" supplies an extended upbeat to a measure on the tonic for "Geh' jetzt" (Ex. 6.3). The lover's presence has become discordant, more an obstacle to the speaker's pleasure than a source of it. The discord resolves—radiantly—when the speaker voices and continually revoices the "now" ("jetzt") of her lover's imminent departure.

Wolf follows the same pattern for the second line of the refrain, but with a telling exception. Here the resolution blends with the radiance of the dawn, marked by a rising vocal leap. With the third statement of "Sieh', der Morgen dämmert," however, the voice immobilizes itself, the piano's energy slackens, and the harmony slips into the tonic minor. Just this once, the speaker's desire seems nostalgically to cling to the lover it characteristically outruns. The fourth and final statement corrects this lapse, restoring both the original piano part and the major-mode resolution. If anything, the momentary hesitation adds to the speaker's suppleness and breadth. Certainly it is in keeping with those qualities that the piano part recurs throughout the song to descending chromatic figures, sonorous and impassioned, that constantly rearise, to descend again (Ex. 6.3). The pattern perhaps suggests a feminine sexuality that self-renewingly transcends the famous "dying fall" of masculine desire. The poor "Geliebter" may simply be too fatigued to move.

Wolf's *Italian Songbook,* its forty-six songs composed in 1890–91 and 1896 to Paul Heyse's translations of brief fifteenth-century popular lyrics,

EXAMPLE 6.3. Wolf, "Geh', Geliebter, geh' Jetzt" (*Spanish Songbook*), mm. 3–9

continues in the amatory vein of the *Spanish Songbook* but at less of a fever pitch. The men's and women's songs are distributed more or less equally, and although the failure of masculine dominance is again a leading topic, it often appears in idealized form in songs of erotic adoration ("Der Mond hat eine schwere Klag' erhoben," "Wenn du mich mit den Augen streifst," "Und willst du deinen Liebsten streben sehn"). Ernest Newman famously observed that the ecstatic songs in the *Italian Songbook* are generally masculine. The women are given to mockery, resentment, or humorous toleration of their lovers; the serious love songs they do have tend to be full of torment. "Hardly ever," Newman writes, "does Wolf allow the women to soar to the heights or compass the depths of forthright passion, as he does the men" (quoted in Walker 1952, 299). This phallocratic judgment, however, is not inevitable. Another way to make the same point is to say that the men's emotional range is narrow and the women's, which does occasionally encompass ecstasy ("Heb' auf dein blondes Haupt," "Wenn du, mein Liebster"), is wide. The sheer versatility of the feminine continually gives the lie to the dream of masculine autonomy.

The frame structure, a coarsened version of its counterpart in the *Spanish Songbook,* makes much the same point. The first song is purely epigraphic, a self-reflexive celebration of "small things," so that the true frame begins with the second song, "Mir ward gesagt." A young woman anxiously anticipates her lover's departure on a journey; "Mit Tränen," she says, "bin ich bei dir allerwarts— / Gedenk' an mich, vergiss' es nicht, mein Herz" (With tears am I with you everywhere— / Think of me, do not forget, my heart). The piano responds with throbbing figuration and "stabbing clashes (seconds) on the first beat of virtually every other bar" (Carner 1982, 61), marking the presence of a "feminine," clinging dependency. Yet the latent presence of a more confident, independent attitude appears when the throbbing suddenly stops and the final line (just quoted) is haloed by a tonal shift from the prevailing E minor to closure in D major. This mild hint of autonomy turns into insouciant sexual bravado in the fleet patter of the well-known closing song, "Ich hab' in Penna," an obvious feminine appropriation of Leporello's catalogue aria in *Don Giovanni.* The promiscuous narrator is a cheerfully de-idealized version of the devoted lover in "Geh', Geliebter, geh' jetzt." She can clearly Don-Juan it as well as, and better than, the next man.

Sampling Oedipus: Four Songs

"In dem Schatten meiner Locken" (Spanish Songbook)

This song is a concert staple, often singled out for its singular lightness and charm. What is most striking about it, however, is that the erotic images to which the lightness and charm attach were weighted down with anxiety for the men of Wolf's day. A young lover lies in a heavy sleep under the shadows of his mistress's hair; three times she asks whether she should wake him—he resents being overwhelmed by languor, even calls her his serpent—and three times she answers "ah, no." In its original early-modern context, the poem plays on the traditional notion that seminal emission saps masculine energy, so that overindulgence unfits a man for worldly action. In its late-nineteenth-century context, the same poem touches on far more comprehensive fears of femininity. For Wolf's contemporaries, women's long hair was emblematic of both narcissistic beauty and a form of feminine art akin to weaving: unbound, flowing, such hair lulled men into a quasi-infantile state of bliss that could be linked to both cultural decadence and biological degeneration. Poets from Baudelaire to Yeats traded ambivalently in the imagery of "Passion-dimmed eyes and the long heavy hair / Shaken out over [one's] breast" (Yeats, "He Reproves the Curlew").

Wolf's song highlights the fact that the serpent-women who coil men in their hair are often represented as doing so unwittingly; they are naive, not malicious, helplessly poisonous in their femininity. The most dangerous women, like the Nana imagined by Zola and Manet, are childlike, capricious, and irresponsible, charming precisely in their narcissism. The voice of "In dem Schatten meiner Locken" belongs to just such a woman. She tries to comb her locks each morning, but the wind dishevels them and her lover succumbs. Her refusals to wake him are unfailingly voiced in a tender pianissimo; her two allusions to his sleeping presence (mm. 3, 46) markedly slow the tempo, suggesting a reluctance to disturb him in which she misrecognizes her hostility as affectionate and her affection as unambivalent. Wolf's piano part limns the beloved's narcissistic charm with a jaunty little tune that halts and hesitates each time she questions whether to wake her lover and resumes after she decides not to. The tune's irrepressibility comes to signify her utter imperviousness to the young man's worldly life.

The piano, however, is less interested in that imperviousness than in the deeper truth it both conceals and reveals. The voice's self-absorbed monologue follows, as if unwittingly, a tonal rhythm that the piano initiates and controls. Three times, reflection begins in B♭ major, shifts to D major at or near the question "Weck' ich ihn nun auf?" ("Shall I wake him now?"), and shifts again to G♭ major at the answer "Ach, nein" (mm. 1–10, 11–32, 33–53). This cyclical movement suggests a mode of temporality that, as Julia Kristeva points out (1988, 191–92), is traditionally associated with feminine subjectivity: the "woman's time" grounded in

cycles, gestation, the eternal recurrence of a biological rhythm which conforms to that of nature ... [a temporality] whose stereotyping may shock, but whose regularity and unison with what is experienced as extra-subjective time, cosmic time, occasion vertiginous visions and unnameable *jouissance* [bliss, orgasm].

Such cyclical time is at odds with the linear time traditionally associated with masculine subjectivity: "time as project, teleology, linear and prospective unfolding: time as departure, progression, and arrival."

Wolf marks the alienation between the two temporal modes both dramatically and structurally. The dramatic instance occurs during the last phase of the woman's monologue, which embraces two rotations of the tonal cycle (mm. 33–42, 43–53). The first of these hesitates over its completion, deferring the shift to G♭ (here F♯) through three pairs of alternating measures on the dominant of B♭ and the tonic of D major (mm. 33–38). It is as if the flow of cyclical time were being interfered with or distorted by pressure from the linear mode. Suggestively, the interference ends just as the women refers to her dark good looks ("diese meine braune Wangen").

The structural mark of temporal difference is Wolf's use of the augmented triad B♭–D–G♭ as the basis for cyclical movement. Movement through an augmented triad lies outside inherited musical modes of linear time and the associated masculinist ideals of mastery and full closure. When the song ends where it began, in B♭, it obeys only its own internal rhythm, not the authoritative tonal paradigm of departure, progression, and arrival. In this context, the piano's jaunty tune, in its own cyclical recurrences, does more than invoke a standard-issue sexist image of empty-headed charm. It both mocks the sleeping lover's distance from, and marks the waking beloved's nearness to, vertiginous visions and unnameable *jouissance*.

"Das Ständchen" (The Serenade)

"Das Ständchen" (Ex. 6.4a) belongs to the one Wolf songbook not yet mentioned, the twenty Eichendorf songs, most of them character sketches of socially marginal figures—students, soldiers, sailors, gypsies, wayfarers—published in 1889. The volume also includes a few Romantic mood pictures, of which "Das Ständchen" is by common consent the most impressive. One summer night, a student plays his lute and serenades his beloved; overhearing him, an old man recalls that in his youth he had often done the like, before his beloved died. The text follows a rhetorical-psychological course typical of the Romantic lyric. The old man compensates for outer losses by inwardly, which is to say rhetorically, merging the past with the present:

> Und die Brunnen rauschen wieder
> Durch die stille Einsamkeit,
> Und der Wald vom Berge nieder
> Wie in alter, schöner Zeit.

> And the fountains once more rustle
> Through the silent solitude,
> And the forest down beneath the hills,
> As in the old, sweet time.

EXAMPLE 6.4.

(a) Wolf, "Das Ständchen" (Eichendorf), mm. 31–33

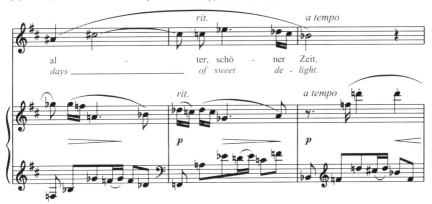

(b) Schubert, "Der Doppelgänger" (Heine), mm. 54–56

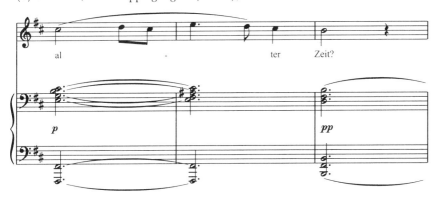

The compensatory vision, however, is unstable, as further reflection proves—and as the old man unconsciously confesses when his vocal line for "in alter, schöner Zeit" echoes the setting of "in alter Zeit" from another, more anguished street scene of nocturnal love remembered: Schubert's "Der Doppelgänger" (Ex. 6.4b). Yet the close does bring reconciliation through an apostrophe that enjoins the student to sing on always ("singe, sing' nur immer zu") and thus to preserve, by personifying, the old man's lost youth, art, and love.

Wolf's piano part anatomizes the play of memory and desire in the old man's mind in order to expose the nostalgic, fantasmatic character of his closing apostrophe. After a brief prelude in which the student can be heard tuning up, the sound of his lute appears as a left-hand ostinato.*

---

*Wolf uses open fifths to evoke a characteristic sound of tuning even though lutes are tuned in fourths and thirds.

This is played pianissmo throughout the song, independent of dynamic changes elsewhere; what we hear is not the lute as such but the lute as overheard and taken as a screen for reflection. The reflection is limned in the right-hand part, which repeatedly tries to piece together "the half-forgotten melody of long ago . . . hover[ing] elusively in the consciousness of the onlooker" (Walker 1952, 239). The result is a bare approximation, the uncertain fiction of a melody that both belongs to the old man and is dispossessingly alienated from him. Wolf makes the point dramatically by having the old man sing "So in meinen jungen Tagen" ("So in my young days") to an imperfect, fragmentary form of the already fragmentary tune. The past cannot be recaptured in the immediacy of voice, nor even by the memory that, this one time, breaks though to voice.

The pitch level of the piano's right-hand melody traces the course of memory from awakening through illusory satisfaction to failure. The opening of this melody is a third higher each time it occurs (F♯ to A♯ to D), reaching its registral peak as the old man recalls his own summer nights of serenading (mm. 33–41). The augmented triad projected by this ascent (D–F♯–A♯) offers a visionary or transcendental alternative to the tonic triad (D–F♯–A), which is outlined recurrently by the ostinato. With the old man's apostrophe, however, the glimmering mnemonic image collapses. The melody drops to its original pitch level and resumes its original form, its evocative power spent (mm. 47–58). What follows is a rather malicious irony: no sooner does the old man bid the student to sing on than the latter propels his lute into a noodling codetta and stops. The apostrophe is hollow to the core. Its gesture of passing the torch presumes a quasi-paternal authority that the old man has pathetically outlived. In second childhood, one becomes an oedipal son again, gawking at the primal scene.

"Auf einer Wanderung" (Mörike Songbook)

Like Eichendorf's "Das Ständchen," Mörike's poem "Auf einer Wanderung" typifies a Romantic genre, in this case the epiphanic lyric. Such lyrics isolate privileged, static-ecstatic moments from the ongoing movement of everyday life. As it does for Mörike's speaker, this rapture often halts a traveler's steps; the narrative time of wayfaring suddenly turns into a lyric time of heightened presence.[13]

Mörike's poem is precipitate in evoking this turnover; Wolf's song is more gradual, transforming what Mörike represents as a near-continuous rapture into a supercharged (male-erotic) consummation. To this end the song divides into two complementary parts, each with its own melodic signature and tempo, and each rising to a big cadential climax; the lesser climax of the first part prefigures the grand climax of the second. The leading melody of the first part is motion incarnate: a cheerful, animated, strongly rhythmic striding or wandering tune. The climax traverses the lines "dass die Blüten beben, dass die Lüfte leben, / dass in hoherem Rot die Rosen leuchten vor" (that the blossoms quiver, that the air quickens, / that with heightened red the roses gleam forth), the early point where Mörike's poem enters its field of bliss. The piano is paramount here, moving molto crescendo and accelerando in sonorous triplets. The voice's rapture is thus interpreted as a quickening of the vital motion embodied from the outset by the striding tune.

The second part of the song is based on a slower, more expressive or reflective theme that evokes a pleasurable sense of melodic and harmonic stasis. As in "Das Ständchen" and "In der Schatten meiner Locken," this stasis is associated with the augmented triad. Here the right-hand piano part makes four consecutive statements of the theme (the third one abbreviated), with each statement a major third higher than the last; the result is a structural projection of the augmented triad D–F♯–A♯–D (mm. 63–76). This melodic cycle meshes with a harmonic counterpart: $B\flat^6_4$–D^6_4–$F\sharp^5_3$–$B\flat^6_4$. Once these cycles have fulfilled themselves, a short crescendo-accelerando leads to the grand climax on "O Muse, du hast mein Herz berührt / mit einem Liebeshauch!" (O Muse, you have touched my heart / with a breath of Love!). This is the privileged moment in the song, introduced by bardic arpeggios and marked by a renewed broadening of tempo in the suspended animation of a prolonged dominant (Ex. 6.5). The vocal line grows expansive, lingering over the words *Muse* and *Liebe* and moving in duplets instead of triplets, two in the time of three. Here the voice, not the piano, is paramount, interpreting the climax not as an enhancement of imaginary motion but as the stilling or sublimation of such motion, beginning with its transformation into the static, "vertical" form of the arpeggios.

But it is just here that the piano exacts a truth disavowed by the voice. The striding and expressive themes are as much continuous as contrasting (Ex. 6.6). Both are based on melodic units that begin and end on the same pitch; both highlight intervals of a third; and the rhythm of the first audibly metamorphoses into the rhythm of the second: ♪♫ | ♪♫♪♩ to ♪♫ ♫ to ♩ ♪♫ . Thus, although the second part of the song immediately begins to orient the voice, longingly, toward stasis, the sound of the expressive theme in the piano recalls the origin of such stasis in vital motion, an origin that can never be fully sublimated. This remains true even during the grand climax, which occurs over a quasi-augmented version of the expressive theme, its link to the striding tune attenuated but still audible. Indeed, the head of the expressive theme returns in its original rhythm just as the voice intones the cardinal term *Liebes*. With the ensuing cadence to *Hauch*, the expressive theme, crossing the threshhold of a trill, is retransformed into the intermediate version of the striding tune at its original tempo, as if the two melodies had become one. At no point does the piano permit the voice the illusion of full transcendence; or, rather, what it permits is precisely that illusion, rendered transparent and thereby the more poignant.

EXAMPLE 6.5. Wolf, "Auf einer Wanderung" (Mörike), mm. 81–91

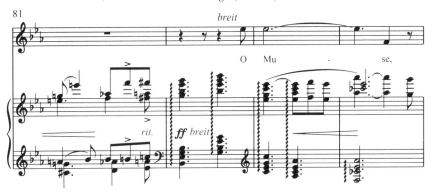

EXAMPLE 6.6. Wolf, "Auf einer Wanderung"
(a) "striding" theme, mm. 1–2

(b) "expressive" theme, mm. 63–66

"Auf einer Wanderung" is a good example of the way in which topics of genuine independent interest are tacitly engaged with ideological formations. The quarrel of stasis and motion belongs to the psychology and philosophy of the Romantic imagination, but it also conforms to a latent oedipal logic. Wandering is a quintessentially virile activity; wandering women in the nineteenth century were identified either as madwomen or prostitutes or both. Men, to steal a phrase, could by contrast be *frei aber froh.* But the stasis of transcendence involves a dangerous proximity to the feminine. Mörike's transformative image, and the substance of Wolf's first climax, is the traditionally feminine image of passional-virginal roses. The closing image is even more explicitly feminine, interpreting the earlier roseate bliss as a Muse-given breath of love. What the piano "says," therefore, while the voice bathes itself in bliss, is that the illusion of transcendence entails the surrender of masculine autonomy. From the sound of that surrender, the piano, disenchantingly, strides away.

"Der Feuerreiter" (*Mörike Songbook*)

Wolf performed this willfully overwrought *Ballade* more often than any other song he wrote. It obviously held a special meaning for him, something hard to separate from its oedipal thematics of heroic transgression and sadistic punishment. A figure from folklore, the fire-rider is mysteriously drawn from afar by fires he is forbidden to extinguish. Mörike's poem recounts the downfall of a "sacrilegious" fire-rider who disobeys this ban by extinguishing fires with a splinter from the true cross. Behind a hill (Golgotha?) there is one last fire; the fire-rider plunges boldly into a burning mill, only to be incinerated while the infernal Foe grins amid hellfire from the roofbeams. Read in oedipal terms, the fire may allegorize either the anger or the passion of the Bad Father enshrined in the superego. The fire-rider can defy these forces by means of the sacred relic or magic charm that uniquely transforms a son's suffering into redemptive power, but he cannot do so and live.

Wolf's song is a study in extremes, wild, noisy, and agitated while the fire blazes, and increasingly hushed and fragmentary as the fire dies. Surplus melodrama deliberately jostles surplus pathos. This extremity is localized in the voice of the narrator, who overidentifies with the fire-rider; the vocal line runs the gamut from whispering to virtual shouting, suggesting panic during the fire and sentimentality in its aftermath.

The piano exploits this hysterical quality in order to invest the voice, ventriloquistically, with the sadistic force of the fire-Father-Foe. The song opens with rampaging triplets suggestive of the moving flames, against which the movements of the fire-rider are narrated. Although the voice, following *Ballade* conventions, asserts less rhythmic independence than usual, Wolf for the most part approximates its usual separation from the piano. At certain critical moments, however, voice and piano implode into unity. Twice the voice cries "hinter'm Berg, hinter'm Berg, brennt es in der Mühle" ("back o' the hill, back o' the hill, the mill's on fire") to a distinctive melodic figure; twice the piano, marked triple forte, accompanies in rhythmic unison, then repeats the melodic figure in the bass while the voice is silent (Ex. 6.7). The violent repetition makes it clear that the voice, in spite of itself, has become the piano's messenger. What is meant as a cry of horror from a partisan of the defiant son is realized as a cry of vindictive triumph from the malicious father; for a moment, the voice catches fire. When the voice later recalls its outcry in order to proclaim the Foe's triumph, "Hinter'm Berg, hinter'm Berg, rast er in der Mühle," the piano does not even bother to join in; the voice is sufficiently alienated without that.

One more repetition of the "hinter'm Berg" outcry, fading out over the gutted mill, remains. The voice utters it in an exhausted pianissimo, in an abbreviated form that serves to place the smoldering fire *sub specie aeternitatis*. "Hinter'm Berg," the phrase now goes, "hinter'm Berg brennt's." Back o' the hill it's burning: the statement is now unconditional, the burn-

EXAMPLE 6.7. Wolf, "Der Feuerreiter" (Mörike), "hinter'm Berg" figure, mm. 23–26

ing perennial. At this juncture, the piano begins to repeat, softly but obsessively, rhythmic and melodic fragments, some literal, some varied, of the "hinter'm Berg" figure (Ex. 6.8). This process continues through the end of the song, endlessly disseminating the same message. The fire, as signifier, may be burned out; the fire it signifies keeps on burning. The career of the fire-rider has been futile; in the end, the voice cannot even bid him rest except by mournfully reinvoking the "hinter'm Berg" figure (Ex. 6.9).

"Der Feuerreiter," its concentration riveted on Wolf's most basic concerns, makes a fitting *envoi* to this survey of his songs. Reporting to a friend on a performance, in 1894, of his arrangement of the work for chorus and orchestra, Wolf wrote (Walker 1952, 331):

> "Der Feuerreiter" struck home like a bomb. . . . It was fearfully beautiful. Everything was at high tension. The effect was shattering. What a shame, what a shame, that you were not there. You would have opened your eyes.

The rhetorical figuration that links eye-opening truth to explosive violence, in the process eliding pleasure and subsuming beauty, is no mere

EXAMPLE 6.8. Wolf, "Der Feuerreiter," mm. 92–96, 116–18

hin - ter'm Berg,   hin - ter'm Berg   brennt's!

immer mehr abnehmend

Husch!   da fällt's in   A - sche ab.

EXAMPLE 6.9. Wolf, "Der Feuerreiter," mm. 122–25

eccentricity. On the contrary; it is the figuration most central to the psychocultural order to which Wolf's work belongs. For that reason it is most often a hidden figuration, obscured by enfranchising beauty and restoring the place of pleasure. The majority of Wolf's songs follow this practice, though often with the intention of being detected at it. But "Der Feuerreiter" is a credo. It is Wolf's most extravagant song precisely because it is meant to be his most truthful.

Notes

1. Criticism not based on the Wolf legend is hard to find. Radcliffe (1960) hews to the legend closely; Stein (1985) departs from it only by bracketing the interplay of text and music in order to take up the analytical question of extended tonality. Youens (1992), published after this chapter was written, appears less to depart from the legend than to refine and historicize it.
2. For a fuller account of this issue, see Kramer (1984, especially the chapter "Song") and Agawu (1992).
3. For an influential account of the plurality of speakers and "personae" in the lied, see Cone (1974) (1–56). Cone arguably is too quick to subsume this plurality under a single "musical persona," something he does even more strongly in Cone (1992). For critiques of Cone, see Kramer (1990b) (187–88) and (1992).
4. See the discussions in Deleuze and Guattari (1983), Thewelheit (1987), and de Lauretis (1983).
5. The formula for inversion was coined in mid-century by Karl Heinrich Ulrichs: *anima muliebris virili corpore inclusa.* For a history, see Chauncey (1982–83, 116), who observes that "inversion . . . did not denote the same conceptual phenomenon as homosexuality . . . [but rather] referred to a broad range of deviant gender behavior."
6. Heinrich's brother-in-law Wilhelm Dlauhy had a small role in the performance, substituting for Wolf as singer-narrator toward the end of the song. Dlauhy does not, "appear" in the fantasmatic scene, the workings of which his presence would help to veil (even if, as may have happened, he was merely a fifth wheel).

7. Goethe writes:

> Ach, dürft ich fassen
> Und halten ihn
> Und küssen ihn
> So wie ich wollt.
> (Ah, might I but clasp him
> And hold him
> And kiss him
> As I wish).

Schubert, having set this, reprises:

> O könnt ich ihm küssen
> So wie ich wollt.
> (O could I but kiss him
> As I wish).

"Könnt" initiates a chain of sforzandos in the piano; a strong expression of desire becomes a fierce one. For a full analysis of the complex text-music relations in this song, see Kramer (1984, 150–55).

8. The domestic piano, by contrast, symbolizes the restricted, heavily regulated subjectivity of women (see Leppert 1992).

9. For a fuller account of "Ganymed," see Kramer (1990b, 166–75).

10. For more on Wolf's harper songs, including "Wer nie sein Brot," see Kramer (1990a).

11. This caution might have been worded, ". . . cannot always keep even its fictitious, male-authored version of femininity from becoming a wild card," were it not that under an oedipal regime *all* femininity is fictitious and male-authored.

12. For further discussion of such man-to-man negotiations across and through the feminine, see Sedgwick (1985, 1–27).

13. For an account of the type, see Hartmann 1964, 3–30.

Bibliography

Agawu, V. Kofi. "Toward a Theory of Song." *Music Analysis* 11 (1992): 3–36.

Benjamin, Jessica. "Master and Slave: The Fantasy of Erotic Domination." In *Powers of Desire: The Politics of Sexuality,* ed. Ann Snitow, Christine Stansell, and Sharon Thompson, 280–99. New York, 1983.

Carner, Mosco. *Hugo Wolf Songs.* London, 1982.

Chauncey, George, Jr. "From Sexual Inversion to Homosexuality: Medicine and the Changing Conception of Female Deviance." *Salmagundi* 58–59 (1982–83): 114–46.

Cone, Edward T. *The Composer's Voice.* Berkeley, 1974.

———. "Poet's Love or Composer's Love?" In *Music and Text: Critical Inquiries,* ed. Steven Paul Scher, 177–92. Cambridge, 1992.

de Lauretis, Theresa. "Desire in Narrative." In *Alice Doesn't: Semiotics, Psychoanalysis, Cinema,* 103–57. Bloomington, IN, 1983.

Deleuze, Gilles, and Felix Guattari. *Anti-Oedipus: Capitalism and Schizophrenia.* Trans. Robert Hurler, Mark Seem, and Helen R. Lane. Minneapolis, 1983.

Faas, Ekbert. *Escape into the Mind: Victorian Poetry and the Rise of Psychiatry.* Princeton, 1988.

Foucault, Michel. *The History of Sexuality.* Vol. 1: *An Introduction.* Trans. Robert Hurley. New York, 1980.

Freud, Sigmund. *The Ego and the Id.* Trans. Joan Riviere. Revised by James Strachey, New York, 1960.

————. *Introductory Lectures on Psychoanalysis.* Trans. James Strachey et al. New York, 1966.

Hartmann, Geoffrey H. *Wordsworth's Poetry: 1787–1814.* New Haven, 1964.

Haywood, Jean I. *The Musical Language of Hugo Wolf.* Ilfracombe, 1986.

Kinsey, Barbara. "Mörike Poems Set by Brahms, Schumann, and Wolf." *Music Review* 29 (1968): 257–67.

Kramer, Lawrence. *Music and Poetry: The Nineteenth Century and After.* Berkeley, 1984.

————. "Decadence and Desire: The *Wilhelm Meister* Songs of Wolf and Schubert." In *Music at the Turn of Century: A Nineteenth-Century Music Reader,* ed. Joseph Kerman, 115–28. Berkeley, 1990. [Kramer 1990a]

————. *Music as Cultural Practice: 1800–1900.* Berkeley, 1990. [Kramer 1990b]

————. "Victorian Poetry, Oedipal Politics: *In Memoriam* and Other Instances." *Victorian Poetry* 29 (1991): 351–64.

————. "Song and Story." *Nineteenth Century Music* 15 (1992): 235–39.

Kristeva, Julia. *The Kristeva Reader.* Ed. Toril Moi. New York, 1988.

Leppert, Richard. "Sexual Identity, Death, and the Family Piano in the Nineteenth Century. In *The Sight of Sound: Music Representation, and the History of the Body,* 119–52. Berkeley, 1993.

McIver, William W. "The Declamation in Selected Songs from Hugo Wolf's *Italienisches Liederbuch.*" *NATS Bulletin* 34 / 2 (December 1977): 32–37.

Newman, Ernest. *Hugo Wolf.* London, 1907. Reprint. New York, 1966.

————. Liner note for *Hugo Wolf Society. The 1931–1938 Recordings,* reissued by EMI on 7 disks (1981), ALP 3996–4002.

Ossenkop, David. *Hugo Wolf: A Guide to Research.* New York, 1988.

Radcliffe, Philip. "Germany and Austria: The Modern Period." In *A History of Song,* ed. Denis Stevens, 228–64. New York, 1960.

Sams, Eric. "Hugo Wolf." In *The New Grove Dictionary of Music and Musicians,* ed. Stanley Sadie, 20:475–92. London, 1980.

————. *The Songs of Hugo Wolf.* 2d ed. London, 1985.

Sedgwick, Eve Kosofsky. *Between Men: English Literature and Male Homosocial Desire.* New York, 1985.

Stein, Deborah J. *Hugo's Wolf's Lieder and Extensions of Tonality.* Ann Arbor, 1985.

Thewelheit, Klaus. *Male Fantasies.* Vol. 1: *Women, Floods, Bodies, History.* Trans. Stephen Conway in collaboration with Erica Carter and Chris Turner. Minneapolis, 1987.

Walker, Frank. *Hugo Wolf: A Biography.* New York, 1952.

Youens, Susan. *Hugo Wolf: The Vocal Music.* Princeton, 1992.

CHAPTER SEVEN

Gustav Mahler: Romantic Culmination

Christopher Lewis

In June 1915, just four years after Gustav Mahler's death, the conductor Willem Mengelberg wrote to Mahler's brother-in-law Alfred Rosé from Amsterdam:

> This season, we have had beautiful Mahler performances—the First—the Second—Third—Fourth—Seventh— Lied von der Erde— Kindertotenlieder—das Klagende Lied and many songs with orchestra. Many of these works were repeated. You see from this that here we have a really strong Mahler cult set in motion.[1]

Although Mahler is known to the modern concert patron chiefly if not exclusively as the composer of gigantic dramatic symphonies, it is clear that in his own time and shortly thereafter his reputation as a creative artist depended equally on his songs. That his mature compositions fall exclusively into two radically different genres mirrors the extent to which his existence as an artist was divided by conflicting necessities that required both private and public expression. His responsibilities as a conductor made it difficult for him to find time for composition; both his professional callings were obstacles to the establishment of a functional family life. Musically, these fundamental dichotomies were reflected in his continual attempts to reconcile the extrovert developmental drama of the symphony with the intimate lyricism of the song, the vast forces of the post-Romantic orchestra and its large audience with the small circle of friends implied by the very concept of chamber music, and the objective musical values of absolute music with the symbolically autobiographical world of music informed by literary and philosophical programs. Furthermore, the songs are informed by two inherited traditions—those of the German art song and the German folk song. Mahler's attempts to fuse the stanzaic structure and simple declamation of the folksong with the more sophisticated tonal design, melodic development, and contrapuntal texture of the art song were a constant barrier to his attempts to find critical acceptance for his songs.

Early Songs

Mahler began composing as a precocious child, perhaps as early as the age of six. By the time he left his home in Iglau, Bohemia, to enter the Vienna Conservatory in 1875, he apparently had composed enough to earn an exemption from the harmony and counterpoint examinations. Unfortunately, Mahler destroyed virtually all his early compositions, and the only evidence we have of his juvenile lieder are two fragments and three songs that waited over a century for publication. These remnants are fascinating evidence that certain of Mahler's artistic attitudes were formed before his twentieth year.

The two fragments, which apparently date from about 1875,[2] are eighteen neatly copied measures of a setting of Heine's "Im wunderschönen Monat Mai" and almost twenty-two measures of a composition draft setting lines from the second and third of three Heine poems collectively titled "Tragödie."[3] "Im wunderschönen Monat Mai" is highly chromatic, remarkable chiefly for its dogged avoidance of the tonic C after the four-measure piano introduction. The "Tragödie" setting is musically very different: rather more diatonic, especially in the melodic line of the second strophe, with a much simpler, more syllabic declamation, a more straightforward phrase structure, a more conventionally metric rhythmic surface, and a much simpler homophonic texture. In short, "Im wunderschönen Monat Mai" is an attempt at a developed art song, whereas "Trägodie" in its relative simplicity resembles a folk setting. Heine identifies the second of the poems in the set (the first part of Mahler's text) as "a real folk song, which I heard in the Rhineland,"[4] but Mahler alters the text in two ways. First, to make the structure and scansion of the two stanzas more closely parallel, he changes the opening couplet of the second stanza from "Ein Jüngling hatte ein Mädchen lieb / Sie flohen heimlich von Hause fort" to "Es hatt' ein Knab ein Mägdlein [lieb][5] / Sie flohen gar heimlich von Hause fort." Second, he writes a new stanza beginning with an altered version of the next poem: "Auf ihren Grab blau Blümelein blühn." In his mid-to-late teens, Mahler therefore already exhibits certain fundamental attitudes to song composition that he would never abandon: an attraction to both lyric poetry and folk texts; an ability to imitate folk style and to mix it with his own chromatic tonality; and a remarkable ease in adapting the poetry—whatever its source—to his creative needs. Mahler's practice is a surprisingly rare literal exemplification of Edward T. Cone's observation (1974, 18) that in song "the composer's persona governs words as well as music. The words, that is, have become part of the composer's message, utterances of his own voice. In sense, he composes his own text."

Early in 1880, Mahler composed three songs of a planned set of five dedicated to the object of one of his earliest passing infatuations, Josephine Poisl.[6] The poems are apparently by Mahler. The first two songs, "Im Lenz" and "Winterlied," are unremarkable except for their stylistic diversity and tonal adventuresomeness, but the third song, "Maitanz im Grünen," is a different matter. A straightforward ländler, with a consistent homophonic texture, a strongly diatonic folklike tone, and a slightly modified strophic structure, it looks ahead not only to many later Mahler songs but also to his characteristic symphonic ländler. Mahler included "Maitanz," slightly revised and now called "Hans und Grete," in his first set of published songs.

Publication and Reception

The history of the publication, first performance, and reception by the public and the press of Mahler's songs reveals some of the reasons for Mahler's attitudes towards his place in the artistic world. There are six groups of published songs (see Table 7.1). The first volume of *Lieder und Gesänge* comprises Group I, a set of five early songs. Volumes 2 and 3 form a completely distinct collection: nine songs with texts from *Des Knaben Wunderhorn*, a collection of German folk texts published by Achim von Armin and Clemens Brentano in 1806 and 1808.[8] Although they appeared in his first publication, these songs were probably composed between 1887 and 1890 and therefore constitute Mahler's third group.[9] The *Lieder eines fahrenden Gesellen*, begun in 1884 (see Roman 1991 and Mitchell 1980b, 92–93, 119–23), constitute Group II.

Almost everything about the *Gesellen-Lieder* is problematical, even to the number of songs. On 1 January 1885, Mahler wrote (to Friedrich Löhr; Mahler 1979, 81):

> My signposts: I have written a cycle of songs, six of them so far, all dedicated to her [Joanna Richter, the current object of Mahler's affection]. She does not know them. What can they tell her but what she knows. I shall send with this the concluding song, although the inadequate words cannot render even a small part.—The idea of the songs as a whole is that a wayfaring man, who has been stricken by fate, now sets forth into the world, travelling wherever his road may lead him.

Since no trace survives of music for more than the published four songs, Donald Mitchell (1980b, 123) suggests that by the word *Lieder* Mahler sim-

TABLE 7.1.
Mahler's Songs

Group	Title	Text	Composed	Date Published (Publisher)
	Fragments and juvenilia			
	a. Im wunderschönen Monat Mai	Heine	?1875	ms.
	b. Es fiel ein Reif	Heine	?1875	ms.
	1. Im Lenz	Mahler	1880	1990 (Schott)
	2. Winterlied	Mahler	1880	1990 (Schott)
	3. Maitanz in Grünen	Mahler	1880	1990 (Schott)
I	*Lieder und Gesänge [aus der Jugendzeit]*, Vol. 1		1880–83?	1892 (Schott)
	4. Frühlingsmorgen	Leander		
	5. Erinnerung	Leander		
	6. Hans und Grethe [cf. No. 3]	Mahler		
	7. Serenade aus Don Juan	de Molina		
	8. Phantasie aus Don Juan	de Molina		
II	*Lieder eines fahrenden Gesellen*	Mahler	1884?–96?	1897 (Weinberger)
	18. Wenn mein Schatz Hochzeit macht			
	19. Ging heut' morgens übers Feld			
	20. Ich hab' ein glühend Messer			
	21. Die zwei blauen Augen			
III	*Lieder und Gesänge [aus der Jugendzeit]*, Vol. 2	Brentano and Arnim	1887–90?	1892 (Schott)
	9. Um schlimme Kinder artig zu machen			
	10. Ich ging mit Lust durch einen grünen Wald			
	11. Aus! Aus!			
	12. Starke Einbildungskraft			
	Vol. 3	Brentano and Arnim	1887–90?	1892 (Schott)
	13. Zu Strassburg auf der Schanz			
	14. Ablösung im Sommer			
	15. Scheiden und Meiden			
	16. Nicht wiedersehen!			
	17. Selbstgefühl			

(*continued*)

TABLE 7.1. (*continued*)

Group	Title	Text	Composed	Date Published (Publisher)
IV	*Lieder aus Des Knaben Wunderhorn*	Brentano and Arnim		1899–1900 (Weinberger)
	22. Der Schildwache Nachtlied		1892	
	23. Verlor'ne Müh		1892	
	24. Trost im Unglück		1892	
	25. Wer hat des Liedlein erdacht?		1892	
	26. Das Irdische Leben		1893?	
	27. Des Antonius von Padua Fischpredigt		1893	
	28. Rheinlegendchen		1893	
	29. Lied des Verfolgten im Turm		1898?	
	30. Wo die schönen Trompeten blasen		1898	
	31. Lob des hohen Verstandes		1896	
	32. Es sungen drei Engel		1895	
	33. Urlicht		1893	
	34. Das himmlische Leben		1892	
V	*[Sieben Lieder aus letzter Zeit]*			
	35. Revelge	Brentano and Arnim	1899	1905 (Kahnt)
	36. Der Tamboursg'sell (DKW)	Brentano and Arnim	1901	1905 (Kahnt)
	37. Blicke mir nicht in die Lieder	Rückert	1901	1905 (Kahnt)
	38. Ich atmet' einen linden Duft	Rückert	1901	1905 (Kahnt)
	39. Ich bin der Welt abhanden gekommen	Rückert	1901	1905 (Kahnt)
	40. Um Mitternacht	Rückert	1901	1905 (Kahnt)
	41. Liebst du um Schönheit	Rückert	1902	1907 (Kahnt)
VI	*Kindertotenlieder*	Rückert		1905 (Kahnt)
	42. Nun will die Sonn'		1901	
	43. Nun seh' ich wohl		1904	
	44. Wenn dein Mütterlein		1901	
	45. Oft denk' ich		1901	
	46. In diesem Wetter		1904	

ply meant "song texts," a common enough German usage. Mitchell's hypothesis makes sense of Mahler's phrase "the inadequate words cannot render even a small part," as a musical setting would have rendered the whole. The *Gesellen-Lieder* were probably orchestrated between 1893 and 1896 (Roman 1991) and were published by Weinberger in versions for voice and piano and for voice with orchestra. The two scores differ significantly, for Mahler revised certain compositional features as he orchestrated. Performers now have the option of singing the cycle with piano using either Mahler's score[10] or a modern reduction of the orchestral score.[11]

Perhaps spurred by the publication of the *Lieder und Gesänge*, in 1892 Mahler turned again to *Des Knaben Wunderhorn* for the texts for the fourth group of songs, all of which were scored for orchestral accompaniment. Having composed thirteen songs (No. 22–34 in Table 7.1), Mahler published them in orchestral score (1899–1900) but omitted "Es sungen drei Engel" because it was part of the Third Symphony. When they were republished by Universal in 1905,[12] "Urlicht," the fourth movement of the Second Symphony, and "Das himmlische Leben," used in the Fourth Symphony, were also omitted, and the now traditional division into two volumes of 5 songs each was established.[13] The piano-vocal volume contained 12 songs (lacking "Das himmlische Leben"), and later Universal Edition volumes also included "Revelge" and "Der Tamboursg'sell," which were composed in 1899 and 1901, respectively.[14]

"Der Tamboursg'sell" was Mahler's last *Wunderhorn-Lied*; all his later songs were to texts by Rückert, and they comprise Groups V and VI. "Blicke mir," "Ich atmet'," "Ich bin der Welt," and "Um Mitternacht" were all composed and orchestrated in the summer of 1901 (Bauer-Lechner 1980, 225n. 11; Mitchell 1985, 122n. 3). "Liebst du um Schönheit" was composed later for Mahler's wife, Alma, as a song for voice and piano (A. Mahler 1990, 60), and it clearly stands apart from the other four, not only in its medium but also in the intimacy of its conception and its realization.[15] The four orchestral *Rückert Lieder* and the last two *Wunderhorn* songs were issued individually in 1905;[16] "Liebst du" followed two years later in a piano version only,[17] and after Mahler's death all seven were gathered together under the title *Sieben Lieder aus letzter Zeit*.[18] This convoluted and at times uncertain history explains why the songs appear in such diverse groupings: as *Four Rückert Lieder* (the orchestral songs); as *Five Rückert Lieder* (the same in piano reduction, with "Liebst du"); and *Seven Late Songs* (the same, with the last two *Wunderhorn-Lieder*).

Mahler's sixth group of songs is, like the *Gesellen-Lieder*, a true cycle. In summer 1901, while working on the first four *Rückert-Lieder*, Mahler composed and orchestrated three *Kindertotenlieder* to poems that Rückert had written after two of his children had died: "Nun will die Sonn' so hell aufgehn," "Wenn dein Mütterlein," and "Oft denk' ich, sie sind nur ausgegangen." "Nun seh' ich wohl" and "In diesem Wetter" were composed and orchestrated in 1904 (Lewis 1987). The first edition appeared almost immediately, in both orchestral and piano versions.[19]

The record shows that, whatever may have been Mahler's difficulties with the symphonies, after the initial breakthrough with the *Lieder und Gesänge* in 1892 he was able to issue song collections at regular intervals, without inordinately long gaps between composition and publication. The sole exception seems to be the *Gesellen-Lieder*. Mitchell (1980b, 112) suggests that the cycle may have been withheld because Mahler was unwilling to reveal the extent to which the First Symphony cannibalized the songs, but Roman (1991) deduces that Mahler did not finish revising the piece until after 1894. In either case, it seems that the late publication was not due to any great reluctance on the part of the publishers.

Notwithstanding the relatively prompt publication, first performances of the songs came sporadically, and in some instances only many years after the appearance in print; audiences were sometimes enthusiastic, but critics were generally uncomprehending. The first known public professional performance of Mahler songs took place at a benefit performance in Prague on 18 April 1886 (see Table 7.2 for a list of the lieder premieres). On a program with twenty-five other pieces, Betty Frank sang "Frühlingsmorgen," "Ging' heut morgen," and "Hans und Grethe," with the composer at the piano. The simple folksong that closed the group was a special success; it was warmly applauded and had to be encored. Perhaps fortunately for Mahler, most of the critics were at another concert (La Grange 1973, 143, n. 48). At the next premiere, three years later, the reviews began to focus more directly on what was heard as the principal defect in Mahler's conception of the lied. His originality was recognized, but he was taken to task because the style of the music did not suit the texts (La Grange 1973, 202). It is surely significant that in both these early performances, the greatest audience response was reserved for the most simple, folklike song in the group.

The orchestral *Wunderhorn-Lieder* fared no better. For the Berlin critics in 1892, the novel and bizarre character of the music offered no point of contact with poems (La Grange 1973, 254). Although the audience at the Hamburg concert the next year enthusiastically applauded the songs, the reviews were brutal. Mahler was again attacked for writing extravagant, contorted music incompatible with his texts (La Grange 1973, 282f).

The *Lieder eines fahrenden Gesellen* were heard for the first time in public on 16 March 1896 in Berlin. The audience in the half-empty hall accorded the song cycle a reasonably warm reception (La Grange 1973, 355). After the concert Mahler admitted that he had attempted to outwit the critics: "The words of the songs are my *own*. I did not give my name in the programme to avoid providing ammunition for adversaries who would be quite capable of parodying the naïve and simple style" (letter to Max Marschalk, 20 March 1896; in Mahler 1979, 178). Nevertheless, the *Gesellen-Lieder* were criticized for being boring, unsingable, too dramatic,

TABLE 7.2.
Premiere Performances of Lieder during Mahler's Lifetime

18 April 1886, Prague.
  Frühlingsmorgen
  Ging' heut Morgens
  Hans und Grethe
Betty Frank (soprano), Mahler (piano)

3 November 1889, Budapest.
  Erinnerung
  Scheiden und Meiden
  [*also* Frühlingsmorgen]
Bianca Bianchi (soprano), Mahler (piano)

29 April 1892, Hamburg.
  Aus! Aus!
  Nicht Wiedersehen
  [*also* Hans und Grethe]
Richard Dannenberg (tenor?), Carl Armbrust (piano)

12 December 1892, Berlin.
  Der Schildwache Nachtlied
  Verlor'ne Müh'
Amalie Joachim (contralto), Raphaël Maszkowski (conductor)

27 October 1893, Hamburg.
  Das himmlische Leben
  Wer hat dies Liedchen [sic] erdacht
  [*also* Verlor'ne Müh']
Clementine Schuch-Proska (soprano), Mahler (conductor)

  Der Schildwache Nachtlied
  Trost im Unglück
  Rheinlegenden
Paul Bulss (tenor), Mahler (conductor)

16 March 1896, Berlin.
  Lieder eines fahrenden Gesellen
Anton Sistermans (bass-baritone), Mahler (conductor)

14 January 1900, Vienna.
  Das irdische Leben
  Wo die schönen Trompeten blasen

(*continued*)

TABLE 7.2. (*continued*)

[*also* Ging het' Morgens über's Feld, Die zwei blauen Augen, *and* Wer hat dies Liedlein erdacht]
Selma Kurz (soprano), Mahler (conductor)

15 February 1900, Vienna.
 Selbstgefühl
 [*also* Wo die schönen Trompeten blasen *and* Die zwei blauen Augen]
Eugen Gura (baritone), Mahler (conductor)

29 January 1905, Vienna.
 Lied des Verfolgten im Turm
 Des Antonius von Padua Fischpredigt
 Ich atmet' einen linden Duft
 Blicke mir nicht in die Lieder
 [*also* Trost im Unglück *and* Rheinlegendchen]
Anton Moser (baritone), Mahler (conductor)

 Der Tamboursg'sell
 Kindertotenlieder
 Ich bin der Welt abhanden gekommen
 Um Mitternacht
 [*also* Schildwache Nachtlied]
Friedrich Weidemann (baritone), Mahler (conductor)

 Revelge
Fritz Schrödter (tenor), Mahler (conductor)

3 February 1905, Vienna.
 Repetition of the program of 14 January 1905, with the addition of:
 Lob des Hohen Verstandes
 [*also* Verlor'ne Müh' *and* Wer hat dies Liedlein erdacht]
Marie Gutheil-Schoder (soprano), Mahler (conductor)

14 February 1907, Berlin.
 Um schlimme Kinder artig zu machen
 Ablösung im Sommer
 [*also* Nicht Wiedersehen, Selbstgefühl, Starke Einbildungskraft, Kindertotenlieder, Gesellen-Lieder, *and* Four Rückert Lieder]
Johannes Messchaert (baritone), Mahler (piano)

and exhibiting faulty declamation and music too ornate for the texts (La Grange 1973, 356f).

At Mahler's first Vienna premiere (14 January 1900), his songs were enthusiastically applauded by the audience; "Wer hat dies Liedlein" had to be immediately encored. Again, the majority of the reviews found fault with the declamation, the incongruity of textual and musical styles, and the unvocal character of the melodic lines (La Grange 1973, 553f). The critic of the *Neue freie Presse*, however, was Eduard Hanslick, and his article, although revealing a certain puzzlement, was considerably more perceptive:

> In the songs we heard yesterday . . . [Mahler] proclaims himself an enemy of the conventional and the customary, a "chercheur," as the French would say, without implying any derogatory criticism by the use of this term. The new "songs" are difficult to classify: neither *Lied* nor aria nor dramatic scene, they possess something of all these forms . . . . [Hanslick compares the *Lieder* to Berlioz's orchestral songs. He recalls Goethe's remarks about the *Wunderhorn* collection's simple character.] Mahler, in the forefront of modernism, shows a desire, as so often happens, to seek refuge in the opposite extreme— in naivity, in unremitting sentiment, in the terse, even awkward language of the old folk song. However, it would have been contrary to his nature to have treated these poems in the simple undemanding manner of earlier composers. Although a folk-like character is retained in the vocal line, this is underlaid by a sumptuous accompaniment, alert in its sprightliness and vivid in its modulation, which Mahler gives, not to the piano, but to the orchestra. . . . It is impossible to ignore the fact that there is a contradiction, a dichotomy, between the concept of the "folk song" and this artful superabundant orchestral accompaniment. Yet Mahler has pursued this venture with extraordinary delicacy and masterly technique. As we stand at the beginning of a new century, we are well advised to say of each new work produced by the musical "Sezession" (Mahler, Richard Strauss, Hugo Wolf, etc.): "It may very well be that the future lies with them."[20]

On 29 January 1905, a concert in the small hall of the Musikverein in Vienna was devoted entirely to Mahler's lieder. Curiously, all the singers were men. In fact, shortly after this concert, Mahler stated that his songs were consistently conceived for the male voice.[21] We cannot know whether he meant all his songs, almost all his songs, or merely a particular group such as the *Kindertotenlieder*. The last seems most likely, since the song movements in the second, third, and fourth symphonies all require a female voice. Mahler often accompanied performances of his songs by women, enjoying the experience to such an extent that he once remarked that he was unable to hear a beautiful female voice without falling in love with the singer (La Grange 1973, 552).

The concert was sold out, and for once the enthusiasm of the public was echoed by the Viennese critics, who almost without exception recognized the extraordinary artistry of the songs, and especially of the *Kindertotenlieder*. The music of the cycle was found "fully worthy" of one of the best-loved German poets, and a number of critics remarked on the close and appropriate linking of the words and music. Nonetheless, the *Wiener Abendpost* decried both the overly refined instrumental effects and the over-reliance on obvious musical characterizations such as the waltz, ländler, and march in the *Wunderhorn-Lieder*; the reviewer also remarked on the music's eccentricity (La Grange 1979, 584–85).[22]

It is ironic that it was not until just before he left Vienna that Mahler achieved some critical recognition for his lieder, and it is doubly ironic that he had devoted himself to a highly restricted poetic repertoire and still not been understood. His poetic tastes were remarkably consistent. On the one hand, the texts of the *Gesellen-Lieder* resemble the tone, structure, and language of the *Wunderhorn* poems; on the other, their symbolic meaning is linked to that of the *Kindertotenlieder*. The two great cycles, which in a sense frame Mahler's mature song production, are both directly expressive of the dilemma of the Romantic artist and of Mahler's situation as a composer constantly struggling against incompatible opposites.

The Dilemma of the Romantic Artist

Being a composer was the source of a fundamental difficulty—alienation. To the Romantics, the artist is, by virtue of his calling, not a normal member of society; yet he must constantly seek acceptance by and recognition from those from whom he is estranged. His life is given meaning only by his art—Schlegel said of himself that he had developed such a literariness of mind that living seemed to be synonymous with writing (Silz 1929, 46). Yet artistic creation no longer provided sufficient means to support life; Mahler earned his living as a conductor, composing primarily in the summer recess from the opera.

The dilemma was more than merely practical, for in the Romantic household art and philosophy dwelt in the same room. Herder had taught the Romantics respect for the irrational; Kant had convinced them of the sovereignty of reason. They never questioned the validity of the instinctive and unconscious, yet neither could they deny the power of the intellect. As philosophers they tried to rationalize their feelings, and as artists they tried to give creative expression to philosophic ideas. They were "tormented by endless dualisms of reason and feeling . . . [and] felt painfully the incompatibility of their poetic mission and their practical careers, the antithesis between them and their families" (Silz 1929, 84). Nineteenth-century song is saturated with expressions of this pervasive Romantic dilemma. The often trivial surface meaning of the verse has an ironic intent and is aimed at an inner circle who, because of their familiarity with the symbolic vocabulary, will understand all that is meant.

To the Romantics, Woman symbolized "the more perfect representative of humanity, and exemplified a union of physical and spiritual qualities which seemed indispensable" for perfect love, and for perfect humanity (Silz 1929, 125). Schubert's miller-maid, Schumann's reluctant *Dichterbraut*, the golden-haired maiden of the *Gesellen-Lieder*, all symbolize stability, acceptance and place. Their rejection of their suitors means loss of family—that is, an estrangement from all that the artist craves of society. It is as a symbol of estrangement that the Romantic song so frequently invokes *Wanderlust*. The wanderer is a metaphor for the process of art, which in turn is a metaphor for the process of life (this is especially true of the *Kindertotenlieder*). Engaged in "a search for meaning prompted by a dissatisfaction with the fragmentary, apparently inexplicable nature of experience" (Brown 1979, 186), the wanderer is a symbol either of artistic escape or of artistic exile from conventional society (Gish 1963, 230, 234).

Many Romantic protagonists plunge into death or madness; the latter is the spiritual analogue of the former. But even death represents an escape, a resolution of the artists' dilemma, since it meant to the Romantics the "satisfaction of their craving for the infinite, a mystical restoration to the original unity of life," a liberation from the world into spiritual freedom (Silz 1929, 155–56). This meaning is explicit in the last of the *Gesellen-Lieder*. "There at last I've found some sleep, under the linden tree. It snowed its blossoms over me, I knew no more the evils of life." Two successive stages of existence—life and death—or two concurrent modes of existence—the real and the imaginary, the physical and the metaphysical—may equally symbolize the central problem of humanity, the problem of the concreteness of human existence (Wellek 1964, 48–49). Thus, complex multiple layers of an existential duality are inherent in this Romantic conceit: the incompatibility of man and woman, on the surface; beneath that, the incompatibility of artist and society; and, under all, the question of the stability of the human self, or, if we like, of the incompatibility of body and soul. In the words of René Wellek, (1964, 50), "it is not *merely* alienation from society, or the question of artist and society: it is a much profounder malaise about the utter elusiveness of reality, the discontinuity of our self, the impossibility of human freedom." Paradoxically, while his art is the source of the artist's earthly estrangement, the permanence of his art is the artist's best hope for continuity of self.

Nature represents the ideal and the norm and is therefore the common source of both art and symbolic love (or, in the broader sense, life). The attraction to folk models is an important indication of the connection between nature and art.[23] Mahler said of the *Wunderhorn* texts, "I have devoted myself heart and soul to that poetry (which is essentially different from any other kind of 'literary poetry,' and might almost be called something more like Nature and Life—in other words the sources of all poetry—than art) in full awareness of its character and tone" (letter of 2 March 1905 to Ludwig Karpath, in Mahler 1979, 284). Mahler here explicitly invokes the crucial trinity of the Romantic artistic conception: Life (or Love), Nature, and Art.[24]

Mahler's poetry and music are thus autobiographical in a special way: They are concerned not with describing the self—with giving poetic currency to the events of a life—but with *defining* it (Goodson 1984)—with finding symbolic and metaphoric language to evoke the practical and philosophic ramifications of the Romantic dilemma, of the condition of being an artist. Life and death, light and dark, speech and silence, are all symbols of creative energy and impotence, since, for the Romantic artist, reality was not what he reported but what he created. It was a failure to understand the seriousness of intent behind the naive surface of the *Wunderhorn* verse that allowed critics to find the sophistication of Mahler's music inappropriate. However, even when the verse is simple, there is usually an attempt at expressing a meaning that relates directly to the experience of being an artist and therefore, in a deeper sense, to the experience of being. "Writing is not a naive phenomenon, and reading requires the deciphering of signs" by means of which the artist attempts consciously to transcend reality (Thalmann 1967, 82). Mahler knew this perfectly well, and he knew also the danger of being read literally. Although real-life experience may be the reason for a work's existence, narration of simple events can never be its true content (see Mahler's letter of 26 March 1896 to Max Marschalk, in Mahler 1979, 179).

The *Wunderhorn* and *Gesellen* Lieder

The poems in Arnim and Brentano's *Des Knaben Wunderhorn* are not pure folk expressions. The anthologists had no qualms about "touching them up," in some cases to a considerable extent; only about a sixth of the collection was published unaltered (Dargie 1981, 100). Goethe, for one, saw no reason why the person who wrote down a folk poem should not have the same right to alter it as did those who passed it along orally.

TABLE 7.3.
"Wenn mein Schatz Hochzeit macht": Structure of text

Stanza 1: Love	*Stanza 2: Nature*	*Stanza 3: Art*
D Marriage of the beloved	**E♭** Blue flowers wither	**D** No singing
B♭ Crying in a dark room	**F** Beautiful world	**B♭** Sleep in sorrow
G The beloved		**G** Sorrow
		[the beloved]

Mahler adopted the same free attitude to the poetry he set, whether the source was folklore or art poetry.

Mahler was very much aware of the "naive and simple style" (letter of 10 March 1896 to Marschalk, in Mahler 1979, 178) in the poems of the *Gesellen-Lieder* and pointed out that they are "in a certain sense related to the *Wunderhorn*" (letter to Karpath, 2 March 1905, in Mahler 1979, 284). But he failed to point out that the first of the *Gesellen* poems is actually a trope on one from *Des Knaben Wunderhorn*; he apparently believed that he had discovered the latter only in 1888, some years after he had composed "Wenn mein Schatz Hochzeit macht."[25] Mitchell's explanation of the discrepancy seems most convincing. Mahler must have known some of the *Wunderhorn* poems as a youth, or even as a child: he "absorbed the *Wunderhorn* spirit and style along with the very air he breathed," and the "happy and fruitful accident that set him off on a solid and extensive exploration of the *Wunderhorn* anthology" was merely "the crystallization of a preoccupation that had long been established."[26]

Mahler was an accomplished versifier. He was able to impose on all the *Geselle* texts the external attributes of *Volkstümlichkeit*: the vocabulary is simple, direct, and informal; the images—blue flowers, singing birds, a red-hot knife of sorrow, golden grain and golden hair, the linden tree losing its blossoms—are conventional; the lines are short and the rhyme schemes uncomplicated. The settings are not folk-song imitations, even though the music bears some resemblance to certain of the simpler *Wunderhorn-Lieder*. Example 7.1 illustrates the surface similarities of the first, second, and last *Gesellen-Lieder* with the *Wunderhorn-Lied* "Ich ging mit Lust." The melodies are all diatonic, the harmonic rhythm is slow, and in all the songs a simple pedal point predominates. The textures are homophonic, and the melodies are either scalar or comprised of triadic arpeggiations. An antique air is lent to "Wenn mein Schatz" by the modal progression to the subdominant and the avoidance of the leading tone. These characteristics of Mahler's "folk" style recur consistently in his music from "Hans und Grethe" to parts of the Ninth Symphony. In the case of "Ich ging mit Lust," little of the remainder of the song contradicts the folk characteristics of its opening, but that is not true of any of the *Gesellen-Lieder*. Not one is cast in strophic form; not one exhibits a conventional tonal design; and not one fails to link its music to its text with a sophistication that absolutely belies the naive surface.

The setting of "Wenn mein Schatz" is explicitly designed to articulate the Romantic trinity and expose the symbolic foundation of the cycle (see Table 7.3). In stanza 1, love has been denied and is cause for sorrow. In stanza 2, the world is lovely, flowers are blue,[27] and a sweet bird sings. In stanza 3, both natural and artistic creation are dead. The repetition of the same tonal plan (indeed, the same music) for the first and third stanzas articulates the parallel between the loss of love and the loss of art. "When my love is married" (D minor) is paired with "Do not sing, do not bloom"; "I'll

EXAMPLE 7.1.

(a) "Wenn mein Schatz," mm. 1–13

(b) "Ging heut' morgen," mm. 1–9

(continued)

(c) "Die zwei blauen Augen," mm. 1–7

From the Collected Edition, Vol. 13/1 (Joseph Weinberger, Vienna—Frankfurt/Main—London). Used by permission.

(d) "Ich ging mit Lust," mm. 1–12

From 24 Songs Vol. ii (International Music Co., N.Y.). Used by permission.

go in my gloomy little room" (B♭) is answered by "In the evening, when I go to sleep," and "Weeping for my dear love" (G minor) is balanced by "I'll think upon my sorrow." The blue eyes of the beloved are mirrored in the blue flowers and connect to the third element of the trinity by virtue of their symbolic reference to artistic vision: the grief-stricken crying over loss of love occurs in a darkened room. In the final song of the cycle, all three images return. The blue eyes—the loss of love—have sent the protagonist as a wanderer to cross a gloomy heath at night (even more explicitly than in the Schubert cycles, loss of love is directly identified as the symbol for alienation); the blue flowers, now bereft of all color and life, return as the snow-white linden blossoms falling to earth; the protagonist's night becomes eternal.

Many musical details articulate textual cross-references in the cycle. Example 7.2 shows one of the most powerful melodic links among the four songs (noted by Dargie 1981, 102). The texts associated with this recurrent gesture reveal the crucial moments of the plot: "my saddest day . . . no more singing . . . can never bloom for me . . . knife in my breast . . . on a black bier . . . taking leave . . . restful sleep [death] . . . all is good again [life's evils past]." The intricacy of the musical-textual structure of the *Gesellen-Lieder* belies the folk spirit that sometimes marks the surface of Mahler's songs. The critics who objected to this eclectic spirit did not understand that the fusion of the folkish and the artistic was for Mahler a powerful symbol representing the natural source of his art. If certain Schubert lieder are attempts to create folksong[28] and Brahms's folk settings are recreations of real folk material, then Mahler's *Gesellen-* and *Wunderhorn-Lieder* represent a third attitude: the desire to transform folk material and make of it true art songs.

The *Gesellen-Lieder* provide much of the thematic material for the First Symphony; the songs must have been more to Mahler than a source of good tunes. The real-life event that was their immediate cause, an unhappy love affair, was not one he wished to commemorate publicly (La Grange 1973, 119–20). Having apparently been reminded of the affair, Mahler wrote (to Marschalk, 14 January 1897; in Mahler 1979, 207): "At any rate—please, my dear fellow—do not touch on the 'fahrenden Gessellen' episode in my life. (The connection with the First Symphony is purely artistic.)" Indeed it was; what Mahler wished to perpetuate as an "inner programme" for the symphony was the cycle's symbolic recreation of the conditions rather than the events of his life. Through the 1880s and 1890s, his letters are studded with references to himself as a *fahrender Gessele* by which he always means his lack of *artistic* place. Having left home at the age of fifteen, in his journeyman years, he then served successive terms at Bad Hall (1880), Laibach (1881–82), Olmütz (1883), Kassel (1883–85), Prague (1885–86), Leipzig (1886–88), Budapest (1888–91), Hamburg (1891–97), Vienna (1897–1907), and New York (1907–11). Just before he opened the formal negotiations that led to his appointment at the Vienna

Opera House, Mahler wrote to Anna von Müldenberg (March 1897, in Mahler 1979, 216), "Thank God my *Wanderzeit* is drawing to an end."

The *Wunderhorn* songs that are incorporated in various ways into the Second, Third, and Fourth Symphonies likewise relate directly to Mahler's personal experience of the Romantic dilemma—the alienation of the

EXAMPLE 7.2.

(a) "Wenn mein Schatz," mm. 14–17   (b) "Wenn mein Schatz," mm. 71–74

(c) "Ging heut' morgen," mm. 119–22

(d) "Ich hab' ein glühend Messer," mm. 6–9

(e) "Ich hab' ein glühend Messer," mm. 68–71

(f) "Die zwei blauen Augen," mm. 4–8

(g) "Die zwei blauen Augen," mm. 40–44

(*continued*)

EXAMPLE 7.2. (*continued*)

(h) "Die zwei blauen Augen," mm. 50–57

Da wusst' ich nicht wie das Le - ben tut, war al - les

al - les wie - der gut! Ach al - les wie - der gut!

From the *Collected Edition*, Vol. 13/1 (Joseph Weinberger, Vienna—Frankfurt/Main—London). Used by permission.

artist—and, at a second level of symbolism, to more metaphysical questions. "Des Antonius von Padua Fischpredigt" is, on the surface, a frothy phantasy, set to music with, as Mahler noted, a slightly Bohemian flavor (see La Grange 1979, 1004). In its reincarnation as the scherzo of the Second Symphony, it appears powerful, sardonic, perhaps even tragic. The music of the two versions is essentially the same: in the scherzo, two modestly different statements of the first four-and-a-half strophes of the song frame a newly composed (but related) developmental trio section; the whole is concluded by an expansive coda. In the absence of the amusing verses, Mahler's music is revealed as the setting of the subtext, rather than the text, of the *Wunderhorn* poem.

That subtext, not very deeply concealed, has Mahler at its core. While working on the song, "he imagined eels, carps, and sharp-nosed pikes pushing their inexpressive faces out of the water and gazing at the saint with empty eyes before swimming away, not having understood a single word of his sermon. This image made him laugh aloud: he saw in it a delightful satire on human stupidity" (La Grange 1973, 275). That image must surely still have been in the back of his mind just a few years later as, at the *Gesellen-Lieder* premiere, Mahler refused to encore one of the songs: "No. They haven't understood anything" (La Grange 1973, 355). Presenting his gospel to the serried ranks of the uncomprehending public and the hostile critics, Mahler must have felt for St. Anthony not merely sympathy but downright fraternity. In his hands, the amusing folk tale becomes simultaneously a personal joke and a metaphysical statement. The same meaning is even more amusingly carried by "Lob des hohen Verstandes," in which a donkey judges a singing contest between a nightingale and a cuckoo—and awards the prize to the cuckoo.

The two irreconcilable worlds of St. Anthony and his fish are more explicitly the poetic point of "Das himmlische Leben," the *Wunderhorn-Lied* that eventually became the finale of the Fourth Symphony. Mahler regarded the song as crucial to his work of the 1890s (La Grange 1983, 249); no *Wunderhorn* text is more explicitly dualistic: "We revel in heavenly pleasures / Leaving all that is earthly behind us." In late 1909 Mahler wrote to Bruno Walter (Mahler 1979, 346):

> The day before yesterday, I did my First here [in New York]. Apparently without getting much reaction. However, I myself was pretty pleased with that youthful effort! All of these works give me a peculiar sensation when I conduct them. A burning pain crystallizes: what a world this is that rejects such sounds and patterns as something antagonistic! Something like the funeral march and the storm that then breaks out seems to me like a burning denunciation of the Creator. And in each new *work* of mine (at least up to a certain period) this cry again and again goes up: "Not their father art thou, but their Tsar!" That is—what it is like *while I am conducting!* Afterwards it is all instantly blotted out. (Otherwise one just could not go on living.) This strange reality of visions, which instantly dissolve into mist like the things that happen in dreams, is the deepest cause of the life of conflict an artist leads. He is condemned to lead a double life, and woe betide him if it happens that life and dream flow into one—so that he has appallingly to suffer in the one world for the laws of the other.

The existential duality that so tortured Mahler is openly expressed in the Second Symphony when "Urlicht" prepares for the transfiguration of the Finale: "Man lies in deepest need, / Man lies in deepest pain, / Yes, I would rather be in heaven!" The Third Symphony draws extensively on two *Wunderhorn* sources, in addition to "Das himmlische Leben." "Ablösung im Sommer" is, in a way, a sequel to "Lob des hohen Verstandes"; the cuckoo is dead, but the nightingale still lives, "and when the cuckoo's time is up / She'll start singing!" In "Es sungen drei Engel," heavenly joy provides surcease from earthly pain.[29] It is hardly incidental that in all these songs, the "other," transfigured, world is the world of art—implicitly in the gift of light (i.e., vision) in "Urlicht," explicitly in the singing of the nightingale and the angels.

Rückert

Mahler's turn from the *Wunderhorn* texts to the poems of Friedrich Rückert in summer 1901 marked a watershed in his career. As a poet, Rückert can hardly be classed with Eichendorff or Heine; his language is sometimes clumsy, and the structure of the verse rather self-conscious. But Mahler expressed for the simple homeliness of Rückert a "profound affinity" (La Grange 1983, 346), writing to Webern and Schoenberg that, after the *Wunderhorn*, he "could not set any poet except Rückert—it is above all lyric poetry, and everything else is secondary" (La Grange 1983, 576). As late as 1907, two years after his last Rückert setting, he wrote to Alma as she was about to join him, "Don't forget my *Oberon* stuff. Bring my bicycling suit too, also Mommsen, Beethoven's Letters. In fact, of the books, leave only Goethe and Shakespeare there. Bring Rückert" (A. Mahler 1990, 291).

Mahler found in Rückert a voice that spoke about things that mattered to him, in a tone very different from that of the often sardonic and satirical *Wunderhorn-Lieder*. As in the earlier collection, it was the songs' poetic message that compelled Mahler to weave them into his symphonies. To inform the inner program of the Fifth Symphony, "Ich bin der Welt abhanden gekommen" was transformed into the famous Adagietto.[30] The reference to artistic transfiguration could hardly be more explicit:

> I am dead to the tumult of the world
> And at rest in a quiet place.
> I live alone in my own heaven,
> In my love, in my song.

"Ich atmet' einen Linden Duft" turns on the image of a delicate fragrance wafted from another world to color and bring life to this one. Mahler here anticipates the final cadence of *Das Lied von der Erde*, also carrying an image of eternal suspension between the earthly and the otherworldly. The feeling of being suspended between the two worlds is created by the song's dissonant tonic sonority—a combination of D-major and B-minor triads—that never resolves. This tonic sonority is structural rather than merely decorative. Portions of the song are harmonized by the prolonged double-tonic chord; at times, the dominants of D major and B minor are overlaid, or D and B are directly juxtaposed. A drastic plunge into Eb articulates a change of address in the poetry, as the impersonal "a beloved hand" becomes personally directed: "the spray of lime *you* gently plucked." Implications of both D major and B minor are delicately overlaid on Eb before the final cadence returns to the double-tonic (see Ex. 7.3).

This beautifully crafted song demonstrates clearly the distinction between Mahler's mature tonal idiom, founded on background structures derived from paired tonics, and the "progressive tonality" of some of the early songs (especially the *Gesellen-Lieder*). These early songs simply start and end in different keys, a dramatic device linked to the text and not uncommon in Schubert songs (see Krebs 1981, 1985). With the orchestral *Wunderhorn* settings of the early 1890s, Mahler begins exploring the structural possibilities of true paired tonics. The most fully developed experiments in this vein carry sufficient tonal weight to become symphonic movements: the C/Eb pairing of "Des Antonius von Padua" and the E/G of

EXAMPLE 7.3. Harmonic plan of "Ich atmet' einen linden Duft"

D/B   V/B   (B)   V/D&B V/D   D - - B   E♭   (D)   (B)   V/B&D B/D

"Das himmlische Leben" both reflect and are integrated with the larger tonal schemes of their respective symphonies (see Lewis 1984, 1–8 and 103). There is, of course, a fundamental difference between a song that is scored for orchestra and one that is conceived symphonically.[31] A symphonic conception may be thought to presuppose a certain formal breadth, a textural depth, and a thematic character allowing development as well as statement of ideas. A symphonic movement may, however, be quite short (as the Adagietto of the Fifth) and texturally very simple (as the Tempo di Menuetto of the Third). One sign of a master composer such as Mahler is that virtually any thematic material can be successfully developed; however, the symphonic movement must be founded upon a continuous tonal plot that will provide the dramatic underpinning of the structure. This is especially true for Mahler, since he relied to a great extent on a technique of constant thematic variation (Roman 1974, 158). The paired-tonic structures developed in the *Wunderhorn-Lieder* of the 1890s are the fundamental musical aspect that allowed the songs to migrate wholesale into the symphonies and the principal reason they constitute a new genre, developed from the intimate piano lied but radically different from it.

Mahler's turn from the *Wunderhorn* texts to Rückert constituted not an about-face but a gentle veering along a broad path. Nonetheless, the *Kindertotenlieder* pose a special problem, for it is difficult to understand why Mahler should have been attracted to such a peculiar subject. When he started them, he was a childless bachelor; he was in full command of his creative powers, having just completed the Fourth Symphony, in which he finally solved the difficult tonal-structural problems that had plagued the first three, and as director of the Vienna Opera he held one of the most important musical posts in Europe. Mahler was fully aware in the summer of 1901 that he had achieved a remarkable mastery of his craft. He wrote to Natalie Bauer-Lechner, "My present creative work is that of an adult, a man of ripe experience. Although I no longer attain my former heights of enthusiasm, I now feel I'm in full possession of my powers and technique, that I'm master of my means of expression, and capable of carrying out anything I put my hand to" (La Grange 1995, 362). The *Kindertotenlieder* seem to contradict this mature confidence.

Edward Kravitt (1978, 333–34) has suggested that the songs are a symbolic, prescient dirge for Mahler's own death, thoughts of which were engendered by a serious illness in February 1901. According to Kravitt, Mahler's crisis shocked him into the thought of having children as a gateway to immortality; in the *Kindertotenlieder*, he symbolized this wish, in the form of a mourning parent, and his panicked desire for heirs sparked the flame of his whirlwind courtship of Alma. Intriguing as Kravitt's thesis is, it is not improbable that the forty-year-old Mahler was simply swept off his feet by a cultured and very beautiful young woman. And it is curious that fear of death and a need to have progeny should find expression in songs about *dead* children. Mahler did suffer a serious hemorrhage early in 1901 and was frightened by it, but he did not become morbidly obsessed. The day after the attack, he remarked that the thought of dying did not frighten him in the least, so long as his affairs were in order. An operation the following June dispelled all anxiety for this health, and throughout the following summer he seemed peaceful and relaxed (La Grange 1995, 334–36, 358–70). Indeed, in late June he wrote to Max Kalbeck (22 June 1901; in Mahler 1979, 251): "Scarlet fever is not very noticeable here by the lake; and even if it were, *j'y reste!* You can see that, too, is an article of faith with me; though it is also knowledge that a man's real enemies are not outside him, but within himself." The comment is particularly significant, as scarlet fever had taken Rückert's children. An interpretation of the poems that depends on real—though unborn—children and a real—though anticipated—death ignores both Mahler's familiarity with the literary context of Romanticism and the symbolic content of his earlier songs. On the other hand, verses focused on the loss of family encompass all the estrangements and incompatibilities of the Romantic condition.

The second of the *Kindertotenlieder*, "Nun seh' ich wohl," is an open doorway into this private world, for Mahler gave especially cogent musical and textual clues to its interpretation. When the text of "Nun seh' ich wohl" is read as figurative poetry, with creative vision symbolized by images of light, it reveals a portrait of the artist no longer a young man. The portrait is not drawn from life, but like that in the *Gesellen-Lieder*, it is a sketch in very personal terms of the artistic dilemma.

Nun seh' ich wohl, warum so dunkle Flammen	Now I understand well why you flashed at me
Ihr sprühtet mir in manchem Augenblicke,	Such mysterious flames in many a look,
O Augen! Gleichsam, um voll in einem Blicke	O Eyes! As if in one look
Zu drängen eure ganze Macht zusammen.	To concentrate your whole influence.
Doch ahnt' ich nicht, weil Nebel mich umschwammen,	Yet I did not foresee, for mist surrounded me,

Gewoben vom verblendenden Geschicke,	Woven by a blinding fate,
Dass sich der Strahl bereits zur Heimkehr schicke,	That the ray already sought to return
Dorthin, von wannen alle Strahlen stammen.	There, whence all such bolts come
Ihr wolltet mir mit eurem Leuchten sagen:	You wanted to say with your glow:
Wir möchten nah dir bleiben gerne,	We would like to stay by you,
Doch ist uns das vom Schicksal abgeschlagen.	But this is denied us by fate.
Sieh' uns nur an, denn bald sind wir dir ferne!	Look at us for soon we will be far from you.
Was dir nur Augen sind in diesen Tagen:	What are but eyes to you in these days
In künft'gen Nächten sind es dir nur Sterne.	In future nights will be but stars.

The first quatrain of the sonnet exposes a state of present knowledge, looking back to a time when a powerful source of artistic authority was not understood. In the second quatrain, the failure to understand the "mysterious flames" is attributed to the blinding delusions of superficial accomplishment, through which, however, the truth can be glimpsed. The next four lines reflect nostalgically on the past and on the truth that, whether as artists or as ordinary people, we can never remain what we are now, for that inevitably becomes what we have been; and that, as we grow and learn, what we are becomes farther and farther removed from what we were.

In Rückert's poem the last six lines comprise two tercets. But the tonal design, phrase articulation, and orchestration make the last two lines a couplet following a quatrain, greatly intensifying the poetic effect. At the beginning of the poem, the eyes are a source of light. The figure is inverted in the second quatrain as the eyes attempt to perceive light, despite being blinded. In the closing couplet, a second inversion transforms the eyes into unseeing stars, a source of light in future darkness: incomprehension will give way to knowledge; youth will grow to maturity; life will fade into death; the inspired will become the inspiration. These lines resound in our ears with echoes of Mahler's famous epigram, "My time will come."

V. Kofi Agawu has pointed out that the crucial words *Strahlen, Leuchten,* and *Sterne* are linked by the prominently articulated $^6_4$-chords that underlie them, and that shifts of mode are correlated with changes in the poetic voice. Agawu refers to the *Tristan*-like harmonies of the song; Mitchell (1985, 97) likewise finds that certain passages exude a "*Tristan*-derived ecstasy." In fact, the music does more than allude to *Tristan.* Mahler made his usual small textual revisions for this song. The most crucial is the repetition of the words *O Augen* and their separation from the

EXAMPLE 7.4. *Tristan* parody in "Nun seh' ich wohl"

surrounding clauses. The music exaggerates this rhetorical invocation, and the passage shown in Example 7.4 makes the reference explicit. The music shown in the box is quoted exactly from Mahler's song; what follows is a hypothetical continuation based on his musical source. The point made by the coincidence of text and music hardly requires emphasis. The second *O Augen*, the form of the motive towards which the music has been striving since its opening measures, directly quotes *Tristan*. The conductor for whom that opera was a sacred trust, kept always under his hand and eye (see A. Mahler 1990, 96), could not have written the passage unknowingly. It stems from the poetic references to sources of artistic vision,[32] which Mahler identifies as Wagner.[33]

The paired-tonic structures of which Mahler demonstrates such knowing mastery by the turn of the century, and which were first systematically explored in *Tristan* (see Bailey 1985, 121), inform the language of "Nun seh' ich wohl." The complex harmonic foreground derives from the pairing of C minor with A♭ major, and its modally changed analogue of C major with A minor (see Ex. 7.5). The upper-part voice-leading of mm. 6–8 elaborates the underlying V of C, but the powerfully articulated A♭ triad, prolonged by passing motion, is at this point a stronger point of reference than is C. Even in m. 9, when the bass of the supposed V of C resolves, a 6–5 displacement in the upper voice causes the A♭ triad to supplant the presumed principal tonic. This unresolving is immediately followed by the *Tristan* parody of mm. 10–14—as if to say, "This is where I

EXAMPLE 7.5. Sketch of "Nun seh' wohl," mm. 1–10

learned it." At the beginning of the ensuing C-major section, concatenated and consecutive couplings of C and A reiterate the point.

The words articulated by the recurrences of the *Tristan/Augen* motive comprise a summary of the poem's references to artistic vision, providing a direct link from the abstract symbolism of the poetry to the specific artistic sources identified by the music: "O Augen! O Augen!" (mm. 10–14); "The ray sought to return" (mm. 28–29); "From whence all such rays come" (35–37); "You wanted to say" (mm. 38–40); "We will be far from you" (44–47); postlude (voice absent). Table 7.4 summarizes the meanings encompassed by the textual and musical references. We see clearly that the literal sense of Rückert's poem is as a framework for symbolic reference to

TABLE 7.4.
Levels of Poetic Meaning in "Nun seh' ich wohl"

The Romantic paradigm	*Interpretation*	*Vehicle*	*Scope*
1. Escape from reality into art	Ruckert's grief for his lost children poetically expressed	Literal sense of the words	General to the whole cycle
2. The "Romantic dilemma"	Estrangement of artist from society	Symbol of loss of family	General to the whole cycle
3. The human self as artist	(a) The passing of journeyman years and the arrival at artistic maturity	Symbols of blindness and sight; mist and clarity	Specific to "Nun seh' ich whol"; others are similar
	(b) The source of that mature vision	Musical references	Specific to 'Nun seh' ich whol"
4. The existential problem	(a) The discontinuity of self	Layers of time in the poem: past, present, future; symbols of estrangement.	The vehicle specific to "Nun seh' ich wohl"; the sense general to the whole cycle.
	(b) Immortality through Art	Eyes become stars as days turn to nights.	

the Romantic dilemma of the artist estranged from society; we see that the symbols by which that meaning is expressed are interpreted by Mahler as specifically referential to his own mature confidence in his powers; and we see that at the very bottom of the structure "are still the old basic questions of human existence, of love and loss, of life and death, of speaking and being silent" (Thalmann 1967, 110).

Every artist, married or single, has children: they are his art.[34] Every human adult has a child: it is himself, always living in his own memory. It is such a child—the self of his journeyman years, and the products of those years—to whom Mahler is bidding a nostalgic farewell. As he achieved his artistic maturity around the turn of the century, Mahler thus testified, in the last songs he wrote,[35] that he knew where he was and by precisely what road he had traveled. The powerful voice that cried out to him from Rückert's poetry, the voice with which he felt such affinity, was his own, and it spoke to him of the one thing that mattered to him above all else—his existence as a creative artist.

For Mahler, only *artistic* mortality was to be feared (see Bauer-Lechner 1980, 171). Ironically, while assuring the continuity of his own creative work, he contributed not a little to the death of the intimate Romantic piano lied he had inherited from Schubert and Schumann. This is only fitting, for Mahler's whole life was a history of entrapment in irony. Perhaps the most literary of song composers, he was constantly attacked for having misunderstood his texts; his faith in himself as an artist was met with almost unanimous critical disdain; the demands of ordinary life made the achievement of the dream-world that was so necessary to him almost impossible; only his death brought him recognition in his own city. The opening lines of one of Rückert's best-loved lyrics might have been written as Mahler's epitaph; they perfectly capture the flavor of his life and the meaning of his art:

Zwischen Lied und Liebe war mein Leben,	I lived between song and love,
Aber, schwebend zwischen Lieb' und Liede	Yet, suspended between love and song,
Wusst' ich nie die beiden auszugleichen.	I knew not how to reconcile the two.

Notes

1. Willem Mengelberg to Alfred Rosé, 24 June 1915, E5 CAr6 280, The Mahler-Rosé Collection, The Gustav Mahler-Alfred Rosé Room, The Music Library, The University of Western Ontario, London, Canada. I am grateful to William Guthrie, the head of the music library at the University of Western Ontario for allowing me to examine musical holographs and certain letters in the Mahler-Rosé Collection.

2. The handwriting is as obviously immature as the compositional technique. Donald Mitchell ascribes a date of "1875 or earlier" (Mitchell *Early*, 302).

3. The holographs of these two songs are in the Pierpont Morgan Library, New York. I am grateful to J. Rigbie Turner, Curator of Music Manuscripts for allowing me the privileges of the Library. The full text of the last two poems of Heine's "Tragödie" is:

II

Es fiel eir Reif in der Frühlingsnacht,
Er fiel aur die zarten Blaublümelein,
Sie sind verwelket, verdorret.

Ein Jüngling hatte ein Mädchen lieb,
Sie flohen heimlich von Hause fort.
Es wußt' weder Vater noch Mutter.

Sie sind gawandert hin und her
Sie haben behabt weder Glück noch Stern,
Sie sind verdorben, gestorben.

III

Auf ihren Grab da steht eine Linde,
Drin pfeifen die Vögel und Abendwinde,
Und druntar sitzt, auf dem grünen Platz,
Der Mülle 'sknecht mit selnem Schatz.

Die Winde die wehen so lind und so schaurig,
Die Vögel die singen so süß und so traurig,
Die schwatzenden Buhlen, die werden stumm,
Sie weinen und wissen selbst nicht warum.

(Heinrich Heine, *Neue Gedichte,* vol. 2 of *Historisch-kritische Gesamtausgabe der Werke* [Hamburg 1983], 73–74.) In view of the probable date of composition of this song, the references to death and graveside flowers may have sounded in Mahler's ears as reminders of the recent death (13 April 1874) of his younger brother, Ernst. de La Grange says Mahler later told Natalie Bauer-Lechner that no other death had so deeply affected him (*Mahler,* vol. 1, 45).

4. Heine, *Neue Gedichte,* 73. See Jack Diether's discussion of these songs.

5. Mahler forgets the underlay of this word.

6. See Mahler, *Selected Letters,* 386–87 n. 5. The holographs are in the Mahler-Rosé Collection, the University of Western Ontario. The dedication and the numbers, but not titles, of the fourth and fifth songs are given on the title page. Each of the songs is dated on its last page: 19 February 1880, 27 February 1880, and 5 March 1880. First publication was in *Verschiedene Lieder,* vol. 13/5 of the *Collected Works,* ed. Zoltan Roman (Mainz, 1990).

7. On the engraver's copy Mahler entered the word "Volkslied" under the title (Roman's preface to *Verschiedene Lieder,* ix), but whether as an identification of a source or merely as a characterization is unknown. Mahler said that both music and words of the song came to him in the middle of the night (Bauer-Lechner, 150–51).

8. The three volumes were called *Lieder und Gesänge aus der Jugendzeit* when reissued after Mahler's death. Donald Mitchell's characterization of *Lied* as art

song and *Gesang* as unsophisticated air almost reverses the distinctions that likely existed in Mahler's mind. To the German-speaker, *Lied* is a generic term and means simply "song"; it does not have the connotation of sophistication it now has for the English-speaking world. *Gesang* carries implications of formality and artifice. Nonetheless, the terms are not always used in these distinct ways and are sometimes even employed simultaneously; e.g., the poster for the *Kindertotenlieder* premiere carried the dual heading "Ein Lieder-Abend mit Orchester" and "Gesänge von Gustav Mahler" (see Mitchell 1985, 40).

9. The compositional history of these works is most uncertain. See Mitchell 1980b, 113–17.

10. *Gustav Mahler: Lieder eines fahrenden Gesellen,* Zoltan Roman, vol. 13/I of his *Sämtliche Werke* (Vienna, 1982).

11. *Gustav Mahler: Lieder eines fahrenden Gesellen,* ed. Colin Mathews (London, 1977). The *Gesellen-Lieder* may indeed have been planned as an orchestral cycle (see Mitchell 1980, 93) but composed pianistically. On 12 April 1896, Mahler offered some compositional advice to Max Marschalk: "Next you must shake off the *pianist!* None of this [Marschalk's score] is a movement for an *orchestra*—it is conceived for the piano—and then rearranged for orchestra without getting free of the trammels of that *instrument.*—I suffered from *that* ailment once myself.—All of us nowadays start out from the piano, whereas the old masters' origins lay in the *violin* and the *voice*" (Mahler 1979, 182). Mahler's final intentions may well have been that the orchestral version should differ in some respects from the much earlier piano version because of the differences in the sonority, resonance, power, and textural flexibility between the two accompanying media.

12. See Richard Specht's preface to the Philharmonia series miniature score, *Des Knaben Wunderhorn* (Vienna, n.d.).

13. Mitchell (1980b, 249–50). Universal continued to issue the Weinberger scores individually, with an Universal-Edition sticker covering the Weinberger logo on the title page.

14. Mitchell (1980b, 142). The full piano-vocal version was published as *14 Lieder aus Des Knaben Wunderhorn* by Universal-Edition, Vienna. From 1892 to 1893, Mahler referred to the five songs of 1892 as "Humoresken" (La Grange 1979, 996).

15. The song was apparently later orchestrated by Max Puttmann, an employee of the publisher C. F. Kahnt (La Grange 1983, 1117; Mitchell 1985, 123–24).

16. The publisher was C. F. Kahnt. The piano versions were published in one volume; the title page is reproduced in Blaukopf (1976, plate 231).

17. Mitchell (1980b, 112); *Gustav Mahler: Lieder nach Texten von Friedrich Rückert,* ed. Zoltan Roman vi, vol. 13/4 of *Sämtliche Werke* (Leipzig, 1984).

18. Perhaps in 1913, by C. F. Kahnt, undated edition; see Mitchell (1985, 69).

19. Leipzig: C. F. Kahnt, 1905.

20. *Neue freie Presse,* 15 January 1900. The review was reprinted in full in Eduard Hanslick, *Aus neuer und neuester Zeit: Musikalische Kritiken und Schilderungen* (Berlin, 1900), 70–80. The excerpt relating to the songs is given in Mitchell (1980b, 430–31).

21. Mein Gesänge sind durchwegs für ein Männerstimme gedacht" (Mahler to Oscar Fried, [Spring] 1905; in Mahler 1983, 52).

22. The frequency with which hostile critics invoked words like "bizarre," "eccentric," "extravagant," "contorted," and so on leads one to speculate upon the extent to which these expressions were coded references to Mahler's Jewishness. Sometimes critics were more directly antisemitic: "One could hardly expect Mahler to possess the true German spirit" (cited in La Grange 1979, 553).

23. Certain visual and musical symbols from folk sources were transferred to opera (see Bailey 1981).

24. I am indebted to Robert Bailey for my understanding of this secular trinity.

25. The most accessible publication of the two texts is in Mitchell's preface to A. Mahler (1990, xxvi).

26. Mitchell (1980b, 119). For discussions of the evidence relating to Mahler's introduction to the *Wunderhorn* collection, see also A. Mahler (1990, xxv–xxvii), Dargie (1981, 112–13), and La Grange (1979, 986).

27. The line "Blümlein blau! Verdorre nicht," are reminiscent of Mahler's old Heine "Tragödie" fragment.

28. Bailey (1981, 436). In fact, several Schubert songs have achieved the status of folk songs in German-speaking countries.

29. In this case, it is more accurate to say that the song is derived from the symphonic movement, rather than the other way around; the text, of course, precedes both (see Mitchell 1980b, 129–32).

30. See the comparative analysis of foreground and middle-ground in Lewis (1987).

31. This discussion is necessarily brief; for a fuller treatment of the subject with respect to Mahler, see Tibbe (1971) and Mitchell (1985), 25–143.

32. While the references are most direct in "Nun seh' ich wohl," images of light pervade all the songs of the cycle.

33. Bruckner's many Wagner references are similarly motivated.

34. While composing the Rückert songs of 1901 (including the first batch of *Kindertotenlieder*), Mahler said to Bauer-Lechner: "They were the most blissful days of my life, those of my honeymoon with my muse! Since then, our marriage has produced one child after another, and it hardly even occurs to us to thank each other for this happiness" (La Grange 1983, 96).

35. "Nun seh' ich wohl" one of the two last songs Mahler composed. It is curious that after his marriage Mahler embarked on virtually no new song projects; he merely finished the *Kindertotenlieder* cycle and, in 1902, composed "Liebst du um Schönheit."

36. "A work whose bounds are clearly apprehended, reeks of mortality—and that's just what I can't stand in art!" in Bauer-Lechner, *Recollections*, 171.

Bibliography

Editor's Note: Originally, all references were to the three-volume French biography by La Grange (1979, 1983, 1984). But now that the second volume (1995) of a projected four has appeared in English (volume 1 was published in 1973), most of the references have been transferred to the English versions. A few citations for which counterparts could not be found in the English volumes are left to the French sources.

Agawu, V. Kofi. "The Musical Language of *Kindertotenlieder* No. 2." *Journal of Musicology* 2 (1983): 81–92.

Bailey, Robert. "Visual and Musical Symbolism in German Romantic Opera." In *International Musicological Society: Report of the Twelfth Congress, Berkeley 1977*, ed. Daniel Heartz and Bonnie C. Wade, 436–44. Kassel, 1981.

———. *Richard Wagner: Prelude and Transfiguration from "Tristan and Isolde."* New York, 1985.

Bauer-Lechner, Natalie. *Recollections of Gustav Mahler*, Ed. Peter Franklin. Trans. Dika Newlin. London, 1980.

Blaukopf, Kurt. *Mahler: A Documentary Study.* Oxford, 1976.

Brown, Marshall. *The Shape of German Romanticism.* Ithaca, 1979.

Cone, Edward T. *The Composer's Voice.* Berkeley, 1974.

Dargie, E. Mary. *Music and Poetry in the Songs of Gustav Mahler.* Bern, 1981.

Diether, Jack. "Notes on Some Mahler Juvenalia." *Chord and Discord* 3 (1969): 3–100.

Gish, Theodore. "*Wanderlust* and *Wanderlied*: The Motif of the Wandering Hero in German Romanticism." *Studies in Romanticism* 3 (1963): 225–39.

Goodson, A. C. "Hölderlin and the Bounds of Romantic Metaphor." In *Deutsche Romantik and English Romanticism*, ed. Theordore Gish and Sandra Frieden. Munich, 1984.

Heine, Heinrich. *Neue Gedichte.* Vol. 2 of *Historisch-Kritische Gesamtausgabe der Werke.* Hamburg, 1983.

Kravitt, Edward F. "Mahler's Dirges for his Death: February 24, 1901." *Musical Quarterly* 64 (1978): 329–53.

Krebs, Harald. "Alternatives to Monotonality in Early Nineteenth-Century Music." *Journal of Music Theory* 25 (1981): 1–16.

———. "The Background Level in Some Tonally Deviating Works of Franz Schubert." *In Theory Only* 8/8 (1985): 5–18.

La Grange, Henry-Louis de. *Gustav Mahler.* Vol. 1. London, New York, 1973. Vol. 2. New York, Oxford, 1995.

———. *Gustav Mahler: Chronique d'une vie.* Vol. 1. Paris, 1979. Vol. 2. Paris, 1983. Vol. 3. Paris, 1984.

Lewis, Christopher. *Tonal Coherence in Mahler's Ninth Symphony.* Ann Arbor, MI, 1984.

———. "On the Chronology of the *Kindertotenlieder*." *Revue Mahler* 1 (1987): 22–25.

Mahler, Alma. *Memories and Letters.* Ed. Donald Mitchell and Knud Martner. Trans. Basil Creighton. 4th ed. London, 1990.

Mahler, Gustav. *Gustav Mahler: Selected Letters.* Ed. Knud Martner. Trans. Eithne Wilkins, Ernst Kaiser, and Bill Hopkins. New York, 1979.

———. *Gustav Mahler: Unbekannte Brief.* Ed. Herta Blaukopf. Vienna, 1983.

Mitchell, Donald. *Gustav Mahler: The Early Years.* Rev. ed. London, 1980. [Mitchell 1980a]

———. *Gustav Mahler: The Wunderhorn Years.* Berkeley, 1980. [Mitchell 1980b]

———. *Songs and Symphonies of Life and Death.* Berkeley, 1985.

Roman, Zoltan. "Structure as a Factor in the Genesis of Mahler's Songs." *Music Review* 35 (1974): 157–66.

———. "The Chronology of Mahler's *Gessellen-Lieder*: Literary and Musical Evidence." Paper read before the American Musicological Society, Chicago, 10 November 1991.

Silz, Walter. *Early German Romanticism: Its Founders and Heinrich von Kleist.* Cambridge, MA, 1929.

Thalmann, Marianne. *Zeichensprache der Romantik.* Heidelberg, 1967.

Tibbe, Monika. *Über die verwendung von Liedern und Liedelmenten in instrumentalen Symphoniesatzen Gustav Mahlers.* 2d ed. Munich, 1971.

Wellek, René. "German and English Romanticism: A Confrontation." *Studies in Romanticism* 4 (1964): 35–56.

CHAPTER EIGHT

Richard Strauss: A Lifetime of Lied Composition

Barbara A. Petersen

Richard Strauss (1864–1949) composed lieder throughout his long career, from the 14-measure "Weihnachtslied" of December 1870 to his crowning achievement of 1948, the orchestral songs now known as the *Vier letzte Lieder*.[1] His more than two hundred songs stand at the end of the great nineteenth-century German lied tradition. Perhaps because Strauss enjoyed a long composing career and lived nearly to the halfway mark of the twentieth century, he is sometimes viewed less as a nineteenth-century figure than as a transitional or even a twentieth-century one (if, toward the end, something of an anachronism). Yet, three-quarters of his lieder—112 songs published in groups with opus numbers, forty-five early songs, and a handful of occasional pieces—were composed by 1904.

As important as the lied was to Strauss, this small-scale genre was often subordinate to larger works—first the tone poems and later the operas—which he himself would conduct. His work as a conductor of operatic and orchestral repertory was far more important to Strauss than his occasional appearances as a pianist in lieder or chamber music, and this is certainly reflected in his compositional priorities. From his first published collection of eight lieder in Op. 10, composed in 1885 and published in 1887,[2] Strauss's songs were issued in groups of two to eight songs—most often four or six—but rarely forming a poetic or musical cycle. Some are settings of a single poet (especially the earliest groups, Opp. 10, 17, 19, 21, 22, 26, and 29), whereas others include a mixture of poets from different periods and even cultures (Opp. 15 and 27 and most of the lesser-known collections from Op. 33 through Op. 44). After his marriage to soprano Pauline de Ahna in 1894, Strauss frequently appeared as piano accompanist for her and other singers. Song recitals (*Liederabende*) mixing songs from different opus groups made up the composer's typical programs, emphasizing the contrasts between individual songs rather than the unity of song groups.

The majority of Strauss's lieder were written for high voice, most often soprano, usually for individuals with whom he was associated. Beginning in his youth he wrote lieder for his aunt Johanna Pschorr, then for Pauline, and later for singers who concertized with him (Elisabeth Schumann, Elena Gerhardt, Maria Reining, Lea Piltti, and others) or who created his leading operatic roles (notably Viorica Ursuleac, Maria Jeritza, Lotte Lehmann, and Elisabeth Rethberg). Strauss's songs through Op. 56 (1903–6) achieved popularity as soon as they were published; editions with translated text (especially into English, but also French, Italian, and Russian), transpositions for other voice categories, and reprints were numerous. The songs were widely performed, frequently arranged, sometimes orchestrated (by Strauss and others), and, from 1898, recorded with increasing frequency.

From 1907 to 1917, Strauss nearly ceased writing lieder; he sketched at least twenty songs but completed only three, none of them published in his lifetime.[3] When he returned wholeheartedly to the song in 1918, both he and the musical world had changed. Yet he continued to turn out songs with either piano or orchestral accompaniment to the end of his creative life. Increasingly, his later songs show the influence of operatic writing in their coloratura vocal style, accompaniments conceived for orchestra instead of piano, and dramatic, expansive scenalike structures.

Writing within a few years of Strauss's completion in 1906 of the last song of Op. 56, such authors as Ernest Newman (1908) and Henry T. Finck (1917) believed that Strauss had completed his contributions to the lied. They were proved wrong in 1918, when Strauss created four groups of songs (Opp. 66–69) in rapid succession.[4] Individual songs, occasional pieces, and two groups with opus numbers (Op. 71 with orchestra, Op. 77 with piano) continued to appear sporadically from Strauss's composing desk, but he never regained his earlier concentration on collections of lieder. Incomplete sketches from the 1930s show him again dabbling with Goethe settings—a lifelong interest—but without the earlier impetus to complete and publish them.

Poets and Poetry

In his lieder, Strauss set the verses of over sixty poets. He found their work in poetry volumes that he owned, often noting in the margins his first compositional ideas; several such volumes are still found in the Richard

Strauss Archive in Garmisch. He often copied poems into his sketchbooks, adding similar marginalia: key signatures, meters, modulations, and melodic or rhythmic motives. Aside from text repetition (and the occasional carelessness in copying), departures from the original poems are unusual in Strauss's settings. Changes enumerated in critical reports of the *Gesamtausgabe der Lieder* (see Editions) usually involve little more than substitutions of single words.[5] Unfortunately, the editor fails to indicate in which literary or musical sources these variants are found, but Reinhold Schlötterer (1988) cites Strauss's poetic sources and indicates those still belonging to the Richard Strauss Archive.

The poetry of Strauss's early lieder is almost exclusively from the late eighteenth and early nineteenth centuries, usually by the same poets whose works were set by countless earlier composers.[6] Strauss's lifelong concentration on poets from Goethe through his own contemporaries is made clear in Schlötterer's arrangement of the lied texts in chronological order by birth of the poets. The earliest include Michelangelo Buonarroti, then William Shakespeare and Pedro Calderón de la Barca. Over 80 percent of the poets represented were born between 1749 (Goethe) and the 1870s (Emanuel von Bodmann, Hans Bethge). Only eleven of the poets were younger than Strauss, from the frequently set Otto Julius Bierbaum (1865–1910) to Betty Knobel (b. 1904), the poet of his last completed song, "Malven."

At least eighty-five of the poems set by Strauss were also used by other composers, including C. F. Zelter, Karl Loewe, Robert Franz, Schumann, Brahms, Konradin Kreutzer, Max von Schillings, Hans Pfitzner, Max Reger, and many others who are virtually unknown today. "Der Fischer" was the most frequently set of all the poems Strauss worked with. Second in popularity was probably Goethe's poem "Gefunden"; at least ninety settings are known, among them Strauss's Op. 56, No. 1 (1903).[7] Strauss created two settings of only one poem, Uhland's "Einkehr"; the first (o. op. 3) dates from 1871, the second from 1900 (Op. 47, No. 4).

Beginning with his first mature group of songs, Op. 10, Strauss turned temporarily to a group of lesser-known writers from the generations just preceding his own. In setting poems by Hermann von Gilm (1812–64) in Op. 10, Count Adolf Friedrich von Schack (1815–94) in Opp. 15, 17, and 19, and Felix Dahn (1834–1912) in Opp. 21 and 22, Strauss sought not high literary quality but expressive verse that personally inspired him. When truly struck by a poem, Strauss could easily dash off a song. An oft-quoted remark from 1895 illustrates his spontaneity:

> For several months I had no desire to compose; then suddenly one evening I took a book of poetry in my hand and leafed through it perfunctorily; one poem struck me so much that before I had read completely through it the musical concept came to me.[8]

So inspired, he could sketch out the entire song in a few minutes. But he admitted that not all his works flowed so easily, and sometimes he would select

> any random poem that happens to be at all suitable for a musical set-
> ting—but the process is slow, the result is artificial, the melody has a
> viscid flow, and I have to draw on all my command of technical re-
> sources in order to achieve something that will stand the test of self-
> criticism.[9]

After concentrated use of works by Gilm, Schack, and Dahn, Strauss again shifted direction and turned to more contemporary poets and to representing various poets within each set.[10] Especially during 1895–1902, Strauss's richest, most concentrated lieder period, he set several poems of Henckell, Dehmel, and Bierbaum, as well as other poets, many of whom he knew, including Mackay, Liliencron, Bodmann, and Busse. Some among them had *Jugendstil* tendencies and created a stir with a new poetic genre, the *Soziallyrik*.[11] Strauss later set even more diverse poems, drawing on translations from Shakespeare and Oriental poets, commissioning spe-cific texts, and using recent verses (by Josef Weinheber, Hermann Hesse, and Betty Knobel) as well as traditional poems.

Traditional Beginnings: The Early Songs

Strauss's youthful songs, prior to Op. 10, fall into two basic types. The first includes straightforward lyrical songs with sectional structures gener-ally including repetitions of music, six of them in strophic or modified strophic design and most of the others in ternary form. The second type includes dramatic through-composed songs with little repetition; three are short, expressing a single mood ("Nebel," "Winterreise," and "Lass ruhn die Toten"), and four are multisectional, expressive lieder in which the po-etry produces the form. The latter four use set texts concerning nature and its power over man; the romantic themes of dreams, death, nature, and water predominate.

A typical example is "Der Fischer," one of over eighty settings of this popular four-strophe poem by Goethe.[12] The ABCA structure is articu-lated by contrasting keys (G minor, B♭ major, E♭ major, G minor), meters ($\frac{3}{4}$ and $\frac{4}{4}$), tempos, and vocal styles. After the first three stanzas a retransi-tion leads to a substantially literal restatement of the A section, echoing the poetic structure, where two of the four lines of the last stanza are iden-tical to those in the first. The lines of the outer stanzas are sung by the nar-rator in a generally low tessitura, with a rippling "water" figure in the accompaniment. The pair of inner stanzas (sung by the mermaid in a higher tessitura) begins lyrically and includes melismatic flourishes, building toward a dramatic climax on *lockt dich dein eigen Angesicht nicht her, in ew'gen Tau* (Does not your own face lure you into the eternal dew?).

Of Strauss's other surviving *Jugendlieder* (somewhat over half of those known to have been composed), the majority are short (13–60 measures) and clearly derive from the lied styles of earlier nineteenth-century composers. These are the composers whose works Strauss knew as the obedient child of a musically conservative father, the Munich court opera horn player Franz Strauss (1822–1905). One practically unknown set of songs, the *Drei Liebeslieder* (1880–83)[13]—"Rote Rosen" (poem by Karl Stieler), "Die erwachte Rose" (Friedrich von Sallet), and "Begegnung" (Otto Friedrich Gruppe), all characterized by traditional poetry and stylistically conservative music—is vocally rewarding but not overly demanding, and can serve as a good introduction to the early Strauss and a prelude to many of his later songs on floral poetic themes. "Rote Rosen," which Strauss described in a letter to its dedicatee as a "kleines Albumblatt mit unterlegter Musik" (a scrapbook page with added music), opens with a diatonic, arpeggiated accompaniment marked *träumerisch* (dreamily).[14] As the poem becomes more emotional in its middle section, Strauss uses increasingly varied harmonies, melodies, and rhythms to convey its passions (Ex. 8.1).

Selected Songs: The 1880s

With his *Acht Gedichte aus "letzte Blätter" von Hermann von Gilm* Op. 10, Strauss created in the course of three months a group of eight lieder that include two perennial favorites, "Zueignung" (No. 1) and "Allerseelen" (No. 8).[15] "Zueignung" is one of his most straightforward songs, without formal or harmonic complexities; its three largely similar strophes, with the refrain "habe Dank!," are supported by an accompaniment of constant triplet eighth-note movement over rich, full chords. "Allerseelen," a typical example of Strauss's through-composed structural approach, becomes progressively more dramatic, as does the text. The accompaniment here has more stylistic variety and introduces new melodic material in the interludes. In both songs Strauss shapes the vocal line so it reaches a high point near the end of the song, then falls suddenly to the lowest part of the range. None of the other songs in Op. 10 has enjoyed the popularity of these two, but "Die Nacht" (No. 3, the first to be composed) is a particularly lovely example of a strophic song, with a sparse, Schumannesque accompaniment, mostly stepwise melody, and syllabic text declamation.

A year after completing Op. 10, Strauss began the first of three groups of lieder—Opp. 15, 17, and 19—on texts by Count Adolf Friedrich von Schack (1815–94), the Munich collector of nineteenth-century paintings, whose gallery still exists. "Winternacht" (Op. 15, No. 2) offers examples of the Straussian word painting found in many of his lieder of all periods. The recurrent piano motive (first stated in mm. 1–2, then immediately re-

EXAMPLE 8.1. "Rote Rosen," o. op. 76, mm. 14–17

peated three times) dramatically anticipates such words as *Sturmgebrause, Nebelgebräu,* and *Wolkengrau* (tumult of the storm, mist-brew, and cloud-greyness). (See Ex. 8.2.) A subtle unifying idea in the vocal line is the simple stepwise quarter-note descent. The first two stanzas in G minor give way to G major and a more lyrical, calmer portrayal of drifting snowflakes and thoughts of love and springtime. The tripartite musical and textual structures coincide at first but become slightly out of phase as the third stanza is interrupted by variants of the stormy piano motive of the opening.

In contrast to the rarely performed "Winternacht" is the popular "Ständchen" (Op. 17, No. 2). Strauss regretted this song's wide appeal, since he considered his text setting and accentuation not the best possible solutions.[16] The orchestration of this song (1912, by Felix Mottl) and its

EXAMPLE 8.2. "Winternacht," Op. 15/2

(a) mm. 1–2

(b) mm. 38–42

availability in many other arrangements, from keyboard solos by Felix vom Rath and Walter Gieseking to Leopold Weninger's version for orchestra without voice, only reinforced its popularity. Strauss wrote to Karl Böhm that "Ständchen" was entirely too accessible, simple, and spontaneous, further regretting Mottl's orchestration, for which he had not given his approval. Nevertheless, this song has appeared frequently on song recitals for over a century and will continue to remain one of the composer's "evergreens."

"Ständchen" divides into four sections: A (stanza 1), A1 (stanza 2), B (stanza 3), and A2 (postlude). The accompaniment consists of one main idea, a sixteenth-note figure heard throughout the entire song. A single accompanimental figure (in thirty-second notes) similarly underlies Strauss's "Wiegenlied" (Op. 41, No. 1), a song in strophic variation form and Strauss's most famous lullaby. These songs—and many others of his more nostalgic, contemplative type—end simply and softly. Elena Gerhardt, a frequent performer of them, claimed (1949, 10) that "the outstanding characteristic of his songs is the absolute simplicity with which he expressed almost every mood."

An Important Opus: *Vier Lieder* Op. 27

During the years he was creating the Schack song collections and two subsequent groups on poems by Felix Dahn (Opp. 21 and 22), Strauss also composed the tone poems *Don Juan, Tod und Verklärung,* and *Macbeth.* He also worked during a five-year period on his first opera, *Guntram.* The leading soprano of that ill-fated opera was Pauline de Ahna (1862–1950), who also performed lieder with him and appeared in leading roles in other operas he conducted (among them Elisabeth in Wagner's *Tannhäuser* for Strauss's Bayreuth debut in 1894). Their sometimes stormy courtship and artistic collaborations, begun in 1887, led to their engagement during the rehearsals for *Guntram.* For their marriage on 10 September 1894, Strauss wrote the *Vier Lieder* Op. 27: "Ruhe, meine Seele!" (Karl Henckell), "Cäcilie" (Heinrich Hart), "Heimliche Aufforderung" (John Henry Mackay), and "Morgen!" (Mackay).

"Ruhe, meine Seele!" was the first of Strauss's ten settings of poems by Henckell. The song begins with a rhythmically static, harmonically unsettled chordal accompaniment that gives way to impetuous, rushing figurations as the soul's storms are likened to the turbulent ocean surf. A more reflective mood settles in for the final two stanzas, broken poignantly by a brief dissonance on *Not* (need, distress). The poet was well satisfied by Strauss's lightly trembling, scarcely surging interpretation of this poem.[17] He felt that Strauss expressed his poetic atmosphere wonderfully, especially in lines 4 and 8 at the phrases *stiehlt sich lichter Sonnenschein* (the bright sunshine steals) and *wie die Brandung, wenn sie schwillt!* (as the breakers, when they swell) (see Ex. 8.3).

EXAMPLE 8.3. "Ruhe, meine Seele!," Op. 27/1

(a) mm. 9–13

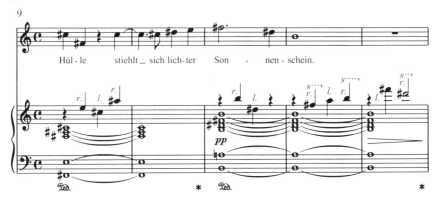

(b) mm. 24–25

"Cäcilie," composed the night before Strauss's wedding (fittingly, to a text that poet Heinrich Hart named for his wife), contrasts markedly, with its difficult but idiomatic piano part and long, expansive vocal phrases. A text-derived rhythmic motive occurs, slightly varied, at each of seven statements of *wenn du es wüsstest* (if only you knew it). Example 8.4 includes variants of the motive and, in mm. 45–52, a typically long, soaring, ecstatic vocal phrase. Such figures are found throughout Strauss's vocal music; a striking example in his operatic writing is the "Agamemnon" motive in *Elektra*.[18]

The dramatic vocal style of both "Cäcilie" and "Heimliche Aufforderung" is frequently described as Strauss's "effusive," "ecstatic" writing (*schwunglich, mit Schwung*). (See Ex. 8.5; Ex. 8.10 illustrates a very different instance of Strauss's wide-ranging, bravura vocal style.) To Strauss's detractors, this style can go beyond fervor of expression to overblown pomposity.

EXAMPLE 8.4. "Cäcilie," Op. 27/2

(a) voice only, mm. 4–5, 13

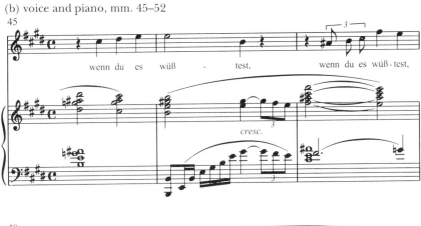

(b) voice and piano, mm. 45–52

EXAMPLE 8.5. *Heimliche Aufforderung,* Op. 27/3, mm. 1–9

"Morgen!," however, exhibits a simpler style of vocal declamation (but one of deep inner intensity) over slow-moving arpeggiated chords. Its introduction is unusually long for Strauss; the voice enters in m. 14 (of forty-three), and the accompaniment of mm. 1–14 repeats as mm. 16–29. Mackay's poem both begins and ends with ellipsis points; Strauss reflects this by beginning and ending the vocal part not on the G-major tonic but a half step on either side of it, and by concluding the accompaniment on a I$_4^6$ chord. The descending chords on *langsam niedersteigen* (slowly descend) offer one of several brief touches of literal word painting (Ex. 8.6). According to Elisabeth Schumann (1952, 56), Strauss wanted these words sung slowly and deliberately, separated by a short breath, and treated with emphasis.[19]

The *Vier Lieder* Op. 27, like most of Strauss's groups of songs, were not intended to be sung together as a unit in their published order. Nor was the order of composition generally related to the sequence of lieder in the printed collections. In Op. 17, Nos. 1, 3, and 4 were completed on 17, 21, and 22 May 1894, respectively; No. 2 followed on 9 September.) In Strauss's song collections through Op. 56, separateness rather than unity was emphasized by his performing practice, as well as his publishers' scattering songs in random order throughout anthologies and transposing songs inconsistently within single opus groups.[20] A rare exception, *Mädchenblumen* Op. 22, might be performed in order as a unit; Strauss accompanied its four flower songs both singly and as a group. But the atypical collection *Krämerspiegel: Zwölf Gesänge von Alfred Kerr* Op. 66 is Strauss's only true song cyle.

Two studies of Op. 27 have challenged the long-held view of Strauss's lieder as unrelated entities. Marie Rolf and Elizabeth West Marvin (1990) argue that "Ruhe, meine Seele!" and "Morgen!" form the outer pillars of a unified opus and exhibit formal schemes that are mirror images of each other.[21] Further points of unity include identical measure lengths, images of nature (the sun breaking through darkness), the poets' common social-

EXAMPLE 8.6. "Morgen!," Op. 27/4, mm. 26–29

EXAMPLE 8.7. "Ruhe meine Seele!," Op. 27/1
(a) original version, mm. 30–31

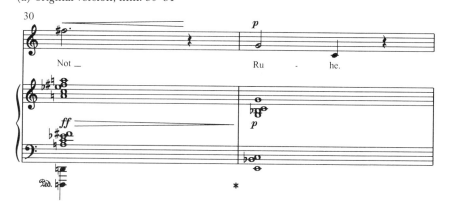

(b) orchestration, mm. 32–3

(*continued*)

EXAMPLE 8.7. (*continued*)

ist leanings, and—for all four songs—dates and circumstances of their composition (from a week after announcing their engagement to a day before the Strausses' wedding). Timothy Jackson (1988) has linked the 1948 orchestrated version of "Ruhe, meine Seele!" to the *Vier letzte Lieder*. The close connections of these five songs were noted by Alan Jefferson as early as 1971,[22] but the detailed analysis by Jackson (1988 and 1992) takes Jefferson's suggestions much further with the support of biographical and circumstantial evidence, analysis of the musical sources, and reconstruction of Strauss's compositional process. The crucial connection between "Ruhe!" and the later four songs is, he argues, the *Notmotiv* that appears at the text *Not* (Ex. 8.7a). This is emphasized in Strauss's orchestration (Ex. 8.7b) and finally finds a resolution in the orchestral prelude of "Im Abendrot." Offering a divergent opinion, Jefferson (1991, 122) quotes Walter Legge on "Ruhe": "the whole atmosphere of this lied is totally out of keeping with the gentle, introspective mood of the *Four*. It would jar—horribly."

Increasingly Varied Lieder: 1895–1906

During the early years of his and de Ahna's marriage and musical partnership, Strauss continued to create many atmospheric, sometimes nostalgic love songs that immediately became—and have remained—popular. Among these are "Traum durch die Dämmerung" (Op. 29, No. 1), "Ich trage meine Minne" and "Sehnsucht" (the first two songs of Op. 32), and "Glückes genug" and "Ich liebe dich" (the pair that begins Op. 37). The stepwise melodies of "Traum durch die Dämmerung" are poignant examples of how Strauss can subtly paint a mood (see Ex. 8.8 for the final phrase, which is yet another example of a typical soft ending).[23] Ever fond

EXAMPLE 8.8. "Traum durch die Dämmerung," Op. 29/1, mm. 28–33

Däm - mer-grau in der Lie - be Land, in ein

mil - des, blau - es Licht.

ppp

of self-quotation, Strauss quoted this song (and "Befreit," Op. 39, No. 4) in the tone poem *Ein Heldenleben* Op. 40 (completed in 1898).

Stiller Gang (Op. 31, No. 4) is important as the first of Strauss's settings of Richard Dehmel's verse and is a rarity within his works, as he created one version with viola obbligato.[24] "Wenn" (Op. 31, No. 2) is noteworthy for its abrupt shift of tonality (E♭ to E major) in mm. 48–49. In a humorous footnote, Strauss advised singers who wished to remain within the nineteenth-century tradition to sing the final seven bars a half step flat, thus ending in the key in which the song began.

Three of Strauss's settings of poetry from *Des Knaben Wunderhorn* date from this period: "Himmelsboten" (Op. 32, No. 5), "Für funfzehn Pfennige" (Op. 36, No. 2), and "Hat gesagt—bleibt's nicht dabei" (Op. 36, No. 3).[25] In "Für funfzehn Pfennige" Strauss deftly contrasts the narrator with the two characters of the story (a clerk and a maiden) and makes much fun of the fifteen pennies or small change with elaborate sixteenth-note melismas. Strauss's diary for 20 August 1897 mentions "at 2:30 composed a joyous little song from *Des Knaben Wunderhorn*."[26] The song's humor is carried further by his marginalia in the Deutsche Staatsbibliothek autograph.[27] He scolds himself for writing octaves between melody and bass (mm. 15–16) and for using "scheussliche Stimmfuhrung!!" (dreadful voice-leading) in mm. 38 and 29, especially the cross relation F♯–F♮. He also challenges the prospective singer about a melismatic passage (mm. 21–22) with the remark, "Whoever can, sing it like [Eugen] Gura!" Finally, he advises in a footnote that if the song does not seem worth enough musically to the listener, he can get a refund for fifteen cents at the box office.

Among the other songs in Op. 36, "Anbetung" (No. 4) is the first of Strauss's lieder on poems by Friedrich Rückert (1788–1866). His interest in setting Rückert began and ended with choral works, resulting in a total of twelve lieder and seven choruses (some incomplete). Six Rückert poems in the Persian *ghazel* form, which strictly incorporates both rhymes and refrains in couplets, usually on the subjects of love and wine, attracted Strauss.[28] The first of these was "Anbetung," with the end rhyme *-anken* and the refrain "wie schön, o wie schön!"

Intermingled with traditional song texts from *Des Knaben Wunderhorn* and poems from earlier generations are poems by Strauss's contemporaries, including two in an altogether more serious vein. These are by Dehmel and Henckell, both of whom contributed to the genre of *Sozial-lyrik*. These two songs, composed in June 1898 and September 1901, did not signal a new direction for Strauss as a lieder composer but remain isolated examples of his brief venture into the realm of social criticism in the lied.

In "Der Arbeitsmann," Op. 39, No. 3, Dehmel's poem becomes an angry, bitter protest song. The dirgelike repetitions of two principal motives in the accompaniment and tritone descents on the refrain "nur Zeit!" contrast with birdsong trills, as the poet declares that the one thing the working-class man lacks in order to be as free as the birds is time.[29]

Henckell's "Das Lied des Steinklopfers" (Strauss's Op. 49, No. 4) expresses the futility of man's social plight, using the example of a stoneworker (literally "stone breaker"). Strauss's atypically non-tonal chord progressions, ponderous rhythmic motives, low range, and relentlessly gloomy E minor reflect the heavy, repetitive work that this stoneworker must undertake "für's Vaterland." The declamatory vocal line is full of chromatic alterations and wide skips. At m. 45, Strauss introduces fragmentary text repetition (not in Henckell's original poem) over a partial repeat of the opening accompaniment. Indicated to be sung in half voice (as if humming to oneself), the second half of the song reflects the despair of Henckell's tormented and hungry laborer (Ex. 8.9). In 1904 an anonymous critic described the song as "extremely striking, extremely novel, expressing in the music the grimness, the hard hopelessness, the anarchistic tendency of the words. There is potent effect in the repetition of the few most significant phrases."[30]

EXAMPLE 8.9. "Das Lied des Steinklopfers," Op. 49/4, mm. 45–51

The Lied in Transition

Biographers have claimed that Strauss wrote lieder as *Handgelenksar-beit* (off-the-cuff creations), as a sort of release after completing larger works.[31] This has some validity for the earlier years, when his major works were symphonic poems. But after completing *Guntram* at the end of 1892, he wrote only a few songs until after the opera's premiere on 10 May 1894. Before trying his hand at a second opera, *Feuersnot*, he created several song groups (Opp. 43, 44, 46, and 47), then tapered off song composition as *Feuersnot* was in progress (1900–1). After completing this opera, he wrote seven of the eight lieder of Op. 49—clustered around another wedding anniversary date. The concentration on song composition during the month of September in several different years is probably due in part to Pauline's influence, but also had to do with available time, because most of his composing had to be relegated to the summer, when he was not conducting. Then the family would retreat to rural villages or alpine settings, where he could concentrate without interruption.

As Strauss worked on *Salome* in 1903–4, only the Op. 56 songs were in progress. He completely abandoned lieder (except for many incomplete sketches) during the creation of his next four operas, *Elektra, Der Rosenkavalier, Ariadne auf Naxos*, and *Die Frau ohne Schatten*. Only after the last of these was completed in 1917 did he return to the lied. By then the *Soziallyrik* was forgotten and a different type of exterior motivation influenced his choice of poetry, especially in the collections of Opp. 66 and 67. In *Krämerspiegel* Op. 66, texts specially written by the poet and critic Alfred Kerr enabled Strauss to express the conflict between the composer as artist and the publisher as businessman. In this autobiographical work, the composer declares war on the publishing industry; the texts of the twelve songs contain the names of publishers as well as references to Strauss's compositions. Musical quotations from the latter reinforce the wit and irony of Kerr's verses. The expansive and virtuosic piano part—with more preludes, interludes, and postludes than in most of Strauss's lieder—vary the mood from ironic and satirical to lyrical, charming, humorous, and dramatic. Strauss originally titled this collection *Die Händler und die Kunst*, changing it to *Krämerspiegel* three years later.[32]

The first half of Op. 67 consists of three slightly mad Ophelia songs from Shakespeare's *Hamlet* (as translated by Karl Simrock); the second half is a trio of "bad-tempered," rather cynical and adversarial songs from Goethe's *West-östlicher Divan*, one of Strauss's favorite sources of poetry.[33] Each half of this opus forms an independent minicyle. The Ophelia songs, clearly intended to be sung by a high female voice, are better known today than the *Divan* songs, which seem more appropriate for male voice. Applying Goethe's words to himself, Strauss comments here on his muse's subservience to a publisher's contract, the problems he had with meeting deadlines, and other business-related obligations.[34]

EXAMPLE 8.10. "Erschaffen und Beleben "("Hans Adam war ein Erdenkloss")

The brief song "Zugemessne Rhythmen," o. op. 122 (1935) also uses a *West-östlicher Divan* poem; it offers another type of criticism, this time musical—but also with deeper political implications. "Zugemessne Rhythmen" is one of several short "occasional" songs Strauss wrote in tribute to a colleague; here he was thanking writer Peter Raabe for his defense of modern German composers in response to a tirade (directed mainly at Hans Pfitzner's opera *Palestrina*) by critic Walter Abendroth. Quoting a melody from Brahms's Symphony No. 1 and principal themes from his own *Arabella* and *Tod und Verklärung*, Strauss contrasted Brahms, as the older talent who enjoys established—if eventually hollow and abhorrent—forms and rhythms, with himself as the spirit who thinks up new forms. In the piano postlude, he introduces a theme from Wagner's *Die Meistersinger*, further contrasting the "talent" of Brahms with the "genius" of Wagner.[35]

Throughout his lifetime of lieder writing, Strauss often used extravagantly wide vocal ranges. In his first song, "Weihnachtslied" (December 1870), the opening vocal phrase rises from b to e″ within two bars. Dramatic leaps and register shifts are Strauss trademarks throughout his lieder, becoming even more prominent after the turn of the century. The resulting difficulties are among the reasons for the infrequent performance of many otherwise worthy songs. Strauss urged Hans Hotter, a favorite interpreter of his works, to take on the challenges of his textually and musically more difficult songs.[36] Free-ranging vocal lines are especially characteristic of drinking songs such as "Bruder Liederlich" (Op. 41, No. 4) and "Der Pokal" (Op. 69, No. 2).[37] The reckless hilarity of the 1922 "Erschaffen und Beleben" (o. op. 106) is a particularly lively example of Strauss's *schwunglich* (excited) style. It begins with wide leaps of tenths and twelfths, continues with challenging vocal acrobatics that aptly mirror the text, and comes to a triumphant close with more leaps and wide-ranging melismas on the words *Gläser* and *Tempel* (see Ex. 8.10).[38]

Orchestral Songs and Orchestrated Lieder

During the years when Strauss was accompanying his wife's performances, they gave solo evenings of his lieder alone or of lieder alternating with chamber works, including sonatas and his two melodramas for piano and narrator. They also performed groups of lieder with piano accompaniment as parts of orchestral concerts that he conducted. Such mixing of genres was accepted in the late nineteenth century, but having access to an orchestra surely led Strauss to think that making use of it would be even more aesthetically appealing.[39] As early as 1878, Strauss had written a song with orchestral accompaniment, the ballad "Der Spielmann und sein Kind" (o. op. 46).[40] This childhood work was probably long forgotten by 1897, when he completed his first group of orchestral songs, the *Vier Gesänge für eine Singstimme mit Begleitung des Orchesters* Op. 33. During the ensuing decade he created two more sets of orchestral songs, obviously not for Pauline: *Zwei grössere Gesänge* Op. 44 for low voice and *Zwei Gesänge* Op. 51 for bass. Generally Strauss used the term *Gesänge* for orchestral songs, restricting *Lieder* to those with piano.[41] Two lieder from Op. 27, "Cäcilie" and "Morgen!," were among the four love songs Strauss orchestrated in September 1897 (a few days after his third wedding anniversary) for his wife to sing. The others were "Liebeshymnus" (Op. 32, No. 3) and "Das Rosenband" (Op. 36, No. 1).[42] This group, which the Strausses performed widely as "Vier Gesänge für Sopran mit Orchesterbegleitung," signaled to the musical world that one of his most significant contributions to the lied genre would become the orchestral song, either initially composed with orchestral accompaniment or with an original piano part expanded.

A few years after the 1897 orchestrations, Strauss created three more drawn from different existing opus groups; the Strausses premiered these with the Berlin Philharmonic on 8 July 1900. Many other performances followed, and the group became commonly known as "Drei Mutterlieder," once again reinforcing the close connection between work and family that runs throughout Strauss's oeuvre. One of the three lieder, "Meinem Kinde" (Op. 37, No. 3), belongs to the collection that Strauss dedicated to Pauline to celebrate the birth of their only son, Franz, on 12 April 1897. Appropriately grouped with it were "Wiegenlied" (Op. 41, No. 1) and "Muttertändelei" (Op. 43, No. 2). A final orchestration in 1906 for Pauline was "Die heiligen drei Könige" (Op. 56, No. 6). The sketchbook for this song includes designations of orchestral instruments, and though it was first published as part of an opus of piano lieder, the orchestral version is clearly preferable.[43] Its many instances of word painting are introduced with a realism reminiscent of the programmatic effects in such orchestral works as the recently completed *Symphonia domestica,* or the tone poems from a decade earlier (especially *Till Eulenspiegel* and *Don Quixote*).

For the next dozen years Strauss completed no more song collections. When he returned to writing lieder in 1918, it was with great concentration and enthusiasm, for he created twenty-nine songs in four opus groups and orchestrated six songs in less than a year.[44] Five of the orchestrations were most likely intended for Elisabeth Schumann, whom he first met in 1917 and for whom he wrote the *Sechs Lieder nach Gedichten von Clemens Brentano* Op. 68. Some of the orchestrations were included in her 1921 tour of America with Strauss as conductor and accompanist. Most of his subsequent orchestrations were made in 1933 (four songs) and 1940 (six songs, five of them from Op. 68) for the soprano Viorica Ursuleac, wife of conductor Clemens Krauss and creator of roles in five of Strauss's operas.[45]

Strauss's continuing creation of orchestrations as well as orchestral songs in the twentieth century was certainly influenced by these singers (among others) and by his increasing devotion to operatic composition. The mutual influences between genres also became stronger, with more operatic writing in his songs—reaching a peak with the florid coloratura of "Amor" Op. 68, No. 5, but also evident in other longer, more dramatic songs, as well as a few humorous "character" songs—and with set pieces in the operas. The latter include the tenor aria "Di rigori armato" in *Der Rosenkavalier,* the Composer's arietta "Du Venus' Sohn" in the prologue of *Ariadne auf Naxos,* and the sonnet "Kein Andres" in *Capriccio.* As Strauss began to abandon the nineteenth-century lied with piano accompaniment, his songs grew in length as well. Up to 1902, the majority have durations of one-and-a-half to four minutes. His orchestral "Gesänge" are usually cast in larger forms, with "Notturno," Op. 44, No. 1, the longest at thirteen minutes.[46] Of the orchestrated songs, "Lied der Frauen" at eight minutes and "Die heiligen drei Könige" at six-and-a-half are not only the longest but also stylistically the most effective in their complete symphonic versions.

Among Strauss's over two hundred lieder are many worthy of study and performance beyond those mentioned here. Having begun as a composer with a traditional Romantic outlook, Strauss expanded the scope of lieder writing with both his large-scale orchestral songs and his small occasional and dedicatory pieces for voice and piano. As his songs from the period between the two world wars become better known, their position as important links between the well-known earlier songs and his final glorious *Vier letzte Lieder* can be better appreciated. However adventuresome and modern some of these intervening songs were, it is the last songs that reaffirm Strauss's reputation as a composer solidly in the nineteenth-century tradition.

Bibliographic and Discographic Notes

First editions of Strauss's lieder were generally issued within a year of their creation. The majority were sold to Joseph Aibl Verlag in Munich, Strauss's first principal publisher, who issued works from the String Quartet Op. 2 (1881) to the *Sechs Lieder* Op. 37 (1898). Aibl published the songs singly and in small collections ("Hefte"). By the time the proprietor Eugen Spitzweg sold the firm in 1904 to Universal Edition in Vienna, Strauss had signed a contract with Adolph Fürstner in Berlin, decided against remaining exclusively with one publisher, and placed songs with many different publishers.

In 1912, Universal Edition reissued in four volumes Strauss's forty-three songs previously published—and often reprinted—by Aibl;[47] the songs were not grouped chronologically or by opus number, with songs from any one opus scattered throughout the four volumes. Later volumes added to the series included songs originally assigned to Daniel Rahter (Hamburg), F. E. C. Leuckart (Leipzig), Bote & Bock (Berlin), and C. A. Challier (Berlin). Adolph Fürstner issued eight volumes of songs around 1909, each volume containing a single opus. The first American publication (edited by Huneker in 1910) included Opp. 10, 15, 17, 19, 21, 22, and 56.

Plans for a complete edition of Strauss's lieder, which had appeared under twelve different German and Austrian imprints, were initiated in the 1940s by Kurt Soldan, but World War II halted the project. For Strauss's centenary, his publishers' collaborations resulted in the four-volume *Richard Strauss: Gesamtausgabe der Lieder*.[48] The inclusion of the *Jugendlieder* made available the surviving songs from 1870 to 1883; another dozen inventoried by Max Steinitzer were lost or destroyed.[49] The songs without opus numbers were reprinted in a practical performing edition (see Editions, *Nachlese*).

Recordings

The available recordings of Strauss lieder are quite comprehensive, beginning with the first wax cylinder of "Zueignung" made in 1898. Of historical interest from the 1940s are issues on the Rococo label (later Preiser) with Strauss as accompanist for various singers. There are also a few examples of the composer as solo pianist (in versions of his songs without voice) and as conductor of orchestrated lieder. The single largest collection of Strauss lieder is Dietrich Fischer-Dieskau's 1970 album *Richard Strauss: Das Liedschaffen* (EMI: Odeon 1 C 163-50043/51, reissued as Angel CD 63995), which includes 134 lieder.

A discography compiled in 1972 (Morse and Norton-Welsh) lists dozens of recordings of the most popular songs (eighty for "Morgen!," seventy-nine for "Ständchen," seventy-six for "Traum durch die Dämmerung," and so forth, to only one private recording of the orchestral *Drei Hymnen* Op. 71). Today, only a few of the lieder without opus numbers remain unrecorded. As previously unknown songs have come to light, they have been performed, published, and recorded; among these are "Wer hat's gethan?," rediscovered in 1973, and "Malven," in 1984.[51] The *Vier letzte Lieder* continue to be favorites of many sopranos, and selected orchestrated lieder are also widely represented in recordings.[52]

Notes

1. Only the *Schneiderpolka* for piano, o. op. 1, predates the "Weihnachtslied" (o. op. 2). Two months after completing the last of the *Vier letzte Lieder* (o. op. 150), Strauss wrote a final song, "Malven" (AV 304), and sketched two further works, "Nacht" (AV 303, probably a song for soprano and orchestra) and "Besinnung" (AV 306, for chorus and orchestra). The cataloging of Strauss's works was systemized in Asow (1959–74), which assigns AV numbers to incomplete and lost works; the designation "o. op." (*ohne Opuszahl*) applies to completed works to which Strauss did not assign opus numbers. A subsequent chronological numbering system was created by Trenner (1993) but these "TrV" numbers are not yet in wide use.

2. Many writers, including Asow (1959–74, 1:39), give 1882–83 as the dates of composition for these songs, but they are now known to date from August to November 1885. Not published with the others was a ninth song, "Wer hat's gethan?" (o. op. 84A), which came to light in the 1970s after the autograph of Op. 10 was given to the Pierpont Morgan Library in New York as part of the Mary Flagler Cary Collection (no. 198). The first publication of "Wer hat's gethan?" (1974; see Editions) includes a facsimile of the autograph and an engraved performing edition.

3. The three are the *Zwei Lieder aus Calderón's "Der Richter von Zalamea"* o. op. 96 and the textless "Der Graf von Rom," o. op. 102. The abandoned sketches began as

early as 1903, when his song output began to dwindle. Op. 56, with six songs composed in 1903–6, would be his last lieder collection for over a decade.

4. The circumstances surrounding Strauss's return to lieder composition have been outlined by many authors; see especially Petersen (1980, 117–21), including the chronological table of songs written in 1918.

5. Some typical examples: in "Morgen!" (Op. 27, No 4): *Seligen* becomes *Glücklichen* (line 3); in "Ständchen" (Op. 17, No. 2), *die über die Blumen hüpfen* becomes *um über die Blumen zu hüpfen.*

6. These poets include Burns, Byron, Chamisso, Geibel, Goethe, Heine, Hoffmann von Fallersleben, Körner, Lenau, and Uhland. Rückert and Eichendorff appear, but later or in works other than solo songs. His Rückert settings, beginning in 1897, include ten lieder, five choruses, and some incomplete works. With the possible exception of "Anbetung," Op. 36, No. 4, Strauss's Rückert lieder have never achieved much popularity. Eichendorff's verses appear in two early choruses (1876 and 1880), in *Die Tageszeiten* op. 76 (subtitled "Ein Liederzyklus für Männerchor und Orchester"), and in a song, "Im Abendrot" (1948).

7. The Goethe settings are catalogued in Schuh (1952). Jefferson (1971, appendix D [p. 125]) lists twenty-one texts (none by Goethe) set by Straus and others.

8. Finck (1917, 287), one of many sources for this quote from Strauss's answer to a questionnaire circulated in 1895 by Friedrich Hausegger.

9. Finck (1917, 287). For the original German, see Schuh (1976, 469; see also pp. 412–13).

10. In the lieder from Op. 10 to Op. 22, only one song (Op. 15, No. 1) is not by the poet of the rest of the opus.

11. Examples include Henckell's "Das Lied des Steinklopfers," set by Strauss as Op. 49, No. 4, and Dehmel's "Der Arbeitsmann" Op. 39, No. 3.

12. "Der Fischer," o. op. 33 is printed in *Gesamtausgabe* 3: 232 and *Nachlese* 14 (see Editions).

13. Sent by Strauss to a girlfriend, Lotte Speyer, in 1883, they remained unknown until published (*Drei Liebeslieder,* see Editions) in 1958 and premiered at Carnegie Hall by Elisabeth Schwarzkopf 30 November 1958. The songs are also in *Gesamtausgabe* 3:159–73, reprinted from the earlier edition.

14. The letter appears in full in the first edition of "Rote Rosen" and in Holde (1958, 3). Although hard to render precisely into English, Strauss's description was obviously intended to personalize Stieler's poem, much as if he were writing verses into the young lady's autograph book, then setting them to music.

15. Joseph Aibl published eight songs, both individually and in two collections of four each, in 1887. A ninth song, "Wer hat's gethan?," o. op. 84A, was written with them but remained unpublished until 1974. The composer's autograph used by the printer (*Stichvorlage*) reveals that it was once considered for inclusion in the group: an editor's hand has marked it as Op. 10, No. 6 (see note 2).

16. Detailed discussions are found in Petersen (1980, 73) and the sources cited there.

17. Letter of 12 December 1895 in Grasberger (1967, 94–95).

18. Several examples are included in the discussion of text-inspired motives in Petersen (1980, 77–81).

19. The soprano's annotations can also be seen in her compilation (Schumann [1952]).

20. Strauss may have had second thoughts about this subject: Hans Hotter reports (in Kohler [1990]) lengthy discussions with Strauss about the important relationship of both text and tonality in constructing a Strauss recital program. See Kohler (1990).

21. Rolf and Marvin plan to continue their revealing analysis (Rolf 1990) and expand this study to include the other two songs of Op. 27.

22. Jefferson 1971, 58–59, and 1991, 118–22. In the latter, Jefferson includes "Malven" because it was the last song Strauss completed, without implying that it be orchestrated or that it has connections to the other five.

23. Max Reger's 1899 setting of the same poem uses ascending, more chromatic, scales to set the same words. He certainly knew Strauss's song, since it was among those he transcribed for piano alone.

24. Strauss set Dehmel's poem within a few days of receiving the as yet unpublished copy with a letter from the poet. The early song "Alphorn," o. op. 29 has an accompaniment of horn and piano; otherwise, only the *Zwei Lieder* o. op. 96, composed for Calderón's play *Der Richter von Zalamea*, have obbligato instruments.

25. "Für funfzehn Pfennige" lacks the usual umlaut on *fünfzehn*, as it is in folk dialect. A fourth *Wunderhorn* song, "Junggesellenschwur," and two Alsatian folksong settings belong to Op. 49 (1900–1).

26. Strauss's unpublished diaries are in the Richard Strauss Archive, along with a card file summarizing the most important musical annotations; at the time I used it the cards covered only the period 1896–1901. The date of 20 August 1897 is confirmed by the date on a sketch of the song; the final manuscript and later diary annotation for its completion are dated 2 September 1897.

27. Berlin, Staatsbibliothek zu Berlin, Mus. ms. autogr. Richard Straus 3.

28. See Petersen (1980, 66–68).

29. The orchestration of this song brings out the birdlike trills even more, foreshadowing the birdsongs in "Im Fruhling" and the larks in "Im Abendrot." Throughout his life, from the 1877 song "Die Drossel," o. op. 34, which begins with an ad libitum piano introduction as the thrush's song, to these two of the *Vier letzte Lieder*, birdsong was a favorite device of Strauss's.

30. Unsigned review of Strauss's Carnegie Hall recital with David Bispham, "Richard Strauss Appears."

31. Stories have long circulated that Strauss even dashed off lieder during intermissions of operas by other composers that he was conducting.

32. For more on these songs and on Strauss's business dealings in general, see Petersen (1980).

33. Strauss used Goethe's poetry in thirteen lieder and brief "occasional" songs (fourteen if the uncertain attribution on "Das Bächlein" is accepted). In addition, eleven incomplete sketches of other Goethe lieder survive in Strauss's sketchbooks (1903–35). See Petersen (1980, 201–5).

34. See Petersen (1992, especially pp. 121–22).

35. See Del Mar (1978, 3: 397–99). A fuller description of the song is given in Schuh (53).

36. See Grasberger, 408. The Hotter-Klien recording of eighteen lieder (see Kohler) includes some of the more difficult and rarely performed songs, notably the *Zwei Gesänge* Op. 51 and the Rückert lieder (o. op. 114, 115, and 121)—premiered by Hotter in 1964, honoring the composer's centenary—along with the usual chestnuts.

37. Three other drinking songs also exhibit this style of vocal writing, as do the suc-

cessive stages of unfinished sketches of two Goethe poems, "Trunken müssen wir alle sein" and "So lang man nüchtern ist." Examples from the sketches are in Petersen (1980, 53).

38. "Erschaffen und Beleben" stands in stark stylistic contrast to the three Rückert lieder (composed in 1929 and 1935) with which Strauss grouped it in a manuscript under a single opus number with the title *Vier Gesänge für Bass mit Klavier.*

39. The mixing of orchestral and chamber forces did not prevent the four orchestrated songs of 1897 from appearing on programs alongside piano-accompanied lieder; see, for example, the 1898 program in Petersen (1980, 149).

40. The seven-minute song (with text by August Heinrich Hoffmann von Fallersleben) is printed with piano accompaniment in *Nachlese* 45, but not in *Gesamtausgabe* 3. It is contemporaneous with several lieder with piano that set texts by Geibel, Goethe, and Fallersleben, as well as fragments for a Goethe-based singspiel *(Lila)* and some short orchestral pieces.

41. An exception is the *Drei Gesänge älterer deutscher Dichter* Op. 43, which is for voice and piano. But his usual distinction of the two terms makes it unlikely that Strauss would have used *Lieder* for the orchestral songs of 1948, which were given their group title not by the composer but by Ernst Roth at Boosey & Hawkes. (Trenner, in Gesantausgabe 3, 282). Will they someday be known as *Fünf letzte Gesänge?*

42. The piano version of "Das Rosenband" was composed on the day of their wedding anniversary.

43. See the discussion of this composition in Petersen (1980, 60 and 112).

44. The orchestrated songs were "Des Dichters Abendgang," "Waldseligkeit," "Winterweihe, Winterliebe," and "Freundliche Vision," all orginally dating from 1899–1900.

45. The first of the Op. 68 lieder to be orchestrated was No. 6, "Lied der Frauen," in the 1933 group. There are also other orchestrations from 1935 and 1943, as well as the previously mentioned "Ruhe, meine Seele!" from 1948.

46. The four songs in Op. 33 range in duration from four to eight-and-a-half minutes; the pair in Op. 44 are thirteen and six, those in Op. 51 are seven and three minutes long, and the durations of the *Drei Hymnen von Friedrich Hölderlin* Op. 71 are approximately ten, six, and seven minutes.

47. Each volume was available for high, medium, or low voice.

48. The first printing was in a large format; the 1972 reprint is in octavo, but volume and page numbers are identical in the two printings.

49. These lost songs belonged to Strauss's aunt, Johanna Pschorr, a singer with whom he performed at family musicales and to whom twenty-six of his youthful songs were dedicated. These family gatherings, where Strauss performed his own works as well as works by Weber, Mendelssohn, and other nineteenth-century composers, were among his first, rather traditional, musical experiences. These song manuscripts seem to have disappeared or been destroyed between the world wars. See Steinitzer (1911, 177–81); in later editions of the book, he moved the information from chap. 31 "Ungedruckte Jugendwerke," to the index of compositions at the end of the book. Steinitzer's incipits are the only surviving music for these songs.

50. Several songs are also available individually or in small groups, for instance a *Song Album* (six songs from opp. 47–69, for high voice only) from Boosey & Hawkes.

51. On "Malven," see Petersen (1985).

52. There is even available a cassette recording (Turnabout CT-4830) of the 22 May 1950 world premiere of the *Vier letzte Lieder* by Kirsten Flagstad with Wilhelm Furtwängler and the London Philharmonia Orchestra.

Bibliography

Anonymous. "Richard Strauss Appears," *New York Times,* 28 February 1904, 7.

Asow, E. H. Mueller von. *Richard Strauss. Thematisches Verzeichnis. Nach dem Tode des Verfassers vollendet und herausgegeben von Alfons Ott und Franz Trenner.* 3 vols. Vienna, 1955–74.

Brosche, Günter, ed. *Richard-Strauss-Bibliographie, Teil 2: 1944–65.* Vienna, 1973.

———, and Karl Dachs, eds. *Richard Strauss. Autographen in München und Wien. Verzeichnis.* Veröffentlichungen der Richard-Strauss-Gesellschaft München 3. Tutzing, 1979.

Del Mar, Norman. *Richard Strauss. A Critical Commentary on His Life and Works.* 3 vols. London, 1962–72. Reprint. 1978. Reprint. Ithaca, NY, 1986.

Finck, Henry T. *Richard Strauss. The Man and His Work.* Boston, 1917.

Gerhardt, Elena. "Strauss and his Lieder: A Personal Reminiscence." *Tempo* 12 (1949): 9–11.

Grasberger, Franz, and Alice and Franz Strauss. *"Der Strom der Töne trug mich fort": Die Welt um Richard Strauss in Briefen.* Tutzing, 1967.

Haider, Friedrich. "Neue Liedereinspielung und Probleme des Notentextes." *Richard Strauss-Blätter* n.s. 23 (1990): 75–77.

Holde, Artur. "Unbekannte Briefe und Lieder von Richard Strauss." *Internationale Richard-Strauss-Gesellschaft, Mitteilungen,* no. 19 (November 1958): 2–6; no. 20 (February 1959): 8–15.

Jackson, Timothy L. "Richard Strauss's *Winterweihe*—An Analysis and Study of the Sketches." *Richard Strauss-Blätter* n.s. 17 (1987): 28–69.

———. "Compositional Revisions in Strauss's 'Waldseligkeit' and a New Source." *Richard Strauss-Blätter* n.s. 21 (1989): 55–82.

———. "The Last Strauss: Studies of the letzte Lieder." Ph.D. dissertation, City University of New York, 1988.

———. "Ruhe, meine Seele! and the *Letzte Orchesterlieder*." In *Richard Strauss and His World,* ed. Bryan Gilliam, 90–137. Princeton, 1992.

Jefferson, Alan. *The Lieder of Richard Strauss.* London, 1971.

———. "Richard Strauss' Six Last Songs." *Richard Strauss-Blätter* n.s. 24 (1991): 118–22.

Kennedy, Michael. *Richard Strauss.* London, 1976. Revised. 1983. 2d rev. 1988.

——— (article), and Robert Bailey (work list, bibliography). "Strauss, Richard." In *The New Grove Dictionary of Music and Musicians* 18:218–39. 20 vols. London, 1980. Reprinted in *The New Grove: Turn of the Century Masters.* New York, 1985.

Kohler, Stephan. Liner note in *Lieder von Richard Strauss,* Preiser SPR 3367, reissued as Preiser CD 93367 (1990).

Krause, Ernst. *Richard Strauss. Gestalt und Werk.* Leipzig, 1955. 7th ed. 1984. 3d ed. Trans. John Coombs as *Richard Strauss. The Man and His Work.* London, 1964.

Morse, Peter, and Christopher Norton-Welsh. "Die Lieder von Richard Strauss— Eine Diskographie." *Richard Strauss-Blätter* o.s. 5 (1974): 81–123.

Newman, Ernest. *Richard Strauss,* London, 1908.

Ortner, Oswald, comp. *Richard-Strauss-Bibliographie, Teil 1.* Completed by Franz Grasberger; covers 1882–1944. Vienna, 1964.

Petersen, Barbara A. "Richard Strauss as Composers' Advocate, oder 'Die Händler und die Kunst.'" In *Richard Strauss: New Perspectives on the Composer and His Work,* ed. Bryan Gilliam, 115–32. Durham, NC, 1992.

———. "Richard Strauss in 1948–49: Malven, September und letzte Briefe an Maria Jeritza." *Richard Strauss-Blätter* n.s. 13 (1985): 3–20.

———. *"Ton und Wort:" The Lieder of Richard Strauss.* Ann Arbor, 1980. Revised German edition. Trans. Ulrike Steinhauser. *"Ton und Wort:" Die Lieder von Richard Strauss.* Veröffentlichungen der Richard-Strauss-Gesellschaft München 8. Pfaffenhofen an der Ilm, 1986. All references are to the English version.

Rolf, Marie, and Elizabeth West Marvin. "Analytical Issues and Interpretive Decisions in Two Songs by Richard Strauss." *Intégral* 4 (1990): 67–103.

Schlötterer, Reinhold, ed. *Die Texte der Lieder von Richard Strauss, Kritische Ausgabe.* Veröffentlichungen der Richard-Strauss-Gesellschaft München 10. Pfaffenhofen an der Ilm, 1988.

Schuh, Willi. *Goethe-Vertonungen. Ein Verzeichnis.* Zurich, 1952.

———, ed. *Richard Strauss: Briefe en die Eltern 1882–1906.* Zurich, 1954.

———. *Richard Strauss: Jugend und frühe Meisterjahre: Lebenschronik 1864–98.* Zurich, 1976. Trans. Mary Whittall as *Richard Strauss: A Chronicle of the Early Years 1864–1898.* New York, 1982.

———. "Zur Vertonung des Divan-Gedichts 'Zugemessne Rhythmen.'" In *Richard Strauss Jahrbuch 1954,* 122–24. Bonn, 1953.

Schumann, Elisabeth, comp. *Liederbuch/Favourite Songs.* New rev. ed. London, [1952].

———. "Richard Strauss. Morgen. A Master Lesson by Elisabeth Schumann." *Etude* (February 1951): 26, 56.

Steinitzer, Max. *Richard Strauss.* Berlin, 1911. Enlgd. ed. 1927.

Strickert, Elizabeth. "Richard Strauss's 'Vier letzte Lieder': An Analytical Study." Ph.D. dissertation, Washington University, 1975.

Tenschert, Roland. *3 x 7 Variationen über das Thema Richard Strauss.* Vienna, 1944.

Trenner, Franz. *Die Skizzenbücher von Richard Strauss aus dem Richard Strauss-Archiv in Garmisch.* Veröffentlichungen der Richard-Strauss-Gesellschaft München 1. Tutzing, 1977.

———. *Richard Strauss. Werkverzeichnis.* Vienna, 1985. Rev. ed. Veröffentlichungen der Richard-Strauss-Gesellschaft München 12. Munich, 1993.

Wilhelm, Kurt. *Richard Strauss persönlich.* Munich, 1984. Trans. Mary Whittall as *Richard Strauss. An Intimate Portrait.* London, 1989.

EDITIONS OF STRAUSS'S LIEDER

Ausgewählte Lieder. Piano Solo. (Mit beigefügten deutschen und englischen Text). Ed. Max Reger. 2 vols. Munich, 1899 (vol. 1); Vienna, 1904 (both).

Drei Liebeslieder. New York, 1958.

Forty Songs. Ed. James G. Huneker. Boston, 1910.

Gesamtausgabe der Lieder. Ed. Franz Trenner. 4 vols. London, 1964–65. I: Opp.

10–41; II: Opp. 43–68; III: Opp. 69–77, 19 Jugendlieder, 20 songs without opus numbers; IV: 21 orchestral songs and the composer's own orchestrations of 20 songs. Reprint. 1972.

Lieder-Album. 10 vols. Vienna, 1912– . Numerous reprints; 43 songs in vols. 1–4 currently in print.

Lieder-Album. 8 vols. London, n.d. [1909?].

Malven. London, 1985.

Nachlese. Lieder aus der Jugendzeit und verstreute Lieder aus späteren Jahren. Ed. Willi Schuh. London, 1968. (21 early songs, 9 o. op. [1896–1942], 3 early sketches.)

Thirty Songs. Ed. Sergius Kagen. New York, 1955.

Wer hat's gethan (H. v. Gilm). Erstausgabe des Liedes mit vollständigem Faksimile. . . . Afterword by Willi Schuh. Tutzing, 1974.

STRAUSS SOCIETY PUBLICATIONS

Mitteilungen der Internationalen Richard-Strauss-Gesellschaft. 1-62/63. Berlin, 1952–69.

Richard Strauss-Blätter o.s. 1–13. Vienna, 1971–79. N.s. Tutzing, 1980– . (Semiannual.)

Veröffentlichungen der Richard-Strauss-Gesellschaft München. Approximately annual series of monographs, catalogues, and collections of correspondence or essays. Tutzing, 1977–84. Pfaffenhofen an der Ilm, 1986–89. Continuing with various publishers (Munich, Berlin).

CHAPTER NINE

The Song Cycle: Journeys Through a Romantic Landscape

John Daverio

The Romantic Song Cycle as a Genre

The song cycle, as a cultural product of nineteenth-century German musical Romanticism, discloses a paradoxical movement between the art-lessness, the noble simplicity demanded by the lied tradition, and the art-fulness that a cyclic form should display. It is this interplay of the naive and the artful, of miniaturism and large-scale grouping, that makes the song cycle a quintessentially nineteenth-century phenomenon. Contraries of this sort served as the point of departure for many early critical accounts. As the reviewer of Schubert's *Winterreise* for the Munich *Allgemeine Musik-Zeitung* put it in an article of 28 July 1828, "the task of a song cycle, if it is to form a beautiful whole, seems to us to be to carry in the detail and variety of its parts the conditions of a continuous and increasing interest." Two years earlier, the reviewer of Heinrich Marschner's *Sechs Wanderlieder von Wilhelm Marsano* Op. 35 similarly noted that, although the cycle's six songs might be sung individually, "nonetheless they also relate so closely to one another that they form a kind of tragic *Liederroman*."[1]

Implicit in the designation as song cycle is an aesthetic claim: we expect that the lieder in question will amount to more than a mere collection, that they will exhibit elements of musicopoetic cohesiveness extending beyond the individual lied to encompass the entire set.

Yet the song cycle has received relatively little close attention from scholars. It remains, as Barbara Turchin comments (1981, 6), "a genre in

search of a history." Even during the nineteenth century, critical commentary was limited. Gustav Schilling's *Encyclopedie der gesammten musikalischen
Wissenschaften* (1837), though containing substantial entries for *Lied,
Liederspiel,* and *Liedertafel,* has none for *Liederkreis,* and Hermann Mendel's
brief definition of *Liedercyclus* in his *Musikalisches Conversations-Lexicon*
(1870–1879, 6:324) (based on the "Liederkreis/Liedercyclus" article in
Arrey von Dommer's 1865 revision of H. Ch. Koch's *Musikalisches Lexicon*)
includes but a passing reference to Beethoven's *An die ferne Geliebte* and
Schubert's *Die schöne Müllerin.* Mendel's description of the song cycle as a
primarily poetic genre ("a series of lyric poems related in content and
character") reflects the orientation of most of the critics of the age, who
stressed the importance of verbal and narrative relationships over musical
factors.[2]

The nineteenth century's equivocal attitude may be further gauged
from the peculiar performance history of many cycles. Complete or near-
complete renditions of cycles were not unknown in the first half of the
century; in February 1818, Conradin Kreutzer performed several of his five
Frühlingslieder Op. 33 (three in Leipzig and four in Berlin), and according
to Joseph von Spaun, Schubert sang the whole of *Winterreise* to his circle of
friends.[3] But the practice of selecting and presenting individual songs was
the norm, in both public and private circles.[4] Even by 1856, when Julius
Stockhausen gave the first documented complete performance of *Die
schöne Müllerin,* Eduard Hanslick felt compelled to assert: "So far as I am
aware, the idea [of singing an entire song cycle] is new"; four years later,
he referred to the practice as an "experiment."[5] A degree of equivocation
over the song cycle's status as genre can also be inferred from publications
like Schlesinger's *Collection des Lieder de Schubert* (1838), which offered up
selections from the composer's great cycles.

This uncertainty has spilled over into our century as well. The term
Liederkreis apparently did not merit a separate entry in the first edition of
Die Musik in Geschichte und Gegenwart, nor does the song cycle figure in Carl
Dahlhaus's magisterial *Die Musik des neunzehnten Jahrhunderts* (1980), a self-
styled history of the musical genres of the age of Romanticism. And although the work of scholars such as Walther Dürr, Luise Eitel Peake, and
Barbara Turchin has shed much light on the Romantic song cycle, vexing
questions remain. In the first place, there is the difficulty of identifying
the sets of songs that should occupy positions in a history of the cycle.
Nineteenth-century commentators, who generally concentrated on the attributes of single songs, offer little help. The review of Schubert's *Winterreise*
in the 17 January 1829 issue of the Vienna *Allgemeiner musikalischer Anzeiger*
is typical; although the reviewer recognizes it as a cycle (*Cyklus*), his song-
by-song description focuses on the detail at the expense of the whole.[6] A
lengthy two-part review of Schumann's songs, in the 1842 volume of the
Leipzig *Allgemeine musikalische Zeitung* does much the same; the discussion
of the Heine *Leiderkreis* Op. 24—a work that satisfies the song cycle's de-

mand for cohesiveness—differs little in approach from the reviewer's comments on the *Drei Gedichte von E. Geibel* Op. 30, which clearly do not.[7]

One must also consider the great variety of terms employed to designate song cycles and collections in the nineteenth-century sources: terms like *Liederkreis, Liederzyklus, Liederreihe, Liedergabe, Liederroman, Liederstrauß,* and *Liederkranz,* none of which can be assumed to reflect a given set's degree of musicopoetic integrity. Schumann's *Myrthen* Op. 25 was published as a "Liederkreis," whereas his *Frauenliebe und -leben* Op. 42 was simply designated as "Acht Lieder für eine Singstimme mit Begleitung des Pianoforte" (in the Whistling print of 1843). Yet few would dispute that the former shows less obvious signs of musical and poetic unity than the latter.[8]

Opinions vary on what characterizes true cycles—roughly speaking, groups of self-sufficient but interdependent works—as opposed to collections: groups of self-sufficient and independent works belonging to the same genre and sharing the same medium. Even Arthur Komar's criteria for establishing "song cyclehood"—unity of poetic content, shared thematic, harmonic, and rhythmic figures, continuity between adjacent songs, coherent tonal planning—represent less a set of prescriptions than a series of possibilities.[9] As Jonathan Dunsby has pointed out (1983, 168), there simply does not exist an analytical system that can adequately deal with works, like the song cycle, that he inelegantly but aptly describes as "multi-pieces."

Thus, for many writers, Schubert wrote only two cycles, *Die schöne Müllerin* and *Winterreise,* whereas others would include smaller-scaled groups, such as the settings of the Harper and Mignon songs from Goethe's *Wilhelm Meister* (D. 478 and 877, respectively) as well.[10] Scholars have even argued for the recognition of "hidden cycles"; Harry Goldschmidt (1974), for instance, has hypothesized that the six Heine songs of Schubert's *Schwanengesang,* if rearranged according to the order in which the poems appeared in Heine's *Heimkehr,* in fact constitute a coherent cycle,[11] and Richard Kramer suggests (1988) that Schubert may have conceived a number of "mini-cycles" (such as his settings of Goethe's "An die Entfernte," D. 765, "Am Flusse," D. 766, "Willkommen und Abschied," D. 767, and "Der Musensohn," D. 764) whose cohesion was later masked by a publication process that served entrepeneurial and not necessarily artistic ends.[12] The point here is not to decide who may be right or wrong. Conflicting views and conjectures on the status of a group of songs as cycle or collection might rather be taken as signs that we are dealing with a genre that is hardly fixed in the same sense as the symphony or sonata. The generic boundaries of the song cycle are fluid, dependent on the critical orientation of the receiver.

This brings us to a final problem: the song cycle is a fundamentally hybrid genre, a *Mischform,* and histories have tended to do less well by these than purer types. Nonetheless, it is probably fair to say that the nineteenth century witnessed a revolution in its attitude to the whole genre question, an aesthetic shift that is apparent in both the criticism and the artistic products of the age. For Friedrich Schlegel, one of the principle apologists for the new poetics, "All of the classical poetic genres are now ridiculous in their generic purity";[13] in fact, it was Schlegel's view that the "modern" genre par excellence, the *Roman* or novel, was so significant precisely because of its potential for bringing together or fusing the classical types— epic, lyric, and drama.[14] The impulse toward generic mixture that informed the novels of Jean Paul, Novalis, and E. T. A. Hoffmann manifested itself in music as well; here too the *Mischgedicht* moved from the periphery to the center of artistic activity. Karl Köstlin, who contributed most of the music volume of Friedrich Theodor Vischer's *Ästhetik oder Wissenschaft des Schönen* (Leipzig, 1857), was perhaps the single nineteenth-century theorist who attempted to cope systematically with the issue.[15] But whereas Köstlin found aesthetically suspect, for example, the mixture of epic and lyric qualities in the ballad, we might allow for the possibility that generic tension was at the very heart of the matter, and concede further that of all the lied-based genres, it was the song cycle that afforded the greatest scope for a creative interplay of this sort.

Clearly, the song cycle resists definition. So far as the choice and arrangement of texts are concerned, we can hardly speak of a norm. A composer might draw on a preexistent lyric cycle (as Schumann drew on Heine's *Lyrisches Intermezzo* for *Dichterliebe*), though few were set complete (the Schubert-Müller *Winterreise* is exceptional in this regard). But the interpolated lyrics in a *Roman* (like Goethe's *Wilhelm Meister*) or a *Kunstmärchen* (such as Ludwig Tieck's *Magelone*) could also provide an appropriate vehicle. A song cycle could also bring together a single author's poems not originally conceived as a unit (Schumann's Eichendorff *Liederkreis*, Op. 39) or draw on a group of texts by many poets (Schumann's *Myrthen* Op. 25). The musical possibilities—tonal disposition, motivic connections, affective sequence, and the like—are equally variable. The only requirement is a demonstrable measure of coherence. Schumann (1982, 262), referring to his Heine *Liederkreis* Op. 24, says as much in a letter to Clara of 24 February 1840: "In the past days I completed a large cycle (coherent) of Heine songs." Critics and analysts should therefore attempt to describe the nature and quality of this coherence as it manifests itself in individual cases.

The Prehistory of the Romantic Song Cycle: Performance or Work of Art?

Commentators have recognized for some time the error of viewing Beethoven's *An die ferne Geliebte* Op. 98 (1815–16) as an absolutely originary work, the first in an impressive line of nineteenth-century song cycles. Beethoven's celebrated work was preceded by a tradition of convivial music-making involving lieder, a practice that continued well into the nineteenth century (its influence may still be felt in works like Schumann's *Spanisches Liederspiel* Op. 74), coexisting with and influencing the cultivation of the song cycle as a high artform. A reviewer of Hans Georg Nägeli's *Liederkranz auf das Jahr 1816*, a collection of twenty-three songs, remarked that the chief purpose of these lieder was "the promotion of sociability" and that they were intended "for small circles [*Kreise*], where several people who are able to sing come together, but who, given the number and quality of their voices, could not make up a choir."[16] Publications like this were directed primarily at *Liederkreise*, social circles devoted to singing, writing poems, composing simple song melodies, and, according to one writer, playing elaborate party games with songs.[17]

In the early nineteenth century, when the institution was at its height, Goethe, Zelter, J. F. Reichardt, and F. H. Himmel all figured as leaders or members of such groups. A number of Müller's *Schöne Müllerin* poems originated as a part of the *Liederkreis* activities centered in the home of State Councillor Stägemann in Berlin (1816–17), and the famed Schubertiades, held in Joseph Spaun's home from 1825 to 1827, and described so vividly in the diaries of Fritz and Franz Hartmann, featured not only performances of lieder and piano duets, but also dancing, meals, acrobatic stunts, and drinking bouts.[18] In a word, the social context from which works like *Die schöne Müllerin* and *Winterreise* emerged represented a mélange of high art and bourgeois entertainment.

Though the nineteenth-century *Liederkreis* (as an institution) provided a social frame for the nurturing of the song cycle, the cyclic idea was present in song composition and publications from some years before. Already in the eighteenth century, prints appeared in which lieder were grouped by poet (witness the many collections devoted to settings from Gellert's *Geistliche Oden und Lieder*) or subject matter (as in the 1747 edition of Sperontes' *Singende Muse an der Pleisse*). With the appearance, in late eighteenth-century England, of publications like James Hook's *The Seasons* (ca. 1783) and *The Hours of Love* (1792), the song cycle can be said to have come into its own. It is tempting to posit a connection between these unpretentious works and the diminutive cycles (or cycles of diminutive songs) that German composers such as Reichardt and C. G. Neefe would produce shortly thereafter; Luise Peake (1980, 522) has in fact suggested that the romantic song cycle emerged from the confluence of the English predilection for setting related texts and the activities of the German *Liederkreise*. But in the absence of firmly documented links, we will have to settle for the notion that the romantic cycle was essentially the product of the convergence of a number of specifically German traditions.

The narrative element that figures in many song cycles can be traced back to the *Liederspiel*, a genre more or less invented by Reichardt, whose *Lieb und Treue* (Berlin, 1800) amounted to a play with interspersed songs—many of them settings of lyric poems by Goethe and Herder. Although this work was performed in public (at the Berlin Royal Opera House), the "play with songs" also figured in private circles. Stägemann's Berlin *Liederkreis* (1816–17) brought together the composer Ludwig Berger and the poet Wilhelm Müller to collaborate on a projected *Liederspiel—Rose, Die Müllerin*—which in turn led to Berger's cycle of ten songs, *Die schöne Müllerin* (Berlin, 1818), Müller's expanded cycle of twenty-three poems with *Prolog* and *Epilog* (published in the *Sieben und siebzig Gedichte aus den hinterlassenen Papieren eines reisenden Waldhornisten*, 1821), and ultimately Schubert's twenty-song cycle (1823). A narrative thread likewise runs through the forty-six lieder of Himmel's *Alexis und Ida: Ein Schäferroman* (1813), a setting of C. A. Tiedge's pastoral idyll *Das Echo*, and Sigismond Neukomm's setting of the same poet's *Aennchen und Robert* (1815).

Associative or affective links, on the other hand, impart a measure of poetic unity to the twenty brief songs of C. G. Neefe's *Bilder und Träume* (1798) and to Ferdinand Ries's *Sechs Lieder von Goethe* Op. 32 (1811). The latter work may well have served as a model for Beethoven's *An die ferne Geliebte*.[19] In addition, it may not be purely coincidental that the song cycle began to flourish in tandem with the rise in popularity of the poetic cycle, a genre cultivated by poets from Ludwig Uhland and Heinrich Heine to Richard Dehmel and Rainer Maria Rilke.[20] In the earlier part of the nineteenth century, Uhland's *Wanderlieder* and *Frühlingslieder* (both published 1815) seem to have had a particularly decisive impact. Conradin Kreutzer was drawn to both cycles, setting all nine poems of the first and five poems from the second. As Barbara Turchin has shown (1987), Kreutzer's *Wanderlieder* (1818) initiated a significant trend in song cycle composition that would resonate in many subsequent works centered on wandering as a poetic theme: Marschner's *Sechs Wanderlieder* Op. 35, Schubert's *Winterreise*, Schumann's Kerner *Liederreihe* Op. 35, and Mahler's *Lieder eines fahrenden Gesellen*.

The purely aesthetic quality of many of the earlier song cycles is slight. Kreutzer's *Wanderlieder*, as important as they may have been in establishing a subgenre within the song cycle, remain unassuming compositions—one might say intentionally unassuming. This is just as true of the cycles of better-known (and perhaps more serious-minded) composers: Weber's *Leyer und Schwert* songs (Opp. 41–43, 1815) come to mind. But it would be a mistake to view the majority of the early song cycles from the aesthetic angle alone; we should also consider the possibilities that they afforded for bourgeois entertainment. Berger's *Schöne Müllerin* songs may pale next to Schubert's, but the circumstances that led to their creation were artistically vibrant by any standard. The plan to mount a "geselligen Liederspiel" based on the story of a journeyman miller lad's fated love for Rose, the miller's daughter, allowed Wilhelm Müller, Wilhelm and Luise Hensel, and Hedwig Stägemann to exercise their poetic talents and to participate as singing actors. Susan Youens has shown (1991) how the complex web of interpersonal relationships that obtained among the members of the Stägemann salon (including the composer Ludwig Berger and the poet

Clemens Brentano) made for intriguing parallels with the drama enacted in the "geselligen Liederspiel."[21] Berger's cycle, then, came to life primarily as a "performance" for the members of a private company of song enthusiasts and should be evaluated only secondarily as a "work" designed for aesthetic contemplation.

It is in this aesthetic sense that Beethoven's *An die ferne Geliebte* does mark a point of origin, or at least a new orientation for the song cycle that would be of singular importance for the Romantics. If there was a genuine connection between this cycle and Beethoven's *Unsterbliche Geliebte*,[22] then we are faced with a transformation of life into art comparable to Goethe's poetic sublimation of his love for Ulrike von Levetzow in the Marienbad Elegy, or Hölderlin's mediation of lived experience and craft in the late hymns. Beethoven, at any rate, may well have been the first composer to stamp the song cycle as a high art form and at the same time to articulate its chief compositional challenge: the fusion of art and apparent artlessness. Here he was certainly aided by Jeitteles's poems, which were probably never published apart from Beethoven's settings. Although each of the six, taken individually, is a rather conventional love lyric, the poetic cycle as a whole displays remarkable symmetries. The overall layout of the strophes in each poem, if songs 3 and 4 are taken as a unit, forms the pattern 4 + 3 + 8 + 3 + 4.[23] In addition, there are alternations of trochaic and anapestic metrical patterns and of four- and six-verse strophes as one passes from poem to poem.

This tension between convention and sophistication is reflected in the music at all levels: tonal, melodic, formal, and generic. The cycle's tightly-wrought tonal plan (E♭–G–A♭–A♭–C–E♭) is counterbalanced by quasi-improvisational transitions of intentional simplicity that emphasize the affective breaks between songs instead of smoothing them over. The melodic unity of the cycle results from the songs' consistency of tone, so that gestural similarity (in particular, the sigh and echo figures that pervade songs 1, 2, 4, and 5) is of greater moment than motivic development.[24] Dynamic, goal-directed processes are avoided at the formal level, too, as witness the prominence of the variation principle in the piano parts of songs 1, 3, and 4. Likewise, the recall of the music of the first song in the last (at "Dann vor diesen Liedern weichet") is less a teleologically conceived gesture than an evocative one. If it underscores the poetic point that spatial and temporal distances can be overcome by singing these songs, it also suggests that the cycle hardly comes to an end: the peculiarly inconclusive gesture in the piano (a modified version of the cycle's opening three measures) is a perfect cipher for infinite continuation. Last, the conflict between simplicity and artfulness is registered in the close of the last song, as the lied melody from the beginning of the cycle is treated in the manner of an operatic stretto, replete with quickening tempo, word repetitions, and fittingly ostentatious piano writing. Conviviality, in other words, gives way to artistic pretensions.

Schubert's Song Cycles: Biedermeier Sensibility and Romantic Irony

An die ferne Geliebte prefigures Beethoven's late style in many telling respects, as Joseph Kerman (1973) has argued. But the song cycle as a genre remained a somewhat peripheral phenomenon in Beethoven's creative oeuvre. For Schubert, on the other hand, the cyclic impulse took center stage in various forms. His predilection for focusing on the works of a single poet and setting clearly definable groups of poems en masse led him between 1814 and 1816 to approach the lyric output of Goethe, Schiller, Klopstock, Hölty, and Mayrhofer in this way. Unfortunately, his plan conceived in 1816 to bring out eight volumes of songs, each devoted to one poet's works, came to naught. From 1821 on, Schubert's songs were instead published in small volumes (*Hefte*), generally comprising three to four songs. For Walther Dürr (1986, 29–30), editor of the lieder volumes of the *Neue Schubert-Ausgabe,* these volumes fall into three categories: songs grouped by poet (twenty-four *Hefte*), songs linked by dedicatee (fifteen) and songs related through musical and poetic content (twenty-four).

The great Müller cycles, *Die schöne Müllerin* and *Winterreise,* clearly belong to Dürr's last category, but so do many publications whose status as cycles is less easy to determine. The published song-groups on texts from Goethe's *Wilhelm Meister* surely merit consideration as cycles, given the poetic interrelatedness of the component songs and the tonal, textural, and gestural ties that bind together each group. It is more difficult to view a publication like Schubert's Op. 108 (1829) in these terms; here the composer (perhaps in consultation with his publisher Leidesdorf) assembled three songs ("Über Wildemann," D. 884; "Todesmusik," D. 728; "Die Erscheinung," D. 229), each the work of a different poet (E. Schulze, Schober, and Kosegarten) and each originally composed at a different time (1826, 1822, and 1815 respectively). Neither key scheme (D minor– G major–E major) nor poetic content suggests a very strong cyclic intent.[25] Many of the smaller cycles, then, may owe their existence to commercial concerns.

The larger cycles, too, are not without definitional problems of their own. There is some justification, for example, in viewing *Winterreise* as an immense double cycle. Schubert probably first encountered Müller's poetic cycle during the winter of 1826–27 in the twelve-poem form in which it appeared in *Urania: Taschenbuch auf das Jahr 1823 (Jahrgang* 15). He must have regarded his settings of these twelve poems as a self-sufficient unit, opening and closing in D minor, for after No. 12, in Schubert's *Winterreise* autograph, is the indication "Fine." At some point before March 1827 Schubert happened on Müller's expanded, twenty-four-poem cycle, in the second volume of the *Gedichte aus den hinterlassenen Papieren eines reisenden Waldhornisten* (1824). As Müller had interspersed his twelve new poems among the *Urania* texts, Schubert had little choice but to pick out those not already set while retaining the ordering of the new poems from the *Gedichte*, except for switching the original order of "Nebensonnen" and "Muth." Schubert's autograph reflects the two-tiered compositional history of the cycle through its numbering of the new lieder, now designated as a "Fortsetzung," as 1–12.[26] Is *Winterreise* one cycle or two? Or are we asking the wrong question? Does not the peculiar history of the cycle rather complement its non-linear poetic progress, its intentional open-endedness?

Die schöne Müllerin (composed 1823; published 1824 as ". . . ein Cyclus von Liedern gedichtet von Wilhelm Müller") does not raise such questions. Müller's twenty-five-poem narrative cycle is probably more coherent in structure than any other cycle of the period, and Schubert set it practically complete, omitting only the *Prolog, Epilog,* and three poems. The concensus on Schubert's less discussed larger cycle is that the poetry is generally simple, even naive in tone, and that the music is correspondingly unpretentious.[27] Eduard von Bauernfeld, in "Some Notes on Franz Schubert" (1869), even commented that the composer's melodies occasionally tended toward the "commonplace," "trivial," and "unrefined," qualities that he detected in several of the *Müllerin* songs.[28] The primary affect of the first half of the song cycle (up to the climactic No. 11, "Mein") is indeed suggestive of naiveté, but this is a "second" naiveté—much as Hegel spoke of a "second" nature—into which we can read premonitions of the coming catastrophe, the miller lad's suicide by drowning.

In retrospect, there is a troubling, sometimes menacing, quality in even the simplest strophic songs, projected in No. 1 ("Das Wandern") through the piano's incessantly repeated "mill-wheel" sixteenths, and in No. 7 ("Ungeduld") through equally insistent triplets. Songs 8 through 10 then move from absolute simplicity of utterance to a brief but clear prefiguration of the final tragedy (the turn to minor at the end of No. 10, "Thränenregen"), so that the verbal and accompanimental repetitions in the apparently joyous No. 11, "Mein," project an element of strain. The text provides Schubert with the opportunity to forge important musical links in the second half of the cycle, most notably in the four "green ribbon" songs: No. 12 ("Pause") and No. 13 ("Mit dem grünen Lautenbande"), both in B♭; No. 16 ("Die liebe Farbe") and No. 17 ("Die böse Farbe"), both in B. In the latter two, Schubert creates a telling disparity between song title and musical affect that perfectly mirrors the miller-boy's bitter attitude toward the color green, his faithless lover's favorite. "Die liebe Farbe" is set in a brooding B minor tinged with major, whereas "Die böse Farbe" reverses the pattern, its jaunty B major tinged with minor. The ironic tone within each song is compounded by the ironic relationship between them.

Schubert's prime means of binding together the entire cycle, however, hinges on the consistent employment of related accompanimental figures in songs poetically centered on the brook: Nos. 2, 3, 4, 6, 15, 19, and 20. These insistently repeating patterns are ultimately and fittingly stilled in the mesmerizing dactyllic rhythms of the last song, "Des Baches Wiegenlied."

Unlike the *Müllerin* songs, *Die Winterreise* does not trace a linear narrative course. Schubert's "laments over a sweetheart's faithlessness," as one of his contemporaries called them,[29] appear to follow a path as aimless as that of the dejected, lovelorn wanderer who sings them. Schubert conceived his cycle (or double cycle) as an interweaving of musicopoetic topoi—chorales, horn calls, echoes—all potentially representative of infinite extension in time and space. Songs 5 ("Der Lindenbaum"), 6 ("Wasserfluth"), and 7 ("Auf dem Flusse") are linked not only by their shared tonal center (E major/minor),[30] but also by horn calls and chorale-style writing, evocations of a less troubled past. But the opening song, "Gute Nacht," introduces the cycle's principal musical topoi: obsessively repeating rhythms and shifts of mode, both familiar from *Die schöne Müllerin,* though intensified here.

These features surface in other cycles that treat similar poetic themes, such as Marschner's *Wanderlieder;* Schubert, however, deploys them on a much broader scale. In *Winterreise,* the steadily repeated rhythms in songs 1, 4, 10, and 13 (all of the *Wanderlieder* type) become musical symbols for rigidification and obsession. Similarly, the major-minor (or minor-major) alternations in songs 2, 11, and 16 can be read as musical expressions of an ironic self-awareness. In No. 11, the wanderer's past state of dreamy blissfulness, represented by an easy-going $\frac{6}{8}$ melody (a parody of a popular *Singspiel* tune) is called into question by flashes of minor at *Und als die Hähne krähen* and by the turn to minor at the close of the third strophe and the last. Mayrhofer's comment, in his 1829 obituary notice, was right on the mark: "The poet's [Müller's] irony [in *Winterreise*], rooted in despair, appealed to him [Schubert]: he expressed it in cutting tones."[31] A similar point can be made by considering formal structures: the fragile strophic design of No. 12 ("Einsamkeit"), for instance, seems at odds with the violent, melodramatic outbursts at "Ach, dass die Luft so ruhig!"

But what of the overall shape and meaning of *Winterreise?* In what sense is it a cycle? Though the poems can in no way be taken to chart a progressive, linear development toward a goal, Schubert's musical plan is not without a logic of its own. Many of the topoi that inform the cycle are brought together in the strategically placed No. 20, "Der Wegweiser," where the wanderer overcomes his preoccupation with and longing for death.[32] This does not mean, however, that the last song, "Der Leiermann," articulates a hopeful statement, that the wanderer's bleak winter may give way to a more comforting spring.[33] The song's numbing tonal stasis, coupled uneasily with its obsessive repetition of the mechanical hurdy-gurdy figure, points to a demystified but grim future given over to the endless rendition of mournful tunes. The accent falls on the painful, not the hopeful, side of self-awareness. If the Biedermeier spirit is colored with irony in the *Müllerin* songs, it is wholly supplanted by an ironic consciousness in *Winterreise.*

Schumann's Song Cycles: The Composer as Poet and Historian

With Robert Schumann's turn to lied composition in 1840, the song cycle reached a crucial turning point in its history. In less than a year, Schumann produced a series of cycles that explore all the possibilities of the genre: the Heine *Liederkreis* Op. 24; *Myrthen* Op. 25 (on texts by Goethe, Rückert, and Byron, among others); the Eichendorff *Liederkreis* Op. 39; *Dichterliebe* Op. 48; *Frauenliebe und -leben* Op. 49; and the Kerner *Liederreihe* Op. 35. On the one hand, these works—especially *Dichterliebe* and *Frauenliebe und -leben*—contributed much to subsequent notions of the ideal or typical song cycle. On the other hand, we should give due emphasis to the radicality of conception that animated Schumann's cycles, a quality that they share with many of his sets of piano pieces from the preceding decade.[34] For Roland Barthes (1985, 295), it was Schumann's structuring of the piano cycles as a continual series of interruptions that makes them so striking.

Indeed, the rapid-fire mood shifts that characterize Schumann's cycles created real problems of comprehensibility for his contemporaries. An 1842 article considering, among other works, Opp. 24, 25, and 35, suggests that the "tangle of musical images" that Schumann was wont to introduce in his large-scale works often made it difficult for listeners to grasp their "logical progress and purposiveness."[35] For a reviewer of *Dichterliebe*, the latter was "a cycle of songs that rushed past fleetingly like butterflies [*papillons*], leaving us little time to take delight, lovingly, in their irridescent colors."[36] The "modernity" of the song cycles lies precisely here, in their employment of a fanciful montage technique that puts them on a par with the enigmatic collections of literary fragments cultivated so assiduously by the early Romantics. This might well have been the technique to which Schumann (1982, 279) referred in a letter to Clara of 31 May 1840, when, having just completed the Eichendorff *Liederkreis,* he proclaimed, "Sometimes it seems to me as if I were charting out wholly new paths in music."

This is not to say that Schumann's application of the montage idea was devoid of musical logic. On the contrary, issues of coherence were of paramount importance for him; in his review of Carl Loewe's *Liederkreis in Balladenform, Esther* Op. 52 (1835–36), Schumann took careful note of the unifying power of a clear tonal plan (centered, in *Esther,* on A minor/ major) and of thematic recall as well (the music of the second song's "Gott Israels, wohin mich kehre" resurfaces in the third).[37] In his own cycles, however, Schumann often causes us to reexamine notions of number and order normally considered requisite for musicopoetic coherence. *Dichterliebe* was published in 1844 as a cycle of sixteen songs but first took shape, in the spring of 1840, as "20 Lieder und Gesänge" from Heine's *Lyrisches*

Intermezzo, and it may have originally been conceived as a setting of twenty-nine poems.[38] The songs of the Eichendorff *Liederkreis* can be shown to form a logical sequence in any one of several orderings: that in which the poems were set to music, that of the published version of 1842, and the slightly altered sequence of the 1850 revision. Experiments with order can likewise be inferred from the source material for a singular and until recently neglected cycle, Robert and Clara's jointly conceived *Zwölf Lieder aus F. Rückerts Liebesfrühling* Op. 37/12.[39]

The Heine *Liederkreis* Op. 24 poses no problem of number or ordering. It was conceived from the start as a setting of a pre-existent cycle, nine poems from the *Junge Leiden* section of Heine's *Buch der Lieder.* Yet it entails an interesting approach to cyclic coherence. It could be said that Schumann actually thought, in this case, in terms of two modes of coherence, the first a "logical" coherence that would bind one song to the second, and an "associative" coherence that would relate non-adjacent songs. A measure of narrative logic is already built into the texts, which trace the poet's progress from dreamy despair (over his treacherous beloved) to a state of self-awareness in which recovery through art seems a real possibility. Schumann's tonal plan, moving by thirds and fifths through D, B, E, A, and back to D, provides a logic of its own, as do the topical links that connect adjacent songs (e.g., the "horn chorale" of Nos. 2 and 3 the echoes of Nos. 3 and 4, or the recitativelike writing in Nos. 5 and 6). On the other hand, the appearance of similar accompaniment figures in songs 5 and 7 and of the chorale topos in songs 3 and 8 belongs to a stratum of associative recurrences that is no less powerful for its evocativeness. The interplay of "logic" and subtle association accounts for the peculiar but compelling character of the affective shifts—Barthes's continual interruptions—that set off one song from the next.

The Eichendorff *Liederkreis* Op. 39, in Schumann's word his *allerromantischstes,*[40] offers perhaps the most sophisticated solution to the problem of imparting melodic coherence to a cycle of songs without violating the ethos of the individual lied as an unrepeatable lyric utterance. Clearly, Schumann wanted to avoid the kind of musical return that Loewe had employed in *Esther:* the recall of a sharply chiseled and syntactically complete motive that might suggest an epic quality antithetical to the lied. Schumann's solution involved introducing, in the piano part of the first song of the 1850 version of the cycle, "In der Fremde," a motive distinctive enough to be recognized on its return in later songs but aphoristic enough to allow for developmental reshaping (see Ex. 9.1a). Though this B–F♯–B motive plays a limited role in "In der Fremde," as part of a countermelody to the vocal line, in the next song, "Intermezzo," it is altered over the course of several bars so that the B–F♯ fifth is expanded to an octave (Ex. 9.1b). The piano sets off "In der Fremde" (song 6) with a variant of the original motive (Ex. 9.1c), which pervades the remainder of the lied, resuming its original form just before the climax and then expanding to a sixth for the closing vocal phrase ("es redet trunken die Ferne," Ex. 9.1d). "Frühlingsnacht," the twelfth and final song of the cycle, then takes up the motive in its new form (Ex. 9.1e). The unfolding of a brief but pliable motive thus arches over what Jürgen Thym (1974, 219–25) has defined as the cycle's two expressive curves, the progress from melancholy to ecstasy marked off by songs 1–6 and 7–12. The motive is not developed with a rigorous, forward-driving logic, nor should it be; its course is audible but understated, in perfect keeping with the lied aesthetic.

Dichterliebe, a musicopoetic compression of Heine's sixty-six poem *Lyrisches Intermezzo* into a cycle of sixteen songs, is Schumann's closest approximation to the literary fragment collection (after the manner of collections like Friedrich Schlegel's *Ideen* of 1800) in the realm of song.[41] First to consider is the cycle's tonal openendedness: though the large-scale harmonic plan favors motion by third or fifth between songs, the first song hovers between F♯ minor and A major, and the final song closes in D♭.

EXAMPLE 9.1. Schumann, Eichendorff *Liederkreis,* Op. 39, Motivic Evolution

(a) No. 1, mm. 10–12 (piano)

(b) No. 2, mm. 3–7 (piano)

(c) No. 6, mm. 1–2 (piano)

(d) No. 6, mm. 20–24 (piano and vocal line)

es re - det trun-ken die Fer - ne wie von künf- ti-gem gros - sen Glück

(e) No. 12, mm. 24, 26–27 (piano)

Some of the songs are so brief or harmonically ambiguous that they invite interpretation as extended upbeats to those that follow. Thus, the inconclusive ending of the first song, "Im wunderschönen Monat Mai," on the dominant-seventh chord of F♯ minor, seems to resolve onto the A major of the second song, "Aus meinen Thränen spriessen," especially given the importance of A in the former.

There is no lack of motivic interconnections among the songs; the point is to decide which ones are substantive. (Compare, for example, the settings of "Ich *liebe dich*, so muß ich weinen bitterlich" in song 4, "*und ich weinte* noch lange bitterlich" in song 13, and "Ich senkte auch *meine Liebe*" in song 16.) But the structural integrity of the work is largely the result of Schumann's interweaving of affective strata. This is not really a new phenomenon in the song cycle—we have noted a similar procedure in Schubert—but here it is controlled by a principal absolute-lyric stratum that reaches from the first song to the last. That is, songs 1, 5, 8, 10, 12, and 16 share similar poetic images (references to flowers, songs, lilies), attenuated accompanimental textures marked by delicate arpeggios, and even thematic material. The varied recall at the close of song 16 of the piano's postlude to song 12 brings a sharp mood contrast; it may be read as a yielding of the extroverted ballad tone of "Die alten, bösen Lieder" to the absolute inwardness of the lyric—a subtle reflection, in musical terms, of what Hölderlin's poetic theory designated as a *Wechsel der Töne*.

Schumann's setting of Adalbert von Chamisso's *Frauenliebe und -leben* was anticipated by Carl Loewe's of 1836–37. (Schumann set all but the ninth and last of Chamisso's poems; Loewe's eighth song exists only in sketch form, and his ninth was not published until 1868). Given Schumann's high regard for Loewe as a ballad composer and his interest in Loewe's *Esther*, it is likely that he knew the earlier work. The many similarities between the two support this idea: both are tonally unified cycles, Schumann's in E♭, Loewe's in A major/minor; both composers highlight the phrase *taucht auf tiefstem Dunkel* from the first song with expressive interval leaps; and the opening gesture of the second song, "Er, der herrlichste von allen," features triadic, trumpet-call motives in both cases. But Schumann's cycle surpasses Loewe's in its use of discreet but recognizable gestural recurrences: the melodic sequences and pulsing accompanimental eighths of the second song at *Wandle, wandle deine Bahnen* are echoed in the fourth at *Ich will ihm dienen* and in the sixth at *Weißt du nun die Thränen,* just as the vocal line's chromatic shift from A to A♭ in song 2 (at *traurig sein*) recurs similarly harmonized in song 4 (on *Ringelein* and *erst belehrt*). Intratextual references are enriched by intertextual ones, specifically at the piano's brief interlude in song 6, "Süsser Freund" (mm. 32ff.), where Schumann alludes to the opening melody of the last song of Beethoven's *An die ferne Geliebte* (Ex. 9.2). Surely the recapitulation of the opening song melody in the piano postlude that concludes the work hearkens to the type of return that Beethoven had employed in his cycle, though there is

EXAMPLE 9.2.
(a) Schumann, *Frauenliebe und leben,* No. 6, mm. 32–34 (piano)

(b) Beethoven, *An die ferne Geliebte,* No. 6, mm. 1–2 (piano)

no operatic posturing here. The web of allusions amounts to nothing less than a historicizing of the song cycle, a lyric pronouncement of its past. Schumann's portrayal, in song, of a woman's love and life, is at the same time a historical account of a genre.[42]

After Schumann: Experiments, Dramatic Cycles, and Orchestral Lieder

Cornelius

Few composers of the late nineteenth century devoted their efforts to the song cycle as did Schumann. One who did was Peter Cornelius, who produced most of his cycles between 1853 and 1856 while an active member of Liszt's circle at Weimar; these include *Vater unser* Op. 2, *Trauer und Trost* Op. 3, *Rheinische Lieder* Op. 7, and *Weihnachtslieder* Op. 8 (two somewhat altered versions of the latter appeared in 1859 and 1870). They constitute an odd corpus of works. From Schumann, Cornelius adopted the idea of casting his cycles as tonal unities; only the *Weihnachtslieder* and *An Bertha* (1862–65/1873) begin and close in different keys. But Cornelius employed a number of his own devices. In most of his lieder, for instance, he drew on his own texts. Each of the *Vater unser* poems, therefore, represents the composer's paraphrase of a line from the prayer. Likewise, each lied in the cycle takes as its point of departure a brief melodic citation from the monophonic *Pater noster*. As Cornelius reported to Liszt, "Nine songs based on cantus firmi! Now that is new."[43]

On the whole, the borrowed material is treated with remarkable variety. In songs 1 and 7 the cantus firmus is restricted largely to the piano bass line, but in songs 3 and 4 it pervades both vocal and accompanimental parts. Songs 8 and 9 bring choralelike harmonizations, and song 6 is a contrapuntal tour de force, with a chromatic version of the cantus treated imitatively, then combined with augmented and doubly augmented forms. The *Weihnachtslieder* also incorporate borrowed material; the second and third versions, for instance, feature the chorale, "Wie schön leuchtet der

Morgenstern" in the piano part of song 3, "Drei Kön'ge wandern aus Morgenland." Archaisms of another sort figure in *Trauer und Trost,* whose sixth song, "Der glückes Fülle," employs harmonic progressions suggestive of the Phrygian mode, particularly through an emphasis on the minor dominant. Cornelius's peculiar blend of chromaticism and modally flavored diatonicism, of sentimentality and Christian moralizing, remains an anomaly in the history of the song cycle.

Brahms

Though more a part of the mainstream as a lied composer, Johannes Brahms maintained an equivocal attitude toward the song cycle. By far the majority of his songs, like Mendelssohn's, were published in groups more accurately described as collections than cycles, a term that he never used in connection with his song publications.[44] Not that Brahms was unconcerned with questions of order—he once complained that "most male and female singers group his songs together [on their programs] in a quite arbitrary manner, considering only what suits their voices, and not realizing how much trouble he had always taken to assemble his song compositions like a bouquet." Similarly, he informed Rieter-Biedermann with regard to the *Lieder und Gesänge* Op. 59: "The two volumes differ in size, but I wish the order, which you will call a disorder, to be kept."[45]

Indeed, one can often detect "minicycles" of songs on texts by the same poet embedded within what appear to be heterogeneously grouped lieder. It was Brahms's practice to begin with clusters such as these, which were only later assembled into larger "bouquets" just prior to publication. Frequently the minicycles on a single author's work share not only poetic imagery but musical material as well. Hence the two Hoffmann von Fallersleben songs entitled "Liebe und Frühling" from Op. 3 are set in the same B-major tonality and are bound together by similar melodic and textural details. In much the same way, the Eichendorff songs from Op. 7, "Parole" and "Anklänge," both concerned with a young girl's separation from her beloved, play on C and E tonalities and bring evocative horn-call figures as musical symbols for distance. Two of the Uhland settings from Op. 19, "Scheiden und Meiden" and "In der Ferne," are based on nearly identical melodies, their motivic parallelism again being generated by poetic content; in the second lyric, the poet, parted from his lover, recalls the melody of the first, itself a song of parting. Similarly, two of the Op. 59 settings of Klaus Groth poems, "Regenlied" and "Nachklang," and the paired Heine songs from Op. 85, "Sommerabend" and "Mondenschein," are linked by clearly related melodies fashioned in response to textual images.

Two of Brahms's song collections, the *Neun Lieder und Gesänge* Op. 32 (on texts from Daumer's *Hafis* and Platen's *Romanzen und Jugendlieder*) and the *Romanzen aus L. Tieck's Magelone* Op. 33, merit close attention, if only because they point up the disadvantages of circumscribing the limits of the song cycle as a genre too narrowly.[46] Eric Sams (1972, 27) is one of the few who treats the Op. 32 *Lieder* (composed and published in 1864) as a cycle, largely because the texts that Brahms assembled convey a "story of lost love, remorse, and undying fidelity." But the songs also use some remarkable harmonically integrative devices, an awareness of which may affect our reading of the overall poetic message. The most significant of these is the Schubertian succession of harmonies that Christopher Wintle calls the "Neapolitan complex"—I(i)–↑VI–↑II–German augmented sixth–I(i)$^6_4$–V–I(i)—a progression that plays an important role, at local and global levels, in Brahms's instrumental music of the 1860s.[47]

Elements of the complex, in its darkly hued minor form, occur in the first of the Op. 32 songs, the somber *Wanderlied* "Wie rafft ich mich auf in der Nacht"; emphasis on the minor Neapolitan at *O wehe, wie hast du die Tage verbracht* makes Brahms's setting of the last strophe particularly poignant. The minor Neapolitan also colors the concluding cadence of the C♯-minor song 4, *Der Strohm, der neben mir verrauschte*, recalling the D-minor tonality of songs 2 and 3. Though the complex does not surface in the immediately following songs, they too are linked by harmonic means: diminished-seventh sonorities are used to dramatic effect in song 5 and in song 6, whose inconclusive ending on C makes for an extended dominant preparation for the next song (in F). But Brahms's setting of the third strophe of the last song, "Wie bist du, meine Königin," brings the Neapolitan complex in its entirety; the line *Und grüne Schatten breiten sich, ob fürchterliche Schwülle* even pairs major and minor forms of the Neapolitan harmony. Thus, by hearkening back to the dark harmonic palette of the cycle's earlier songs, Brahms places his "happy ending" in a questionable light. The deluded poet may be convinced that his unattainable beloved is "wonnevoll"; the composer tells us otherwise.

Brahms's first encounter with the Magelone tale—as first told in the late-twelfth-century poem of Bernard de Treviers and subsequently circulated in chapbooks and *Volksbücher*—may have occurred as early as the spring of 1847, when the young musician was serving as piano tutor to Lieschen Giesemann in Winsen.[48] Perhaps by 1853, during his stay in the Schumann household, Brahms came to know the version in Tieck's *Phantasus* (1812–16), the *Liebesgeschichte der schönen Magelone und des Grafen Peter von Provence,* a recasting of the old tale as a *Kunstmärchen,* each of its eighteen brief chapters culminating in a lyric poem.[49] These poems (excepting those at the conclusion of chaps. 1, 16, and 17) supplied Brahms with the texts for his Magelone *Romanzen* Op. 33, the cycle whose composition occupied him at various points between 1861 and 1869 and which was published by Rieter-Biedermann in five *Hefte* of three songs each in 1865 (*Hefte* 1–2) and 1869 (*Hefte* 3–5).

The work's peculiar compositional and publication history, together with the fact that a clear narrative line cannot be inferred from the lyrics alone, has led some scholars, Walther Dürr (1984, 304–9) and Leon Plantinga (1984, 431) among them, to wonder whether Brahms's *Magelone* is a cycle or should be performed as such.[50] There is strong evidence, however, that Brahms composed songs 7, 8, 12, and 13 before the first six were published, a sign that he was thinking in cyclic terms from the start.[51] In addition, though it is not possible to deduce the story of Peter and Magelone from Tieck's poems alone, they do project a pattern of union, separation, and reunion—the course of true love in the abstract. Therefore, a connecting narrative (a summary of the story for which the poems furnish lyric interludes), such as Otto Schlotke's of 1899, is not absolutely requisite to appreciating the *Romanzen* as a cycle.[52] Brahms's attitude was typically ambivalent. In a letter of March 1870 to Adolf Schubring he stated bluntly: "The *Magelone Romanzen* should not be thought of as a single entity, nor do they have anything to do with [Tieck's] story; it's only due to a certain German thoroughness that I set the poems up through the last number."[53] But in an exchange of 1866 with Max Friedlaender, Brahms came close to reversing himself on both points.[54] Most telling is the composer's rhetorical query, reported by Kalbeck (1912–21, I: 429): "Aren't they [the *Magelone* songs], after all, a kind of theatre?"

A fair amount of criticism has been leveled at the *Magelone Romanzen,* which have been variously described as "sprawling" or "undisciplined" structures, even "failures in the attempted genre." The chief complaint has revolved around Brahms's use of operatic elements such as excessive word repetitions, abrupt tempo shifts, and exaggeratedly declamatory writing, features that have been viewed as antithetical to the lied tradition.[55] For some writers, the cycle's stylistic oddities can be explained only in biographical terms, by conjecturing that Brahms must have identified deeply with the hero of Tieck's tale.[56] It is possible, however, to view the anomalies in another light. An important impetus for Brahms's settings of Tieck's lyrics was certainly provided by his 1861 performances of Beethoven's *An die ferne Geliebte,* Schubert's *Die schöne Müllerin,* and Schumann's *Dichterliebe* with the famous baritone Julius Stockhausen (the dedicatee of the *Magelone* songs).[57] We can readily imagine the tradition-conscious Brahms planning to write a song cycle that could at once withstand comparison with those of his predecessors and assert its own individuality of conception. Thus, Brahms may have modeled his "operatic" Lieder on Schubert's ballads (more so than the songs from his cycles)—works like the Ossian *Gesänge* (in particular, D. 150, D. 282, D. 293, D. 375, and D. 534) or "Atys," D. 585.[58] Similarly, the idea of setting the interpolated lyrics from a prose narrative as a single group might have derived from Schumann's nine *Lieder und Gesänge aus Goethe's Wilhelm Meister* Op. 98a (none of which exhibits operatic structures). It was Brahms's achievement to have created a precise musical analogue to Tieck's generically hybrid *Liebesgeschichte:* if the *Kunstmärchen* occupies a middleground between simpler forms like the *Volksmärchen* and grander ones like the *Roman,* then Brahms's mix of lied and operatic elements mediates between the song cycle as fragment collection and the bolder pretensions of opera.

Although it is possible to hear in the *Magelone Romanzen* a sublimation of Brahms's desire to compose an opera,[59] it is probably more important to realize that here he contributed a startlingly experimental work to a genre whose history is determined by experimental works. Its key scheme, proceeding from and eventually arriving at E♭, moves principally by thirds and fifths, and thus is in line with the concentric plans of Beethoven and Schumann. But the break of a second between the eighth song ("Wir müßen uns trennen," in G♭) and the ninth ("Ruhe, Süßliebchen," in A♭) suggests a division of the whole into two lyric "acts," the first (songs 1–8) tracing the course of Peter and Magelone's blossoming love, the second (songs 9–15) devoted to their separation and reunion. Within each half, Brahms presents a varied mixture of *Romanzen,* some tending toward the ethos of the lied, and others incorporating stylistic and formal traits associated with dramatic music; not every one of the *Magelone* songs is an opera aria in disguise.

Thus, songs 4 and 5 (which, in Tieck's tale, Peter sends to Magelone along with his precious rings) stem directly from the lied tradition. They are unified as a lyric pair by subtle linking devices similar to those employed by Schubert and Schumann: the gentle sighs and accompanimental triplets of song 4 ("Liebe kam aus fernen Landen") reverberate in the more emotionally charged atmosphere of song 5 ("Willst du des Armen"), whereas the contrasting key of the former song's middle section (F) is taken over as the latter's principal tonality. Likewise, Nos. 11 ("Wie schnell verschwindet") and 12 ("Muß es eine Trennung geben"), both nearly perfect examples of the *Lied im Volkston,* are perceived as a distinct pair. Sensitive to their role in Tieck's story as laments sung alternately by Magelone and Peter, Brahms set both in minor keys, compound meter, and simple strophic forms. These *Romanzen im Volkston* furthermore provide a foil for the more operatically conceived No. 3 ("Sind es Schmerzen"), whose two-part, slow-fast design recalls that of the early nineteenth-century virtuoso aria, and for No. 10 ("Verzweiflung"), with its quasi-orchestral piano part and rhetorically heightened vocal line.

Most intriguing, however, are the *Romanzen* that mediate the two qualities songlike and operatic. The ABA' form of No. 8 ("Wir müßen uns trennen"), for instance, concords with patterns that Brahms regularly employed in his lieder, though the slow-fast tempo disposition of the AB unit points, as in No. 3, to the aria. The formal layout of No. 15 ("Treue Liebe dauert lange") is much the same, though here the recurrence and transformation of the A material throughout the song adds another integrative feature. The positioning of the more dramatically styled *Romanzen* is by no means entirely fortuitous; No. 8 closes off the first lyric "act," as No. 15 (a "duet" for the principals, Peter and Magelone) does the second.

Brahms's *Magelone* songs, therefore, do suggest a "kind of theatre," but one of the sort to which Tieck alluded in the *Phantasus,* which "constructs a stage for the imagination within the imagination."[60]

Wagner

If operatic traits are implicit in Brahms's *Magelone,* they are explicit in Richard Wagner's *Fünf Gedichte für eine Frauenstimme mit Pianoforte-Begleitung* on texts by Mathilde Wesendonk, composed between November 1857 and May 1858 and published in 1862. The majority of the songs, then, came into being while Wagner was at work on Act I of *Tristan und Isolde.* Although only two, "Im Treibhaus" (No. 3) and "Träume" (No. 5), are specifically designated "Studien" for *Tristan,* the musicodramatic impulse can be felt throughout. The form of "Der Engel" (No. 1), for example, only superficially adheres to a songlike ABA; the melodic return, at *da der Engel schwebt,* comes at the close of a verbal syntactic unit and receives such ambiguous harmonic support that the join between sections is skilfully disguised. The design of the first song thus approximates that of the revised version of Venus's aria "Geliebter, komm!" for the 1860–61 *Tannhäuser.* Wagner, in other words, had already become a master of the "art of transition" (*Kunst des Übergangs*) that he would describe to Mathilde Wesendonk in a letter of 29 October 1859 (*Selected Letters of Richard Wagner,* trans. & ed. Stewart Spencer and Barry Millington, New York, 1987, 475).

"Stehe still!" (No. 2) likewise proceeds in a continuous, evolving form, the agitated "Rad der Zeit" music of the beginning giving way to a serene, prayerful second half. The principal material of "Im Treibhaus" (No. 3) would resurface in the opening portion of Act III of *Tristan,* but even within the confines of a relatively brief song the operatic pedigree of the music is clear; its freely developing, practically leitmotivic course is only interrupted for a recitativelike setting of *Wohl, ich weiß es, arme Pflanze.* In "Schmerzen" (No. 4), the operatic background is provided by the *Ring,* not *Tristan;* mention of "ein stolzer Siegesheld" calls up a reference to the Sword motive, whereas the close of the song brings dual allusions to Wotan's characteristic cadence and the Sword motive in C, its associated tonality in the *Ring* thus serving as the key of the song.

With "Träume" (No. 5) we return to the world of *Tristan* through the song's prefiguration of the Ab-major love duet music of Act II. It is primarily this overriding dramatic tone that imparts cyclic coherence to the songs, for neither the key scheme (G–C minor/major–D minor–C–Ab) nor the compositional history of the set would seem to support a cyclic interpretation. But the final ordering of the songs (which differs markedly from the order of their conception),[61] is not without a certain logic. The set was arranged to culminate in "Träume," the most evocatively *Tristan*esque of the songs, its appoggiatura gestures on repeated settings of the word *Träume* and strong subdominant coloring having already been foreshadowed in "Der Engel," the first song. At the center of the set, Wagner placed the other *Tristan* study, "Im Treibhaus." The symmetrical disposition of the *Tristan* songs, together with their gradually intensifying expressive effect, makes Wagner's songs a truly musicodramatic cycle.

Wolf

The monumentality of design that came so naturally to Wagner seems to have eluded Hugo Wolf. "What does it signify," he wrote in 1891, commenting on his notoriety as a songwriter, "but the reproach that songs are all I shall ever write, that I am master of what is only a small-scale genre?"[62] Schumann voiced similar feelings when, after completing the Eichendorff *Liederkreis* Op. 39, he wrote to Clara: "But I don't want merely to continue writing so many little pieces; now I can seriously turn to opera."[63] It was a common nineteenth-century disease—not the cultivation of miniatures, but the troubling over their aesthetic integrity—and few artistic figures suffered from it as chronically as did Wolf. Chief among the symptoms was a dialectic interplay of grandiose conceptions and compressed utterance, a dialectic that runs through the whole of Wolf's lied output. He carefully planned the contents of his large song collections, as Eric Sams has pointed out (1983, 36), so that the "artistic unit" was not the individual lyric but the entire songbook, which then served to represent the oeuvre of a single poet, whether Mörike, Goethe, or Eichendorff. Taken as a group, these songbooks—each an embodiment of the tension between anthology and aphorism—brought to fruition the kind of project that Schubert had envisioned but abandoned as early as 1816.

Within several of Wolf's large collections, smaller groupings of songs can be discerned. In the Mörike lieder, for instance, Nos. 2 and 3 ("Der Knabe und das Immlein" and "Ein Stündlein wohl vor Tage") share tempo, key, and thematic material. But pairs of this sort hardly count as cycles. Indeed, the closest that Wolf comes to the song cycle in the Beethoven-Schubert-Schumann sense is in his settings of the *Wilhelm Meister* lyrics that head off his Goethe lieder (1890). Though music is provided for all ten of the *Wilhelm Meister* poems, only six of them are grouped into minicycles of three songs each: *Harfenspieler* I ("Wer sich der Einsamkeit ergibt"), II ("An die Türen will ich schleichen"), and III ("Wer nie sein Brot mit Tränen aß"); and *Mignon* I ("Heiß mich nicht reden"), II ("Nur wer die Sehnsucht kennt"), and III ("So laßt mich scheinen").

A microcosmic history of the song cycle can be read out of the *Wilhelm Meister* lieder alone, for Schubert, Schumann, and Wolf all turned to the interpolated verse in Goethe's *Bildungsroman*. Wolf more nearly approximates Schubert in his fashioning of the lyrics into diminutive cycles; Schumann, on the other hand, set them all (excepting the *Spottlied* "Ich armer Teufel, Herr Baron") as a single group in G minor/major, and an unusual one at that. Schumann's cycle, Op. 98a, requires a baritone for the Harper songs and a soprano for those of Philine and Mignon; the lyrics are further disposed so that songs for high voice and low voice alternate.[64] Lawrence Kramer (1987) has sensitively detailed many of the points of contact and contrast between Wolf's and Schubert's settings of the Harper poems. According to his reading, the affective sequence of the Schubert songs (D. 478) moves from alienation to resignation and finally reaches stoical acceptance; Wolf rather views the poems in terms of a bleaker, late-nineteenth-century *Weltanschauung*, so that his settings project a sense of paralyzing self-consciousness and tortuous immobility.[65] It is possible that the Schumann songs provided a bridge between these varying outlooks. The C-minor tonality and languid chromaticism of Wolf's "An die Türen will ich schleichen" are paralleled in Schumann's setting; likewise, the "frozen insensibility" (to quote Kramer) of Wolf's song is present in Schumann's in the form of a mesmerizing, repeated accompanimental figure. Wolf's "Wer nie sein Brot mit Tränen aß" also may have taken its shape (as a buildup to a mighty climax, followed by a dissolution into near immobility) and ethos from Schumann's song.

Wolf's Mignon songs, however, show fewer affinities with Schubert's and practically none at all with those of Schumann. Schubert's *Gesänge aus Wilhelm Meister* Op. 62 (D. 877) consists of four songs: two settings of "Nur wer die Sehnsucht kennt," the first a soprano-tenor duet for Mignon and the Harper (B minor), the second a completely new setting for solo voice (A minor), followed by Mignon's lieder "Heiß mich nicht reden" (E minor) and "So laßt mich scheinen" (B major). Whereas Schubert's cycle forms a tonal unity (in B minor/major if performed with the duet version of the first song), Wolf's Mignon lieder—"Heiß mich nicht reden" (F), "Nur wer die Sehnsucht kennt" (G minor), "So laßt mich scheinen" (A minor)—clearly do not. The dactylic rhythm that pervades the accompaniment of Wolf's first song, along with the $\frac{6}{8}$ meter of the second, may stem from Schubert, but little else does. The single element that Wolf shares with Schumann involves the placement, in final position, of "So laßt mich scheinen." This is an important detail, for Schubert also reserved Mignon's prophetic utterance on her early death for the close of his cycle.

In this case, in contradistinction to the Harper songs, Schubert and Schumann come forth with essentially positive readings, the former's prayerful, the latter's folklike in tone. Mignon, the mysterious and secretive child, may be destined to die young, but, at least for Schubert and Schumann, hers will be a redeeming death, a serene transfiguration of a naive spirit. Wolf's lieder, in contrast, are unremittingly dark; there is little hope for a sublime afterlife registered here. Even the F major of "Heiß mich nicht reden" is troubled by the intense chromaticism that also runs through the minor-key songs. The latter are marked by an even sharper cleft between advanced harmony, on the one hand, and simple accompanimental patterns and melodic shapes on the other. The naiveté of Wolf's Mignon is more than a little tinged with neurosis. The hopefulness that

Schubert sensed in the *Wilhelm Meister* poems and that Schumann reserved for Mignon has little place in Wolf's darker world.

Mahler

Monumentality and miniaturism, progressive musical techniques and studied naiveté, interact in different ways in Gustav Mahler's song cycles, which belong as much to the history of the symphony as to that of the lied. Indeed, a complex generic interplay is embedded in the compositional history of the *Lieder eines fahrenden Gesellen*, a fin-de-siècle *Winterreise* in which Schubert's troubled wanderer is replaced by a journeyman making his way through "eine schöne Welt," hoping for final peace "unter dem Lindenbaum." Probably composed between 1883 and 1885, the *Gesellenlieder* were not published until 1897, when they appeared in versions for voice and piano and for voice and orchestra. In the meantime, most likely between about 1884 and 1888 and again from 1893 to 1896, Mahler concentrated on his First Symphony, which draws liberally on the material of this cycle. Thus the two works, and the genres they represent, are mutually dependent. This is reflected partly in the fact that, although the songs were probably orchestrated after the main work on the First Symphony was complete, manuscript evidence suggests that Mahler had planned an orchestral song cycle from the start.[66]

The mutual dependence of two genres—lied and symphony—that are in many ways antithetical can lead to knotty compositional problems. How, for instance, can a basically static, reflective form like the strophic song be converted into a dynamic sonata-allegro? This was the challenge that Mahler posed for himself in transforming the second of the *Gesellen* songs, "Ging heut' morgen übers Feld," into the *Immer sehr gemächlich* of the first movement of the First Symphony. The solution entailed casting the opening of the song's second strophe as a sonata-form first group, a reworked version of the third strophe as transition, and a variant of the first strophe as second group. The reason for the reversal of song strophes (the key to Mahler's solution) is obvious: in the song, the third strophe effects a modulation up a fifth, which could be used in the symphonic movement to make the transition from tonic to dominant required by sonata form. Conversely, a song movement conceived as such from the outset might just as easily be informed with symphonic traits. The opening movements of *Kindertotenlieder* ("Nun will die Sonn' so hell auf'gehn") and *Das Lied von der Erde* ("Das Trinklied vom Jammer der Erde") can be heard as strophic song forms, yet each employs developmental and recapitulatory gestures more readily associated with the symphonic allegro.

The relationship noted here between lied and symphonic movement can also be seen as existing between song cycle and symphony. The First Symphony enfolds a song cycle within itself: the first movement refashions the second *Gesellen* song; the trio of the second movement draws on "Hans und Grete" from the first volume of *Lieder und Gesänge* (1880–83); and the third movement invokes "Die zwei blauen Augen," the last of the *Gesellen* songs. *Kindertotenlieder,* though technically an orchestral song cycle, is no less a lyric symphony, as witness its (arguably) sonata-form opening movement, symmetrical tonal plan (D minor–E♭/C minor–C minor–E♭–D minor/major), and employment of large-scale reprise (the recurrence of the first movement's bells in the last). With *Das Lied von der Erde,* which Mahler described as a symphony, the fusion of genres is nearly complete.

Thus the song cycle, which entered the nineteenth century as the most personal of genres, was transformed in the late nineteenth and early twentieth centuries into one of the most public. Though initially its subtle and elusive modes of achieving coherence may have supplied an alternative to symphonic structuring procedures, the song cycle eventually (and ironically) came together with the symphony. But the two genres did not quite "fuse." In *Kindertotenlieder,* and even in much of *Das Lied,* listeners cannot help but feel uncomfortable, as if eavesdropping on the most private of utterances. This sensation is intensified by the discrepancy between the privacy of the message and the size of the forces used to convey it. Mahler thus makes explicit what is implicit throughout the Age of Romanticism: not only the centrality of the lied but the centrality of the poet-composer's "I" straining to express itself.

Strauss

The song cycles of Richard Strauss, whose nineteenth-century *Weltanschauung* persisted into our own times, register a discrepancy as well. The cleft between style and medium that, on occasion, brings the lieder of Schumann, Brahms, and Wolf in touch with the dramatic, becomes the norm for Strauss. Although he once reported to the publisher Eugen Spitzweg that his *Mädchenblumen* Op. 22 (1886–88), a setting of a four-poem lyric cycle by Felix Dahn, included some "very complicated," even experimental songs,[67] we are probably less apt to be taken by the extravagant imagery of the poetry or the harmonic idiom of the music than by the operatic allusions in the final song. The "dreamy-dark" plant growths that "yearn for distant places" from the edge of the pond bring melodic references to the Longing motive from *Tristan,* just as the alluring maiden's attunement to the speech of the stars is suggested by piano figuration reminiscent of the *Waldesweben.*

Strauss's proclivity for self-conscious quotation intensifies in the *Krämerspiegel* Op. 66 (1918), certainly one of the more bizarre products of the composer's imagination. On the one hand, these settings of twelve frivolous and punning verses by Alfred Kerr represent Strauss's closest approximation to the dimensions and cohesiveness of the great nineteenth-century cycles: the compelling if unusual tonal sequence, no less than the carefully graduated affective sequence and concomitant web of motivic connections—the fourth song is built largely on the opening figure of the second, which in turn draws on the beginning of the first; the piano postlude of the last song, in a move recalling *Dichterliebe,* recapitulates the prelude of the eighth song—contributes to the unity of the set. On the other hand, the satirical tone of both text and music—the work was intended as the composer's "revenge" on the Berlin publishers Bote and Bock for an unfortunate contractual arrangement—is markedly at odds with the refined expressivity expected of the song cycle. Hence the sometimes tasteless double entendres of the text (even Strauss's name takes on its actual meaning as "bunch of flowers" in the second song) are matched by a veritable riot of quotations in the music, which includes references to *Rosenkavalier* (songs 2 and 10), *Götterdämmerung* (song 3), *Tod und Verklärung* (song 8), the *Sinfonia domestica* (song 11), *Ein Heldenleben* (song 11), Beethoven's Fifth Symphony (song 11), and *Till Eulenspiegel* (song 12). In addition, the Schumannesque prelude to the eighth song would find a place in Strauss's last opera, *Capriccio,* in the moonlight interlude prefacing the Countess's final scene. In other words, the dramatic manifests itself negatively in *Krämerspiegel,* where the song cycle threatens to dissolve into a tissue of leitmotives.

In the songs of the next set, Op. 67 (1918), quickly drafted to ward off an impending breach-of-contract suit from Bote and Bock, Strauss directs his dramatic impulses toward more serious ends. The second of the collection's two minicycles, a setting of three lyrics of disillusionment from Goethe's *Westöstlicher Divan,* takes shape as an operatic *Gesangszene.* An essentially declamatory and tonally ambiguous setting of "Wer wird von der Welt verlangen" prefaces the E♭-major cantabile, "Hab ich euch denn je geraten," the whole rounded off by the C-minor/major "Wanderers Gemütsruhe," an impetuously driving tour de force for the pianist. Even here, Strauss cannot resist the urge toward self-quotation: the first and second songs both allude to *Die Frau ohne Schatten,* the second to the *Alpensinfonie.* The allusions, however, are maintained within a musically satisfying frame. In addition, the final song of the group makes significant references to the preceding three-song minicycle, a setting of Ophelia's "mad" lyrics from *Hamlet* in Karl Simrock's translation, its *moto perpetuo* triplets echoing the languid chromaticism of "Sie trugen ihn auf der Bahre bloß" (the last Ophelia song), and its closing major-minor flourish evoking the startling mode shifts in "Guten Morgen, 's ist Sankt Valentinstag" (the second Ophelia song).[68] The text of the Goethe lyric enjoins the wanderer to ignore the filth and evil of the workaday world, which Strauss, via the references to the Ophelia songs, depicts as a senseless realm. Musicopoetic substance for the Goethe setting and a measure of coherence for the entire diptych are thus ensured with a single stroke.

Strauss's so-called *Vier letzte Lieder* were completed during the spring and late summer of 1948, yet few would deny that their spiritual locus is in the nineteenth century. Links with the earlier century may be even more tangible; Timothy Jackson argues (1983 and forthcoming) that the germinal idea for the set derives from the 1894 setting of "Ruhe, meine Seele!" (Op. 27, No. 1). Strauss revised and orchestrated the latter in June 1948, just after completing "Im Abendrot" from the *Vier letzte Lieder*. In Jackson's view, the early song and the late orchestral lieder together form a coherent group, the placement of "Ruhe, meine Seele!" just before the terminal "Im Abendrot" making explicit the resolution of the musicopoetic tensions of what Jackson calls the *Not* motive in the final song. Regardless of whether we opt for four or five last songs, there can be little doubt that Strauss's contact with the poetry of Eichendorff ("Im Abendrot") and Hermann Hesse ("Frühling," "Beim Schlafengehen," "September") in the years just before his death elicited musical responses whose blend of lyric introspection and symphonic effusiveness is rivaled only by Mahler's example.

The "public" dimension of the late orchestral lieder reveals itself in a wealth of connections with that most public of genres, opera, specifically represented here by Strauss's final operatic testament, *Capriccio*. The rapturous lyricism of the D♭-major "Beim Schlafengehen," its closing paragraphs serving as affective center for the set, resonates in tandem with the last phases of the Countess's concluding monologue in *Capriccio*. (Another luminous D♭ ending comes to mind: the E♭–D♭ appoggiatura gesture that marks the vocal close in "Beim Schlafengehen" replicates the concluding cadence in the trio of *Rosenkavalier*, Act III.) Strauss's setting of the last words in "Im Abendrot"—*ist dies etwa der Tod*—likewise sets off multiple associations; the often-mentioned allusions to *Tod und Verklärung* intersect with a more subtle reference to the deceptive resolution of the second quatrain of the *Capriccio* sonnet.

Strauss's approach to cyclic organization points to a more private mode of utterance. He left no definitive word on the order in which the songs should proceed, nor is this surprising, for their texts ("Frühling" excepted) tend to circle about the same theme: a final release in death that is neither ultrasensual nor morbid, but rather mystically transformative. Thus, practically all of the last songs are quite literally "last" songs, each with its distinctive orchestral color: a richly differentiated tutti in "Frühling"; *divisi* strings, harp, and horn in "September"; solo violin in "Beim Schlafengehen"; and trilling flutes (to paint the text's pair of larks) in "Im Abendrot." Discreetly wrought connectives criss-cross from one song to another; the larks of "Im Abendrot" are prefigured in "Frühling," much as the terminal vocalise in "September" is echoed in the broad melismas of "Beim Schlafengehen." Unity of tone also issues from a characteristic melodic-harmonic idea of coupling half-step motion in the upper voice with third motion in the bass. Variants of what remains an unstated *Urform* saturate the orchestral preludes to "Frühling" and "September" and likewise figure as emblems for "die gestirnte Nacht" in "Beim Schlafengehen" and for "der Tod," the final conceit in "Im Abendrot."

The same gesture makes a link with the deceptive cadence in the sonnet from *Capriccio,* which closes with a celebrated question mark. Resolved that the argument over the primacy of words or music must remain *unre-*solved, the Countess asks whether there is an ending for the projected opera simultaneously unfolding before us that "is not trivial" (*nicht trivial ist*). Although her dilemma does not bear directly on the poetic theme of the last orchestral lieder, it is clear that Strauss here hit upon an ending—for a career, and for a musical epoch-that was far from trivial. His decision belatedly to bring down the curtain on German Romanticism through the medium of the song cycle rings true indeed.

Notes

1. Quoted from Deutsch (1947, 795) and *Allgemeine musikalische Zeitung,* Leipzig [*AMZ*] 30 (26 July 1826): col. 483. Translations are mine unless noted otherwise.
2. See Turchin (1981, 231).
3. *AMZ* 20 (1818): cols. 198, 211; Deutsch (1947, 613).
4. For references to Schubert's renderings of selected songs from *Die schöne Müllerin,* see Deutsch (1947, 574). The first public performance involving *Winterreise* occurred on 10 January 1828 in Vienna, when the tenor Ludwig Tietze sang only its opening song, "Gute Nacht"; see Deutsch (1978, 577). Still, it should be kept in mind that the public performance of songs was very much a rarity in the first several decades of the nineteenth century; see Kravitt (1965, 207).
5. Hanslick (1870, 208–10). Only toward the end of the century, with the rise in popularity of the Viennese *Liederabend,* did the lied (and with it, the song cycle) begin its double life as private *and* public genre; see Kravitt (1965, 211–13).
6. See Brusati (1978, 23–24).
7. "Robert Schumanns Gesangkompositionen," *AMZ* 44 (January 1842): cols. 33, 58–60.
8. Schumann's autograph manuscript for *Frauenliebe* (Staatsbibliothek zu Berlin, Hans 2, Mus. ms. autogr. Schumann 16/2) does, however, bear the designation: "Cyklus v. acht Liedern" (see Ozawa 1989, 27). Beethoven's *An die ferne Geliebte* presents the opposite situation. Although the work was published in 1816 as a *Liederkreis,* Beethoven's autograph contains the simple designation: "Sechs Lieder von Aloys Jeitteles."
9. Komar (1971, 64–66). The difficulties connected with formulating a workable definition of the song cycle have also been addressed by Ruth Bingham (1993), who convincingly argues that we can best do justice to the pre-Beethovenian repertory, in particular, by taking into account the differing meanings attached to the term *cycle* in the late eighteenth and early nineteenth centuries. For example, Johann Bornhardt's *12 Monate* (ca. 1810) comprises a cycle in that the poetic texts describe a uniformly recurrent series of events. On the other hand, the notion of a cycle as a random grouping of points equidistant from a central locus is represented in topical cycles (where the poems circle about a single theme) like Friedrich Himmel's and Friedrich Hurka's settings of Karl Müchler's *Die Farben* (1795). A third conceptual shape, which Bingham calls a

"sprung circle," involves both topical centrality and fixed linear recurrence, as in Himmel's 1808 cycle *Die Blumen und die Schmetterling.* Bingham further points out that some topical cycles, Weber's *Die Temperamente* Op. 46 (1816) among them, use contrast, as opposed to motivic or tonal recall, to achieve unity.

10. See, for instance, the commentary in Dürr (1984, 261–62).

11. *Schwanengesang* was assembled as a cycle by the publisher Tobias Haslinger, possibly with the aid of Schubert's friends. See also R. Kramer (1985, 213–19).

12. See also R. Kramer (1987).

13. Friedrich Schlegel, *Kritische Fragmente* (1797), No. 60, in Schlegel (1967, 154).

14. See *Fragmente zur Poesie und Litteratur II* (1799–1801), No. 237, in Schlegel (1981, 273): "*Character of the Roman.* (1) Mixture of the dramatic, epic, lyric . . ."

15. See Dahlhaus (1973, 873–877).

16. *AMZ* 18 (November 1816): cols. 810–11.

17. For Luise Eitel Peake (1968, 67ff., and 1982), many of the earlier song cycles embody a riddle that the participants in a "*Liederkreis*-game" must solve. Peake suggests that by following various verbal and musical clues, and drawing the appropriate inferences, the players of the game might learn, for example, that *An die ferne Geliebte* was a representation of a giant teardrop, or that *Die schöne Müllerin* takes the form of a meandering brook. There is little hard evidence, however, for the existence of games like this. Peake (1982, 243) bases much of her case on the 1816 *AMZ* review of Nägeli's *Liederkranz* (see note 16), which, in her translation, states that members of a *Liederkreis* "can entertain themselves with a kind of song game." But the reviewer actually refers to "eine Art von Liederspiel" (*AMZ* 18: 811), where *Liederspiel* is better rendered as "a play with songs" than as "song game."

18. See Hanson (1985, 120–21).

19. See Peake (1982, 253–55).

20. See Mustard (1946).

21. See also Feil (1975, 23–26).

22. See Kerman (1973, 129–32).

23. The fifth strophe of the first song, as Kerman has conjectured (1973, 126), was almost certainly added by Beethoven to help motivate the musical recall at the end of the sixth song and therefore is not included in the count.

24. For a different view of the motivic substructure of the cycle, see Reynolds (1988).

25. See R. Kramer (1987, 670). Kramer also notes that the second song, "Todesmusik," was first composed in G♭.

26. For further commentary on the *Entstehungsgeschichte* of *Winterreise,* see Feil (1975, 28), Stöffels (1987, 182–200), and Youens (1989, vii–xiii, and 1985b).

27. See, for instance, McKay (1977, 94).

28. See Deutsch (1958, 234).

29. Letter (22 January 1828) from Marie von Pratobevera to Josef Bergmann, in Deutsch (1947, 716–17).

30. Song 6 was originally cast in F♯ minor. A directive in the *Stichvorlage* for *Abteilung* I of the cycle calls for its transposition to E minor.

31. Deutsch (1958, 15).

32. See Susan Youens's sensitive account (1987). Walter Everett (1990, 167–72) discusses "Der Wegweiser" as an important center for the elaboration of the "grief" motive (the embellishment of the fifth scale degree by its semitone upper neighbor) that runs through many of the songs.

33. Cf. McKay (1977, 94–100) and Youens (1985a, 128–35).

34. In some cases the links between song cycle and character-piece collection may be quite palpable. For example, Eric Sams (1975, 36) conjectures that some of the Heine *Liederkreis* songs may have originated as sketches for the *Davidsbündlertänze* Op. 6.

35. "Robert Schumanns Gesangkompositionen," *AMZ* 44 (1842): cols. 31–32.

36. *Neue Zeitschrift für Musik [NZfM]* 23 (11 July 1845): col. 14.

37. *NZfM* 5 (1 November 1836): 143.

38. See Hallmark (1979, 18, 110–12).

39. See McCreless (1986, 18–19) and Hallmark (1990, 8–11). Clara contributed songs 2, 4, and 11 to the Op. 37/12 set, perhaps taking Robert's No. 9 ("Rose, Meer und Sonne") as the model for her No. 4 ("Liebst du um Schönheit").

40. Letter to Clara of 22 May 1840 (in Schumann 1982, 278).

41. For a detailed account of Schumann's creation of *Dichterliebe* out of the *Lyrisches Intermezzo* poetry, see Hallmark (1979, 110–25). *Dichterliebe* has probably received more concentrated attention than any of Schumann's other song cycles; significant studies include Hallmark (1977), Komar (1971, especially 63–94), Pousseur (1982), and Neumeyer (1982). Marston (1991) puts forward Beethoven's C♯-Minor String Quartet Op. 131 as a tonal model for Schumann's most often discussed cycle.

42. The portrayal is conceived from a distinctly male point of view; this line of thought is pursued in Solie (1992).

43. Quoted in Sams (1974, 841).

44. The only one of Mendelssohn's song collections that displays cyclic traits is his *Zwölf Lieder* Op. 9 (1830); see Turchin (1981, 122–29). For a discussion of the genre-designating terms employed by Brahms in his lied publications, see Fellinger (1990, 380–82).

45. The first quotation as reported by Heinz von Beckerath; both in Fellinger (1990, 380–85).

46. For a discussion of Brahms's Op. 121 as a cycle, see Whittall (1983).

47. See Wintle's discussion (1982) of the E-Minor Cello Sonata Op. 38 and the A-Major Piano Quartet Op. 26.

48. See Boyer (1980, 267). Brahms's library included a large number of *Volksbücher;* his undated copy of a collection published in Berlin, which contains a *Historia von der schönen Magelona,* is signed "Johs. Brahms 1857." See Hofmann (1974), item 753 (pp. 122–23).

49. Tieck's *Märchen,* which he published under the pseudonym "Peter Leberecht," first appeared in 1797. As the employment of interpolated lyrics was a common feature in the *Romane* and *Novellen* of the literary Romantics, the song cycle may have drawn on an analogous device. Karen Hindenlang (1990, 584–86), for instance, has argued that "Auf einer Burg," the enigmatic seventh song of Schumann's Eichendorff *Liederkreis,* functions much like the lyric digressions in the prose works of the composer's literary models.

50. Brahms's equivocation over the cyclic status of the *Magelone Romanzen* is considered in light of the publication history of the songs in Jost (1990, 43–46). According to Jost, Brahms's interest in fashioning a tightly-wrought cycle waned after he completed the first six settings.

51. For a detailed account of the cycle's complex history, see Bozarth 1978 (4–6, 34–40) and 1983 (209–10, 215–18).

52. See Kalbeck (1912–21, 1: 428). For a more recent attempt at a connecting narrative, see Daverio (1989, 361–65).
53. Brahms (1920, 219). According to Kalbeck (1912–21, 1: 428), Brahms was "generally opposed to the performance of all the Lieder as a cycle," and when Brahms learned that the first two *Hefte* of *Romanzen* were not selling well, he suggested that Rieter reissue them mixed with some of his more popular songs (Kalbeck 1912–21, 2: 271)—hardly an indication that the cyclic integrity of the work counted for much. The songs were, however, performed as a cycle during Brahms's lifetime; Kalbeck (1912–21, 4: 224) reports Ludwig Wüllner's Meiningen performance during spring 1891 with the composer in attendance.
54. Friedlaender (1928, 39–40).
55. See Musgrave (1985, 38), Sams (1972, 25–26), Plantinga (1984, 431), Jost (1990, 48–49), and MacDonald (1990, 187).
56. Cf. Kalbeck (1912–21, 1: 429, 439), Sams (1972, 25), and Boyer (1980, 269–86). Jost (1990, 46–61) provides a provocative alternative; his analysis of *Romanzen* Nos. 3, 4, 9, and 13 purports to show just how far Brahms *distanced* himself from Tieck's poetic world by employing musical devices that seem to contradict the sense of the poetry. Of course, any musical setting will transform to some degree the meaning embodied in a poetic text. The perfect fit between word and tone that both composers and critics have held up as an ideal for the lied is a chimera. Moreover, the force of Jost's argument depends on the degree to which we are willing to accept that Brahms's transformations of Tieck's poetic meanings amount to out-and-out contradictions. For Tieck, the Sulima lyric (No. 13) may have been intended to suggest that Peter's exotic admirer represented a real alternative to his love for Magelone; Brahms's music, on the other hand, may hint at Peter's ultimate unwillingness to respond to Sulima's overtures (Jost 1990, 52–53). But whether the two points of view are mutually exclusive, as opposed to complementary, remains open to debate.
57. See Kalbeck (1912–21, 1: 424).
58. See also Krones (in *Brahms: Kongress Wien 1983*, ed. Susanne Antonicek and Otto Biba, 317–20, Tutzing, 1988).
59. On Brahms's abortive attempts to find a suitable opera libretto, see Wirth (1983).
60. Tieck (1844–45, 2: 4). Ludwig Finscher has demonstrated that several of Brahms's early Eichendorff settings ("Lied," Op. 3, No. 6; "Parole," Op. 7, No. 2; and "Anklänge," Op. 7, No. 3) must be viewed not only as musical responses to the individual poetic texts, but also as evocations of the scenes in the *Romane* from which the lyrics were drawn. According to Finscher (1990, 339), this amounts to "an internalization of Eichendorff's poetic world from which the songs surface as arrested moments of an internal monologue." Although Finscher maintains that Brahms never again took this approach to lied composition, it is in fact the basis for the "internalized theatre" of the *Magelone* settings.
61. The dates of completion are as follows: "Der Engel," 30 November 1857; "Stehe still," 22 February 1858; "Im Treibhaus," 1 May 1858; "Schmerzen," 17 December 1857; Träume," 5 December 1857. (*Richard Wagner, Sämtliche Werke*, vol. 17, *Klavierlieder*, ed. Egon Voss, 119–20, Mainz, 1976).
62. Letter of 12 October 1891 to Oskar Grohe, quoted in Sams (1983, 36).
63. Letter of 22 May 1840, in Schumann (1982, 278).
64. This may also have been the mode of performance for Conradin Kreutzer's *Frühlingslieder;* see Peake (1979, 92).
65. Schubert and Wolf set the *Wilhelm Meister* poems in different orders; Wolf fol-

lowed the order established by Goethe in his *Gedichte:* "Wer sich der Einsamkeit," "An die Türen," "Wer nie sein Brot" (this differs from the order in
the novel); Schubert reversed the order of the last two poems.

66. For a summary of the tangled history of song cycle and symphony, see Mitchell
(1975, 27–32, 91–112) and chap. 7 of this volume.

67. See Schuh (1982, 141).

68. Brahms also set five Ophelia lyrics (in the A. W. Schlegel–Tieck translation) for
an 1873 performance of *Hamlet* in Prague. Strauss's songs have little in common with these unassuming, quasi-folklike pieces, which in all probability he
did not know. Karl Geiringer's 1935 edition (G. Schirmer, New York) includes
the melodies and the simple piano accompaniments that Brahms intended for
rehearsal purposes only.

Bibliography

Barthes, Roland. "Loving Schumann." In *The Responsibility of Forms,* trans. Richard
Howard, 293–98. New York, 1985.

Bingham, Ruth. "The Song Cycle in German-Speaking Countries 1790–1840: Approaches to a Changing Genre." Ph.D. dissertation, Cornell University, 1993.

Boyer, Thomas. "Brahms as Count Peter of Provence: A Psychosexual Interpretation of the Magelone Poetry." *Musical Quarterly* 66 (1980): 262–86.

Bozarth, George S. "The Lieder of Johannes Brahms: Studies in Chronology and
Compositional Process." Ph.D. dissertation, Princeton University, 1978.

———. "Brahms's 'Liederjahr of 1868.'" *Music Review* 44 (1983): 208–22.

———. ed. *Brahms Studies.* Oxford, 1990.

Brahms, Johannes. *Briefwechsel.* Vol. 14. Ed. Wilhelm Altmann. Berlin, 1920.

Brusati, Otto. *Schubert in Wiener Vormärz: Dokumente 1829–1848.* Graz, 1978.

Dahlhaus, Carl. "Zur Problematik der musikalischen Gattungen im 19. Jahrhundert." In *Gattungen der Musik in Einzeldarstellungen: Gedenkschrift Leo Schrade,* ed.
Wulf Arlt, 840–95. Bern, 1973.

Daverio, John. "Brahms's *Magelone Romanzen* and the Romantic Imperative." *Journal of Musicology* 7 (1989): 343–65.

Deutsch, Otto Erich. *The Schubert Reader.* Trans. Eric Blom. New York, 1947.

———. ed. *Schubert: Memoirs by his Friends.* London, 1958.

———. *Franz Schubert: Thematisches Verzeichnis seiner Werke in chronologischer Folge.* Kassel, 1978.

Dunsby, Jonathan. "The Multi-Piece in Brahms: *Fantasien* Op. 116." In *Brahms: biographical, documentary and analytical studies,* ed. Robert Pascall, 167–89. Cambridge, 1983.

Dürr, Walther. *Das deutsche Sololied im 19. Jahrhundert: Untersuchungen zu Sprache und
Musik.* Wilhelmshaven, 1984.

———. "Die Lieder-Serie der neuen Schubert-Ausgabe." *Musica* 40 (1986): 29–30.

Earl, D. L. "The Solo Song in Germany: 1800–1850." Ph.D. dissertation, Indiana
University, 1952.

Everett, Walter. "Grief in *Winterreise*: A Schenkerian Perspective." *Music Analysis* 9
(1990): 157–75.

Feil, Arnold. *Franz Schubert: Die schöne Müllerin—Winterreise.* Stuttgart, 1975.

Fellinger, Imogen. "Cyclic Tendencies in Brahms's Song Collections." In Bozarth
(1990, 379–88).

Ferris, David. "From Fragment to Cycle: Formal Organization in Schumann's Eichendorff Liederkreis." Ph.D. dissertation, Brandeis University, 1993.

Finscher, Ludwig. "Brahms's Early Songs: Poetry versus Music." In Bozarth (1990, 331–44).

Finson, Jon. "The Intentional Traveler: Romantic Irony in the Eichendorff *Liederkreis* of Robert Schumann." In *Schumann and His World*, ed. R. Larry Todd, 156–70. Princeton, 1994.

Friedlaender, Max. *Brahms's Lieder*. Trans. C. Leonard Leese. London, 1928.

Goldschmidt, Harry. "Welches war die ursprüngliches Reihenfolge in Schuberts Heine-Liedern?" *Deutsches Jahrbuch für Musikwissenschaft 1972* 17 (1974): 52–62.

Hallmark, Rufus. "The Sketches for *Dichterliebe*." *19th-Century Music* 1 (1977): 110–36.

———. *The Genesis of Schumann's Dichterliebe: A Source Study*. Ann Arbor, MI, 1979.

———. "The Rückert Lieder of Robert and Clara Schumann." *19th-Century Music* 14 (1990): 3–30.

———. *Schumann's Frauenliebe und Leben: Context, Composition, and Interpretation*. Oxford, forthcoming.

Hanslick, Eduard. *Aus dem Concertsaal: Kritiken und Schilderung aus den letzten 20 Jahren des Wiener Musiklebens*. Vienna, 1870.

Hanson, Alice M. *Musical Life in Biedermeier Vienna*. Cambridge, 1985.

Hindenlang, Karen A. "Eichendorff's *Auf einer Burg* and Schumann's *Liederkreis, Opus 39*." *Journal of Musicology* 8 (1990): 569–87.

Höckner, Berthold. "The 'Multiple Persona' and Robert Schumann's Heine-*Liederkreis*, Op. 24." Paper read at the 59th Annual Meeting of the American Musicological Society. Montreal, 1993.

Hofmann, Kurt. *Die Bibliothek von Johannes Brahms—Bücher und Musikalienverzeichnis*. Hamburg, 1974.

Jackson, Timothy. "The Last Strauss: Studies of the *Letzte Lieder*." Ph.D. dissertation, City University of New York, 1983.

———. "'Ruhe, meine Seele!' and the *Letzte Orchesterlieder*." In *Richard Strauss and His World*, ed. Bryan Gilliam, 90–137. Princeton, 1992.

Jost, Peter. "Brahms und die romantische Ironie." *Archiv für Musikwissenschaft* 47 (1990): 27–61.

Kalbeck, Max. *Johannes Brahms*. 4 vols. Berlin, 1912–21.

Kerman, Joseph. "An die ferne Geliebte." In *Beethoven Studies*, ed. Alan Tyson, 123–57. New York, 1973.

Knaus, Herwig. *Musiksprache und Werkstruktur in Robert Schumanns "Liederkreis."* Schriften zur Musik, 27. Munich, 1974.

Komar, Arthur, ed. *Schumann: Dichterliebe*. Norton Critical Scores. New York, 1971.

Kramer, Lawrence. "Decadence and Desire: The *Wilhelm Meister* Songs of Wolf and Schubert." *19th-Century Music* 10 (1987): 229–42.

Kramer, Richard. "Schubert's Heine." *19th-Century Music* 8 (1985): 213–25.

———. Review of *Franz Schubert: Lieder* (Neue Ausgabe Sämtlicher Werke, IV/5), ed. Walther Dürr (Kassel, 1985). *Music Library Association Notes* 43 (1987): 670–71.

———. "Distant Cycles: Schubert, Goethe and the *Entfernte*." *Journal of Musicology* 6 (1988): 3–26.

———. *Distant Cycles. Schubert and the Conceiving of Song*. Chicago, 1994.

Kravitt, Edward F. "The Lied in 19th-Century Concert Life." *Journal of the American Musicological Society* 18 (1965): 207–18.

MacDonald, Malcolm. *Brahms.* New York, 1990.

Marston, Nicholas. "Schumann's Monument to Beethoven," *19th-Century Music* 14 (1991): 247–64.

Massenkeil, Günther. "Cornelius als Liederkomponist." In *Peter Cornelius als Komponist, Dichter, Kritiker und Essayist,* ed. Hellmut Federhofer and Kurt Oehl, 159–68. Regensburg, 1977.

McCreless, Patrick. "Song Order in the Song Cycle: Schumann's *Liederkreis,* Op. 39." *Music Analysis* 5 (1986): 5–28.

McKay, Elizabeth Norman. "Schubert's *Winterreise* Reconsidered." *Music Review* 28 (1977): 94–100.

Mendel, Hermann, ed. *Musikalisches Conversations-Lexicon.* 11 vols. Berlin, 1870–79.

Mitchell, Donald. *Gustav Mahler: The Wunderhorn Years.* Berkeley, 1975.

Musgrave, Michael. *The Music of Brahms.* London, 1985.

Mustard, Helen Meredith. *The Lyric Cycle in German Literature.* Columbia University Studies in German Literature, new series, 17. New York, 1946.

Neumeyer, David. "Organic Structure and the Song Cycle: Another Look at Schumann's *Dichterliebe.*" *Music Theory Spectrum* 4 (1982): 92–105.

Ozawa, Kazuko. *Quellenstudien zu Robert Schumanns Liedern nach Adelbert von Chamisso.* Frankfurt, 1989.

Peake, Luise Eitel. "The Song Cycle: A Preliminary Inquiry into the Beginnings of the Romantic Song Cycle and the Nature of an Art Form." Ph.D. dissertation, Columbia University, 1968.

———. "Kreutzer's *Wanderlieder.* The Other *Winterreise.*" *Musical Quarterly* 45 (1979): 83–102.

———. "Song Cycle," in *The New Grove Dictionary of Music and Musicians,* ed. Stanley Sadie, 17: 521–23. London, 1980.

———. "The Antecedents of Beethoven's Liederkreis." *Music and Letters* 63 (1982): 242–60.

Petersen, Barbara. "Richard Strauss as Composers' Advocate, oder 'Die Händler und die Kunst.'" In *Richard Strauss: New Perspectives on the Composer and His Work,* ed. Bryan Gilliam, 115–32. Durham, NC, 1992.

Plantinga, Leon. *Romantic Music.* New York, 1984.

Pousseur, Henri. "Schumann ist der Dichter: Fünfundzwanzig Momente einer Lektüre der *Dichterliebe.*" In *Musik-Konzepte Sonderband: Robert Schumann II,* ed. Heinz-Klaus Metzger and Rainer Riehn, 3–128. Munich, 1982.

Reynolds, Christopher. "The Representational Impulse in Late Beethoven, I: An die ferne Geliebte." *Acta Musicologica* 40 (1988): 43–61.

Rosen, Charles. *The Romantic Generation.* Cambridge, MA, 1995.

Sams, Eric. *Brahms Songs.* Seattle, 1972.

———. "Peter Cornelius." *Musical Times* 115 (1974): 839–42.

———. *The Songs of Robert Schumann.* 2d ed. London, 1975.

———. *The Songs of Hugo Wolf.* London, 1983.

Schilling, Gustav, ed. *Encyclopedie der gesammten musikalischen Wissenschaften, oder Universal-Lexicon der Tonkunst.* 7 vols. Stuttgart, 1835–42.

Schlegel, Friedrich. *Kritische Friedrich Schlegel Ausgabe.* Vol. 2: *Charakteristiken und Kritiken I (1796–1801).* Ed. Hans Eichner. Zurich, 1967. Vol. 16: *Fragmente zur Poesie und Literatur I.* Ed. H. Eichner. Munich, 1981.

Schuh, Willi. *Richard Strauss: A Chronicle of the Early Years 1864–1898.* Trans. Mary Whittall. Cambridge, 1982.

Schumann, Robert and Clara. *Briefe einer Liebe.* Ed. Hanns-Josef Ortheil. Königstein, 1982.

Solie, Ruth. "Whose Life? The Gendered Self in Schumann's *Frauenliebe* Songs." In *Music and Text: Critical Inquiries,* ed. Steven Scherr, 219–40. Cambridge, 1992.

Stöffels, Ludwig. *Die Winterreise.* Vol. 1: *Müllers Dichtung in Schuberts Vertonung.* Bonn, 1987.

Thym, Jürgen. "The Solo Song Settings of Eichendorff's Poems by Schumann and Wolf." Ph.D. dissertation, Case Western Reserve University, 1974.

Tieck, Ludwig. *Phantasus.* Berlin, 1844–45.

Turchin, Barbara. "Robert Schumann's Song Cycles in the Context of the Early Nineteenth-Century Liederkreis." Ph.D. dissertation, Columbia University, 1981.

———. "Schumann's Song Cycles: The Cycle within the Song." *19th-Century Music* 8 (1985): 231–44.

———. "The Nineteenth-Century Wanderlieder Cycle." *Journal of Musicology* 5 (1987): 498–526.

Whittall, Arnold. "The *Vier ernste Gesänge,* Op. 121: Enrichment and Uniformity." In *Brahms: biographical, documentary and analytical Studies,* ed. Robert Pascall, 191–207. Cambridge, 1983.

Wintle, Christopher. "The Sceptred Pall: Brahms's Progressive Harmony." In *Brahms 2: biographical, documentary and analytical Studies,* ed. Michael Musgrave, 197–222. Cambridge, 1987.

Wiora, Walter. *Das deutsche Lied: Zur Geschichte und Ästhetik einer musikalischen Gattung.* Wolfenbüttel, 1971.

Wirth, Helmuth. "Oper und Drama in ihrer Bedeutung für Johannes Brahms." In *Brahms Studien.* Vol. 5, pp. 117–39. Hamburg, 1983.

Youens, Susan. "Retracing a Winter Journey: Reflections on Schubert's *Winterreise.*" *19th-Century Music* 9 (1985): 128–35. [Youens 1985a]

———. "*Winterreise:* In the Right Order." *Soundings* 13 (1985): 41–50. [Youens 1985b]

———. "*Wegweiser* in *Winterreise.*" *Journal of Musicology* 5 (1987): 357–79.

———. Introduction to *Franz Schubert—Winterreise—The Autograph Score.* New York, 1989.

———. "Behind the Scenes: *Die schöne Müllerin* before Schubert," *19th-Century Music* 15 (1991): 3–22.

CHAPTER TEN

Performing Lieder:
The Mysterious Mix

Robert Spillman

Upon hearing the soprano Victoria de los Angeles, Giacomo Lauri-Volpi was moved to state: "When listening to her, one perceives that ideal point at which, when words are sung, the thought and the sound meet; the point at which two otherwise irreconcilable worlds find a common ground."

This is high praise; it also describes perfectly what is so magical, elusive, and satisfying in concert singing. Most voice students aspire to the operatic stage, dazzled by the possibility of singing full-throated, passionate performances in costume, with orchestra and with scenery. There is a certain comfort in being onstage with many other performers, partially anonymous behind the costume and the assumed character. For those who fall under the spell of the art song, however, there is nothing comparable to the intimacy, vulnerability, and connection with an audience that can be found in the solo recital.

Feeling the lure of the concert stage does not guarantee success on it. A more compelling motivation for a musician to study, perform, and understand any repertoire is love of the repertoire itself. Dreams of glory can be useful in getting started in music study, but the intensity of devotion required to continue is enough to discourage many would-be stars. The material studied must provide the justification for the study.

The German lied is a genre that rewards its students and devotees with almost limitless riches. The music is as varied as it is beautiful; both voice and accompaniment are involved in its subtleties and glories. The texts deal with an enormous range of subjects but emphasize intimate, personal choice and emotion, a characteristic that corresponds to the intimacy of most lied performances: one singer and one pianist, facing an audience and armed with nothing but text, music, and personality. The vulnerability required for lied performance becomes one of its greatest assets when grasped by intelligent performers and listeners and reflects the goal of personal expression inherent in the medium. The Romantic lied is, by definition, an attempt at presenting words and music in an equal marriage of expressiveness. The search for increased personality and truer expression led the great composers of lieder to find solutions that were honest, daring, and personal, resulting in a body of work that requires an exceptional level of personal commitment from its interpreters.

Those who aspire to the successful performance of German lieder soon discover the complexity of their task; they must possess not only a dependable technique and a sense of what is beautiful, but also the understanding of two languages, one musical and the other literary. It has always been the goal of great composers for the voice to bring together text, musical sense, and performing skill, but the proportions have varied. In the Western musical tradition there is room for the recitative of Caccini and the formal phrases of J. S. Bach. The idea of singing can range from the limpid lyricism of Bellini's bel canto to the speaking on pitch of a cabaret artist such as Lotte Lenya. Somewhere between these two lies the performance of lieder.

The boundaries of the lied repertoire are easily defined: songs in the German language written in or around the nineteenth century, having its roots in the era of Romanticism. The overwhelming majority of the repertoire is written for one singer and one pianist; any discussion of lied performance must start from this reference point. Since the latter half of the nineteenth century, lieder have been commonly performed in a concert setting: singer and pianist dressed more or less formally, the singer standing, facing the audience and performing from memory, the pianist seated at right angles to the audience before the keyboard. Visual aids are kept to a minimum—no scenery or costumes, only the facial expression and body language of the singer and ideally a printed text and/or translation in the program (song recitalists should present the material in the original language). Given these stringent constraints, it is a tribute to the power of the material that anyone should be willing to invest the time and effort needed to become an accomplished lied singer. What follows is a discussion of some of the necessary skills.

Communication

Performing a song is nothing more or less than telling a story. It is the particular genius of Romantic lied that the accompanist is integrated in this task. The accompaniment supports, comments on, and illustrates the text; this presupposes a characteristic of music that has been a sticking point of music criticism for more than a century: that music can of itself express, indicate, or represent extramusical things, whether thoughts, emotions, objects, or actions. This also presumes that both singer and pianist are continually engaged in getting their point across, making understandable their concept of the action and emotion of the material. In lieder it is not merely the accepted meaning of a word or phrase that communicates; the presentation of that word or phrase through a particular harmony, interval, rhythm, timing, color, nuance, facial expression, and body language either supports that accepted meaning or comments ironically on it. The elements of melodic interval, harmonic language, and rhythm are the work of the composer; to achieve effective nuance in presentation requires the thought and commitment of the performer.

This commitment to the concept that a work of music can be expressive requires more than a generalized earnestness; otherwise a folksinger who sings in a flat monotone could easily become a lied performer. It also requires more than generalized perkiness or gloom, a level of expressiveness beyond which many students of singing never venture. In addition, it requires more than the enjoyment of vocalism, for the success of a lied performance depends not on the beauty of the voice but on how beautifully the beauty of the voice accords with the meaning of the text. If the poem talks of beauty, we rejoice in the ravishing sounds presented by singer and pianist; if the text speaks of anguish, pain, or ugliness, then limpidity or opulence alone will not suffice. Nor will the simple desire to make one's meaning clear; this desire must be fulfilled by faithfulness, understanding, and technique.

Faithfulness

The lied is not very rewarding for the singer who wishes to be praised for vocal prowess—Handel and Verdi have provided better and more appropriate opportunities for that. It is also not a genre congenial to the pianist whose highest goal is to play some works of, say, Liszt faster and louder than anyone else. It is also a difficult medium for those who seek fame by reinterpreting masterpieces; composer and poet provide enough subtlety, irony, hidden meaning, and shading so that anyone trying to make white black and black white is doomed to failure.

Perhaps because the material is so complex and the work so arduous, the great performers of lieder are remarkable in their unanimous devotion to being faithful—to reproducing the music accurately and understanding the poem thoroughly; personal expression that does not fit the music or text is intrusive. The lied singer also discovers very quickly that there is no place to hide on the concert stage, and that the audience has a disconcerting ability to read a performer's mind. If he or she is not in accord with the words and music of the song, there had better be an excellent reason for such ambiguity or irony. If the performer is concentrating on his or her technique, the audience will, too; if fear is uppermost in his or her mind, that fact will reach the audience instantaneously. No costume, no scenery, no diverting collegue will come to the rescue of the concert performer who does not remain attentive to the words and music at hand, and who does not have the means of presenting them clearly. The aspirant who wishes to succeed as a lied interpreter is thus forced to seek tools that will aid in understanding the meanings of the poet and the wishes of the composer.

Understanding

Once a musician commits to a path of fidelity to a composer's wishes, a number of questions present themselves, along with several practical considerations.

Appropriateness of Material

For all practical purposes, this presents questions for the singer rather than the pianist: Do I have the range for this song? Do I have the ability to sustain the tessitura? Do I have the ability to sustain the tempo asked for? Would it require me to sing more loudly than I can? Am I of the same gender as the persona, and if not can I bring it off anyway?

In the case of range, the song recital is at least one place where it is perfectly acceptable to transpose a piece of music in order to make its performance feasible. Transposition of individual pitches is generally frowned upon unless a composer expressly writes alternatives, as in "Der Tod und das Mädchen" by Schubert and "Ballade des Harfners" by Schumann. On the other hand, piano passages are more likely to be altered to fit a transposition, taking a low note up if it would be off the keyboard, for example.

In the case of tessitura or phrase length, the singer must decide whether personal limitations would work against the effectiveness of the song. There is no room in this genre for taking a lied such as "Sapphische Ode" presto just because a singer is short of breath. Actually, there is no allowance for such a feat anyway, since Brahms marks this lied to be performed andante, and the genre requires a certain level of honesty from its practitioners.

In the case of a tessitura that is too high or too low, the singer's self-interest will probably protect the composer, as the singer is not likely to expose a weak part of his or her voice. The same is true of material that requires extremes of dynamics. If, however, someone decides to perform a song with *pp* and *ff* markings, such as "Gretchen am Spinnrade," the singer's dynamic range must go from the softest to the loudest that is comfortably possible for that individual.

In the case of gender-specific material, such as Schumann's *Dichterliebe* (dedicated to a female singer) or *Frauenliebe und -leben,* great artists such as Lotte Lehmann, Dietrich Fischer-Dieskau, and Christa Ludwig have transcended gender boundaries. This is again a question of the comfort level of the singer; no one seems to care if a male pianist plays *Frauenliebe und -leben* or a female pianist *Dichterliebe,* and if a singer can feel comfortable and dramatically involved while presenting words spoken by someone of the opposite sex, there is precedent for this practice. We should be careful, however, that this does not lead to a performance that is no more than uninvolved vocalization; just because a man thinks "Du Ring an meinem Finger" is a beautiful song does not mean he has the ability to carry it off successfully in performance. Rather, the performance must be convincing dramatically; this requires empathy for the speaker of the text that transcends simple narration.

Concept of Text

Both singer and pianist have a duty and responsibility to consider the meaning of the poem, both of its individual words and of the moods, thoughts, or narrative being presented. This requires a large amount of homework, for the German speaker as well as the foreigner. The performer who is not aware of the direction the text is taking every moment will fall into the trap of generalization, projecting either an expressionless vocalization or some generic gray area of meaning. For example, someone presenting "Die Forelle" of Schubert must have understanding on several levels: what *zappelt* means, for example; what the phrase *so lang dem Wasser Helle . . . nicht gebricht* means (and why that phrase and grammatical construction are used); and, considering the song as a whole, whether it is about fishing or about somebody stealing one's girlfriend.

Point of View

Closely related to one's understanding of the text is the decision of how closely one wishes to identify with it during a performance. There is a degree of *Distanzierung* in any performance of lieder; the well-dressed mature woman standing in front of us is not poor, half-crazed Gretchen sitting at her spinning wheel. The text of "Gretchen am Spinnrade," however, is written in the first person singular, and the listener will be cheated if he or she goes away from a performance of this song without comprehending at least some of Gretchen's words, attitude, emotions, and situation.

Most lied texts have an "I" in them somewhere; some are composed of simple narrative. These narratives give performers opportunities to find points of view congenial to themselves and to the texts. In "Heidenröslein," for example, how tragic are those repeated *Rösleins*? Is the final line of each verse "Röslein auf der Heiden") sympathetic, sorrowful, flippant, or a mixture? In Schubert's "Meeresstille," is the narrator terrified along with the sailor, and is he or she a voice of doom or (perhaps more farfetched) a soothing, comforting voice? Decisions about one's point of view need not be simple or automatic in first-person-singular texts. In "Heidenröslein," again, is the boy careless, infatuated, or malicious? Is the hero of *Winterreise* slowly going mad, or is he painfully aware of his situation at all times? Does he meet Death in the last song, or must he go on living?

Almost everyone performing lieder loves contemplating the problem of finding and presenting a point of view. This is perhaps because this issue, no matter how enthusiastically contested, is much less painful and thorny than the task of successfully presenting the material. For that one needs technique.

Technique

Diction

Essential to any good lied performance is a clear, accurate presentation of the text. The singer must have a good ear for phonetic sounds and the technique and willingness to reproduce them faithfully. The pianist should have an ear for vocal color in order to modulate dynamics and timing to complement the various vowels and many thicknesses of consonants in the German language. Unless a coach, and therefore a teacher of singers, the pianist has less responsibility for the diction than the singer, who is frequently asked to do things that go against basic bel canto training.

VOWEL FORMATION

German has few diphthongs and many vowels held constant throughout their duration; this requires a singing technique with true attacks and an unwavering delivery. German also has a large number of vowel sounds; in addition to the regular vowels a singer must be able to distinguish among all the umlauted ones. Just because the voice is most resonant in a certain register when singing a closed *e* does not mean that one may sing a closed *e* there when an open *e* is written. Conversely, the fact that a composer sets a closed vowel in a register that is uncongenial to a singer's concept of good basic singing does not allow the substitution of some generic open "univowel." A singer is not allowed to change *Wonne* to *wohne* or *Sohne* to *Sonne;* such a transference changes the meaning of the word.

On a more basic level, faithfulness requires that, for example, *ist* may not, in any register, sound like the English word *east*. Of course, all good singers modify their vowels; a listener, however, must believe that he or she hears the correct vowel, and this requires more flexibility than many non-German speakers are willing to learn. All great composers have great ears, and if they wish to hear a certain word in a certain register they probably have a certain color in mind; altering a vowel can alter a composer's intent as well as the poet's.

CONSONANTS

Compared to the Romance languages, German has a high consonant content. Consonants often appear in clusters, and a singer aspiring to fluency must come to grips with such terrors as *wo greift's hin?* ("Erstes Liebeslied eines Mädchens," Wolf/Mörike) and *dazwischen schluchzen und stöhnen* ("Es ist ein Flöten und Geigen," Schumann/Heine, from *Dichterliebe*). Correct production of unvoiced consonants contradicts the misguided idea that correct Italianate vocal production requires a steady stream of vowels. Even Italian, as vowel-heavy as it is, has unvoiced consonants, including those which, when doubled, require that the phonation of the vocal cords be interrupted. In German, consonants may be expressively thickened more (randomly) than in Italian. All these considerations suggest that a singer regard a vocal line as being made up of a variety of sounds, not all of which require the phonation of the vocal cords. Fears that this is destructive to sound vocal technique are unfounded; it is instructive to listen to singers known for superior beauty of tone and technique, such as Fritz Wunderlich and Christa Ludwig, who pronounce every *t* and flip every *r* in a text.

ELISIONS

It is a basic tenet of good Italian diction that words should be run together as if they form a single longer word that stretches from cesura to cesura. It is also characteristic of French diction that the final sound of each word is attached to the beginning of the next one. In opposition to this, German diction requires that every word and word-stem that begins with a vowel be separated from the preceding sound. This is anathema to those true to the "Italian" ideal of continuous vocalization. Their antipathy is to some degree due to the harmful effect a violent use of the glottal stop can have on the throat. One need not, however, bang one's glottis like a frog in order to attack a vowel; a gentle release of breath will suffice to effect the separation. The separation must, however, be there.

VOCAL "LINE"

There are secret chapels at which singers, especially voice teachers, worship a sectarian idol known to initiates as "line." This is commonly regarded as the product of the minimization of consonants plus the manipulation of vowels to give the impression of each sound's being of equal size and weight, with—here is the really deadly point—as little "distance," or variation of color, between them. Again, however, great composers know what a word sounds like; if they want a closed vowel on a particular low pitch, for example, it is likely that they do not want a loud sound. Everyone can learn from the palette of sounds produced by great artists such as Elly Ameling and Dietrich Fischer-Dieskau.

The Pianist

As the preceding suggests, lieder require the singer to produce every sound of the German language in any register and over a wide range of dynamics. An equal command of technique is required of the pianist. A very wide range of dynamics and balances (often called tone colors) with special emphasis on the lower range of dynamics, is necessary, as is a hair-trigger sense of timing, used to shade phrases rhythmically as well as to provide tight ensemble. Very desirable for a pianist working in the German Romantic song repertoire is the cultivation of a so-called singing sound: a touch that mimics the singing line through legato shadings and connections, and which avoids harshness.

For both singer and pianist, therefore, the study of lieder should expand one's technique and expressivity. Thus enhanced, the palette of sound of both performers enables them to communicate the meaning of the poem to the listener. Although a medium as complex as the lied favors those who approach musical decisions through analysis and detailed thought, there are and have been great artists who achieve wonderful results intuitively. Using either approach or a combination of the two, the study process is even more exciting than the selection of a point of view. Musicians, like any artists, love to deal with the manipulation of the medium itself.

Style

Many important musical decisions must be made in preparing a lied for performance; most deal with general musical categories such as articulation or tempo, whereas others pertain to the style of the composer. The latter are the most problematical, as great composers can rarely be kept in a box of our defining.

A Composer's Characteristic Style

One must be careful in labeling a performance technique or a sound as typical of a composer. If we say that Schubert's style is more detached and Strauss's more legato, what are we to do with "Litanei" or "Für fünfzehn Pfennige"? If Brahms is a "legato" composer, how does one sing "Der Schmied"? If Mahler is even more of a "legato" composer, how does one perform "Des Antonius Von Padua Fischpredigt"? If Strauss is less florid and heavier than Schubert (the Schubert of "Ellens zweiter Gesang"), what do we make of "Amor" or "Ständchen"?

We must be careful not to generalize. We can safely say that the pianos used by Brahms, Wolf, and Strauss were richer than those of Schubert's time and that their singers were equipped to sing Wagner. It is probably correct to sing the long phrases in Brahms's "Die Mainacht" with a somewhat heavier tone than the long phrases in Mozart's "Abendempfindung" or Schubert's "Litanei." It is probably correct to say that Mozart relies more on terrace dynamics than Wolf does. Attacks are quicker in most lieder by Schubert than in most lieder by Mahler. We must, however, be prepared to deal with exceptions. If we say that "Komm, lieber Mai" is "typical" Mozart, that is, light in tone color, piano in dynamics, and slender of line, we must also remember that Mozart gave us "Das Veilchen," "Die Alte," and "Abendempfindung," and that his lightness need not be monochromatic.

Despite these caveats, intelligent choices can be made. We can refrain from performing "Abendempfindung" slowly, thickly, intensely legato, and *molto rubato* so that it sounds like one of Mahler's *Kindertotenlieder*. We can perform the *Ernste Gesänge* of Brahms with warm, opulent sound, without haste, so that they need not be mistaken for Schubert's "Der Rattenfänger." With some trepidation, we might offer some examples of what is typical for a composer. Schubert sounds slender and buoyant, as in "Der Musensohn"—but he also wrote "Das Wirtshaus" and "Prometheus." Let Schumann be represented by the tender lyricism of "Du bist wie eine Blume," but remember that he also wrote "Ich grolle nicht." Brahms composed the dark, rich sounds of "Sapphische Ode"—but he also composed "Botschaft," which combines the buoyancy of Schubert with the smooth, soaring line of Schumann. Wolf's style is often associated with the legato and drama of a song like "Verborgenheit," but he is also the composer of such comic works as "Ich hab' in Penna" and "Zur Warnung." It would seem that the performers of the nineteenth century, as they progressed toward the weight and intensity of Wagnerian singing, were also required to retain the agility and finesse required for Rossini. Thus we find both "Um Mitternacht" and "Wer hat dies Liedlein erdacht?" among the works of Mahler, and "Ich wollt' ein Sträusslein binden" and "An die Nacht" within the same group of songs by Strauss (and these are not the most extreme of the Brentano lieder).

Choice of Tempo

In the selection of an effective speed for a performance, clarity must remain of primary importance. "Der Musensohn" is a rapid song, but it should not be frantic and unclear. "Mein!" is likewise lively, but the eighth notes must be heard. Most great lied performers gravitate to speeds that are not extreme, making sure that the text is clear in rapid songs and that phrases do not drag in slow ones. If pitches or words become either slurred or too clipped, it is likely that the tempo is too fast. In the world of lieder, there are no prizes for the fastest "Die Rose, die Lillie," or the slowest "Die Mainacht," only for the most interesting and communicative performance. One generality that does seem to apply is: a slow song by later composers such as Brahms, Wolf, and Mahler tends to be taken more slowly than one by Mozart, Schubert, or Schumann, because of the heavier sound and texture typical of these composers.

Choice of Dynamics

A basic rule almost always applies: the later the year of composition, the more extreme the dynamics can be. For example, Schubert's "Liebesbotschaft" and Strauss's "Ständchen" share many characteristics—rapid, light figuration in the piano, a generally low dynamic level, and a wide vocal range. But Schubert nowhere allows himself the expansive forte climax that builds so naturally in Strauss's composition.

Vocal Weight

Because of the intimacy of most lied performances, extremes of soft singing are available that would not be feasible in opera. An accomplished interpreter will take advantage of this and will not be satisfied with mezzoforte where pianissimo is appropriate. This extended range of dynamics can point up the shortcomings of those singers who have been schooled for opera. More people can sing "Verborgenheit" at a steady mezzoforte than can produce a true, spinning pianissimo and a full, rich fortissimo while performing that particular lied, and singers in the first category probably should avoid material such as "Auch kleine Dinge."

A group of lieder in performance should be notable for great variety of weight, dynamic, and color. As the performers move from "An den Mond" to "Die Allmacht," or from "Nachtigallen schlagen" to "Immer leiser," or from "Anakreons Grab" to "Mühvoll komm' ich," each song will have its particular family of sounds.

Articulation

Some songs call for a legato technique of a classical, "Italianate" nature, whereas others are more parlando. For example, "Das Wandern" and "Wohin?" sound best when performed bouncily and semi-detached, with the exception of certain phrases in "Wohin?" that Schubert marks with slurs. Elsewhere, Schubert indicates that the right hand (and presumably the voice) of "Gretchen am Spinnrade" is to be performed *sempre ligato,* while the left hand is *staccato.* "Ich hab' in Penna" is an obviously parlando lied, whereas "Mir ward gesagt," despite the repeated notes, works best extremely legato. A singer of lieder must develop the versatility necessary to be able to choose, employ, and switch articulations as called for.

Rubato

The amount of rubato employed in lied performance is again a matter of avoiding excess. Self-indulgence is one trap; rigidity is another. The best singers bend a tempo or a phrase not to hide a technical limitation but because of expressive musicality. There is no reason to believe that laws of historical progression dictate that Strauss is more congenial to rubato than Schubert; "Morgen" and "Allerseelen" work well when counted rather steadily, whereas "Ganymed" can stand a number of changes and displacements. Schumann is the lied composer most likely to write tempo changes into the music, with Mahler a distant second.

There is no reason to keep the tempo steady if the text can be made more meaningful by bending it. "Das Wandern," the opening song of Schubert's *Die schöne Müllerin*, seems quite motoric; the sixteenth notes of the piano part proceed in regular patterns without interruption. Almost all leading interpreters of this song, however, sing the fourth verse (describing the millstones) slightly more slowly than the preceeding ones. This suggests that meaningful emphasis of the text can be important. Also, almost every singer needs to take a fraction of a second of extra time to breathe before starting the last phrase (the fourfold *das Wandern*). This demonstrates that phrasing and breath can be more important than a steady tempo. This may shock musical purists, who would prefer a literal interpretation of the score. A lied is a musical presentation of text and thought that must both be made clear. A good interpreter will avoid excess; younger lied singers probably need to be encouraged toward rhythmic freedom than toward greater severity.

Phrasing

Without sensitivity to phrasing, any performance of lieder is disappointing. Both singer and accompanist must be aware at all times of the direction of the music, and must be shading both dynamics and speed to enhance that directional pull. If a song is well written, important words and syllables will fall on important notes within a phrase. The performers must group what goes before these small climaxes so that the phrase moves in that direction. Then they must emphasize these points, by making them louder, by changing color, by delaying the attack, or by extending or thickening the initial consonant. It is simple but effective to make a particular stressed syllable stand out by making it louder; sometimes a softer dynamic could be used to make the same point. A richer, more intense sound can underline a passionate moment in the phrase, whereas less crucial words can receive less intensity. Especially effective is the use of varying attack times to underline the relative importance of words. A singer in German has the freedom to delay the onset of the word in various ways: a word can gain importance by being late; a word starting with a vowel can be separated from the proceeding sound by a greater break in the sound (*ewig* or *allein*); and unlike Italian, an initial consonant in German can be extended, as in *süss* or *müde*.

Performers must also make decisions about how much to "let the music breathe," that is, how much freedom to allow between phrases. Composers sometimes write vocal lines with no rests; Schubert's "Auf dem Wasser zu singen" is a good example. Here the pianist should bend the flow of sixteenth notes a bit so that the singer is not forced to gulp for air and jerk the phrase endings. Other songs have written-in rests, where the vocal and piano lines intertwine and exchange positions in a continuous flow.

Presentation

After expanding his or her technique and grappling with dramatic and interpretive issues, a performer arrives at the act of performing. The program will have been well chosen to suit the singer and be worthy of the extended commitment—even devotion—she or he must give it. The two performers will have polished it until it becomes their personal possession. Thus readied, how is it best presented?

In general, singer and pianist should bring to a lieder recital the same preparation and disposition with which musicians ideally approach any performance. Both should, for example, be satisfied that in rehearsal they have achieved a proper dynamic balance in the concert space. Some singers like working in front of a fully open piano because they can hear themselves better; others find it intimidating. But the piano should always be open a bit, either on short stick or with a block placed under the lid, for a completely closed lid muffles the piano's sound.

The singer must have the added readiness to place him- or herself on intimate terms with the audience. The singer becomes the persona of each song and must be willing and able to open up, become confessional, intimate, vulnerable; he or she must make eye contact—if the text calls for it—with members of the audience in order to communicate sincerely. The singer must remember that he or she is in toto an expressive instrument. Dress should be elegant, yet comfortable. Awkwardness or stiffness will be noticed and will detract from the effectiveness of the performance; they must be avoided. Hands and arms should be used expressively, but sparingly, otherwise resting comfortably at the singer's side or with one occasionally propped on the piano.

If a singer likes to move around, he or she should do so. Chaliapin marched while singing Schumann's "Die beiden Grenadiere," and Fischer-

Dieskau looks for birds in the trees during Wolf's "Fussreise"; Hermann Prey plays drunk during Wolf's "Zur Warnung." Janet Baker stood practically frozen in place during Schubert's "Gretchen am Spinnrade" until the climax, and then at "Ach, sein Kuss!" she raised her hand slightly and took one step forward; the effect of the modest movement was shattering. This kind of acting helps, especially when singing in German to a non-German-speaking audience. In addition, it is an essential courtesy to the audience to provide texts and translations in the program and to leave the house lights up enough for the audience to be able to read them.

The lieder on the program must be ordered in a way that makes sense. A group of an entire program should have variety, including points of high intensity contrasting with more gentle moments. The performers should be comfortable in passing from one song to the next because the changes in mood and character must be instantaneous; no lied is long enough that one can get focused anywhere later than the beginning. The first song in a group or program must be congenial for the singer and inviting for the audience; a later song can be the most intimate. In choosing the last song one should remember that it may determine the audience's departing mood and judgment.

There is, of course, a special case in which the order of a group of songs has already been decided by the composer: that is the song cycle. John Daverio, in his essay (chapter 9, p. 279), discusses how varied the nature of song cycles can be and how resistant the genre is to simple definition. For the present purpose it will suffice to distinguish between those cycles that are narrative and those that are not, regardless of whether the poems were written by one or more poets, constitute a preexistent cycle themselves, or represent a selection made by the composer.

Cycles with a story line require a preparation similar to that of an opera singer. The protagonist of a cycle almost always is given opportunity to grow, develop, and change during the course of the several songs, and the performers must follow the clues and directions given in this regard. The length of time the performers must hold the stage in character also dictates that identification with the protagonist's character be deep and well thought-out. Decisions must be made, just as in the theatre, about the age, background, and beliefs of the protagonist. For example, the heroine of *Frauenliebe und -leben* must age during the course of the eight songs; she may not, however, become an empty-headed flirt. The pause between lieder becomes vitally important during a cycle. Between contrasting songs of a heterogeneous group, the interval is used to shift mood and assume a different personality. In the cycle, this space is where the protagonist reacts to the preceding text and moves forward with his or her life. Two performers might decide to minimize a particular pause between songs, for example, by jumping directly from the end of "Der Jäger" into the beginning of "Eifersucht und Stolz" during a performance of *Die schöne Müllerin*.

Just as there is usually one particular climax of a song, there is often a turning point in a cycle. In *Dichterliebe,* something radical occurs before "Ich grolle nicht" to turn bliss into bile. Does this mean that the preceding song ("Im Rhein, im heiligen Strome") still expresses the poet's happy devotion, or has the rejection already occurred, causing the poet to seek solace in the cathedral? Starting with "Ich grolle nicht," the poet alternates between grief (lieder 8, 10, 12) and anger (lieder 7, 9, 11). Songs 13, 14, and 15 describe the poet's dreams and hallucinations—providing a type of therapy that enables him to bury the past in song 16. The postlude of the final song quotes from "Am leuchtenden Sommermorgen" (No. 12), repeating the phrase that originally followed the speech of the flowers: "Don't be angry at our sister, you sad, pale man." Similarly, singer and pianist must decide where in *Winterreise* and *Die schöne Müllerin* the protagonist gives up hope; in both cases it may be possible for a single measure, chord, or word to provide the turning point toward the final tragedy.

For those groups of songs that do not tell a story, the performers can imagine a narrative or psychological context as long as this plot does not betray the text of the poems. It is easy to present Schumann's Op. 24 as a story of rejection similar to *Dichterliebe;* it requires considerably more imagination to make a viable story out of Schumann's Eichendorff *Liederkreis.* Such looser collections can be presented as various experiences of a single character, or as merely extended groups of lieder.

Whether acting out a story or portraying a series of lyrical moods, the projection of the text is obviously important. This brings up a critical question: If German is not the native language of the performer or the audience, why sing lieder in the original language? It is hard enough for an American audience to understand the wordplay of a Stephen Sondheim, much less that of Heinrich Heine. Mörike's poetry is as beautiful as that of Keats, but it is not the native language of the American singer. So why not perform lieder in translation?

The justification for singing in German is not solely the communication of the text as words, but of the fusion of words and music that the composer has created. We should aspire to sing Strauss's "Morgen" in German not because we wish to imitate the sound of Fischer-Dieskau singing it beautifully, but because we have discovered for ourselves how inseparable the sensual sounds of the words and their meanings are from the notes composed for them and how inadequate and less pleasing any English equivalent would be. We must come to the conclusion that the fusion of words and music are so necessary and integral that the two cannot be separated. Like the Countess in Strauss's opera *Capriccio,* we find ourselves unable to sacrifice either words or music.

For a singer whose native tongue is not German, the proper performance of lieder is difficult; one is working in a strange and difficult language, in a musical style of a different era, presenting thoughts and attitudes which may seem distant or naive in late twentieth-century, postmodern Western culture. There is, however, no other body of the vocal literature that so magically combines carefully wrought and deeply felt music and poetry to evoke the universals of human emotion and expression. In any of thousands of lieder one is likely to encounter a miracle.

Bibliography

Adler, Kurt. *The Art of Accompanying and Coaching.* Minneapolis, 1976.

Boyle, Nicholas. *Goethe: The Poet and the Age.* New York, 1991.

Brod, Max. *Heinrich Heine: The Artist in Revolt.* Trans. Joseph Witriol. Westport, CT, 1976.

Coffin, Berton. *The Singer's Repertoire.* 2d ed. 5 vols. New York, 1960–62.

Daverio, John J. *Nineteenth-Century Music and the German Romantic Ideology.* New York, 1993.

Emmons, Shirlee, and Stanley Sonntag. *The Art of the Song Recital.* New York, 1979.

Fischer-Dieskau, Dietrich. *The Fischer-Dieskau Book of Lieder.* New York, 1977.

Flores, Angel, ed. *An Anthology of German Poetry from Hoelderlin to Rilke.* New York, 1960.

Greene, Harry Plunkett. *Interpretation in Song.* London, 1912.

Helfgot, Daniel. *The Third Line.* With William O. Beeman. New York, 1993.

Kagan, Sergius. *On Studying Singing.* New York, 1960.

Kramer, Lawrence. *Music and Poetry; The Nineteenth Century and After.* Berkeley, 1984.

Lehmann, Lotte. *More than Singing.* New York, 1945.

——. *Eighteen Song Cycles.* New York, 1972.

Mare, Margaret L. *Eduard Mörike.* Westport, CT, 1973.

McGlatheny, James, ed. *Music and German Literature.* Columbia, SC, 1992.

Miller, Philip. *The Ring of Words.* New York, 1973.

Moore, Gerald. *Singer and Accompanist.* New York, 1954.

——. *Poet's Love, The Songs and Song Cycles of Schumann.* New York, 1981.

Moriarty, John. *Diction.* Boston, 1975.

Prawer, Siegbert S., ed. *The Penguin Book of Lieder.* New York, 1964.

Schiotz, Aksel. *The Singer and his Art.* New York, 1970.

Schwartz, Egon. *Joseph von Eichendorff.* New York, 1972.

Siebs, Theodor. *Deutsche Aussprache.* Berlin, 1969.

Spillman, Robert. *The Art of Accompanying.* New York, 1985.

Stein, Deborah, and Robert Spillman. *Poetry into Song.* New York, 1994.

Stevens, Denis. *A History of Song.* New York, 1961.

Wilcke, Eva. *German Diction in Singing.* New York, 1930.

Index

Note: references for musical examples or poetic excerpts are designated with the letter e, tables with the letter t; references found in notes are designated with an n.